Anglo-Saxon England 3

Her mon mæg giet gesion hiora swæð

ANGLO-SAXON ENGLAND

3

Edited by

PETER CLEMOES

MARTIN BIDDLE   JULIAN BROWN

RENÉ DEROLEZ   HELMUT GNEUSS

STANLEY GREENFIELD LARS-GUNNAR HALLANDER

PETER HUNTER BLAIR   JOHN LEYERLE

PAUL MEYVAERT   BRUCE MITCHELL

RAYMOND PAGE   FRED ROBINSON

CAMBRIDGE UNIVERSITY PRESS

Published by the Syndics of the Cambridge University Press
Bentley House, 200 Euston Road, London NW1 2DB
American Branch: 32 East 57th Street, New York, NY10022

Library of Congress Catalogue Card Number: 74-79139

ISBN: 0 521 20574 3

First published 1974

Printed in Great Britain
at the University Printing House, Cambridge
(Brooke Crutchley, University Printer)

Contents

Contents

*Abbreviations listed before the bibliography (pp. 233–4) are used throughout
the volume without other explanation*

Figures

Preface

This volume continues the policy of its predecessors. Only one point needs to be made about its contents: it had been intended to include an article on the use of colour by Anglo-Saxon artists alongside the one on Old English colour words, but this aim had to be abandoned when the expected author fell ill. It is hoped that the article in question will be published in a forthcoming issue, perhaps the next.

Once again I am much indebted to Mrs Janet Godden for help with the editing.

PETER CLEMOES
for the editors

CONTRIBUTIONS FOR FUTURE ISSUES ARE INVITED

Material may be submitted to any of the editors, but it would be appreciated if the one most convenient regionally were chosen (Australasian contributions should be submitted to Bruce Mitchell) unless an article deals mainly with archaeology, palaeography, art, history or Viking studies, in which case the most suitable editor would be Martin Biddle (archaeology), Julian Brown (palaeography and art), Peter Hunter Blair (history) or Raymond Page (Viking studies). A potential contributor is asked to get in touch with the editor concerned as early as possible to obtain a copy of the style sheet and to have any necessary discussion. Articles must be in English.

The editors' addresses are

Mr M. Biddle, Winchester Research Unit, 13 Parchment Street, Winchester, Hampshire (England)

Professor T. J. Brown, Department of Palaeography, King's College, University of London, Strand, London WC2R 2LS (England)

Professor P. A. M. Clemoes, Emmanuel College, Cambridge CB2 3AP (England)

Professor R. Derolez, Rozier 44, 9000 Gent (Belgium)

Professor H. Gneuss, Englisches Seminar, Universität München, 8 München 40, Schellingstrasse 3 (Germany)

Professor S. B. Greenfield, Department of English, College of Liberal Arts, University of Oregon, Eugene, Oregon 97403 (USA)

Dr L.-G. Hallander, Lövångersgatan 16, 162 21 Vällingby (Sweden)

Dr P. Hunter Blair, Emmanuel College, Cambridge CB2 3AP (England)

Professor J. Leyerle, Centre for Medieval Studies, University of Toronto, Toronto 181 (Canada)

Mr P. Meyvaert, Mediaeval Academy of America, 1430 Massachusetts Avenue, Cambridge, Massachusetts 02138 (USA)

Dr B. Mitchell, St Edmund Hall, Oxford OX1 4AR (England)

Dr R. I. Page, Corpus Christi College, Cambridge CB2 1RH (England)

Professor F. C. Robinson, Department of English, Yale University, New Haven, Connecticut 06520 (USA)

Cross-Channel language ties

R. DEROLEZ

Ever since the question of the origin of the Old English dialects was first raised, Bede's brief account of the Anglo-Saxons' tribal origins (*HE* I. 15) appears to have been a stumbling block as much as a help. Considering that scholars have been investigating the dialect origins for almost a century now, with a very limited set of data supplemented by varying degrees of insight and imagination, one may wonder whether the present body of facts warrants yet another approach. It seems, however, that not all possible sources of information have been tapped. The admittedly marginal material which I propose to examine here may perhaps serve to place the whole question in a somewhat different perspective from that which has been usual so far.

The basic alternative has been formulated often enough: the linguistic correspondences between England and the continent are due either to pre-invasion tribal connections (as suggested by Bede's account) or to post-invasion trade and other contacts. The third possibility, namely that they are due to pure coincidence, though regularly mentioned, seems to have had little appeal. Instead of a survey of the many attempts made so far to solve the problem, a brief discussion of three articles may serve as a starting point. Differing as they do in their approach and conclusions, they suffice to define our present predicament.

William H. Bennett traces the voicing of the initial consonants [f s þ], typical of the southern dialects, back to the continent.[1] Finding the situation in early Middle English absolutely parallel to that in Middle Franconian, he suggests only two explanations: either this parallelism must be put down to a remarkable coincidence (which Bennett does not seem to favour) or else it must be ascribed to a period of inter-tribal contact between the Low Franconians and the later inhabitants of Kent, the Juto-Frisians. Bennett traces the Jutes or Juto-Frisians – the exact meaning of these terms is not always clear – through a series of successive habitats: (i) Jutland; (ii) the Frisian islands and the coastal areas behind them; (iii) the Lower Rhine; and (iv) Kent. In the same way the Saxons are mapped (i) between the Elbe and the Baltic coast; (ii) in the vicinity of present-day Niedersachsen; (iii) on the *Litus Saxonicum*; and (iv) in Wessex. It must have been in the region of the

---

[1] 'The Southern English Development of Germanic Initial [f s þ]', *Language* 31 (1955), 367–71.

Lower Rhine that the Jutes and the Saxons came into contact with the Low Franconians, and to these contacts Bennett suggests that the presence of voiced initial spirants in both Low Franconian and southern English could be ascribed; in which case 'the speech of the first Germanic settlers in southern England already possessed the initial voiced spirants [v z ð]'[1] although these found no adequate expression in Old English spelling. The idea of later contacts being responsible for the voicing does not appeal to him:

> The possibility that the common voicing may have arisen from later cross-Channel relations between southern England and the lower Rhenish area seems extremely remote. Even with the facilities of present-day travel and communication, the Channel and the Straits of Dover are still effective barriers against the ingress of linguistic influences. Furthermore, there is no reason for supposing that only the southern part of England was involved in relations with the lower Rhenish district: yet the English voicing of initial [f s þ] is confined to southern and south-western counties.[2]

Bennett's prerequisite, then, for linguistic influence is close geographical contact: 'Unlike the Angles, the Jutes migrated southward along the North Sea coast as far as the lower Rhine, and the Saxons continued even farther south to the *Litus Saxonicum*.'[3] The historical basis for these assumptions is provided by Bede, *Beowulf* and the 'lower Rhenish cultural traits' that the Juto-Frisians brought to Kent. What strikes one most when examining Bennett's map is the wide gap between positions S² ('Saxons in Niedersachsen'), and S³ ('Saxons on the *Litus Saxonicum*', which is identified with 'numerous colonies near Bayeux on the northern coast of France'). Bennett leaves out of consideration the whole stretch of coast that is closest to England, and whatever linguistic evidence it might provide. Nor, of course, is there any but circumstantial evidence to support his view: the earliest recorded instances of voicing of initial spirants on either side of the Straits of Dover are half a millennium (or more) later than the date suggested by Bennett.

Whilst calling in question the very existence of continental Jutes, David DeCamp is prepared to assign a central position to the Frisians in the development of the Old English dialects.[4] With Jerrold he holds that 'the Jutish race and civilization, as described by Bede and as we know it from the graves of the late fifth and sixth centuries, was made in Kent',[5] a view which entails the outright rejection of the hypothesis of a continental origin of the Old English dialects. Taking his inspiration from dialect geography,

[1] *Ibid.* p. 371.   [2] *Ibid.* p. 371, n. 9.   [3] *Ibid.* p. 370.
[4] David DeCamp, 'The Genesis of the Old English Dialects. A New Hypothesis', *Language* 34 (1958), 232–44.
[5] *Ibid.* p. 238. This bold assertion will have to be revised in the light of J. N. L. Myres's Raleigh Lecture on History 1970 ('The Angles, the Saxons, and the Jutes', *Proc. of the Brit. Acad.* 56 (1971), 145–74).

DeCamp believes that a number of linguistic changes, which can account for the basic features of English dialect distribution, result from post-invasion linguistic diffusion. A series of five phonological innovations would have followed the economic and cultural mainstream (on which see below) and reached Kent between the sixth century and the eighth.[1] Their penetration into England was proportionate to and, indeed, conditioned by, the rise and decline of Kentish ascendancy. First, in the sixth century or the early seventh, $\bar{æ}$ (< WGmc $\bar{a}$) was raised to $\bar{e}$ in Frisia, whence the change was adopted in Kent and spread over all of England, except the south-west (*dǣd*:*dēd*). Not long afterwards, the *i*-umlaut was carried from Frisia to Kent, spreading throughout England probably during the first half of the seventh century. In the south-west the resulting $\bar{æ}$ (< $\bar{a}$ < *ai*, as in *dǣl*) coincided with the older $\bar{æ}$ (from WGmc $\bar{a}$), but elsewhere the two were phonemically distinct (*dǣl*, but *dēd*). The third innovation, the raising of short *æ* to *e* (*wæter* > *weter*), is also traced to Frisia: it was carried to Kent in the late seventh century and hence spread northward, but owing to diminished Kentish prestige did not penetrate north of the Wash; moreover the diffusion must have been very slow. The fourth innovation, the lowering and unrounding of $\breve{y}$ (< $\breve{u}$) to $\breve{e}$, penetrated no further than East Anglia, whilst the fifth and last, the raising of $\bar{æ}$ (< $\bar{a}$ < *ai*) to $\bar{e}$ (*dǣl* > *dēl*), which DeCamp dates to the seventh century or early eighth, did not spread much beyond Kent itself. This linguistic hypothesis is placed against an economic and cultural background which, however, lacks precision, as does the linguistic background.[2] Due stress is laid on the ascendancy of Kent under Æthelberht (560–616), but the Franks enter DeCamp's picture almost as often as the Frisians, no distinction being made, for example, between those on the Lower Rhine invoked also by Bennett, and Æthelberht's father-in-law, Charibert I (561–7), whose capital was Paris. It is none too clear either what area or areas DeCamp means by 'Frisia'. More important still, he offers no evidence for the dating of the Frisian innovations. To some of these points we shall have to return later on. The second phase of DeCamp's hypothesis, the diffusion of linguistic features characteristic of the Saxon south-west into areas formerly under Kentish hegemony, need not delay us here. In DeCamp's view, this is an internal English development, without impulses from outside.

Essentially, DeCamp presents the somewhat extreme expression of a fairly general consensus, an expansion of views put forward by Chadwick and Stenton amongst others.[3] It is against this consensus that M. L. Samuels reacts with his thesis that 'the dialect distributions of periods much later

---

[1] DeCamp, 'Old English Dialects', p. 233.　　　　　[2] *Ibid*. pp. 238f.
[3] H. Munro Chadwick, *The Origin of the English Nation* (Cambridge, 1907), pp. 67–71; F. M. Stenton, *Anglo-Saxon England* (Oxford, 1947), p. 9.

than the invasion must always be considered as potentially relevant to the invasion period'.[1] Samuels points out that 'phonetic change is determined largely by the suprasegmental features of juncture, stress, pitch and intonation, which are never recorded in early writings'; one must always take account of 'the possibility of wide allophonic variation'.[2] More specifically, he finds that the features which distinguish Anglian and West Saxon agree perfectly with the position of pre-Old English on the pre-invasion dialect map of the continent: 'Old English possessed some of the very pairs of variants that would be expected of its geographical position on the continent, notably both *eom* and *beo*, *hwæþer and hweþer*.'[3] There is no reason, in Samuels's view, for discounting the language of the Kentish settlers as 'something wholly transient'; 'the language of Kent may owe as much to its continental origins as to post-invasion contacts, and there is no evidence that compels us to prefer the latter to the former'.[4] He agrees with Bennett that the successive continental homes of the Jutes may well be reflected in linguistic features found in southern England.

The main body of Samuels's article is devoted to Middle Kentish features which can be traced back to Dutch or specifically to Flemish influence. Although his summing-up applies to a later period than to the one under consideration here, it may serve as a convenient conclusion to this preliminary survey:

In any consideration of cross-Channel influence on the language of Kent, Flanders in the Middle English period provides a better-substantiated source than Frisia in the Old English period. While, therefore, there is no reason to deny such Frisian influence, it may have been supplanted by that of Franconian earlier than has been hitherto supposed.[5]

Samuels's enlistment of diachronic linguistic mechanisms does not absolve us from looking for evidence earlier than the Middle English period: his own reference to the 'modern Dutch and Flemish dialect distributions of *reg, rek* "back" and *pet* "well"' (to which he might have added such isolated forms as [meːʒə] 'gnat', cf. OE *mycg*, and *ik weste* 'I wish', lit. 'I wished', cf. OE *ic wyscte*) points in that direction.[6] His conclusions, as far as the Middle English period is concerned, are convincing enough, but his treatment of the background suffers from the indefiniteness of such terms as 'Frisian' and 'Franconian' (as well as from a certain neglect of recent findings).

What we need in the first place is a sharper definition, or at any rate a more circumspect use, of the terms 'Frisian' and 'Franconian', both geographically and linguistically. Only a few points can be raised here in passing. As a language Frisian is documented only at a very late date. Even if the early evidence provided by place- and personal names is taken into account, Frisian remains an unwieldy entity, owing, partly at least, to the varying

[1] 'Kent and the Low Countries', *Edinburgh Studies in English and Scots*, ed. A. J. Aitken, Angus McIntosh and Hermann Pálsson (London, 1972), pp. 3–19.
[2] *Ibid.* p. 4.   [3] *Ibid.* p. 6.   [4] *Ibid.* pp. 8 and 14.   [5] *Ibid.* p. 14.   [6] *Ibid.* p. 9.

location and size of Frisia itself.[1] In Roman times the *Frisii* and the *Frisiavones* (if the latter may be identified with the *Frisii minores* and considered as a more or less distinct group) were located between the Ems (D Eems) and the Rhine. East of them were the Chauci, south-west the Cannenefates and the Sturii. Parts of their later territory in the Netherlands were inhabited by the *Marsaci* and the *Menapii*. In the eighth century and the ninth, when evidence again becomes available, *Fresia* or *pagus Fr(i)esensis* extends from the Weser in the east to a point near the south-western end of the frontier between Belgium and the Netherlands (*Sincval* = a navigable channel near the present village of Cadzand). It comprises the present provinces of Zeeland, North and South Holland, Utrecht, Friesland and Groningen, as well as the western part of Gelderland and probably also Drenthe. The Frisians must have subjected such other tribes as remained within their boundaries. In consequence their territory may have been linguistically less homogeneous than is usually assumed: a number of subject tribes retained their identity long enough for their names to survive in territorial divisions, e.g. Humsterland 786/7 (*Hugumarchi* inhabited by the *Hugas*).[2] On the other hand this seafaring and trading nation made its presence felt well beyond the boundaries of the kingdom (later duchy) and this presence may have had linguistic consequences. The question is, however, whether we can make any statement about the Frisian language in, say, the seventh century, that would not also apply to a vast 'North Sea Germanic' area reaching from the north of France to the north of Germany.[3] Some 'Frisian' features, as we shall see, are documented earlier in non-Frisian territory than in Frisia proper. It will also be prudent to bear in mind the possibility that language movements may have crossed the sea from north to south, not just from south to north, as is usually assumed. This need not entail tracing the origin of medieval Frisia back to an Anglo-Saxon invasion,[4] but it will prevent us from overlooking such place-name evidence as *Engelum* in the province of Friesland and *Englum* in Groningen, which both point to Anglian settlements.

A word remains to be said about the Franks, whose linguistic situation appears to be even more complicated than that of the Frisians. Whilst Frisian may be defined as the language characteristic of the *pagus Fresensis*, 'Franconian', or even a more restricted term such as 'Low Franconian' or 'West Franconian', lacks a useful correlate on the political map of the period. The situation may become clearer if the hypothesis proves acceptable that the

---

[1] Recent surveys will be found in A. Russchen, *New Light on Dark-Age Frisia*, Fryske Akademy Nr 311 (Drachten, 1967), and Paolo Ramat, *Il Frisone. Introduzione allo Studio della Filologia Frisone* (Florence, 1967).

[2] M. Gysseling, 'De oudste Friese toponymie', *Philologica Frisica Anno 1969* (Grins, 1970), 41–51 (Humsterland: p. 46). I owe special thanks to Dr Gysseling for his valuable help on a number of points, bibliographical and other.

[3] Russchen, *Dark-Age Frisia*, p. 31. See also below, p. 13, n. 1.   [4] *Ibid.* pp. 23ff.

Franconian dialects which show the second consonant shift to varying degrees are in fact franconized Alemannic.[1] From the Franconian place-name material in northern France, the Low Countries and north-west Germany an expert can extract an impressive amount of information on the chronology of the settlements,[2] but the link-up of the language data thus provided with the language used during the 'Middle' period will still present problems.

The area with which we are concerned here is marginal in more than one sense – geographically but also linguistically. It has attracted the attention of Anglo-Saxonists on account of a small fraction of its place-name material, no doubt an important fraction, but one which tends to obscure, rather than reveal, its total significance.[3] Research during the last two decades has done much to provide more reliable material and to shed fresh light on a number of old problems. As a look at the map of the area corresponding to the present Département du Pas-de-Calais and Département du Nord (fig. 1) shows, there is good toponymic evidence for assuming that an old frontier runs through this area from Étaples to a point north of Lille (on the map this frontier appears as a zone rather than as a line). It is defined to the south by a string of names in -court: Ramecourt (Verton, 12 kms S of Étaples),[4] Blaucourt (Estrée), Ecquemicourt, Wambercourt, Azincourt, Tramecourt, Ambricourt, Gricourt (Bours), Grandcourt (Houdain), Haillicourt, Vaudricourt, Manchicourt (Essars) and Gondecourt (10 kms SW of Lille). Further south numerous other -court names confirm this impression: Erembeaucourt, Guinecourt, Héricourt, Framecourt, Séricourt, Herlincourt, Ramecourt, Bermicourt, Sautricourt, Hernicourt, Orlencourt, Tachincourt, Magnicourt etc. Parallel to the most northerly -court names we find a string of names in -hem and especially in -inghem: Fromessent (3 kms NE of Étaples; 1207 Fremehesem), Tubersent (864 Thorbodessem, Thorbodeshem), Bréxent (*1115 Brekelesent, *1170 Brechelessem),[5] Ixent (838 Anineshem, Aineshem), Beussent,

---

[1] Hans Kuhn, 'Das Rheinland in den germanischen Wanderungen', *Siedlung, Sprache und Bevölkerungsstruktur im Frankenreich*, ed. Franz Petri (Darmstadt, 1973), pp. 447–83.

[2] Maurits Gysseling, 'Die fränkischen Siedlungsnamen', *ibid.* pp. 229–55.

[3] How far this area has been neglected may be seen from the recent (and otherwise very well documented) study of place-names in south-east England by John McN. Dodgson ('Place-Names from *hām*, Distinguished from *hamm* Names, in Relation to the Settlement of Kent, Surrey and Sussex', *ASE* 2 (1973), 1–50). Dodgson refers only to 'place-names from OHG -heim and those from OHG -ing' (on the authority of A. Bach's *Deutsche Namenkunde*), not to the -hem, -inghem and -hamm names just across the Straits of Dover.

[4] For the place-name material, see Dr M. Gysseling's toponymic dictionary, which registers all names recorded until 1225, *Toponymisch Woordenboek van België, Nederland, Luxemburg, Noord-Frankrijk en West-Duitsland (voor 1226)*, Bouwstoffen en Studiën voor de Geschiedenis en de Lexicografie van het Nederlands VI, 1 and 2 (1960). The name between brackets is that of the 'commune' on whose territory the preceding name is found.

[5] Forms whose date is preceded by an asterisk will be found in Auguste de Loisne, *Dictionnaire Topographique du Département du Pas-de-Calais Comprenant les Noms de Lieu Anciens et Modernes* (Paris, 1907). This work is not always reliable; see below, p. 11, n. 1.

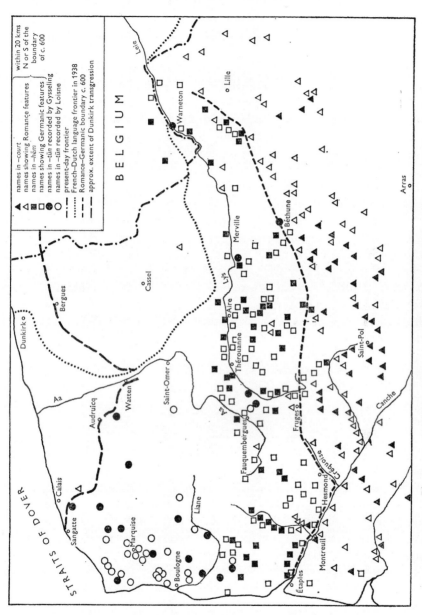

FIG. 1 Place-names in north-east France (based mainly on M. Gysseling's map in *Naamkunde* 2)

Maninghem (1206 *Maningehem*), Radinghem (s. xii ex. *Radingehen, Radin-chehem*), Matringhem (1120 *Matrinkehem*, 1129 *Matringehem*), Mazinghem (Anvin; 1119 *Masinghem*; cf. *id.* near Aire, 1136 *Masingehem*), Blaringhem (Pernes-en-Artois; 1069 *Blaringehem*, ± 1092 *Bladringehem*), Floringhem (1145 *Floringuehem*), Quenhem or Epiquenhem (Calonne-Ricouart; *1307 *Phikene-hem*, *1323 *Piquenehem*), Lozinghem (1147 *Losengehen*), Oblinghem (1147 *Amblingehem*), Radinghem-en-Weppes (1163 *Radigneham*, 1177/91[1] *Radinge-hem*), Erquinghem-le-Sec (1124 *Erchingehem*), Capinghem (1124 *Campingem*, 1144 *Campingehem*), Verlinghem (1066 *Euerlingahem*) and Frélinghien (1066 *Fredlenchehem*, 1080/85 *Ferlingehem*). These last two places are situated respectively six and twelve kms north-west of Lille. For practical reasons I consider here only the area west of the Belgian frontier, which forms the fourth side of our quadrilateral.

To judge by the surviving place-names, the area north of the -(*ing*)*hem* line must at one time have been almost solidly Germanic. First, there are the numerous names in -*hem* and especially -*inghem* (going back to *-haim* and *-ingahaim*), which are by far the largest group. The long list of those in -*inghem* is headed by Assinghem (1139 *Hessingehem*), Audinghem (1221 *Odingheham*), Autinghem (1164 *Hantinguehem*), Bainghen (1121 *Bainghem*), Balinghen (1109 *Baulingkehem*), Barbinghem (844/64 *Bermingahem*), Bayeng-hem-lès-Eperleques (1129 *Bainghem*), Bayenghem-lès-Seninghem (844/64 *Beinga villa*, 877 *Beingahem*), Bazinghen (1156 *Busingehen*, 1164 *Basinguehem*), Bazinghien (1136 *Bazimgehem*, 1212 *Basinghem*) etc. Among those in -*hem* are Audrehem (844/64 *Aldomhem*, with orig. dat. *aldum*), Dohem (1123 *Dalhem*), Étrehem (1193 *Strathem*), Norrent (1207 *Norhem*), Westrehem etc. The variety of other place-name elements is just as significant: *-baki-* (Fourdebecques, 1164 *Furkadebeca*; Honnebecque, 1174 *Hunesbecca*; Rebec-ques, 1084/92 *Resbecca*; etc.; cf. OE *bece, bæce*); *-berga* (Audembert, 1180 *Hundesberch*; Brunenbert, 1190 *Brunesberc*; Colembert, 1121 *Colesberg*; Fauquembergues, 961 *Falcoberg*, 1065 *Falcanberga*; Inglebert, 1129 *Ingelberga*; etc.; cf. OE *beorg, berg*); *-brōka-* (Le Breucq, 1164 *de Bruco*, 1210 *de Broco*; D Broksele = F Broxeele,[2] 1072 *Brocselo*; etc.; cf. OE *brōc*, with the meaning 'watermeadow, marshy land' surviving in Kent and Sussex dial.); *-gatwōn-* (Enguinegatte, 1140 *Inchenegata*, 1170 *Inkenegata*, on the road from Thérouanne to Enquin-les-Mines, etc.; cf. OE *geat* (and ON *gata*?)); *-hamma-* (not always easy to distinguish from -*hem*;[3] Cohem, 1072 *Colshem*, 1194/96 *Coham*;

---

[1] In punctuating dates I distinguish between, e.g., 671/722 = 'in a document dated sometime between 671 and 722' and 671–722 = 'the period from 671 to 722'.

[2] Where two forms of a name (or two names of a place) are given, they are distinguished by the addition of D (Dutch) and F (French).

[3] Gysseling, *Toponymisch Woordenboek*, distinguishes between -*hem* and -*hamm* names on the basis of topographic considerations. See now also Dodgson, 'Place-Names from *hām*'.

Contehem, 1157 *Condeham*; Gonnehem, 1142 *Goneham*; Pitgam, 1115 *Tidecham*; etc.; cf. OE *hamm*); *-*hulta*- (Bécourt, 1170 *Becolt*; Bouquehault, 1164 *Bocolt*; Arquingout, s. xii *Erchingehot, Herchingehout*; etc.; cf. OE *holt*); *-*laidu*- (D Nieuwerleet = F Nieurlet, 1127 *ad Niuuerledam*; cf. OE *lǣd*, *lād*; also *lǣt(e)*?); *-*stadla*- (Darnetal, s. xii *Darnestal*; cf. OE *stall, steall*); *-*widu*-(Colwède, 1164 *Colewide*; cf. OE *widu, wudu*); etc.

There is also a fair sprinkling of names derived by means of the suffix -*ingas*: Affringues, Autingues, Bonningues, Haffringue (1225 *Hafrenges, Hafrengues*) etc. Finally, the place-names surviving from the Gallo-Roman period show typically Germanic sound developments (though some will be given Romance forms in the course of the subsequent romanization of the region).[1] Thus the names in -*iacum*/-*iacas* retain intervocalic *k*, e.g. Coyecques (844/64 *in Coiaco*), Crecques (1119 *Kerseca*), Embry (826 *in Embriaco*, 838 *Embreka*, but 1156 *Embri*), Herly (s. x ex. *uillam Herlecham*, but 1162 *Herli*) and Menty (877 *Menteca*).

There can be little doubt, then, that the line Étaples–Frélinghien marks an old linguistic frontier, going back to the migration age: it was probably well established by about 600. The traces of Germanic which we find south of it, for example the personal names combined with -*court*, -*ville* or -*villers*, or such names as Roussent (11 kms S of Montreuil, ±868 *Hrosam*, 1169/73 *Rossem*, cf. E Horsham) are easily compatible with the Franks' domination over that area established in the late fifth and early sixth centuries. In this vast bilingual area the language of the new settlers was to disappear at an early date (though not without leaving many traces of its presence in the form of loan words). The almost homogeneous Germanic area north of the linguistic frontier could be expected to offer more resistance to the influence of French. Yet as early as the ninth century that influence manifests itself in place-names. A case in point is the name of the village Hesmond on the Créquoise. In 826 its name appears as *Hethenesberg*, in 838 as *Hethenasmont*, in 856 again as *Hethenasberg*, after which only forms in -*mont* or -*munt* are found.[2] The details of this romanization are difficult to ascertain, nor need they concern us here. But the fact that Calais was still an essentially Flemish town at the end of the thirteenth century (see below) is not without importance for an evaluation of the possibilities of linguistic contacts across the Straits of Dover.

From the late ninth century, when the county of Flanders took shape, to the late twelfth, when a large tract of territory fell into the hands of the French king, the Canche marked the extreme south-west frontier of the

[1] M. Gysseling, *Toponymisch Woordenboek* II, 1130; Gysseling, 'De verfransing van Noord-Frankrijk', *Naamkunde* 4 (1972), 53–70 (esp. 54).

[2] Gysseling, *Toponymisch Woordenboek* I, 490, *s.v.* Hesmond; Gysseling, 'De verfransing', p. 57.

domains of the Count of Flanders, which also comprised the counties of Ternois (Saint-Pol) and Artois (Arras). Near the estuary of the Canche was the port of Quentawic (Bede's reference to Theodore of Tarsus having rested there in 669 before crossing the sea is one of the first references to the place). During the Dunkirk transgression (fourth century to eighth),[1] which seems to have caused the eclipse of Gesoriacum-Boulogne, Quentawic gradually took the place of the latter as the main port of north-eastern Gaul for traffic to and from England, serving as the headquarters of the customs administration and sheltering one of the principal mints of the kingdom of the Franks (several mintmasters of Quentawic bear English names).[2] The name Quentawic itself points to Germanic name-giving, both by the presence of *e* for *a* in the name of the river Canche (*Quantia*, but *Cuent* in the *Vita S. Bonifatii*) and by the element *-wīk*. After its mysterious decline in the tenth century it was succeeded by Étaples (first mentioned 1026 *Stapulas*, by which time, however, the northern shores were regaining importance).

The Germanic area outlined above was not uniform, even if we leave out of consideration the south-east, with Lille as its focal point, where French must have been in a stronger position from the beginning. The Dunkirk transgression had created a shallow bay which penetrated deeply into the land between Sangatte ('Sand gate') and Dunkirk. This bay, called Aa Bay after the River Aa, separated what remained of the old coastal strip from the inland areas, reaching as far inland as Watten, whence an arm extended to Saint-Omer. After the transgression period this area was reclaimed, but for obvious reasons its place-names are of little importance in the present context, though Audruicq (1164 *Alderwic*), F Craywick = D Kraaiwijk (1139 *Craierwic*) and others still attest the presence of the bay. The area south-east of the inundations as far as the Belgian frontier differs from the rest of the region under consideration by the appearance of a large number of names in *-sali*, D *ʒe(e)le*, *sele*: Bissezeele, Bollezeele, Broxeele, Herzeele, Lederzeele, Ochtezeele, Oudezeele, Strazeele, Winnezeele and Zermezeele.[3] These names connect the area with more easterly regions (cf. Voormezele, Dadizele, Moorsele etc. in Flanders). As to the area west and south of the Aa Bay, apart from its impressive array of early Germanic names, it presents a type of place-name that has been only alluded to so far, the names in *-tūn* (now

---

[1] Abel Briquet, *Le Littoral du Nord de la France et son Evolution Morphologique* (Paris, 1930).

[2] Jan Dhondt, 'Les Problèmes de Quentovic', *Studi in Onore di Amintore Fanfani* (Milan, 1962) I, 183–248 (p. 213: 'la vocation anglaise de Quentovic'). On the names *Dutta, Ela* etc., see M. Gysseling, 'De vroegste geschiedenis van het Nederlands: een naamkundige benadering', *Naamkunde* 2 (1970), 157–80 (esp. 178).

[3] There is a small group of *-sali* names south and east of Cap Gris-Nez: Audresselles, *1150 *Odersele*, *1208 *Odressele*; and the hamlets Floringuezelle, Framzelle, Goningzelle, Haringuezelle and Waringuezelle, which belong to Audinghem. Otherwise names of this type seem to be very rare south-west of the Aa Bay: Hingueselle (Quelmes), Fauquezelle (Clerques).

mostly spelled -*thun*).[1] The greatest concentration is found in a relatively small area extending from south of the Liane to the high ground east of Cap Gris-Nez, and only about fifteen kms inland. The names found further north (Fréthun, 4 kms SW of Calais), east (*Fouquetun*, now Saint-Venant, and Warneton (D Waasten), both on the F Lys (D Leie)) and south (Béthune, and a small cluster east of Fauquembergues) look very much like outposts for a large-scale occupation which never took place. These -*tūn* names have often been commented upon in connection with the Old English ones,[2] but by now it will have become obvious that there are other reasons for examining the regions north and south of the Straits of Dover together. In view of the large measure of typological agreement and the numerous parallel formations to be found on either side of the Straits (not only Bainchthun: Bainton, but also Barbinghem (844/64 *Bermingahem*): Birmingham, Audrehem (844/64 *Aldomhem*): Aldham, Dohem (1123 *Dalhem*): Dalham, Étrehem (1193 *Strathem*): Streatham[3] etc.), the interpretation given to the material found in north-eastern France must necessarily have consequences for the English material and vice versa.[4] Thus it will be interesting to see the reaction of experts on English place-names to Gysseling's theory on the origin of the -*ingahaim* names. Briefly summarized his view is as follows.[5] The common Gallo-Roman suffix -*iacum*, attached to a variety of names, remained in use

[1] A complete list of these names is not easy to draw up, as part of Loisne's material still awaits critical sifting. Names listed by him in his *Dictionnaire*, but not by Gysseling in his *Woordenboek*, are marked here with an asterisk: Alenthun (Pihen), Alincthun, *Audenthun or Audinthun (Zudausques), Audincthun, Baincthun, *Baudrethun (Marquise), Béthune, *Colincthun (Bazinghen), *Connincthun (Beuvrequen), Dirlincthun (Hames-Boucres), Fouquetun (Saint-Venant), *Florincthun, Fréthun, *Godincthun (Pernes), *Guiptun (Tardinghen), *Hardenthun (Marquise), *Honnincthun (Wimille), *Imbrethun (Wierre-Effroy), Landrethun-le-Nord, Landrethun-lès-Ardres, *Ledrethun (Beuvrequen), *Létrethun (Wimille), Offrethun, *Olincthun (Wimille), *Painchthun (Echinghen), Pélincthun (Verlincthun & Nesles), *Raventhun (Ambleteuse), *Rocthun (Longueville), Samblethun (Coyecques), *Sombrethun (Wimille), *Tardingthun (Tardinghen), *Terlincthun (Wimille), Todincthun (Audinghen), Loisne: Audincthun), *Tourlincthun (Wirwignes), *Verlincthun, *Wadenthun (Saint-Inglevert), *Wainchthun (Saint-Leonard), *Warincthun (Audinghen), *Wincthun or Wingthun (Tardinghen), *Witerthun or Witrethun (Leubringhen) and Zeltun (Polincove). When the question '-*ingtūn* or -*ingatūn*' arises older forms point mostly to -*ingatūn*: Ellingentun (Alenthun), Odingetun (Audincthun), Bagingatun (Bainchthun), Dioruualdingatun (Dirlincthun) etc. See O. Arngart, 'On the *ingtūn* Type of English Place-Name', *SN* 44 (1972), 263–73.

[2] E.g. by Eilert Ekwall, *The Concise Oxford Dictionary of English Place-Names*, 4th ed. (Oxford, 1960), p. 482, *s.v.* OE *tūn*.

[3] In this case the parallelism is almost perfect: Streatham is on Stane Street (Ekwall, *Dictionary*, p. 450, *s.v.*); there was a *Stenegate* in the village of Tatinghem, next to Étrehem (Leulinghem). Gysseling, *Toponymisch Woordenboek*, *s.v.* Étrehem.

[4] A. H. Smith, *English Place-Name Elements*, Eng. Place-Name Soc. 25–6 (Cambridge, 1956), 1, 282, *s.v.* -*ing*: 'In Scandinavia the problems are not quite as complicated as elsewhere and have been adequately treated . . . but those of continental Germanic names, which appear to be as complex as those of England, have not been studied in any detail . . . and until that has been done the final solution of English -*ing* names cannot be reached.'

[5] Gysseling, 'Die fränkischen Siedlungsnamen'.

after the conquest of northern Gaul by the Franks, but was then attached to Germanic names. North of the Seine, however, a form *-iacas* appears, which can hardly be explained as a Lat. fem. acc. pl. in *-as*, but rather as a Germanic masc. nom./acc. pl. form with the same ending as *-ingas*. The suffix *-iacas*, then, would be the result of the Romance–Germanic symbiosis typical of the early Merovingian period. Names in *-iacas* do not seem to occur, however, in Ponthieu–Ternois–Artois, where their place is taken by *-iaca curtis* and *-iaca villa*. It is this latter type, implying the equation *-iaca*: *-inga* (cf. *-iacas*: *-ingas*), which gave rise, north of the linguistic border described above, to the *-ingahaim* type. That the two were considered equivalent may be inferred from such doublets as Merville (s. x *Manriuilla*): Meregem (s. xi *Merengehen*). As early as 649 Saint-Omer provides both *Laudardiaca villa* and *Tatinga villa* (826 *Tatingahem*, Tatinghem); cf. 844/64 *Pupurninga villa*, *Beinga villa* (877 *Pupurninga hem*, *Beinga hem*, now respectively Poperinge and Bayenghem). The *-iaca curtis/-iaca villa* type disappeared at an early date, but the *-ingahaim* type spread to Flanders and Brabant and, to a lesser extent, to Holland and Frisia; in Gysseling's view it also provided the prototype for the Old English *-ingahām* names.[1] This bold linking of place-name developments in England and in the Germanic (or shall we say, 'Saxon'?) area of north-eastern France will perhaps not stand unchallenged, but it ought to set the discussion going.

So far I have carefully avoided using any term more precise than 'Germanic' for the language spoken by the settlers north of the language frontier. The question is, of course, whether one can be more specific. So far good reasons have been found for extending the search for evidence beyond Frisia proper. By the same token the chronological framework will have to be completed. A case in point is the appearance of $\bar{e}$ corresponding to WS $\bar{æ}$, Anglian and Kentish $\bar{e}$ (traditionally held to derive from WGmc $\bar{a}$[2]). As we saw, DeCamp dates the diffusion of this $\bar{e}$ from Frisia to Kent in the sixth century or early seventh, but the earliest recorded instance of *rēd* is in the eighth century and comes from Saint-Omer: 723 *Leodredingas mansiones*, now Ledringham (20 kms S of Dunkirk; perhaps originally a name in *-ingas*, but the present name goes back to **Leodredinga hem*). Also recorded from non-Frisian territory is 830 *Fletuualdus* (Ghent). In the Flemish coastal region from Calais eastward (1290 *Vronemet*) $\bar{e}$ still appears at a time when $\bar{a}$ has become the rule farther inland: ± 1084 *Bolredus*, 1087 *Elvredus* and 1130 *Herred*; and with *mēd*: 1130 *Avinemed*, 1176 *Bertild med*, 1220 *Breda med* etc.[3]

---

[1] *Ibid.* p. 244.

[2] There is evidence for $\bar{a}$ having originated in south-west Germany and for Franconian still having had $\bar{e}$ at the time of the Franks' conquest of Gaul. Gysseling, 'De vroegste geschiedenis van het Nederlands', p. 173; see also Gysseling, 'Proeve van een Oudnederlandse grammatica', *Studia Germanica Gandensia* 3 (1961), 9–52.

[3] Gysseling, 'Oudnederlandse grammatica', esp. p. 31.

The other features listed by DeCamp present the same chronological difficulties; nor should one forget that Frisian does show different developments for the diphthongs *ai* (> *ā* in a limited number of environments only, otherwise *ē*) and *au* (regularly > *ā*). In the case of other 'Anglo-Frisian' developments we are again faced with such a wide diffusion that a more general term is needed to refer to them. The ending of the gen. pl., for example, is -*a* not only in Old English and Frisian, but in the whole area we have considered, as proved by the many place-names containing -*inga*. The change of *a* followed by nasal + voiceless spirant does appear in Frisian territory in the ninth century: *Osgeresgest* (Oegstgeest, near Leiden), but also in Ghent between 768 and 814: *Osgarda* and *Osgiva* (names of *mancipia* in the region of Ghent); from a later date we have examples near Dunkirk (1093 *Goselant*) and in West Flanders (± 1218 *Gosbelec, Gosbelc*).[1]

Neither the place-name material quoted in the course of this article nor the early instances of 'Frisianisms-outside-Frisia' can provide us with a decisive answer to the question 'pre-invasion tribal connections or post-invasion contacts?'. On the contrary they tend to prove that the 'or' may have to be replaced by 'and'. The place-names point to very close tribal connections, the details of which remain to be elucidated (the distribution of the -*tūn* and -*sele* names, for example, looking like a promising source of information). On the other hand, the late, post-invasion, date of common language features may (but need not) indicate post-invasion contacts. Of course, linguistic contacts, as distinct from political, economic and cultural ones, will be difficult to trace with certainty. Often we shall be able to do no more than discover a favourable climate, if possible so favourable that Bennett's objection to cross-Channel relations (see above, p. 2) can be set aside. In the area we have examined, matters are complicated by the advancing romanization, the changes in the configuration of the land (inundation, reclamation, resettlement), the rise of new ports and towns with the accompanying movements of population, and, finally, by the almost total lack of language material – apart from place-names – contemporary with Old English. Fortunately the following period provides ample evidence for the closeness of the dialects spoken north and south of the Straits. From Calais, which became a town of importance in the latter half of the twelfth century, receiving its charter from Count Matthew of Boulogne, enough material in the form of by-laws and lists of tax-payers survives from the late thirteenth

[1] M. Gysseling, 'Chronologie van enkele klankverschijnselen in het oudste Fries', *Fryske Studzjes oanbean oan Prof. Dr J. H. Brouwer* (Assen, 1960), pp. 77f. H. T. J. Miedema would place the beginnings of Frisian as a distinct language in the reign of King Redbad, about 700. 'De tweetalige naam van de Friese koning Rêdbâd-Râdbôd aan het begin der Friese en Nederlandse taalgeschiedenis', *Mededelingen van de Vereniging voor Naamkunde te Leuven* 44 (1968), 38–54; 'Noordzeegermaans en Vroegoudfries', *Leuvense Bijdragen* 60 (1971), 99–104.

century to give an insight into the local language situation. Although the texts in question are drawn up in Latin or French, Flemish words are used abundantly, for example, the by-laws of 1293:[1]

[3] Quod nullus delve worm dbesuden bome, sicut boem extendit intost et intuist. ('Let nobody dig for worms south of the boom, as far as the boom goes in the east and in the west.')

[8] Quod nullus teneat suem portantem neque ber, nisi teneat infra suum beloke, vel zoghe et ber perdantur. ('Let nobody keep a sow in pig or a boar, unless he keeps them within his enclosure, or the sow and the boar will be confiscated.')

[14] Quod nullus drive nec ride nec meine super dic nec over den dic inter murum et slus. ('Let nobody drive nor ride nor lead a horse on the dike nor across the dike between the wall and the sluice.')

And a few years later (before February 1298):

[4] Quod nullus latre nec latigghe teneant porcum. ('Let no "blood-letter", male or female, keep a pig.')

No wonder that these documents, until properly identified, had been filed as belonging to 'une ville non désignée, mais qui doit être un port de mer flamand'.[2] The dialect of Calais no doubt shows the pressure of Flemish as used in the more central parts of the county. There are, however, a number of morphological features such as the -s plural of masc. substantives (als, aels 'eels', houcs 'hooks'), the fem. suffix -igghe (latigghe, lokigghe vs. lat(e)re, lokere), the prefix je- or i- (jegharwet, 'prepared', jemene, ymene 'common' etc.) which correspond to contemporary English, as does the distinction between lengthened e and i in open syllables (spelled e, ei and i, e respectively). The vocabulary, too, points to the proximity of England, both in common nouns (baet 'boat', baetman, berman 'porter', wale, voetokes 'futtocks' etc.) and names of persons (Boid de Dovere, Rogier de Zanduic (Sandwich), Willelmus de Scoram (Shoreham), d'Ingelsche and Sc(r)ipwrictere (Shipwright)).[3]

Calais may have been exceptional in that such abundant documentary evidence has survived; it can hardly have been exceptional in maintaining close contacts with England or in its dialect showing traces of such contacts; nor can those contacts have been as recent as the rise of the town.[4] If this rapid tour of the region between the Canche and the Straits can persuade Anglo-Saxonists to have a closer look at the linguistic and toponymic information which this district offers, it will have served its purpose.

[1] M. Gysseling and C. Wyffels, 'Diets in schepenverordeningen van Calais uit het einde der XIIIde eeuw', *Studia Germanica Gandensia* 4 (1962), 9–30.

[2] *Ibid.* p. 10, n. 1.

[3] For the names see M. Gysseling and P. Bougard, *L'Onomastique Calaisienne à la Fin du 13e Siècle*, Anthroponymica 13 (Leuven–Brussel, 1963), and for a survey of dialect characteristics see M. Gysseling, 'Dialectkenmerken van Calais in de 13e eeuw', *Taal en Tongval* 18 (1966), 147–63.

[4] Philip Grierson, 'The Relations between England and Flanders Before the Norman Conquest', *TRHS* 4th ser. 23 (1941), 71–112.

Old English colour classification: where do matters stand?

NIGEL F. BARLEY

Various attempts have been made by Anglo-Saxonists to deal with the Old English colour vocabulary but the subject remains far from clear. In the present article I shall try to show some of the reasons why this is so and offer a re-interpretation of the Old English colour words *as a system*, treating the Anglo-Saxons simply as a standard ethnographic corpus of anthropological data and therefore amenable to the techniques applied to those present-day communities that are the concern of the anthropologist.

The phenomenon of colour vision involves many fields of study, including physics, psychology and physiology. Anthropologists have long been concerned with colour classification as just one of the cognitive systems that mediate the social perception of reality.[1] Such colour systems have become the standard example of the 'complete relativist' approach to world views.[2] Recently, however, this line has been questioned, specifically with reference to colour systems,[3] and certain universal colour categories have been proposed. The involvement of so many disparate sciences and philosophical dogmas goes a long way to explaining the controversy that still surrounds this topic. Several points are, however, generally accepted and must be briefly reviewed before we consider the specifically Anglo-Saxon features of colour classification.

For the idealized standard colour receptor, the colour perceived depends on three variables – hue, saturation and brightness. Hue can be expressed in terms of the wavelength of the light, saturation in terms of the purity of hue, and brightness in terms of the amount of light transmitted. It is thus clear that hue is a *qualitative* dimension concerned with what sort of light is perceived, while saturation and brightness are *quantitative*, being concerned with the amount of light reaching the eye. This information is traditionally represented visually by means of the colour solid (see fig. 2). Since, however, this three-way opposition can be resolved into a simple binary one between

---

[1] E. Durkheim and M. Mauss, *Primitive Classification* (Chicago, 1963).
[2] B. Whorf, *Language, Thought and Reality*, ed. J. Carroll (Cambridge, Mass., 1964).
[3] B. Berlin and P. Kay, *Basic Color Terms, their Universality and Evolution* (Berkeley and Los Angeles, 1969).

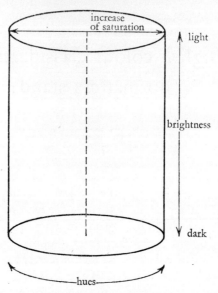

FIG. 2   The colour solid

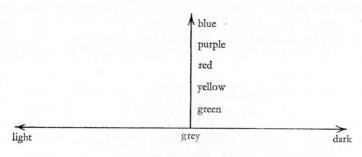

FIG. 3   The Munsell colour chart

the qualitative dimension and those that are quantitative, the normal means of presentation for comparative purposes is the Munsell colour chart where saturation and brightness are absorbed into a single (horizontal) axis. This gives us a much more practical diagram (see fig. 3).

Our own Modern English colour classification is firmly biased towards the differentiation of hues, so much so in fact that we even term extremely light surfaces 'white' and extremely dark surfaces 'black' and treat them as hues. The primacy of hues is shown, moreover, by the fact that we reserve the noun category for their designation and use 'pale' and 'dark' as qualifiers to express the brightness dimension. Hue names are thus the fixed points on which we hang our whole colour system.

Old English colour classification

Once we appreciate how lopsided and idiosyncratic is our own colour system, we shall not be surprised to find that the Anglo-Saxon approach to colour was quite different and that attempts to treat the latter as a hue-stressing system have resulted in a rare confusion. The main stress of the Old English system falls firstly, not upon hue, but upon brightness. This is far from a new insight and has been remarked upon by nineteenth-century writers[1] and more recently by Lerner.[2] For some reason, however, modern Anglo-Saxonists have not recognized the fundamental nature of the light–dark opposition in Anglo-Saxon culture. Nineteenth-century scholars were much more sensitive to the paradigmatic structural implications[3] of this opposition and their insights have been neglected to the great detriment of the subject. Mead[4] remarks that Old English poetry is a literature of light and dark, white and black. Even one whose interests are principally anthropological cannot but be struck by the fact that *Beowulf* is a poem of bright day and darkest night, light ale-hall and gloomy wasteland. That this has a symbolic load is evident. Let it be noted also that black is far and away the most common 'colour' in Old English poetry. It finds expression in a rich vocabulary: *blæc, deorc, dun, sweart, wann* etc. Opposed to black we have the second most common 'colour' term, white, and here again we have a striking profusion of terms: *blac, hwit, beorht, leoht, scir* etc. It is thus apparent that there is an equation of brightness and whiteness, darkness and blackness, or, more accurately, an absence of the distinction that follows from our own hue-stressing system.

Gummere[5] argues that in 'Common Germanic' times, light and dark were associated with joy and sadness only – the extension to good and evil being the result of eastern influence via Christianity. We now know much more about such patterns of thought in primitive society and would be much less willing to accept this line of argument. However this may be (and Gummere's evidence is far from conclusive), by that part of the Anglo-Saxon period for which we have documentary evidence this association is firmly established. Christ and the angels are always *scir, beorht* etc., hell and the devils are always *sweart, wann* and so on. One of the neatest examples of this comes in the poem *Daniel* (448), as pointed out by Gummere: the Jews have just been saved from the flames – the dazzling fire having been described – but the angel who rescues them is 'se þe hie of þam mirce generede' ('he who saved

---

[1] W. Mead, 'Color in Old English Poetry', *PMLA* 14 (1899), 169–206.
[2] L. Lerner, 'Colour Words in Anglo-Saxon', *MLR* 46 (1951), 246–9; repr. in *Essential Articles for the Study of Old English Poetry*, ed. J. Bessinger Jr and S. Kahrl (Hamden, Connecticut, 1968).
[3] I use these terms not simply in their linguistic sense but also in the anthropological sense referring to abstract cognitive structures.
[4] 'Color in Old English Poetry'.
[5] F. Gummere, *On the Symbolic Use of the Colours Black and White in Germanic Tradition*, Haverford College Studies 1 (Haverford, 1899).

white/light	grey	black/dark
blac	*græg*	*blæc*
hwit	*hasu*	*deorc*
beorht	*har*	*dun*
leoht		*sweart*
scir		*wann*

FIG. 4 The light–dark axis

them from the darkness'). The contrast between light and dark is extended to cosmic proportions in the opposition between heaven and hell and reduced to anthropomorphic proportions in the opposition between joy and sadness. It is thus not without significance that *glæd* means both 'joyful' and 'bright'. This binary opposition, then, serves as a basic structuring device ordering the fields of experience and ethics. We can sum it up diagramatically in terms of the light–dark axis (see fig. 4).

The fact that the Anglo-Saxon colour system was not hue-stressing does not, of course, mean that hues were not distinguished. Let us now consider the hue axis. It is perhaps most easily compared with that of Modern English if presented in tabular form after the manner of Ardener[1] (see fig. 5). Although excluded from the 'basic colour vocabulary', words indicating overlapping categories are of interest in any attempt to recreate the Old English system. Thus terms such as *hæwen-grene* and *brun-baso* are valuable for the corroboration they can offer the ordering that we set up. More particularly, a glance at fig. 5 is sufficient to show how simple is the solution to that most perennial of old disputes in Anglo-Saxon – the use of *read* to describe gold. Recourse is often had to highly ingenious and learned explanations urging that gold in medieval times had a relatively high copper content and that it was consequently redder than modern gold. We are told that the adjective was used only for the alliteration or because it had become a set phrase. As elsewhere, such explanations lack an anthropological perspective and so fail to realize that Old English 'red' is not our red and that we cannot blandly equate the two categories. Even the new universalist approach to colour systems[2] assumes that there will be substantial variation from culture to culture in the position of boundaries. That the solution to the 'red gold' problem lies in the lack of fit between two sets of categories and not in differences in the 'reality' described is clear from the use of 'red' cognates in other Germanic languages, such as ON *raud mani*, '"red" moon'.

The basic material on the Anglo-Saxon use of colour words is contained

[1] E. Ardener, *Social Anthropology and Language*, Assoc. of Social Anthropologists Ser. 10 (London, 1971).
[2] Berlin and Kay, *Basic Color Terms*.

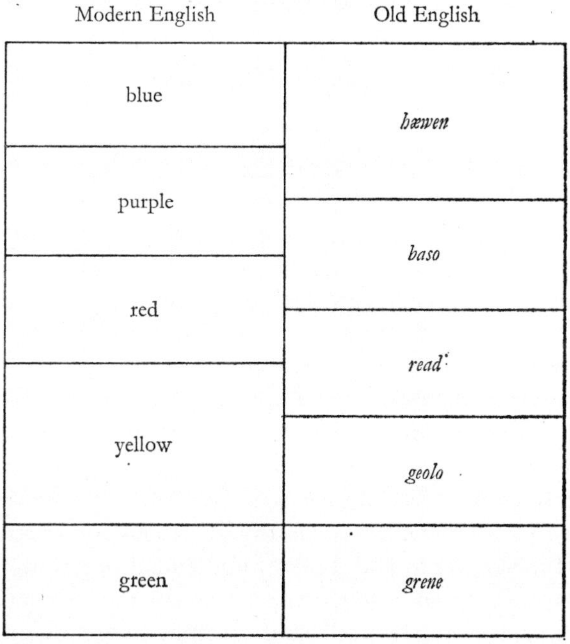

Modern English	Old English
blue	*hæwen*
purple	*baso*
red	*read*
yellow	*geolo*
green	*grene*

FIG. 5   The Old English hue axis compared with that of Modern English

in Mead[1] and Willms.[2] Both offer useful accumulations of data but are lacking in interpretation. It is a sad fact that many Anglo-Saxonists tend to study their people not as thinking members of a social community but as generators of scribal errors and manuscript traditions. Lerner is a rare exception.[3] He takes a most promising line, denouncing previous approaches as bound by the classificatory prejudices and preconceptions of their authors. He suggests a fresh approach from an anthropological perspective to the vexed colour terms we have not yet treated, *fealo, wann* and *brun*. These words have long earned their Anglo-Saxon users much opprobrium. They are held to be vague, imprecise and – even by Lerner – 'unscientific'. He suggests that

[1] 'Color in Old English Poetry'.

[2] J. Willms, 'Der Gebrauch der Farbenbezeichnungen in der Poesie Altenglands', Inaugural Dissertation (Münster i. W., 1902). Since this article was completed, I have come across G. König, 'Die Bezeichnungen für Farbe, Glanz und Helligkeit im Altenglischen', D.Phil. thesis (Mainz, 1957). This offers by far the most comprehensive and accessible collection of data on the subject so far available. Dr König is very much concerned with collocation restrictions and makes many useful points, partly in agreement with my own views. We differ chiefly in the treatment of the 'problem words' (see below), where Dr König's atomistic approach is opposed to any attempt to set up wider correspondences between members of lexical sub-sets. It is my contention that only through the reconstruction of such sub-systems can we ever arrive at an understanding of the processes at work and at an appreciation of the logical consistency of the Old English colour system.

[3] 'Colour Words'.

they can be dealt with only by a third axis of 'brightness'. His use of this term seems itself somewhat vague, since he already has a light–dark axis in his model. Furthermore he seems to be thinking in terms of a scale of absolute, not relative, 'brightness', since he remarks that this quality 'being largely the product of circumstances, the word would apply to objects only in certain circumstances'. In view of what colour specialists have to say on adjustative mechanisms[1] in colour perception this seems inherently unlikely. Lerner has made the mistake of not sorting out his basic colour terms from more elaborated sub-systems. It is unfortunate, moreover, that he has brought the data together only from the poetry, as this is exactly where we should expect most deliberate flouting of the normal collocation restrictions and use of paradigmatic associations.[2] The descriptions of 'brown' waves, 'wan' clouds and 'fallow' flames are *a priori* just as likely to be intended to achieve that shifting of normal apperception that constitutes part of the poetic experience as they are to serve the interests of accurate depiction. Thus, when we find the expression '*harne stan*' (*The Ruin* 43a), 'hoar (grey with age) stone', it is important to know whether *har* normally had an animate application (as is implied by the Bosworth and Toller Supplement, especially the substantivized meaning of *Beowulf* 2988a). In a poem on the transience of earthly things, the poignancy of this word could well be due to such paradigmatic associations. I shall be returning to this problem later.[3]

---

[1] E.g. R. Evans, *An Introduction to Color* (New York, 1948).

[2] See Ardener, *Social Anthropology*, esp. p. lxxvii.

[3] If we wish to regard *har* as limited to contexts marked 'animate', there is a problem in the BT Suppl. entry IIa, 'the word occurs often as epithet of stones and trees used as boundary markers'. The other uses, however, can be safely dismissed as late or consciously poetical. For example, 'of clife harum' in *The Metres of Boethius* (5113a) is not in the prose version, and we would have to be extremely careful if we drew any conclusions from use in the riddles, since, as I show elsewhere (N. Barley, 'Structural Aspects of the Anglo-Saxon Riddle', *Semiotica* 10 (1974), 143–75), riddles manipulate just such restrictions to deceive or help the solver.

Are we, then, to regard the use of *har* with stones and trees as an example of a word already partly freed of collocation restrictions, pointing the way for the other colour terms in their drift towards more general applicability? To adopt this view, it would be necessary to show that such occurrences are relatively late or colloquial. This may, indeed, be the case. The limitation of this phenomenon to boundary symbols suggests, however, another explanation and immediately warns the anthropologist that he is in danger of being misled. Boundary symbols, perhaps more than anything else, are likely to hold a special place in a people's world view. Modern works on classifications and taboos have noted the power of lines of demarcation; see, e.g., M. Douglas, *Purity and Danger* (London, 1966), and A. Van Gennep, *Les Rites de Passage* (Paris, 1909; trans. into English, London, 1960). Elsewhere ('Anglo-Saxon Magico-Medicine', *Jnl of the Anthropological Soc. of Oxford* 3 (1972), 67–77) I have shown that the Anglo-Saxon magico-medical system is based largely upon the manipulation and reaffirmation of boundaries. We see further concern with such matters in the concept of the outlaw, cast outside the social world and symbolically identified with the wolf. It is doubtless no coincidence that the charters that contain the *har stan* phenomenon also indicate the presence of 'wolfshead-trees' on the liminal areas between properties. (An interestingly late case is of a dispute between the abbots of St Albans and Westminster in 1437, recorded in the *Annales Monasterii S. Albani*. The latter abbot complained that the former had destroyed a gallows erected by immemorial custom in a place called

There is every reason to think that the three 'problem words', *fealo*, *brun* and *wann*, can be understood only when reintegrated into the sub-systems of classification of which they form a part. They then become of fundamental importance as part of the study of diachronic category shifts within the Germanic speech community. As far as the essential nature of these words is concerned, it should serve as a warning that there is no Old English word that can be regularly translated as 'colour'. There are several words, such as *færþu*, *hiw* and *bleo*, that *can* be translated 'colour', but often a better rendering is 'appearance'.[1] The Anglo-Saxons had neither colour charts nor a large range of dyes.[2] For them, colours were attributes of objects and had not reached the level of abstraction that they have in our own society. There is good reason to believe that many colour words originate as comparisons with concrete referents.[3] Thus the word for 'red' will often be derived from a term meaning something like 'blood-coloured'. Gradually such words may detach themselves from this original referent, become etymologically obscure and take on a separate lexical existence. Some of them may even reach the basic colour vocabulary.[4] Hence we may expect to find words bound, to a greater or lesser degree, to concrete referents.[5] Also I should like to emphasize that in adducing historical information I am by no means unaware of the distinction between the diachronic and synchronic planes. In the absence of informants, however, the Anglo-Saxonist of anthropological bent must fall back on secondary sources, including philological evidence from related dialects.

If we look at *fealo* in its full Germanic context, it is clear that it formed part of a lexical sub-set originally restricted to horses. The existence of such a sub-set should not surprise us. An extensive cattle vocabulary amongst the Nuer has been well studied.[6] Modern English still contains such a group, e.g. bay, roan, palamino etc. It seems that those areas in which there is greatest interest in developing a system for communicating fine distinctions

---

Nomannesland in order to destroy his boundary marker.) Worship of such plants and trees is attested in the laws (II Cnut 5, 1). This complex problem cannot be fully treated here, but perhaps enough has been said to show that this usage of *har* may be explicable only by reference to other systems of belief that would remove certain stones and trees from the 'non-animal' category. Once more we see the impossibility of dealing with all colour words on a single level.

[1] See A. Cameron, 'The Old English Nouns of Colour: a Semantic Study', unpub. B.Litt. thesis (Oxford, 1968). I am grateful to Dr Bruce Mitchell of St Edmund Hall, Oxford, for bringing this thesis to my attention. For a note on *færþu*, see O. Szemerényi 'A New Leaf of the Gothic Bible', *Language* 48 (1972), 1–10.

[2] E. Ploss, 'Die Färberei in der germanischen Handwirtschaft', *Zeitschrift für die Philologie* 75 (1956), 1–21.

[3] Berlin and Kay, *Basic Color Terms*, p. 37.   [4] *Ibid.* p. 5.

[5] It is regrettable that anthropologists have largely neglected investigation of this aspect of colour classification, since it provides an excellent means of access to other systems of classification operating within a culture.

[6] E. Evans-Pritchard, *The Nuer* (Oxford, 1940).

will tend to evolve a specialized vocabulary.[1] I suggest that horses constituted such a field for the Germanic peoples. The extension of words from a favoured field into more general use is well attested historically and psychologically.[2] For the anthropologist it is yet another example of that universal human tendency to calque one system of classification on another.

Gmc *falwa-[3] occurs as ON *fǫlr*, OS *falu*, OHG *falo* and OE *fealo*. It is used in Old Norse of the human complexion and is used of human hair and gold only in the Old High German glosses. By far the clearest cross-dialectal use is of the horse: (1) There is the Old Norse form quoted by de Vries,[4] *fǫlski*, 'rotes Pferd' (bay horse). (2) There are upper German, Rhenish Franconian forms such as *falch*, 'bay horse or cow'. (3) There is evidence of a continuing struggle between generalization and specialization of sense in Old High German and Middle High German cognates. Two forms from *val* and *valwer* finally parted company, ceasing to be in free variation, and Modern German *falb* has retained its purely equine reference. (4) There is preserved a document of Byzantine origin, *Corpus Hippiatricorum Graecorum* that correlates the colours and temperaments of horses. For once history has been kind to us. Whereas we hitherto had no evidence for a Gothic *falwa-* cognate, this source proves that there was indeed one. The word, moreover, seems to have been applied specifically to horses and was presumably introduced by Gothic troops in the employment of the Empire.[5] The relevant Greek term is ψάλβας, which Schwyzer derives from the Gothic weak substantive form *falwa-*. As elsewhere, the narrow meaning of the substantivized form is further evidence that the word was firmly bound to an equine context.

None of this evidence is conclusive if taken piecemeal, but if considered as a whole it amounts to quite a strong case for assigning *falwa-* to a lexical sub-set of horse words.[6] That such a horse set did indeed exist can be easily demonstrated:

Gmc *blanka-* occurs as ON *blakkr*, OS *blanc*, OHG *blanch* and OE *blanca*.

---

[1] A good study of such a specialized sub-system is C. Frake, 'The Diagnosis of Disease among the Subanum of Mindanao', *Amer. Anthropologist* 63 (1961), 113–32.

[2] S. Ullmann, *The Principles of Semantics* (Oxford, 1959).

[3] For what follows I draw heavily on the evidence in E. Schwentner, 'Eine sprachgeschichtliche Untersuchung über den Gebrauch und die Bedeutung der altgermanischen Farbenbezeichnungen', Inaugural Dissertation (Göttingen, 1915), to which the reader is referred for more detail. This pioneering work brings together much of the available data on comparative Germanic colour studies. It is quite clear that Schwentner realized the existence of collocation restrictions on Germanic colour words but the absence of a structuralist approach prevented him from seeing these as anything but an arbitrary series of disjointed irregularities.

[4] J. de Vries, *Altnordisches etymologisches Wörterbuch* (Leiden, 1961).

[5] E. Schwyzer, 'Germanisches und ungedeutetes in byzantinischen Pferdenamen', *ZDA* 66 (1929), 93–9.

[6] Unfortunately it would be misleading to use the evidence of Vulgar Latin forms as these are relatively late and the dangers of reciprocal borrowing and mutual influence are too great.

In all dialects it is used almost exclusively of horses, in Old High German as an adjective, in Old English and Old Norse as a noun. The postulated Germanic meaning is '*shining white (horse)'. It occurs as βλαγχας in the *Corpus Hippiatricorum* from Gothic *blagka-.

Gmc *blasa- occurs as ON *blese*, OS *blas* and ModE *blaze*. It refers in all dialects to a horse with a white patch on its forehead. In the *Corpus Hippiatricorum* it appears as βάλας.

Gmc *dunna- occurs as OS *dun* (etymologically related are OS *dosa* and OHG *tusin* from which are derived MedLat *dosinus* and *dosius*[1] and OE *dunn*. All forms are firmly associated with horses, with some application to other animals.

Gmc *grawa- occurs as ON *grar*, OS *grao*, OHG *grao*, OFris *gre* and OE *græg*. Cross-dialectally it is restricted mainly to (1) human hair and animal fur and (2) iron. In the animal category it is applied chiefly to horses and wolves. It occurs in the *Corpus Hippiatricorum* as γρίβας and is found again in Modern Greek with the meaning 'grey horse'. It is my contention that Gmc *falwa- was part of this group of colour words, limited originally to horses.

Gmc *bruna- occurs as OS, OFris and OE *brun*. It is common of animals, especially horses. Its other chief use is of metal. Structurally, then, its closest relation is Gmc *grawa-. Unlike *grawa-, however, it is not clearly recorded as applied to human hair. It occurs only rarely of the human complexion. Two factors argue against its inclusion in the horse words: it does not occur in the *Corpus Hippiatricorum* and it seems etymologically connected with Gmc *beron, 'bear'. But neither is conclusive. The absence of the word is not necessarily significant, while the use of the word with reference to the bear might be an early example of that extension of the term to all animals that we observe in the case of *grawa-. I would therefore include it in the horse words.[2]

If, as I have argued, *fealo* and *brun* were originally part of the horse set, how far was this still true in the Anglo-Saxon period? This, of course, is difficult to answer. I have pointed to the problem caused by the fact that the majority of our material is from the poetic corpus. We are really asking how

---

[1] E. Schwentner, 'Eine altgermanische Farbenbezeichnung', *Beiträge zur Geschichte der deutschen Sprache und Literatur* 49 (1925), 423–9.

[2] This raises the question of other colour sub-groups in Common Germanic times. I believe we can detect another group in *erpa, *blunda- and *haira-. Gmc. *erpa- occurs as ON *jarpr*, OHG *erpf* and OE *earp*. It remains fully active only in Old Norse, where it is almost totally restricted to human hair. Gmc. *blunda- is a vexed term that has, however, been traditionally accepted as a Germanic word borrowed early into Latin and referring to the hair of the typical Germanic warrior (see Ploss, 'Die Färberei'). Gmc. *haira- occurs as ON *harr*, OHG *her* and OE *har*. It is applied to human hair and animal fur. Although the evidence for these terms is less convincing than that for the horse words, it is at least enough to suggest that Common Germanic contained a group of colour words limited to human hair.

far a word could be 'normally' applied to the waves etc. and how far such usage constituted a deliberate circumvention of standard collocation restrictions. We are more likely to be able to give a clear answer to this problem if we relate these words to the third member of their set in Anglo-Saxon times. I should therefore like now to consider *wann*.

This is a word without an obvious history and was apparently an Anglo-Saxon creation. We may, therefore, discount the possibility of its forming part of any Common Germanic colour sub-set. If it were a new formation, it would be reasonable to expect it to conform to the colour system at the time of its creation and to shed light on the underlying rationale of that system. In Old English it is homonymous with *wan-* expressing deprivation or negation. It is used of such things as the raven, dark waves and dark chain-mail. In other words, it is applied to things negatively specified for hue, dark things which are glossy to the point of having highlights rippling across their surface. It is this quality of variegated surface-reflectivity, that takes in the whole external appearance, that Lerner was groping for under the term 'brightness'. *Wann* is a word of complex sense impression including information that we would not include under 'colour' at all.

Turning to *fealo*, we find that the things to which it is applied have the same basic quality. It is applied to horses, glinting shield edges, the waves of the sea, flame etc. If we accept this view, the old bone of contention, the *fealwe stræte* of *Beowulf* 916b, ceases to trouble us, as the reference is to the gravel glinting or (see below) to the parched grass. The objects to which *brun* is applied – helmets, swords, waves, feathers – also have the same component. Dal[1] has suggested that in *brun* we have two words that have coalesced. There seems no need to postulate this. The word has always had two components, one hue, the other surface reflectivity. Medieval French courtly verse took over only the latter sense, rediffused it to the other countries of Europe and so made possible those references to 'brown' mirrors and diamonds that occur in the fourteenth and fifteenth centuries.

Given the presence of such marked formal patterns, I suggest that OE *fealo*, *brun* and *wann*, and also *græg*, are terms generally applicable to glossy things. In other words the original horse terms have been extended and generalized to fit the restrictions on *wann*. Adapting the approach of Katz and Fodor,[2] we can encode this as two changes in the semantic markers of the terms concerned:

(1) (Colour) – (Animate) – (Non-human) – (Horse) → (Colour) – (Animate).
(2) (Colour) – (Animate) → (Colour) – (Glossy).

[1] I. Dal, 'German. *brun* als Epitheton von Waffen', *Norsk Tidskrift for Sprogvidenskap* 9 (1938), 219–30.
[2] J. Katz and J. Fodor, 'The Structure of a Semantic Theory', *Language* 39 (1963), 170–210.

The attraction of this presentation is that it enables us to establish a sequence of transformations. Its chief disadvantage is that it fails to deal adequately with relations between elements in a sub-set.[1] For example the above description does not account for the frequent use of the term *fealo* to describe plant-life, where it is applied to brown leaves, dying vegetation. This is to be explained by the fact that *fealo* has entered here into opposition with *grene*. *Fealo* means the fallow land as opposed to the green fields, the winter aspect as opposed to the summer.[2] It is to be expected that any Old English poet worth his salt would exploit these paradigmatic associations. Hence the frequent occurrence of 'fallow waves' in the more elegiac parts of the poetic corpus that has so often been explained as merely 'there for the alliteration'.

Another group of words collocationally distinct in the Old English period is what I would term the '*baso* group'. *Baso* was apparently an Old English coinage. It is glossed *purpureus, phoenicus, coccineus*, i.e. 'crimson/purple'. It should be deleted from the basic colour vocabulary on the grounds that it is a secondary formation from *baso*, 'berry'. Ploss[3] tells us that a favourite dye of the Germanic peoples was produced by crushing blackberries. The broad range of colour covered by this term thus represents a specialized dye-term. It is significant that it is only Old English, regularly applied only to fabrics and occurs as a substantive, meaning 'purple cloth'. Similar is OE *wæden*, meaning 'purple/blue'. It is regularly applied only to fabrics, and, being etymologically related to woad, refers to dye from that plant. The various reflexes of Gmc **salwa-* in the different dialects all have the dominant referent human clothing. Although applied to animals and birds in Old English, even here we find signs of collocation restrictions. A regular feature of its use is its combination with *-pada-*. Thus we have 'saluwigpadan, þone sweartan hræfn' (*The Battle of Brunanburh* 61) and 'earn... / salowigpada' (*Judith* 210–11a). This compound, meaning something like 'sallow-coated', avoids violation of the limitation to clothing. I therefore suggest that the '*baso* group' is a specialized sub-set limited to fabrics, dyes and clothing.

[1] This is why it has to be supplemented by an approach that is structural in the sense of A. Greimas, *Semantique Structurale* (Paris, 1966). One does not, however, have to adopt as extreme a view of the differences between these two models as does E. Coseriu, 'Zur Vorgeschichte der strukturellen Semantik: Heyses Analyse des Wortfeldes "Schall"', in *To Honor Roman Jakobson* (Paris, 1967), esp. p. 493 n. Symbolic systems being of a multi-level order, we must expect to find nesting.

[2] For a further example of this see H. Conklin, 'Hanunoo Color Categories', *Southwestern Jnl of Anthropology* 11 (1964), 339–44. We should note a similar phenomenon in Modern English whereby wine is either 'red' or 'white' regardless of the fact that its actual colour may be purple, green or yellow.

[3] 'Die Färberei'.

In fig. 6 I attempt to formalize, albeit tentatively, the collocation restrictions on some of the principal Old English words.[1] In fig. 7 I attempt to locate the 'problem words' on the hue axis and on the light–dark axis. We have come far since our first consideration of the Old English colour system, but this has at least made clear the grave danger of carrying *our* prejudices into a consideration of *their* categories. The Anglo-Saxon approach to colour was far different from our own biaxial, hue-stressing system. It was concerned chiefly with the differentiation of light and dark. It contained many words of specialized sub-sets that were collocationally restricted. It also had words of complex sense impression that were specified not only for hue but also for light and dark and general surface quality. If I have regretted that scholars have restricted themselves to the poetic use of colour words, this is not to plead merely for a full statistical treatment of the whole Old English corpus. One hopes that the current Old English dictionary project of Cameron and Ball will look at just this sort of problem. At the end of such a laborious undertaking, we should know a lot more about actual usage but would not be necessarily any the wiser concerning the underlying system. We shall have to weigh each occurrence in the light of a system, allowing for random historical omissions, deliberately 'poetic' usage and so on. Cameron[2] argues specifically against such a generative approach, seeking to limit analyses to listing recorded occurrences. This is to condemn the subject to a false, stultifying sterility. It would be as pointless as to seek to describe the English language by a list of recorded utterances. It would, moreover, make it impossible to treat calques of one symbolic system on another, such as we have mentioned with reference to the light–dark axis in Anglo-Saxon society. It is, therefore, not surprising that Cameron's own treatment of *bleo* and *hiw* is excellently structural and so, inevitably, tacitly a generative model without arrows.

The collocation restrictions I have proposed for certain key Old English words are only tentative. They represent only a programme for research. A full investigation would include those colour words that I have not treated and investigate structural relationships between groups at all levels. Thus the study of the evolution of the colour system through time will

---

[1] Lest it should be thought that collocationally restricted sub-systems are unusual, let us note that Modern English again offers a parallel – besides the horse words already mentioned – in its (female) hair sub-set: blonde, brunette, auburn etc. The similarity of this to the Gmc **erpa*-group is striking. It should be observed that the Anglo-Saxons were primarily concerned with the light–dark opposition even here, giving the system: fair = English = beautiful = freeborn, opposed to dark = Celtic = ugly = slave. In this way we can build up a picture of the way in which the Anglo-Saxons calqued a number of cognitive systems on a single axis of the colour system. I have suggested elsewhere ('Anglo-Saxon Magico-Medicine') that the hue axis may be used as a frame on which to hang a classificatory system of disease.

[2] 'The Old English Nouns of Colour', introduction, *passim*.

Word	Horses	Other animals	Birds	Metal	Fabrics	Human hair	Human skin	Water	Plants	Stone
fealo	PG	OE	OE	OE		ME		OE	OE	
blanca	PG		OE mori- bund	OE mori- bund						
dunn	PG	OE			OE					OE
græg	PG	OE	*baso*[a]	PG		PG? not OE		OE		
brun	PG	PG?	OE	PG		ME	OE	OE		
wann	*sweart*[b]	OE rare	OE	OE		OE		OE		
wæden					PG					
baso					OE					
salo			*salo- padig*		PG					
erpa	OE v. rare	OE v. rare	OE v. rare	OE v. rare		PG				
har		PG?	*baso*[a]	OE rare		PG				OE?

FIG. 6 Some key Old English colour words and their collocation restrictions. This is not an attempt to tabulate every *occurrence* of these terms but seeks to outline the underlying system. PG = positively specified in Primitive Germanic; OE = positively specified in Old English; ME = positively specified in Middle English. Unless it is otherwise stated, positions tenable in Primitive Germanic remain so in Old English

[a] The whole subject of OE *græg* remains to be investigated. It seems to be the case, however, that where birds are concerned *baso* is the collocationally appropriate word.
[b] The question of the various restrictions on OE words for 'black' has not been adequately investigated. Mead, 'Color in Old English Poetry', has several suggestive remarks that would reward further study. Meanwhile *sweart* seems to be the collocationally appropriate word for horses.

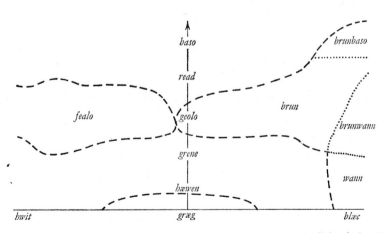

FIG. 7 Location of the 'problem words' on the hue axis and on the light–dark axis

27

become another part of the semiotic science that concerns itself with the processes by which all sorts of systems of classification are shattered, reinterpreted and restructured by a sort of popular etymological gloss.[1]

[1] C. Lévi-Strauss, *La Pensée Sauvage* (Paris, 1962). Proof in such matters is impossible, but it seems not unlikely that the breaking down of collocation restrictions in the Old English period was connected with the great enrichment of material culture experienced by the Anglo-Saxons, firstly as a result of their invasion of these Romanized islands and secondly through their contacts with Mediterranean Christianity. M. Mauss (*The Gift* (London, 1954)) made the point that the fewer material possessions a people have the greater is the symbolic load carried by each. The converse also applies.

Germanic and Roman antiquity and the sense of the past in Anglo-Saxon England

MICHAEL HUNTER

Nothing is more characteristic of the Dark Ages than the ease with which the barbarians assimilated Latin culture. Within a century of Augustine's mission to the pagan English, 'a barbarous, fierce and unbelieving nation' who 'paralysed [him] with terror',[1] Ceolfrith had attempted to make Jarrow a second *Vivarium*[2] and Northumbria could boast scriptoria with an uncial hand superior to the contemporary products of Rome herself.[3] No less striking is the career of a barbarian prince like Cædwalla, who emerged from the forests of Wessex on a pilgrimage to Rome, where he was baptized in St Peter's and had his epitaph written in classical metres by the archbishop of Milan.[4] Yet the Christianity which thus introduced the Saxons to Mediterranean classicism did not cut them off from their native cultural inheritance. The Northumbria which produced the *Codex Amiatinus* was also the home of Cædmon and of the Lindisfarne Gospels, whose rich mixture of Roman and barbaric elements exemplifies the Saxons' success in turning vernacular poetry and insular art to Christian themes.

The two traditions so successfully fused in this way, had, however, been divided in the past. In the imperial period a 'moral barrier' on the Rhine and the Danube had marked a 'fundamental antithesis between civilized mankind under Roman rule and the world of barbarians on the outskirts'.[5] Outside dwelt the uncouth tribes from whom the Anglo-Saxons were descended, with their traditions of divine descent and heroic exploits remembered 'in their ancient songs, their only form of recorded history'.[6] Their way of life contrasted dramatically with the complex and literate civilization of imperial Rome. Even in the provinces the Romans left buildings, roads and artifacts which exemplified the organization and civility of the Roman world in contrast to the barbarian wastes beyond the frontiers.

---

[1] Bede, *Historia Ecclesiastica* 1.23.
[2] P. Hunter Blair, *The World of Bede* (London, 1970), pp. 224–5.
[3] See E. A. Lowe, *English Uncial* (Oxford, 1960).
[4] *HE* v.7.
[5] A. Alföldi, 'The Moral Barrier on Rhine and Danube', *Transactions of the Congress of Roman Frontier Studies, 1949*, ed. E. Birley (Durham, 1952), p. 12.
[6] Tacitus, *Germania*, 2.

In this article I intend to examine the surviving evidence for the Anglo-Saxons' awareness of these contrasting elements in the history of their culture. I have limited my treatment largely to the Christian period, since the evidence from pagan Saxon times, which I have summarized in a short appendix, is less easy to assess. First I shall deal with the Christian Saxons' interest in the Germanic north and then I shall discuss their concern with the history and culture of ancient Rome. I have intentionally separated the Germanic and Roman traditions because significance has sometimes been attached to the Saxons' appeal to one or the other. But in a final section I shall consider how far it is legitimate to divide the two elements in this way, and thus draw more general conclusions about the sense of the past in Anglo-Saxon England.

In pursuing this theme I have consciously neglected one of the most significant elements in the Christian Saxons' approach to the past, their use of the bible. The Old Testament gives a lengthy history of the world before the birth of Christ which was studied throughout the Saxon period. But it was more than mere history for it was seen as part of the unfolding of God's purpose: its divine inspiration gave it claims to examination in a Christian context which the profane history of ancient Rome and Germany lacked. Every aspect of Anglo-Saxon thought was pervaded with Old Testament precedents and parallels.[1] Only when they were 'not content merely to lend an attentive ear to hear the words of Holy Scripture'[2] were Christian Saxons likely to show the concern for secular antiquity examined in this article.

Christianity had a further effect on men's concern with the past, for after the church came to northern Europe it was always more interested in the Christian culture that it had created than in the earlier history of the traditions that formed it. Thus in the most elaborate historical work written in Anglo-Saxon England, Bede's *Ecclesiastical History of the English People*, Roman history appeared only to set the scene for the founding of the English church, and Germanic history only briefly to chronicle the origin of the English people. The Old English version of Bede's *History* took this single-mindedness further still by excising much of this material.[3] Bede's historiography had a primarily didactic end, as he explained to Ceolwulf in the preface to his *History*. He was always concerned to point to the moral lessons of the past, and it is no coincidence that most extant Anglo-Saxon historical writing is hagiography: by the improving study of recent saints the historian best

---

[1] They are, for example, a recurrent motif in J. M. Wallace-Hadrill, *Early Germanic Kingship in England and on the Continent* (Oxford, 1971).

[2] Bede, preface to *HE*.

[3] D. Whitelock, 'The Old English Bede', *Proc. of the Brit. Acad.* 48 (1962), 62.

served the useful function of teaching people in the present. To writers like these, the pre-Christian past might have seemed all but irrelevant.

But, though Bede devoted hardly more than a paragraph to the Germanic origins of the English,[1] this scarcely did justice to the strength of feeling binding Englishmen to their ancestral continental homes. This may be gauged by the frequent appeals from the eighth-century missionaries to their compatriots to help convert the continental Saxons. 'Even they themselves are wont to say, "we are of one blood and one bone"', wrote Boniface, a West Saxon, appealing to all who were 'sprung from the stock and race of the English'[2] and echoing the earlier sentiments of Egbert, a Northumbrian exile in Ireland, who 'knew that there were very many peoples in Germany from whom the Angles and Saxons, who now live in Britain, derive their origin'.[3] One Mercian bishop went even further, rejoicing in the hope that this nation of his own race ('gens nostra') should believe in Christ.[4] The ancient ancestry of the Anglo-Saxons always remained fresh in their memory.

It was made particularly vivid by songs and stories of the old Germanic heroes. King Offa of Mercia may have deliberately modelled his career on his illustrious namesake, 'the prince of heroes...the best between the seas of human kin'.[5] More explicitly, St Guthlac's ungodly career as a soldier was inspired by his memories of 'the valiant deeds of heroes of old', and he was converted to Christianity when 'with wakeful mind, he contemplated the wretched deaths and the shameful ends of the ancient kings of his race in the course of past ages'.[6]

Evidently we owe our knowledge of the kind of stories that left this impression to the work of churchmen, for texts of secular Old English poetry survive only in the transcriptions of monastic scribes. And while the vernacular songs which Aldhelm and Bede composed and sang were doubtless all Christian,[7] other clerics went further and enjoyed secular poetry to an extent which sometimes shocked their peers: the Canons of Edgar forbade priests to sing profane songs, even to themselves,[8] and Alcuin wrote to the bishop of Lindisfarne at the end of the eighth century, 'When priests dine

[1] *HE* i.15.
[2] *English Historical Documents* i, ed. D. Whitelock (London, 1955), 748.
[3] *HE* v.9.
[4] Monumenta Germaniae Historica, Epist. Sel. i, 76. Cf. Wigberht to Lull, *ibid.* p. 276.
[5] C. Fox, *Offa's Dyke* (London, 1955), pp. 289–90. Cf. *Widsith* 35ff. and *Beowulf* 1954ff. Fox also suggests that Wat's dyke may have been named after the hero Wade.
[6] *Felix's Life of Saint Guthlac*, ed. B. Colgrave (Cambridge, 1956), cc. xvi and xviii.
[7] On Aldhelm see C. E. Wright, *The Cultivation of Saga in Anglo-Saxon England* (Edinburgh, 1939), pp. 21–2. Cf. Bede's death-song in Cuthbert's 'Epistola de Obitu Bædae' in *Bede's Ecclesiastical History of the English People*, ed. B. Colgrave and R. A. B. Mynors (Oxford, 1969), p. 582.
[8] *Wulfstan's Canons of Edgar*, ed. R. Fowler, Early Eng. Text Soc. 266 (London, 1972), no. 59, p. 14, and no. 18, p. 6.

together let the words of God be read. It is fitting on such occasions to listen to a reader, not to a harpist, to the discourses of the fathers, not to the poems of the heathen. What has Ingeld to do with Christ?'[1]

Clerics and laymen alike appreciated such stories, and the story of Ingeld must have been widely popular in Saxon England, for it is briefly mentioned in *Beowulf*, one of many allusive accounts of events and personalities in the heroic past which were thrown off without explanation to an audience who could be assumed to understand them.[2] *Widsith* and *Deor*, too, are closely packed with stories of the heroic age, epitomes of larger epics familiar to the poets' audiences, and the surviving fragment of *Waldhere* alludes to Weland and to Theodoric while telling a tale of Attila and the Huns.[3] Above all, *Beowulf* and the *Finnesburh* fragment show the deep affection that the Saxons felt for legends of life and adventure in the heroic age, an enthusiasm running deeper than mere curiosity about the early history of Denmark. Only a few such stories survive from Saxon England, but frequent depictions of them reveal how widespread they must have been. Narrative sculpture appears on a small work-box from the cemetery at Burwell (Cambridgeshire)[4] and on the Swedish helmet from Sutton Hoo,[5] while the legend of Weland the Smith, well-known from northern mythology, occurs on the Franks Casket, a Northumbrian work of about 700. The casket also shows a scene in which a character named Egil heroically defends his house against overwhelming odds, and another which may relate to the story of Sigurd.[6]

In the tenth century St Dunstan was criticized for his interest in 'the

---

[1] Cited in P. Hunter Blair, *An Introduction to Anglo-Saxon England* (Cambridge, 1956), p. 331.

[2] These allusions, and the evidence that survives to elucidate them, are discussed in D. Whitelock, *The Audience of Beowulf* (Oxford, 1951), esp. pp. 34ff., and in R. M. Wilson, *The Lost Literature of Medieval England*, 2nd ed. (London, 1970), ch. 1. See also Alistair Campbell, 'The Use in *Beowulf* of Earlier Heroic Verse', *England before the Conquest: Studies in Primary Sources presented to Dorothy Whitelock*, ed. Peter Clemoes and Kathleen Hughes (Cambridge, 1971), pp. 283–92.

[3] The legends alluded to in *Widsith* are dealt with in R. W. Chambers, *Widsith* (Cambridge, 1912). Note also the reference to Ing in the runic poem in *Runic and Heroic Poems*, ed. B. Dickins (Cambridge, 1915), p. 20.

[4] T. Lethbridge, *Recent Excavations in Anglo-Saxon Cemeteries in Cambridgeshire and Suffolk* (Cambridge, 1931), p. 56; H. R. Ellis Davidson mentions a lost bowl from Sandwich which was repaired with plates stamped with figure ornament; *The Early Cultures of North-West Europe* (H. M. Chadwick Memorial Studies), ed. Bruce Dickins and Sir Cyril Fox (Cambridge, 1950), pp. 135–6.

[5] R. L. S. Bruce-Mitford, *The Sutton Hoo Ship-Burial*, 2nd ed. (London, 1972), pp. 30–1.

[6] For a general account of the casket, see R. W. V. Elliott, *Runes: an Introduction* (Manchester, 1959), pp. 96f. For some more recent theories see A. C. Bouman, 'The Franks Casket: Right Side and Lid', *Neophilologus* 49 (1965), 241f.; S. R. T. O. D'Ardenne, 'Does the Right Side of the Franks Casket Represent the Burial of Sigurd?', *Études Germaniques* 21 (1966), 235f.; C. J. E. Ball, 'The Franks Casket: Right Side', *ESts* 47 (1966), 119f.; Karl Hauck, 'Vorbericht über das Käastchen von Auzon', *Frühmittelalterliche Studien* 2 (1968), 415f.; and M. C. Ross, 'A Suggested Interpretation of the Scene Depicted on the Right-Hand Side of the Franks Casket', *MA* 14 (1970), 148f. See also below, p. 34, n. 6.

vain songs of ancestral heathendom',[1] and a piece of figure sculpture of this period, found during the recent excavations at Winchester, probably depicts the story of Sigmund and the Wolf, as told in the *Vǫlsunga saga*.[2] The chronicler Æthelweard showed his knowledge of the early history of the Germanic peoples by adding to the genealogy of his family the names of Baldr and Withar, not known from any other English source, and by recording traditions about the legendary Sceaf.[3] Æthelweard's additions to the topography of Saxon origins also illustrate his fascination with 'the arrival of our ancestors', as he put it,[4] and with the Germanic past.

Comparable are a series of genealogies, which trace the origins of the royal houses of England back to remote Germanic forebears and eventually even to pagan gods. Bede recorded the descent of the kings of Kent in noting the racial origins of the English people,[5] and St Guthlac derived his ancestry 'through the most noble names of famous kings, back to Icel in whom it began in days of old'.[6] Such genealogies were collected and consolidated in eighth-century Mercia, and lists in BM Cotton Vespasian B. vi and chapters 57–61 of Nennius's *Historia Brittonum* trace the descent of the English royal houses back to the Germanic past, to Woden, to Frealaf and to Geat. Their uniform length[7] and their random combinations of noble-sounding old names[8] suggest artificiality, and they were clearly important to contemporaries less for their historical accuracy than for the impression of age they conveyed. Like the pagans who boasted that their gods were 'legitimate and in existence from the beginning',[9] as though the two were synonymous, such proof of antiquity emphasized the worthiness of the royal houses of England. Alcuin complained in 797 that 'scarcely any of the ancient royal kindred remains, and by as much as their origin is uncertain, by so much is their fortitude less'.[10]

The purpose of the Mercian genealogies may have been partly political, as the English answer to the Carolingians' imperial pretensions, emphasizing Offa's kinship with his prehistoric Germanic ancestors on the continent. 'I, Offa, king of the Mercians, sprung from the royal stock of the Mercians', one charter runs,[11] asserting his hereditary dignity as a member of the oldest

[1] *Memorials of St Dunstan*, ed. W. Stubbs, Rolls Series (1874), p. 11.
[2] Appendix to M. Biddle, 'Excavations at Winchester 1965', *AntJ* 46 (1966), 329f.
[3] *The Chronicle of Æthelweard*, ed. and trans. A. Campbell (London, 1962), pp. 9, 18 (Withar) and 33 (Baldr and Sceaf).
[4] *Ibid.* p. 1. On his additions, see pp. xxxv–vi.   [5] *HE* i.15.
[6] Felix, *Vita Sancti Guthlaci*, trans. Colgrave, c. 2.
[7] K. Sisam, 'Anglo-Saxon Royal Genealogies', *Proc. of the Brit. Acad.* 39 (1953), 327.
[8] *Ibid.* pp. 305–6.
[9] Daniel of Winchester's letter to Boniface, in *English Historical Documents* i, 733.
[10] MGH, Epist. Karol. Aevi, 2, 192.
[11] Quoted by F. M. Stenton, *Preparatory to Anglo-Saxon England, being the Collected Papers of Frank Merry Stenton*, ed. D. M. Stenton (Oxford, 1970), p. 381.

dynasty in Europe against the upstart claims of Charlemagne. The Wessex kings were equally interested in their descent from Germanic heroes, and pedigrees appear in the *Anglo-Saxon Chronicle*, in Æthelweard's Chronicle, in Cambridge, Corpus Christi College 183, in BM Cotton Tiberius B. v and in Asser's *Life of King Alfred*.[1] Some of these traced the dynasty's descent beyond Woden, an elaboration almost certainly of Christian date. But it is significant that names from Germanic mythology were used for these extensions,[2] proving that the genealogies were not mere fossils from the pagan era, and illustrating how greatly links with the barbaric past were valued long after the Saxons' conversion to Christianity. Woden and other figures from Germanic mythology were seen as worthies in a dim heroic past, and it was to these that the Wessex kings claimed to be linked, not to pagan gods. Knowing that the Scandinavians worshipped Woden, Æthelweard explained that he was 'a king of a multitude of the barbarians' who had been deified by the ignorant.[3] In the same manner Daniel of Winchester and other churchmen, in England as elsewhere, declared that the heathen gods were no more than men.[4]

Thus the Germanic past survived into the Christian period without the taint of paganism, despite the censorious attitude of Christians like Bede, who, having recorded the Anglo-Saxon names of the months, added: 'Thanks be to you, O Jesus, who have turned us away from these vanities and granted that we should offer sacrifices of praise to yourself.'[5] Euhemerized, stories with pagan overtones in Scandinavia could appear in Saxon England in conjunction with Christian ones: probably the Weland scene on the Franks Casket was seen by its carver merely as a good story from heroic times, not as anti-Christian,[6] just as the Sigmund scene from Winchester need not imply a revival of pagan cult.

Tangible relics of the Germanic past were rare. *Beowulf* is full of references to ancient weapons and ancestral swords, and it is possible that the sword of Offa bequeathed by Athelstan the Atheling in 1015 was thought to have belonged to King Offa of Angel, not to the eighth-century king of Mercia.[7]

---

[1] *The Anglo-Saxon Chronicle*, Preface (A), and *s.a.* 552, 597 and 855; Northumbrian genealogies are given *s.a.* 547 and 560 and Mercian *s.a.* 626 and 757; *Chronicle of Æthelweard*, p. 33; Asser, *De Rebus Gestis Ælfredi*, 1. See also Sisam, 'Anglo-Saxon Royal Genealogies'.

[2] Sisam, 'Anglo-Saxon Royal Genealogies', p. 308.

[3] *Chronicle of Æthelweard*, pp. 9 and 18.   [4] *English Historical Documents* 1, 732.

[5] Cited in H. Mayr-Harting, *The Coming of Christianity to Anglo-Saxon England* (London, 1972), p. 22.

[6] As is suggested in H. E. Ellis Davidson, 'The Smith and the Goddess', *Frümittelalterliche Studien* 3 (1969), 216f. Cf. Mr Ryan's view of the appearance of Woden in the genealogies, 'Othin in England', *Folklore* 74 (1963), 462.

[7] As suggested in F. Barlow, *Edward the Confessor* (London, 1970), p. 35. Might the 'inlaid sword which belonged to Withar' possibly have been comparable? See *Anglo-Saxon Wills*, ed. D. Whitelock (Cambridge, 1930), p. 61.

But no surviving Saxon sword can be proved to have been valued for such great antiquity, and very few objects can have seemed as venerable as the shield at Sutton Hoo, already ancient when it was buried.[1]

Relics of the Roman past, on the other hand, survived in profusion both at home and abroad. The city of Rome was their natural focus, but the Saxon pilgrims who flocked there were piously intent on Christian Rome and the papacy,[2] and the only evidence that they did not ignore the relics of the imperial past is a single 'sublime proverbial expression'[3] which one of them recorded: 'Quandiu stat Colisæus, stat et Roma; quando cadet Colisæus, cadet et Roma; quando cadet Roma, cadet et mundus.'[4] Some at least were impressed by ancient Rome and others were well informed; Bede knew about the Pantheon.[5]

At home several references to Roman ruins show continuing interest and knowledge throughout Saxon times. Cuthbert was shown 'the city wall and the well formerly built in a wonderful manner by the Romans' at Carlisle in 685,[6] Bede often referred to the relics of Roman Britain[7] and Alcuin mentioned the Roman remains at York in his *De Pontificibus et Sanctis Ecclesiæ Eboracensis Carmen*.[8] A document of 839 referred to London as 'that celebrated place built by the skill of the ancient Romans and commonly known throughout the whole world as the great city of London',[9] and Æthelweard recorded that the Romans 'made cities, forts, bridges and streets with wonderful skill, and these are to be seen to this day'.[10] Vernacular poetry shows the same respect for Roman remains: 'Wondrous is this wall-stone', begins *The Ruin*, and this awe for towns and towers 'broken by fate' was widely shared among the Anglo-Saxons, as is shown by the numerous references to *enta geweorc* in Old English poems.[11]

The Saxons' constant use of *mirabilis* expressed their awareness that they were unequal to such works, but their competent and well-informed interest is reflected by other evidence. Thus Roman sites were used for early monas-

[1] Bruce-Mitford, *Sutton Hoo Ship-Burial*, p. 24.
[2] See W. J. Moore, *The Saxon Pilgrims to Rome and the Scola Saxonum* (Freiburg, 1937). An itinerary survives of a visit to Rome by Sigeric in 990/4, but his description of the city is confined to a list of churches: see F. P. Magoun, Jr, 'The Rome of Two Northern Pilgrims', *Harvard Theol. Rev.* 33 (1940), 267f.
[3] E. Gibbon, *The Decline and Fall of the Roman Empire*, ch. 71.
[4] It appears in the *Collectanea* of the Bede corpus. See H. V. Canter, 'The Venerable Bede and the Colosseum', *Trans. and Proc. of the Amer. Philol. Assoc.* 61 (1930), 150f.
[5] *HE* II.4.
[6] 'Anonymous Life of St Cuthbert', *Two Prose Lives of St Cuthbert*, ed. and trans. B. Colgrave (Cambridge, 1940), IV.8.
[7] *HE* I.5, 11, 12 and 26 and III.2 and 22.
[8] *Historians of the Church of York* I, ed. J. Raine, RS (1879), lines 19f. (pp. 349–50).
[9] *Cartularium Saxonicum*, ed. W. de G. Birch (London, 1885–93), no. 424.
[10] *Chronicle of Æthelweard*, trans. Campbell, pp. 5–6.
[11] E.g. Cotton Gnomic Poem 2, *The Wanderer* 87 and *Andreas* 1235 and 1495.

teries at Reculver, Bradwell, Burgh Castle and elsewhere,[1] perhaps partly out of this veneration for the 'wonderful', but probably also because the ramparts were a ready mode of defence or of ritual demarcation and the structures within them a source of building material. Elsewhere Roman remains were used as a quarry for current needs. Bede records that the monks of Ely searched the ruins of Roman Cambridge for a sarcophagus for St Æthelthryth,[2] and the use of antique pottery or glass late in the Saxon period is proved by a reference to 'haec vascula arte fabricata Gentilium' in the Anglo-Saxon *Ritual of the Church of Durham*, and by a benediction: 'Cleanse by the amplitude of thy grace these vessels, which, by the indulgence of thy piety, after a length of time being taken from the gulph of the earth thou hast restored to the use of men.'[3] Roman intaglios and cameos were also valued in Christian Saxon contexts, and a particularly fine one in the treasury of St Albans was said in the time of Matthew Paris to have been given to the abbey by King Æthelred.[4] These gems carved with subjects such as Minerva or *Dea Romana* may have attracted the Saxons by their delicacy, for there is no evidence that magical properties were attributed to them until later in the Middle Ages.[5]

For Saxon architecture Roman Britain was again a convenient quarry. Roman stones and tiles were often re-used as rubble for Saxon buildings,[6] while at Daglingworth, Gloucestershire, for example, a pair of Saxon windows were cut through a Roman inscribed slab, and a Roman inscription was used as a palimpsest for the Jarrow rood.[7] But elsewhere Roman masonry was reset with some understanding of what Saxon architecture owed to

---

[1] Reculver: *ASC, s.a.* 669; Bradwell: *HE* III.22; and Burgh Castle: *ibid.* III.19. See *HE*, ed. Colgrave and Mynors, p. 270, n. 2 for other examples. For the use of Roman sites for churches, see Joan Evans, 'Anniversary Address', *AntJ* 40 (1960), 127.

[2] *HE* IV.19. Cf. Sebbi's coffin, *ibid.* IV.11, where the fact that the coffin turned out to be too small may suggest that it too was being re-used.

[3] 'Benedictio super vasa reperta in locis antiquis', *The Durham Ritual* (ed. T. J. Brown, EEMF 16 (1969), 46v), cited in T. Wright, 'On Antiquarian Excavations and Researches in the Middle Ages', *Archaeologia* 30 (1844), 440. It is, of course, possible that these remains were native rather than Roman.

[4] Matthew Paris, *Chronica Maiora* VI, RS (1882), pp. 387–8. There is no evidence that it was brought from Italy, as suggested in F. Barlow, *The English Church 1000–1066* (London, 1963), p. 20. For an intaglio set in a late Saxon ring from Faversham, Kent, see O. M. Dalton, *Franks Bequest Catalogue* (London, 1912), no. 206. The St Martins, Canterbury, hoard, which contained an intaglio set in a pendant, is probably early-seventh-century (see S. C. Hawkes, J. M. Merrick and D. M. Metcalf, 'X-ray Florescent Analysis of Some Dark Age Coins and Jewellery', *Archaeometry* 9 (1966), 105–6; also Philip Grierson, 'The Canterbury (St Martins) Hoard of Frankish and Anglo-Saxon Coin-Ornaments', *BNJ* 3rd ser. 7 (1955), 48). So too is the boat grave at Snape, Suffolk, which produced an intaglio set in a Saxon ring (*Proc. of the Suffolk Inst. of Archaeology* 26 (1952–4), 13–14). On intaglios from pagan Saxon graves, see below, p. 49, n. 6.

[5] J. Evans, *Magical Jewels of the Middle Ages and the Renaissance* (Oxford, 1922), pp. 95–6 and 120.

[6] H. M. and Joan Taylor, *Anglo-Saxon Architecture* (Cambridge, 1965) I, 12 and *passim*.

[7] R. G. Collingwood and R. P. Wright, *The Roman Inscriptions of Britain* I (Oxford, 1965), nos. 130 (Daglingworth) and 1051a (Jarrow). Cf. no. 262 (from Lincoln, possibly post-Conquest).

Roman. Thus a Roman decorated slab may have been employed with Saxon ones to decorate Wilfrid's church at Hexham[1] and a piece of Roman entablature was adapted to serve as an impost to the chancel arch of Selham church, Sussex.[2] Columns from Roman sites were probably used in the churches of St Pancras, Canterbury, and of Ickleton, Cambridgeshire,[3] and it has even been suggested that the chancel arch of Escomb, County Durham, and the tower arch of Corbridge, Northumberland, are merely Roman arches rebuilt in their present positions.[4]

Such re-use of Roman material in its proper structural function has a certain significance, but Roman remains were neglected and contemporary sub-Roman exemplars preferred as models for imitation.[5] Bede was thinking of Italy and Gaul when he wrote that churches in Britain were built 'iuxta morem Romanorum',[6] as he was evidently thinking of contemporary southern Gaul in explaining that Æthelberht's law was drawn up after the Roman manner.[7] There was no conscious antiquarianism in this field although a sense of community with Roman culture might exist, and wherever Romano-British models have been suggested as the direct inspiration of Saxon art they can be confidently dismissed. There is no reason to link the seventh-century Kentish churches with the Roman basilica at Silchester,[8] and claims that Romano-British art influenced that of seventh- and eighth-century Northumbria[9] have only illustrated the common effect of barbarian art in linearizing classical naturalism in two separate contexts. Foreign fashion was paramount, and the Mediterranean inspired the classicism of Northumbrian art in the age of Bede, while that of the Mercian and Wessex schools in the later Saxon period was probably wholly due to the influence of the

---

[1] Implied by Taylor and Taylor, *Anglo-Saxon Architecture* I, 304. However W. G. Collingwood is negative: 'we do not know that it was used as ornament there' (*Northumbrian Crosses of the Pre-Norman Age* (London, 1927), p. 22).

[2] Taylor and Taylor, *Anglo-Saxon Architecture* II, 537–8.

[3] *Ibid.* I, 146 and 331 (dated as 'Saxo-Norman').

[4] G. Baldwin Brown, *Anglo-Saxon Architecture* (London, 1925), pp. 140 and 143. Cf. Taylor and Taylor, *Anglo-Saxon Architecture* I, 412 (Market Overton, Rutland) and II, 661 (Wickham, Berkshire) and R. M. Butler, 'A Roman Gateway at Portchester Castle?' *AntJ* 35 (1955), 219ff. (Titchfield, Hants.).

[5] But on the question of whether the 'Escomb fashion' of jamb construction was learnt from Gallic masons or Roman remains, see H. M. Taylor, 'The Origin, Purpose and Date of the Pilaster-Strips in Anglo-Saxon Architecture', *North Staffordshire Jnl of Field Stud.* 10 (1970), 30.

[6] *HE* v.21 and *Historia Abbatum*, 5.

[7] *HE* II.5. Cf. J. M. Wallace-Hadrill, 'Rome and the Early English Church: Some Questions of Transmission', *Settimane di Studio del Centro Italiano di Studi sull'Alto Medioevo* 7 (1960), esp. 528–9, and Wallace-Hadrill, *Early Germanic Kingship*, pp. 32ff. On Roman law in Saxon England see also A. S. Cook, 'Aldhelm's Legal Studies', *JEGP* 23 (1924), 105f. and W. Senior, 'Roman Law in England before Vacarius', *Law Quarterly Rev.* 46 (1930), 191f.

[8] As suggested in F. Saxl and R. Wittower, *British Art and the Mediterranean* (London, 1948), pl. 13, fig. 7.

[9] F. Saxl, 'The Ruthwell Cross', *Jnl of the Warburg and Courtauld Insts.* 6 (1943), 1f., and R. L. S. Bruce-Mitford, *Evangeliorum Quattuor Codex Lindisfarnensis* II (Olten, 1960), 115–16 and 283.

Carolingian renaissance and no deliberate antiquarianism can be proved. The same is true of inscriptions like those of Jarrow and Deerhurst,[1] however boldly classical their form.

More striking is the evidence from coinage. Frequent finds of coin hoards perhaps best explain the entry in the *Anglo-Saxon Chronicle* for 418 that 'in this year the Romans collected all the treasures which were in Britain, and hid some in the ground, so that no one could find them afterwards, and took some with them into Gaul'. By the end of the Saxon period the law of Treasure Trove was apparently taken for granted,[2] while already in the pagan period numerous Roman coins preserved in graves show how attractive the Saxons found them.[3]

Many such coins carried powerful designs – Romulus and Remus suckled by the wolf, or seated winged victories, or the *Gloria Exercitus* type. These clearly impressed the Saxons, for when the earliest gold coinage was established in this country several designs were based on imperial coin types of the third and fourth centuries: a *solidus* from Markshall imitated the *Beata Tranquillitas* issue of 320–1, while the 'Licinius' group in the Crondall hoard reproduced the portrait from the coins of the sons of Constantine which appeared at Trier in *c.* 324–6, and another type copied the *Victoria Augg* 'Two Emperors' *solidus* of the late fourth century.[4] The copying continued during the transition to *sceattas*. The 'Pada' coins reproduced both the helmeted bust and the legend from a bronze of Crispus of *c.* 319, while the 'Standard' group of *sceattas* also followed types of Crispus and Marius or Carausius and the 'London' group show the influence of the '*Fel. Temp. Reparatio* Galley' type of *c.* 348–50.

With the pennies Saxon copying of Roman coins became more sporadic, but at the same time it became more unnatural and therefore more deliberately antiquarian, for contemporary exemplars were always available.[5] A penny of Æthelberht of East Anglia (*c.* 790) has a reverse depicting Romulus and Remus suckled by the wolf and Offa's 'Gold Penny' was closely based on a *Lugdunum aureus* of the emperor Augustus.[6] Of the Wessex kings, Alfred copied the reverse of one of his coins from a fourth-century *Victoria Augg* type; Edward the Elder produced a penny whose reverse, with a fortified gate, directly imitated a Roman coin; and a York type of

[1] E. Okasha, *Hand-List of Anglo-Saxon Non-Runic Inscriptions* (Cambridge, 1971), nos. 61 and 28.
[2] D. Whitelock, 'The Numismatic Interest of an Old English Version of the Legend of the Seven Sleepers', *Anglo-Saxon Coins*, ed. R. H. M. Dolley (London, 1961), p. 189.
[3] See below, p. 50, n. 1. On the insertion of late imperial coins in jewelled pendants, see R. Jessup, *Anglo-Saxon Jewellery* (London, 1950), pl. 28.
[4] These coins and their prototypes are discussed in J. P. C. Kent, 'From Roman Britain to Saxon England', *Anglo-Saxon Coins*, ed. Dolley, pp. 10ff.
[5] The pennies are illustrated in M. Dolley, *Anglo-Saxon Pennies* (London, 1964).
[6] C. E. Blunt and M. Dolley, 'A Gold Coin of the Time of Offa', *NC* 7th ser. 8 (1968), 151f.

Athelstan's based its reverse on the *Consecratio* type of Constantine the Great.[1] Other coins adapted their busts from Roman examples – including Æthelred II's 1003 issue and Harold II's – while, earlier, Offa's diademed and draped bust had been borrowed from a Roman coin. Indeed, Mr Kent would 'go so far as to assert that the predominance, and ultimate triumph, of the royal effigy in profile on the Early English coinage was conditioned by respect for Roman practice'.[2]

The devices on Roman coins had originally been political in intent, and at least some of the Saxons' copies, in deliberately harking back to ancient Roman precedent, must have been similarly inspired.[3] They are part of the context of self-conscious Romanisms like the titles given to Saxon dignitaries witnessing Mercian charters of the eighth century, including 'Offa the patrician' and *tribuni*, *præpositi* and *viri consulares*.[4] Such titles certainly originate in book-learning, but they are significant, for, like the coins, they illustrate a search for dignity in the traditions of imperial Rome. They perhaps provide a background to the use of the term *imperium* to describe the hegemony of the most powerful English kings, whether it reflects a true aspiration to imperialism or no more than a learned gloss on a vernacular title.[5]

Ancient Rome appeared elsewhere in a regnal context. Caesar became the son of Woden and an ancestor of the East Anglian kings in their genealogy,[6] and both Caesar and Alexander – 'mightiest of all the race of men' – were familiar to the author and audience of *Widsith*.[7] A vaguer awareness of ancient Rome is reflected in another context. Professor Deanesley pointed out that in the seventh century 'baptism was looked on as in some way conveying association with the Roman inheritance as well as initiation to Christianity, and was sought at the hands of foreign missionaries in the old Roman centres, Canterbury, York, Catterick, Campodunum, Lincoln, Dorchester'.[8] Recent excavations have shown that the grand buildings of Roman York were still standing when Edwin held court there,[9] and it is

---

[1] The penny of Athelstan is illustrated in G. C. Brooke, *English Coins*, 3rd ed. (London, 1950), pl. xiv, fig. 15; that of Edward is discussed by M. Dolley, *North Staffordshire Jnl of Field Stud.* 10 (1970), 42–3. Mr Dolley has also suggested to me that the flower type of Edmund may be typologically devolved from Alfred's *Victoria Augg* type.

[2] 'From Roman Britain to Saxon England', p. 13.

[3] It is interesting in this connection that Alfred's *Victoria Augg* type was the only coin on which he claimed the title 'Rex Anglorum'.

[4] M. Deanesley, 'Roman Traditionalist Influence among the Anglo-Saxons', *EHR* 58 (1943), 129–30.

[5] See below, pp. 47–8.

[6] R. W. Chambers, 'The Mythical Ancestor of the Kings of East Anglia', *MLR* 4 (1908–9), 508–9.

[7] Lines 76 and 15–16.

[8] 'Roman Traditionalist Influence', p. 130.

[9] 'York Minster', *CA* 2 (1969–70), 163.

even possible that his *vexilla* had Roman precedents,[1] while Alfred was greatly impressed by his investiture as a consul in 853, whatever he believed it to be about.[2]

Any real knowledge of classical history may have been more rare than this vague conception of the Roman past, but at an elementary level some knowledge was quite common. Aldhelm knew something of Roman history, for one of his riddles puns laboriously on the name of the consul Camillus,[3] and he knew what 'the books that tell of Romulus narrate'.[4] Alcuin pondered ancient histories as well as reading the holy scriptures before considering the fortune of the world.[5] Bede incorporated much profane history into his *Chronicle*,[6] and he read Roman historians extensively, especially Orosius, for the introductory chapters of his *History*,[7] displaying his familiarity with the classical past in isolated references elsewhere.[8] The interest of these scholars is, perhaps, predictable. More surprising is the Franks Casket, whose vernacular runic inscription suggests that it was made for a layman rather than an ecclesiastic, for, in addition to its themes from northern mythology, this shows two scenes from Roman history, the finding of Romulus and Remus nursed by a she-wolf and the sacking of the temple at Jerusalem by Titus. The legend of Romulus and Remus may have had a wide circulation in Saxon England, perhaps oral: the scene of the wolf with the twins is also depicted on a bone plaque recently found in Norfolk, probably part of the cover of a service book dating from *c.* 800.[9]

Curiosity about Mediterranean history in the later Saxon period is reflected by brief allusions made by Æthelweard[10] and by the inclusion of a section 'De Dignitatibus Romanorum' amongst miscellaneous matter at the end of

---

[1] See Bruce-Mitford, *Sutton Hoo Ship-Burial*, p. 21, and *Proc. of the Suffolk Inst. of Archaeology* 25 (1949–51), 13ff. (where he links the standards with their appearance on the *sceattas*). But much remains hypothetical, as does Mr Hunter Blair's suggestion that the suppression of names from the Northumbrian regnal lists was inspired by the Roman practice of *damnatio memoriae* (*Early Cultures of North-West Europe*, ed. Dickins and Fox, pp. 248–9). On building E at Yeavering, which Dr Bruce-Mitford considers the 'most astonishing demonstration' of the Northumbrian kings' revivalism, 'obviously based on a *cuneus* of a Roman theatre' (*Codex Lindisfarnensis*, p. 115), see B. Hope-Taylor, 'The Site at *Ad Gefrin*', unpub. Cambridge Ph.D. thesis, pp. 273f. But it is difficult to assess so unusual a feature and there is no evidence of conscious revivalism.

[2] See below, p. 47.

[3] *The Riddles of Aldhelm*, ed. J. H. Pitman, Yale Stud. in Eng. 67 (New Haven, 1925), no. 99.

[4] *Ibid.* no. 35.

[5] *English Historical Documents* 1, 776.

[6] He used Jerome, Rufinus, Isidore and others; see Mommsen's edition, MGH, Auct. Ant. 13, 247ff.

[7] Quotations are noted and printed in italics in *Baedae Opera Historica*, ed. Charles Plummer (Oxford, 1896) 1, 9ff.

[8] E.g. in *Grammatici Latini* VII, ed. H. Keil (Leipzig, 1880), 245, he refers to the war between Caesar and Pompey.

[9] Barbara Green, 'An Anglo-Saxon Bone Plaque from Larling, Norfolk', *AntJ* 51 (1971), 321f.

[10] *Chronicle of Æthelweard*, trans. Campbell, pp. 11 and 18.

the *Durham Ritual*.[1] More substantial is the Old English translation of Orosius's history of the world, of late-ninth- or early-tenth-century date, probably associated with Alfred's circle,[2] and therefore perhaps one of the books which he considered 'most necessary for all men to know'.[3] The translator showed considerable interest in Roman history; probably using a lost commentary, he added to Orosius's narrative information concerning Roman institutions, notably the consulate and triumph, and personalities, including Julius Caesar.[4]

Roman literature and classical myths were more cultivated tastes which were discouraged in Saxon England, where Latin poets were often condemned for their paganism: 'quia pagana erant', wrote Bede, 'nos tangere non libuit.'[5] But they were not unknown, although this is often only revealed by attacks on those who studied them. Thus Aldhelm wrote to a friend: 'What, think you, does it profit a true believer to inquire busily into the foul love of Proserpina . . . to desire to learn of Hermione and her various betrothals, to write in epic style the ritual of Priapus and the Luperci? Beware, my son, of evil women and their loves in legend.'[6] Aldhelm was apparently well aware of what he was condemning; his close familiarity with ancient poets extended at least to Vergil, and his riddles display a considerable knowledge of classical culture, with allusions to mythological figures like Circe and the Cyclopes.[7] The riddles of Tatwine, Boniface and Hwætberht show a comparable, if more limited, schooling in classical literary culture, acquired through such authors as Porphyrius.[8]

All these Saxon scholars were familiar with the subject matter of classical literature, although it is difficult to prove their deep knowledge of particular writers. The same is true of Bede, for, though his direct knowledge of any classical poet has recently been questioned,[9] he certainly knew Pliny,[10] and he displayed some awareness of ancient literature, not least through his

---

[1] Ed. T. J. Brown, EEMF 16, 86v–87r.

[2] So E. M. Liggins, 'The Authorship of the Old English Orosius', *Anglia* 88 (1970), 290 and 321. But see J. M. Bateley, 'King Alfred and the Old English Translation of Orosius', *ibid.* pp. 433ff. and Bateley, 'The Classical Additions in the Old English Orosius', *England before the Conquest*, ed. Clemoes and Hughes, pp. 237ff.

[3] Preface to 'Pastoral Care', *English Historical Documents* I, 819.

[4] Ed. H. Sweet, EETS o.s. 79 (London, 1883), 70–2 (Book 2, 4) and 234 (Book 5, 18).

[5] *Grammatici Latini* VII, 258; see also G. Bonner, 'Bede and Medieval Civilization', *ASE* 2 (1973), 71–90.

[6] Letter to Wihtfrid, quoted in E. S. Duckett, *Anglo-Saxon Saints and Scholars* (London, 1947), pp. 39–40.

[7] Ed. Pitman, nos. 95 and 100.

[8] All ed. Fr Glorie, Corpus Christianorum Series Latina 133 (1968). On Porphyrius, see W. Levison, *England and the Continent in the Eighth Century* (Oxford, 1948), p. 145.

[9] Hunter Blair, *World of Bede*, pp. 289–90.

[10] *Ibid.* p. 290 and M. L. W. Laistner, 'The Library of the Venerable Bede', *Bede, his Life, Times and Writings*, ed. A. Hamilton Thompson (Oxford, 1935), pp. 243–4.

conscious policy of removing pagan illustrative quotations from his school-books.[1] Alcuin evidently knew Vergil well,[2] and his description of the library at York,[3] if true, shows that it contained several classical authors, or, if imaginary, is still significant in showing that he considered that an ideal library ought to possess such texts. Even the most sceptical of recent writers admits that in Saxon England, as in the Visigothic Spain of Isidore, there existed 'une sorte de culture poétique au second degré'.[4] But it remains paradoxical that such doubt reigns about the knowledge of classics in Bede's England, when the rôle of insular continental foundations in transmitting such classical authors as Ammianus Marcellinus, Cicero, Vitruvius, Statius and Valerius Flaccus[5] implies that interest in such writers was exported to the continent from England.

In the later Saxon period texts of Cicero and Persius are known to have circulated in England,[6] while St Dunstan read book I of Ovid's *Ars Amatoria* in a manuscript which still survives.[7] Recent study of Anglo-Latin poems of the tenth century suggests that certain authors, including Horace, were directly known to members of Æthelwold's circle,[8] and Professor Campbell and others consider that *Beowulf* was influenced by Vergil, 'the best known of all poets in the Anglo-Saxon monasteries'.[9]

Later Saxon glosses on Aldhelm's works show that his mythological references were still understood,[10] and Hisperic invocations to classical deities are common in charters of the tenth and eleventh centuries.[11] In the late ninth century Alfred showed his interest in classical myths by incorporating

---

[1] Hunter Blair, *World of Bede*, p. 249.

[2] Cf. MGH, Epist. Karol. Aevi 2, 39; O. F. Long, 'The Attitude of Alcuin towards Vergil', *Studies in Honor of B. L. Gildersleeve* (Baltimore, 1902), pp. 377ff.; and E. M. Sanford, 'Alcuin and the Classics', *Classical Jnl* 20 (1925), 526f.

[3] *Historians of the Church of York* (ed. Raine), pp. 395–6.

[4] J. Fontaine, *Isidore de Séville et la Culture Classique dans l'Espagne Visigothique* (Paris, 1959), p. 743.

[5] Cf. L. D. Reynolds and N. G. Wilson, *Scribes and Scholars* (Oxford, 1968), p. 79 and Levison, *England and the Continent*, p. 144. Irish influence should, however, perhaps be considered: it was because Wihtfrid was bound for Ireland that Aldhelm warned him against the seductions of classical literature (see above, p. 41), and Irish scholars are often said to have had fewer inhibitions about such reading than English. See W. B. Stanford, 'Towards a History of Classical Influences in Ireland', *Proc. of the R. Irish Acad.* 70(C) (1970), 13f. and L. Bieler, 'The Classics in Celtic Ireland', *Classical Influences on European Culture AD 500–1500*, ed. R. R. Bolgar (Cambridge, 1971), pp. 45ff.

[6] Cambridge University Library, Gg.5.35, an eleventh-century Canterbury manuscript, once contained some of Cicero's orations, but these are no longer there. See J. D. A. Ogilvy, *Books Known to the English 597–1066* (Cambridge, Mass., 1967), p. 111. Two late Saxon manuscripts of Persius survive, Cambridge, Trinity College o.4.10 and Oxford, Bodleian Library, Auct. F.1.15.

[7] Oxford, Bodleian Library, Auct. F.4.32, ed. R. W. Hunt (*St Dunstan's Classbook from Glastonbury*, Umbrae Codicum Occidentalium 4 (1961)).

[8] M. Lapidge, 'Three Latin Poems from Æthelwold's School at Winchester', *ASE* 1 (1972), 109.

[9] 'The Use in *Beowulf* of Earlier Heroic Verse', p. 283.

[10] *Old English Glosses*, ed. A. S. Napier (Oxford, 1900), *passim*.

[11] E.g. *English Historical Documents* I, 553, a charter of Cnut, invokes Neptune.

allusions to them into his translation of Boethius from an earlier commentary on the *De Consolatione Philosophiae*, giving his readers an account of Apollo, Saturn and Jove.[1] So too did Ælfric in his vernacular homily *De Falsis Diis*:[2] 'A man was living in the island of Crete, called Saturn, so violent and savage that he ate his children . . . This Jove was so lustful that he married his sister, who was named Juno, a very exalted goddess . . . Mars, who always stirred up conflicts, and liked constantly to cause contention and woe . . .'[3] and so on. These 'pedantic remembrances of Roman heathendom', as Kemble put it,[4] however imperfect, are a warning against underestimating the extent of the Anglo-Saxons' awareness of classical culture.

For, though the evidence consists only of passing allusions and sporadic imitations, it is strikingly widespread throughout the Christian Saxon period. There is no evidence, for instance, of any significant change due to influence from the Carolingian empire after the eighth century, although it may have made classicism fashionable in English art, and new texts of classical authors may have reached England from continental centres of learning. The Saxon monastic scholars of the age of Bede were apparently quite as knowledgeable about the classical past as their successors, and knowledge among laymen can be documented too, as consideration of the Franks Casket has shown. It was Waga the reeve who 'explained' to St Cuthbert that the remains at Carlisle were Roman;[5] his knowledge must have been part of oral lore that may have gone back to the pagan period, just as the East Anglian genealogy and *Widsith* apparently look back to pre-Christian tradition in their rudimentary knowledge of classical personalities. Detailed discussion of sources is generally fruitless in a period from which more has disappeared than has survived, but speculations like these illustrate the extent of knowledge of ancient Rome in Saxon England.

Of course it is easy to overemphasize the depth of the Saxons' concern with the Roman past. Mrs Ellis Davidson has pointed out the appeal of the scenes from Roman history that appeared on the Franks Casket to laymen nurtured in a heroic tradition;[6] there is no need to assume that their appearance there implies as detailed and varied a knowledge of ancient classical culture among laymen as existed among scholars with access to Latin books.

[1] *King Alfred's Old English Version of Boethius*, ed. W. J. Sedgfield (Oxford, 1899), esp. ch. xxxviii (pp. 115–16). On their source, see B. S. Donaghey, 'The Sources of King Alfred's Translation of Boethius's *De Consolatione Philosophiae*', *Anglia* 82 (1964), 23f.

[2] *Homilies of Ælfric: a Supplementary Collection*, ed. J. C. Pope, EETS 259–60 (London, 1967–8), 676f. A small section of Ælfric's homily was adapted by Wulfstan, *The Homilies of Wulfstan*, ed. D. Bethurum (Oxford, 1957), pp. 221f.

[3] *Homilies of Ælfric*, ed. Pope, pp. 682–3.

[4] *The Dialogue of Salomon and Saturnus*, ed. J. M. Kemble (London, 1848), p. 125.

[5] 'Anonymous Life of St Cuthbert', trans. Colgrave, iv.8.

[6] 'The Smith and the Goddess', p. 225 (though there is no need to accept her 'Wodenic' over-tones).

Moreover, interest in pre-Christian Rome was negligible compared with the much fuller concern with the Christian era. If evidence of knowledge of ancient Roman authors is hard to come by, there is no shortage of evidence for the Saxons' use of late Roman Christian poets like Juvencus, Prudentius, Sedulius and Paulinus of Nola.[1] With godly authors like these before him, Bede was free to ignore their pagan predecessors, just as the Saxons copied contemporary Christian, rather than ancient imperial, exemplars in their art, architecture and law.

Among the imitations of Roman coins, Offa's is unusual in reproducing an *aureus* of Augustus, for most of the antique exemplars used were issues of Christian emperors of the fourth century. It is even possible that certain types were purposely avoided; Mr Michael Dolley has pointed out to me that some very common coins of that period which show bearded busts were never imitated, perhaps because the Saxons associated them with the bearded Julian the Apostate and Roman paganism. So too, Ælfric's and Wulfstan's knowledge of classical deities shows no deep appreciation of classical culture, for both found the gods squalid lechers, about whom they wrote with pronounced distaste. Moreover the events from Roman history recorded in the *Anglo-Saxon Chronicle* were limited to those concerning the history of Roman Britain and to the history of Christianity, to which it may have been felt that regnal dates of emperors (which alone are also included) were relevant.

The translator of Orosius's *History* into Old English was equally selective. His intention was to show how the whole of history led to the universal empire of Rome, so that Christ could be born in the universal peace of Augustus's reign and the faith could spread through a universal empire: this scheme, which he inherited from Orosius, he emphasized by omission and rearrangement.[2] The theme of Bede's *Chronicle* was similar, that of the development of the past from the creation towards its central event, the incarnation, and the subsequent progress of Christianity. Secular history, of the Greek and Roman Mediterranean, was knitted to the biblical theme of the unfolding of God's purpose, and thus the framework for a universal past was provided. The result was a polarization of history into the relevant and the irrelevant to this scheme of 'apocalyptic history': in the imperial period, the translator of Orosius saw all things Christian as germane to his argument and all else as negligible. The Christian past could alone be allowed significance.

Not only could it claim a universality of significance. The Old Testament account of the early history of man also taught a universality of fact. The

---

[1] Ogilvy, *Books Known to the English*, pp. 190, 230–2, 239–40 and 217.
[2] Cf. D. Whitelock, 'The Prose of Alfred's Reign', *Continuations and Beginnings*, ed. E. G. Stanley (London, 1966), p. 90.

Book of Genesis provided an infinitely satisfying account of the origin and early history of the human race. In the Dark Ages, as long afterwards, the scriptures were the basis of a synthesis of diverse elements in the history of the world; from the time of the Fathers, as earlier in Jewish thought, there was a tendency for Christian writers to join pagan elements of different heathen cultures with the demons of the bible in 'one confused rabble of malevolent spirits'.[1]

All this tended to conflate the Saxons' view of different elements in the past, and this is nowhere more marked than with the ancient Roman and Germanic traditions examined in this article. For to examine them separately, though convenient, is artificial. Not only did all those who knew most about ancient Rome, such as Bede, Alfred, Dunstan and Æthelweard, dabble in the Germanic past as well, but in addition there is a certain clumsiness in separating the different strands in the Saxons' consciousness of the past, for it is clear that they themselves did so only imperfectly. So Caesar and Alexander could appear in *Widsith* and in the East Anglian genealogy among barbarian heroes, as if they were of the same type themselves, and Asser, in the first chapter of his *Life of King Alfred*, inserted after the name 'Geat' in Alfred's pedigree a passage from Sedulius describing the slave Geta, who appears in Terence, apparently assuming that he and the Germanic god were identical. The context of both was biblical: the compilers of the *Anglo-Saxon Chronicle* thought it only proper to relate Woden and his companions to Noah, Enoch, Seth (who could be identified with the Germanic Sceaf) and Adam.[2] And in *Beowulf* and elsewhere the giants and monsters of northern legend were identified with the progeny of Cain.[3]

Ælfric's *De Falsis Diis* shows a similar synthesis, linking these giants of biblical origin with the gods of classical mythology, who are also identified with the pagan gods of the northern nations. Indeed so sure was Ælfric of their identity that he actually combined the traditions of the two, attributing to the classical gods traits of their northern counterparts and denying the theological opinions of the worshippers of the Scandinavian gods on the basis of what he had read about the classical deities in ancient texts: 'Now the Danes heretically say that Jove (whom they call Thor) is the son of Mercury (whom they call Othon). But they are wrong, for we read in both heathen and Christian books that the evil Jove was really Saturn's son, and the books that the old heathen wrote about him cannot be wrong.'[4]

[1] J. Seznec, *The Survival of the Pagan Gods* (New York, 1953), p. 44.
[2] *ASC*, s.a. 855 and see F. Magoun, 'King Æthelwulf's Biblical Ancestors', *MLR* 46 (1951), 249–50. Asser identifies Sceaf and Seth: *De Rebus Gestis Alfredi*, 1.
[3] O. F. Emerson, 'Legends of Cain, Especially in Old and Middle English', *PMLA* 21 (1906), 831ff, esp. 878f.
[4] Mercury was said to be worshipped in high places, an attribute of Othin's. See *Homilies of Ælfric*, ed. Pope, pp. 715 and 684–5 (lines 141f.).

The same conflation of Teutonic and classical mythology occurs in Alfred's translation of Boethius, which renders 'ubi nunc fidelis ossa Fabricii [a proper name] manent?' as 'where now are the bones of the famous and wise goldsmith, Weland?',[1] while the metrical version elaborates this to 'who knows now the bones of the wise Weland, under what mound of earth they may be concealed?'[2] This substitution of a famous northern legend for a Roman proper name, and the mention of burial rites familiar in Germanic tradition, show how little Alfred differentiated the classical world of Boethius from the legendary barbaric past of Weland.[3] Similarly the poets' 'work of giants' included both Roman ruins and prehistoric barrows,[4] and the same attitude is illustrated by the lack of clear localization of the past. The earlier Offa had become naturalized in England by the time of the St Albans story of the two Offas[5] and place-names associating Weland and other Germanic heroes with ancient sites in England apparently illustrate the same process at an earlier date.[6]

The ancient past of Weland and his like was assumed to be the only possible one; all relics of the remote past were their preserve, and the existence of antiquities like prehistoric barrows never made the Saxons curious about the pre-Roman natives of Britain.[7] All the strands of the past, Roman, Germanic, biblical or native, were knitted into a single, comprehensive fabric. The artist of the Franks Casket saw nothing incongruous in combining on a small box scenes from Germanic heroic legend, from Roman history, and from the bible, while on one panel he depicted side by side the adoration of the magi and one of the more barbaric scenes of Germanic mythology, the vengeance of Weland on King Nithad.

This confusion of different periods and cultures was enhanced by an imperfect awareness of the difference between the past, however alien, and the present – a trait common throughout medieval Europe. Thus on the casket all the figures in all the scenes are depicted in the dress of the period in which the casket was made, and this lack of a sense of anachronism is

---

[1] Ed. W. J. Sedgfield, ch. xix (p. 46).

[2] *Ibid.* 'The Lays of Boethius', ch. x (p. 165).

[3] For a different view, see Donaghey, 'The Sources', p. 40.

[4] Cf. P. J. Frankis, 'The Thematic Significance of *enta geweorc* and Related Imagery in *The Wanderer*', *ASE* 2 (1973), 253–69.

[5] Whitelock, *Audience of Beowulf*, pp. 60–1.

[6] On a group of place-names derived from the Weland legend surrounding Wayland's smithy, see L. V. Grinsell, 'Wayland's Smithy, *Beahhild's Byrigels* and *Hwittuc's Hlaew*: a Suggestion', *Trans. of the Newbury District Field Club* 8 (1939), 136f. On places named after Wade, see Chambers, *Widsith*, pp. 97–8. The association of earthen barrows with the giants and dragons of Germanic mythology is comparable. See B. Dickins, 'English Names and Old English Heathenism', *Essays and Stud.* 19 (1934), 148ff.

[7] Except for Bede's remark that the traces of the stakes in the Thames with which the Ancient Britons resisted Julius Caesar's advance 'are visible even today' (*HE* i.2) and his suggestion that the Britons originally came from Armorica (*ibid.* i.1).

found throughout Old English literature. Saxon vernacular poetry shows how the past was visualized in terms of a heroic, idealized present, as in *The Ruin*, where heroes and Roman ruins are poetically correlated in a vision of 'many a man light of heart and bright with gold, adorned with splendours, proud and flushed with wine'.[1]

Similarly Constantine is shown as a Germanic king, with his hearth-troop and his boar-banner, in the Old English *Elene*, and Labienus appears as the 'emperor's reeve' during Julius Caesar's invasion of Britain in the *Anglo-Saxon Chronicle*,[2] an assimilation with present experience rather than a direct translation. Likewise the Old English Orosius steadily converts Roman terms into Saxon concepts through its translation: Attalus, for example, was said to have entrusted his lands to Rome 'to boclande' as if he were a Saxon ealdorman;[3] and in the Old English Bede *consul* is treated as a synonym for *cyning*.[4]

In these circumstances there was even a tendency to blur the most obvious contrast between the Christian Saxons and their Germanic ancestors, that of the old paganism. *Beowulf* is set in the heroic age, yet in all but one passage it seems to show the Danes as Christian. Moreover this passage depicts them as consciously pagan so clumsily that it has sometimes been considered an interpolation and shows how difficult it was for the poet to conceive the difference between the heroic age and his own.[5]

This tendency to translate the past into terms of an idealized present also explains how ancient offices were modified when they were re-evoked in comtemporary dress. It is not unlikely that the four-year-old Alfred himself mistook his investiture to the consulate in 853 as his coronation,[6] and it is wrong to see in the problematic *imperium* of the Anglo-Saxons the reflection of any aspiration beyond the actual political situation of seventh-, eighth- or tenth-century England. Bede, like others, employed *regnum* and *imperium* indiscriminately to describe the Anglo-Saxon kingdoms, though he preferred to use *imperium* when referring to the king who held the hegemony,[7] and phrases like 'rector et imperator Merciorum regni'[8] suggest a similar confusion of nomenclature. Mere terminology rather than aspiration to imperial

---

[1] *Anglo-Saxon Poetry*, trans. R. K. Gordon, rev. ed. (London, 1954), p. 84.
[2] Preface to D text. [3] Ed. H. Sweet, p. 224 (v.4).
[4] Quoted by H. R. Loyn, 'The Term *Ealdorman* in the Translations Prepared at the Time of King Alfred', *EHR* 68 (1953), 518.
[5] Lines 175ff. Discussed in Whitelock, *Audience of Beowulf*, pp. 77f.
[6] *ASC*, *s.a.* 853. Cf. Asser, *De Rebus Gestis Alfredi*, VIII and *English Historical Documents* I, 810. But see J. L. Nelson, 'The Problem of King Alfred's Royal Anointing', *Jnl of Eccles. Hist.* 18 (1967), 145ff.
[7] P. F. Jones, *A Concordance to the Historia Ecclesiastica of Bede* (Cambridge, Mass., 1929), p. 252. Cf. on the later Saxon period the sources quoted in E. John, *Orbis Britanniae* (Leicester, 1966), pp. 52–5.
[8] Birch, *Cartularium Saxonicum*, no. 289.

dignity is reflected here, just as in the mid-sixth century Jordanes used the term *imperium* to imply the overlordship of one barbarian king over another in the pre-Italian Gothic past.[1] It is dangerous to lay too much stress on the terminology of those who confused imperial offices with tribal ones.

This anachronistic conflation of contrasting past cultures makes it less surprising that those who sought dignity by appealing to ancient traditions constantly combined those of Rome and Germany. For the most interesting aspect of the eighth-century Mercians' pretensions is that, while the Carolingians looked to Rome for their aspirations, or even to Troy for their ancestry,[2] Offa probed back into the past of native legend and felt that to emphasize his kinship with his remote Germanic forefathers was an effective and equally respectable answer to the classical pretensions of the Franks. Yet in other fields the Mercians, like the Franks, looked to the Roman past: 'Offa the patrician' was a signatory to a charter of Æthelbald's and his fellow *tribuni* and *viri consulares* were also Mercian. Moreover Offa had deliberate recourse to ancient Roman exemplars for his coin types, and the effect of this revivalist propaganda may have been widely felt on the continent –his coins were copied as far afield as Lucca.[3]

The Wessex kings also appealed to both the Germanic and the Roman past. Alfred directly copied at least one Roman type for his coinage and as a translator he showed concern for the culture of the ancient world. Yet he followed Offa in proudly tracing his ancestry to the heroic past of Germany, and this genealogy was prefixed to Asser's biography, which looked back, through Einhard, to the classical example of Suetonius. So too Edward the Confessor, the self-conscious restorer of the ancient lineage of Cerdic, imitated ancient Roman coins in at least some of his own.[4] And Æthelweard, though greatly impressed by his kinship with the ancient Germans, devised an extravagantly revivalist Roman title for himself at the opening of his chronicle – 'Patricius consul Fabius quaestor Ethelwerdus'.[5]

All that the past offered was the nobility of antiquity, and the origins of the traditions that were valued or of the titles and motifs that were revived were irrelevant. To see in such awe for either the Germanic or the Roman past a conscious preference for one over the other is to be guilty of anachronism. Anglo-Saxon England was aware of both, but it was not fully conscious of the difference between them and it respected and copied both without conceiving them as separate. Thus it becomes a semantic point whether the

[1] R. Folz, *L'Idée d'Empire en Occident du Ve au VIIe Siècle* (Paris, 1953), p. 22.
[2] Cf. R. W. Southern, 'Aspects of the European Tradition of Historical Writing: 1 The Classical Tradition from Einhard to Geoffrey of Monmouth', *TRHS* 5th ser. 20 (1970), 189–90.
[3] C. E. Blunt, 'The Coinage of Offa', *Anglo-Saxon Coins*, ed. Dolley, p. 42.
[4] *Ibid.* pp. 14 and 215.
[5] *Chronicle of Æthelweard*, trans. Campbell, p. 1.

precedents for Edwin's *tufa*[1] were Roman or Germanic, for Edwin would not have felt the implications of the difference between the two and all that need be said is that he derived majesty from the object. So too it is impossible to wrest information about either Germanic origins or the 'barbarous imitation of imperial dignity'[2] from the vernacular *bretwalda* or the Latin *imperium*, for men who believed that Caesar was related to Woden would not have appreciated the distinction. It is worse still to see the Mercian or Wessex genealogies as conscious rejections of the classical past or to imagine that these 'conflicted' with an appeal to the traditions of ancient Rome in the use of its coin types.[3] There was only one past for the Anglo-Saxons, one in which many traditions were vaguely confused; both in their genealogies and in their coins it was age rather than connotation that appealed to them.

Such an attitude was characteristic of the Christian culture with which they were imbued. In an age preoccupied by precedent it is not surprising that the Saxons were fascinated by the ancient traditions of Europe and the Mediterranean. But it is significant that these were more or less consciously fused into a single, composite picture, dominated by the Christianity which provided a matrix for Anglo-Saxon thought, with a universal past and an apocalyptic future. Only within this was there room for the relics of ancient Rome and Germany, suitably Christianized and inevitably confused, but hallowed by an awesome antiquity.

APPENDIX

THE PAGAN SAXON PERIOD

Archaeology gives some indication of the attitudes of the pagan Anglo-Saxons towards relics of the past in post-Roman Britain; they were apparently primarily (though not exclusively) utilitarian, and not limited to the remains of any particular period. Some objects were re-used: finds of Roman pottery and glass are common from early Saxon cemeteries and settlements,[4] while smaller objects found in Saxon graves include Roman brooches, presumably worn by the Saxons,[5] intaglios in a variety of settings[6] and coins, often pierced for use as weights or

---

[1] *HE* ii.16. On its possible 'Roman' connotations, see above, p. 40, n. 1; on its Germanic associations, see W. A. Chaney, *The Cult of Kingship in Anglo-Saxon England* (Manchester, 1970), pp. 141ff.

[2] F. M. Stenton, *Anglo-Saxon England*, 3rd ed. (Oxford, 1971), p. 35. He considers this view of the title to be mistaken.

[3] While Professor Deanesley has been the chief claimant of Roman revivalism (see 'Roman Traditionalist Influence'), Professor Chaney's stress on pagan Germanic traditions is more misleading (see Chaney, *The Cult of Kingship*).

[4] A. Meaney, *A Gazetteer of Early Anglo-Saxon Burial Sites* (London, 1964), *passim*. On settlements, e.g. Sutton Courtenay, Berkshire, see *Archaeologia* 73 (1923), 179 and *ibid.* 76 (1927), pl. 8.

[5] Meaney, *Gazetteer*, pp. 53, 97, 124, 189 and 268. Also pp. 107 and 115 (rings), p. 275 (buckles) and pp. 139 and 294 (beads).

[6] In rings, from Alfriston, Sussex, *Sussex Archaeol. Collections* 56 (1914), 24, and from Milton-near-Sittingbourne, Kent, F. H. Marshall, *Catalogue of the Finger Rings in the British Museum* (London,

ornaments.[1] In one instance graves in a cemetery were marked with piles of Roman tiles[2] and in another with part of a Roman column.[3] Other evidence shows the Saxons treating the remains of Roman Britain as merely the *disiecta membra* of a culture that meant little to them: they avoided some Roman sites and elsewhere misused Roman villas[4] and roads[5] as graveyards. The latter may at least have been convenient landmarks, and perhaps for the same reason they buried their dead in Neolithic long barrows and in Bronze Age round barrows;[6] they also made cemeteries of the Bronze Age ritual site at Abingdon and a number of Iron Age hill-forts.[7]

At Abingdon J. N. L. Myres has suggested that the Saxons may have felt reverence for the site,[8] and it appears that they sometimes combined superstition for old objects with a concern for the magical properties of their materials. Saxon graves have produced a range of Roman nick-nacks, from broken skillet-handles to strap-ends,[9] as well as Iron Age pins and ring terrets[10] and flint axes[11] and arrow-heads.[12] Mr David Brown considers that many Saxon women were buried with a bag slung round the waist and filled with a collection of objects of a wide range of materials, probably for magical purposes, among them usually at least one old object, either Roman or Iron Age; rings seem to have been especially valued, apparently as amulets.[13]

Finally, place-names occasionally illustrate early Saxon attitudes towards antiquities.[14]

1907), no. 1651 and perhaps no. 1652 (but see G. Payne, *Collectanea Cantiana* (London, 1893), pp. 86–7, apparently referring to this ring with no mention of Saxon context). In a brooch from Alveston, Warwickshire, E. T. Leeds, *Anglo-Saxon Square-Headed Brooches* (Oxford, 1949), no. 116; in a buckle from Lyminge, Kent, *Archaeologia Cantiana* 69 (1955), 24; in pendants from Epsom, Surrey, *Illustrated London News* 6860 (1971), 31, from Pakefield, Suffolk, *VCH Suffolk* 1 (1911), 347, and from Sibertswold Down, Kent, B. Fausett, *Inventorium Sepulchrale* (London, 1856), p. 131; and loose from Ozingell, Kent, C. Roach Smith, *Collectanea Antiqua* III (London, 1854), pl. 5, and Sleaford, Lincolnshire, *Archaeologia* 50 (1887), 404. Dr Martin Henig has kindly informed me of two further examples, neither of them published: British Museum 1936 5–11.22 (from Howletts, Berkesbourne, Kent) and Worthing Museum 3452 (from Highdown, Sussex), both in rings.

[1] Meaney, *Gazetteer, passim*. At Gilton, Kent, a pair of scales was found with eighteen weights, some of them Roman coins, *VCH Kent* 1 (1908), 354.

[2] Meaney, *Gazetteer*, p. 229 (Lackford, Suffolk). [3] *Ibid.* p. 159 (Lovedon Hill, Lincolnshire).

[4] E.g. Denton, Lincolnshire, *Reports and Papers of the Lincolnshire Architectural and Archaeol. Soc.* n.s. 10 (1963–4), 94f., and North Stoke, Lincolnshire (a bath-house), *Archaeologia* 22 (1892), 32. Cf. Meaney, *Gazetteer*, pp. 54, 91 and 301. [5] Meaney, *Gazetteer*, pp. 200 and 259–60.

[6] *Ibid.* pp. 18–19 and *passim*. [7] *Ibid.* pp. 44, 144–5, 250 and 265.

[8] J. N. L. Myres, *Anglo-Saxon Pottery and the Settlement of England* (Oxford, 1969), pp. 121–2.

[9] Skillet-handle, Meaney, *Gazetteer*, p. 262; skillet base, *ibid.* p. 115; part of spoon, *ibid.* p. 265; pin, *ibid.* p. 134; disc, perhaps lid of seal box, *ibid.* p. 88; scale of armour, *ibid.* p. 62; lock, perhaps Roman, *ibid.* p. 119; and bronze tag, *ibid.* p. 95. Some objects may have been valued for their moulded ornament, e.g. a metal ornament with a figure of winged Cupid as reaper, *ibid.* p. 210; enamelled hare-shaped ornament, *ibid.* p. 95; knife handle with hare and hounds design, *ibid.* p. 115. Cf. a portion of a stone plaque carved with a winged figure found at Sutton Hoo (Mound 3) in 1938, *Proc. of the Suffolk Inst. of Archaeology* 30 (1964), 16–17.

[10] Cf. P. D. C. Brown, 'The Ironwork', *Excavations at Shakenoak* III, ed. A. C. C. Brodribb, A. R. Hands and D. R. Walker (Oxford, 1972), 109.

[11] J. Douglas, *Nenia Britannica* (London, 1793), p. 92 (from Ash (Gilton), Kent).

[12] Meaney, *Gazetteer*, pp. 58, 170 and 300. [13] Brown, 'The Ironwork', p. 109.

[14] See Kenneth Cameron, *English Place-Names* (London, 1961), esp. pp. 110–11.

The influence of the catechetical *narratio* on Old English and some other medieval literature

VIRGINIA DAY

In medieval literature there are a number of examples of a type of writing which provides an outline of Christian cosmology and Christian history. These works deal, usually briefly, with the following: God and his creative powers, the creation, the fall of the angels, the creation and fall of man, biblical history, the redemption, Christ's life, the crucifixion, the descent into hell, the resurrection, the ascension, and the second coming and last judgement. The subjects vary somewhat; the fall of man and his redemption are of central importance, and some outline versions are reduced to these essentials.[1]

The inspiration behind this type of writing (at least in the west) is Augustine's *De Catechizandis Rudibus*, written about 405. This work provides instruction and advice for priests on the subject of catechizing. The catechetical instruction should begin, says Augustine, with a *narratio*,[2] consisting of an exposition of Christian cosmology and history: 'Inde iam exordienda narratio est, ab eo quod fecit deus omnia bona valde, et perducenda, ut diximus, usque ad praesentia tempora ecclesiae; ita ut singularum rerum atque gestorum quae narramus, causae rationesque reddantur, quibus ea referamus ad illum finem dilectionis unde neque agentis aliquid neque loquentis oculus avertendus est.'[3] Augustine laid down some more detailed advice on the composition of the *narratio*:

Narratio plena est, cum quisque primo catechizatur ab eo quod scriptum est, *in principio fecit deus caelum et terram*, usque ad praesentia tempora ecclesiae. Non

---

[1] For example, Alcuin, *De Fide Sanctae et Individuae Trinitatis*, Lib. III Prologus, Migne, Patrologia Latina 101.

[2] J. P. Christopher (*The First Catechetical Instruction*, Ancient Christian Writers 2 (Westminster, Maryland, 1946), p. 95) points out that 'the rhetorical term *narratio* must have been applied long before Augustine's time to the historical exposition at the beginning of the catechetical instruction'.

[3] 'At this point we should begin our narration, starting out from the fact that God made all things very good, and continuing, as we have said, down to the present period of church history, in such a way as to account for and explain the causes and reasons of each of the facts and events that we relate, and thereby refer them to that end of love from which in all our actions and words our eyes should never be turned away' (trans. Christopher, *Catechetical Instruction*, pp. 26–7); *De Catechizandis Rudibus*, ed. Adolf Wolfhard (Freiburg, 1892) 7.1.

tamen propterea debemus totum pentateuchem, totosque, iudicum et regnorum et Esdrae libros, totumque evangelium et acta apostolorum, vel, si ad verbum edidicimus, memoriter reddere, vel nostris verbis omnia, quae his continentur voluminibus narrando evolvere et explicare; quod nec tempus capit, nec ulla necessitas postulat; sed cuncta summatim generatimque complecti, ita ut eligantur quaedam mirabiliora quae suavius audiuntur, atque ipsis articulis constituta sunt, ut ea tanquam in involucris ostendere, statimque a conspectu abripere non oporteat, sed aliquantum immorando quasi resolvere atque expandere, et inspicienda atque miranda offerre animis auditorum: cetera vero celeri percursione inserendo contexere.[1]

The narration is to be centred on the redemption.[2] After the narration is finished '. . . spes resurrectionis intimanda est, et pro capacitate ac viribus audientis, proque ipsius temporis modulo, adversus vanas irrisiones infidelium de corporis resurrectione tractandum, et futuri ultimi iudicii bonitate in bonos, severitate in malos, veritate in omnes; commemoratisque cum detestatione et horrore poenis impiorum, regnum iustorum atque fidelium et superna illa civitas eiusque gaudium cum desiderio praedicandum est.'[3]

Augustine's own version of the catechetical *narratio*[4] is too complex, too philosophical, to have provided more than a useful model to later writers; they needed something even simpler, an even more basic narrative, and following Augustine's instructions they produced their own outlines. It is not to be expected that many *narrationes* actually used in catechetical instruction would have survived. Presumably they would have been in the vernacular and mostly would not have been written down at all. Catechism was

---

[1] 'The narration is complete when the beginner is first instructed from the text: *In the beginning God created heaven and earth*, down to the present period of church history. That does not mean, however, that we ought to repeat verbatim the whole of the Pentateuch, and all the books of Judges and Kingdoms and Esdras, and the entire Gospel and the Acts of the Apostles (if we have learned them by heart), or relate in our own words all that is contained in these books, and thus develop and explain them; for which neither time serves nor any need calls. But we ought to present all the matter in a general and comprehensive summary, choosing certain of the more remarkable facts that are heard with greater pleasure and constitute the cardinal points in history: these we ought not to present as a parchment rolled up and at once snatch them out of sight, but we ought by dwelling somewhat upon them to untie, so to speak, and spread them out to view, and offer them to the minds of our hearers to examine and admire. But the remaining details we should weave into our narrative in a rapid survey' (trans. Christopher, *Catechetical Instruction*, p. 18); *De Cat. Rud.* 3.1.

[2] 'Neque enim ob aliud ante adventum domini scripta sunt omnia, quae in sanctis scriptoris legimus, nisi ut illius commendaretur adventus, et praesignaretur ecclesia . . .' (*ibid.* 4.1).

[3] '. . . we should make known to him the hope in the resurrection, and with due regard for the capacity and powers of our hearer and the time at our disposal, combat by discussion the vain scoffings of unbelievers about the resurrection of the body, and speak to him of the last judgement to come, with its goodness towards the good, its severity towards the wicked, its certainty in relation to all. And after the punishments of the wicked have thus been recounted with loathing and horror, we should describe with eager longing the kingdom of the good and faithful, and that city in heaven with its joys' (trans. Christopher, *Catechetical Instruction*, pp. 27–8); *De Cat. Rud.* 7.4.

[4] *De Cat. Rud.* 24–39.

always a predominantly oral activity.[1] Our evidence is likely to come from works of advice to those who would be carrying out this form of instruction, from narratives in which teaching of this kind is reported and from the influence of the *narratio* detectable in literature. The *De Fide Catholica* attributed to Boethius is a perfect example of a *narratio*.[2] Others in Latin are two sermons reported in missionary Lives. In the *recensio Vaticana* of the acts of Andrew, the apostle, when converting the heathen, preaches a sermon on the Christian cycle from the creation to the ascension.[3] In the *Vita Sanctorum Barlaam Eremitae et Josaphat Indiae Regis*, Barlaam, at the heathen court, preaches a sermon in which he describes the Trinity and the Christian cycle from creation to ascension,[4] with a reference to the second coming. Then there is the sermon supposedly preached by St Gall near Constance;[5] the sermon is not certainly by St Gall and is probably to be attributed to Notker the Stammerer, who lived in the ninth century.[6] The author deals with the complete Christian cycle. Two other versions of the *narratio* are clearly to be connected with the *De Cat. Rud.* and with catechetical and missionary contexts. One is the first part of the *De Correctione Rusticorum* by Martin of Bracara (*c.* 515–80),[7] which is followed by references to baptism, the creed and renunciation of the devil.[8] The other is at the beginning of the *Scarapsus* of Pirmin of Reichenau (d. 753)[9] and is followed with matter on baptism, a version of the creed and a full discussion of the renunciation of the devil.[10] Pirmin's career involved missionary work among the Alamanni and no doubt he felt the need for such a manual of instruction in the basic features of the Christian faith. In producing the *Scarapsus* Pirmin used the *De Cat. Rud.* and was also strongly influenced by Martin's work, copying some passages almost word for word from Martin.[11] Martin's *narratio*, which contains especially detailed material about false gods and idols, continues as far as the last judgement. Pirmin follows a more strictly *narratio* structure in not

[1] See *Dictionnaire de Théologie Catholique, s.v. catéchèse*.
[2] *De Fide Catholica, The Theological Tractates of Boethius*, ed. H. F. Stewart and E. K. Rand (London, 1918; rev. ed. 1973). The attribution to Boethius is the subject of controversy; *ibid.* p. 52 n.
[3] Franz Blatt, *Die lateinischen Bearbeitungen der Acta Andreae et Matthiae apud anthropophagos* (Giessen, 1930), p. 121, line 13 – p. 136, line 11.
[4] *Vita Sanctorum Barlaam Eremitae et Josaphat Indiae Regis*, ch. VII, PL 73. Franz Dölger ('Der griechische Barlaam-Roman; ein Werk des H. Johannes von Damaskos', *Studia Patristica et Byzantina* I (1953), 1–104) has argued that the ascription of the Greek original to John of Damascus is correct. [5] *Sermo Habitus Constantiae*, PL 87.
[6] See W. E. Willwoll, *Die Konstanzer Predigt des Heiligen Gallus: ein Werk des Notker Balbulus* (Freiburg, 1942).
[7] *Martin von Bracara's Schrift De Correctione Rusticorum*, ed. C. P. Caspari (Christiana, 1883), 1–14. References are to sections. Martin's debt to the *De Cat. Rud.* is noted by Claude W. Barlow, *Martini Episcopi Bracarensis Opera Omnia* (New Haven, 1950), pp. 163–4.
[8] *De Corr. Rust.* 15.
[9] *Scarapsus* Part I, ed. Gall Jacker, *Die Heimat des hl. Pirmin, des Apostels der Alamannen* (Münster, 1927).
[10] *Ibid.* Part II.   [11] *Ibid.* introduction, pp. 90–3, and notes.

dealing so expansively with false gods, and concludes with the preaching of the apostles and the foundation of the church, including only a very brief allusion to the end of the world.

The influence of the *narratio* on literature can be plainly traced. So far as Latin is concerned, the *Libelli de Spiritalis Historiae Gestis*[1] of Avitus of Vienne (d. 518) could be considered a *narratio* concluding with an allusion to the redemption. The rhythmical poem, *De Fide Catholica*,[2] of Hrabanus Maurus (784–after 856) is certainly an example. This poem is based on the Hiberno-Latin *Altus Prosator*[3] and therefore shares some material with it, but Hrabanus reorganized this source and added substantially to it to produce a complete version of the *narratio* centred on the redemption. The poem *Occupatio*[4] of Odo of Cluny (879–942) has the same structure.

The Irish *Voyage of Snegdus and MacRiagla* provides evidence of the use of the Christian cycle in Ireland. A great bird tells the travellers 'tales of the creation of the world, and tells them of Christ's birth from Mary Virgin, and His Baptism and His Passion and His Resurrection. And he tells tidings of Doom . . .'[5] The Irish poem, the *Saltair na Rann*,[6] and the related prose version in the *Lebar Brec*[7] are further examples.

When we turn to Old English it seems that the *narratio* exercised a decisive influence on the composition of Christian vernacular poetry at the very start, or at least so Bede thought, for his famous description of the corpus of Cædmon's poetry is no less than a description of the catechetical *narratio* as well:

Canebat autem de creatione mundi et origine humani generis et tota Genesis historia, de egressu Israel ex Aegypto et ingressu in terram repromissionis, de aliis plurimis sacrae scripturae historiis, de incarnatione dominica, passione, resurrectione et ascensione in caelum, de Spiritus Sancti adventu et apostolorum doctrina; item de terrore futuri iudicii et horrore poenae gehennalis ac dulcedine regni coelestis multa carmina faciebat. Sed et alia perplura de beneficiis et iudiciis divinis, in quibus cunctis homines ab amore scelerum abstrahere, ad dilectionem vero et sollertiam bonae actionis excitare curabat.[8]

[1] *Alcimi Aviti Opera*, ed. Rudolfus Peiper, Monumenta Germaniae Historica, Auct. Ant. 6.2.
[2] *Carmina* 31, PL 112.
[3] *Altus Prosator*, ed. Clemens Blume, Analecta Hymnica Medii Aevi 51 (1908), 275–7.
[4] *Occupatio*, ed. A. Swoboda (Lipsiae, 1900).
[5] Whitley Stokes, 'The Voyage of Snegdus and MacRiagla', *Revue Celtique* 9 (1888), 21.
[6] *Saltair na Rann*, ed. Whitley Stokes (Oxford, 1883). A new edition with translation is being prepared by the Dublin Institute of Advanced Studies. I owe my access to this translation to the kindness of Mr Fergus Kelly. The *Saltair* goes as far as Christ's ascension.
[7] *Lebar Brec*, ed. and trans. B. MacCarthy, *The Codex Palatino-Vaticanus no. 830*, R. Irish Acad. Todd Lecture Ser. 3 (Dublin, 1892).
[8] *Bede's Ecclesiastical History of the English People*, ed. Bertram Colgrave and R. A. B. Mynors (Oxford, 1969) IV.24. S. J. Crawford ('The Cædmon Poems', *Anglia* 49 (1926), 279–84) points out the similarity of the subjects of this passage of Bede's to the *De Fide Catholica* attributed to Boethius, and also (p. 284) notes a parallel with the structure of the mystery plays, on which see below, pp. 59–61.

We should note especially the break marked by *item* at the end of the cate-chetical *narratio* proper, according to Augustine's definition, and before the subject of the future judgement, which Augustine says, with its attendant description of the punishments of the wicked and the joys of heaven, is to be raised *narratione finita*. Augustine also advises that this be followed by moral exhortation[1] and the last lines of Bede's description show that this is what he thought Cædmon did also. We should observe too that the surviving lines of Cædmon's poetry concern the praise of God for his work of creation,[2] and thus coincide with the expected opening of the *narratio*, which is to begin, Augustine says, with instruction from the text, 'In the beginning God created heaven and earth'. No doubt Cædmon's own religious education, before he received his gift and became a monk, had included instruction by means of a *narratio*. Certainly after his miraculous ability was discovered he was taught, as Bede tells us, *seriem sacrae historiae*.[3] Although some of the versions of the *narratio* are long, as for instance Odo's *Occupatio*, in essence the genre, with its background of instructing the unlearned, demands an outline that is brief. Therefore it is possible that Bede's description of Cædmon's poetry implies only a relatively short work. Bede saw the great importance of the use of the vernacular for basic instruction in the faith and provided ignorant priests with his own English translations of the creed and the Lord's Prayer.[4] To him and his contemporaries vernacular verse techniques would have seemed to offer an effective way of arousing in the unlettered the admiration which Augustine advocated they should be made to feel for the cardinal points of history. Evidently the first, momentous application of these techniques was regarded as nothing short of a miracle.

Old English poetry kept its concern with the basic events of Christian world history – witness, for example, the amount of Old Testament narrative in the extant corpus. More specifically the influence of the *narratio* is probably to be seen in *Genesis*,[5] especially in its opening section (1–102) on God, the creation of the heavens, the fall of the angels and the decision to create man; in the remainder of the poem the influence of the hexameral and Genesis traditions seems stronger. The opening of *Christ and Satan*[6] (1–18), which deals with the creation of the world by God, may also show the influence of the beginning of the *narratio*.

[1] *De Cat. Rud.* 8.2.
[2] Bede gives a translation of these lines of Cædmon's poetry, *HE* IV.24. A version of the Old English lines appears in *The Old English Version of Bede's Ecclesiastical History of the English People*, ed. Thomas Miller, Early Eng. Text Soc. o.s. 95, 96, 110 and 111 (London, 1890–8), I, 344.
[3] *HE* IV.24.
[4] *Epistola Baedae ad Ecgbertum Episcopum*, ed. Charles Plummer, *Venerabilis Baedae Opera Historica* (Oxford, 1896) I, 409.
[5] Ed. George Philip Krapp, *The Junius Manuscript*, Anglo-Saxon Poetic Records I (New York, 1931). [6] Ed. *ibid*.

Three Old English prose homilies are clear examples of the *narratio* genre. Part of Vercelli XIX, without rubric in the Vercelli Book but assigned to Rogationtide in other manuscripts,[1] is one. This homily does not include an outline of the complete cycle, from creation to Doomsday, but, as an introduction to Rogationtide penitential themes, the homilist describes the Trinity and its powers of creation, the creation of heaven, earth and the angels, the fall of the angels, the creation and fall of man and his ultimate redemption. Another example is the sermon, *De Initio Creaturae*, with which Ælfric began his series of *Catholic Homilies*.[2] It is one of the few of his sermons for which no source has yet been discovered.[3] It is an outline of the whole Christian cycle: beginning with an invocation to God and the Trinity and some remarks on God's nature and powers, it runs from the creation to the end of the world. The third example is Wulfstan's reworking of this sermon by Ælfric (Bethurum VI).[4] Although different in style and to some extent in content, Wulfstan's version preserves the essential nature of Ælfric's.

All three Old English homilies are probably connected with the versions of the *narratio* found in the *De Corr. Rust.* and the *Scarapsus*. Owing to the similarity between these two works it is often not possible to tell which of them the influence comes from. The *De Corr. Rust./Scarapsus* could have provided a pattern for the series of events described in Vercelli XIX. A short passage in Vercelli XIX is close to one in *De Corr. Rust./Scarapsus*; compare '. . . þe eva hatte. Of ðam twam þurh godes mihte is ealles middaneardes folc fram cumen'[5] with '. . . dicta est Eva. Ex istis duobus hominibus omne genus humanum propagatum est.'[6] And the passage in which the devil's allies are described, '7 ealle þa þe æt þæm ræde mid him wæron 7 him æfter besawon'[7] could be a version of *De Corr. Rust./Scarapsus* 'illi angeli qui consentientes illi fuerunt'.[8] But the account of the fall of the angels and man in Vercelli XIX contains material, such as the references to Lucifer's name,

[1] See N. R. Ker, *Catalogue of Manuscripts containing Anglo-Saxon* (Oxford, 1957), no. 394, item 24. The passage which I discuss here is on 106v–107r25 of the Vercelli Book; reproduced M. Förster, *Il Codice Vercellese* (Rome, 1913). For the group of items to which this homily belongs in the Vercelli Book see D. G. Scragg, 'The Compilation of the Vercelli Book', *ASE* 2 (1973), 189–207, esp. 194–5 and 203–4.

[2] *De Initio Creaturae, The Homilies of the Anglo-Saxon Church: the First Part, containing the Sermones Catholici, or Homilies of Ælfric*, ed. Benjamin Thorpe (London, 1844–6) I, 8–28 (referred to subsequently as *De Initio*).

[3] *Homilies of Ælfric: a Supplementary Collection*, ed. John C. Pope, EETS 259–60 (London, 1967–8), I, 473.

[4] *The Homilies of Wulfstan*, ed. Dorothy Bethurum (Oxford, 1957), no. VI. Professor Bethurum's note (p. 293), 'This kind of sermon is at least as old as Augustine (*De Genesi ad Litteram*)', is misleading. As she says, it is an 'outline of Christian history', whereas the *De Genesi* is not, although, as a commentary on Genesis, this work overlaps with the first part of the catechetical *narratio*.

[5] Vercelli XIX, 107r, lines 3–5. I have supplied the punctuation.   [6] *De Corr. Rust.* 5; *Scarapsus* 4.
[7] Vercelli XIX, 106v, lines 22–3.   [8] *De Corr. Rust.* 3; *Scarapsus* 2.

his throne in the north, the sending of the rebellious angels to hell rather than into the air and the curious fact that the forbidden tree is the Tree of Life, which could not derive from *De Corr. Rust./Scarapsus*. As to the *De Initio*, it is not possible to define with certainty its relationship to *De Corr. Rust./Scarapsus*. Ælfric knew the *De Corr. Rust.* and used it, for instance, in his sermon *De Falsis Diis*.[1] The *De Initio*, the *De Corr. Rust.* and the *Scarapsus* all treat of similar events in the Christian cycle in a similar order, but this agreement does not extend to the more detailed level of the words and phrases employed by Ælfric. Sometimes Ælfric's work appears to be closer to Martin's than to Pirmin's: for instance, in the passage on idols[2] both Ælfric and Martin go into details (although Ælfric's handling of this theme is far briefer than Martin's), whereas Pirmin does not, and both Ælfric and Martin describe the second coming and the last judgement,[3] but Pirmin does not. On the other hand, both Ælfric and Pirmin mention the harrowing of hell,[4] whilst Martin does not, and both Ælfric and Pirmin have passages on the Law, the patriarchs and the prophets,[5] but Martin does not. Since there is no detailed agreement and Ælfric's sermon contains material found in neither Martin's work nor Pirmin's,[6] Ælfric could have been using the *De Corr. Rust.* or the *Scarapsus*, or both, to provide a model on which to compose freely a version of his own. Wulfstan, however, as Jost has shown,[7] certainly used the *Scarapsus* when reworking Ælfric.

Ælfric produced other versions of the Christian cycle. There is one at the beginning of his *Letter to Sigeweard*[8] and another at the beginning of his *Letter to Wulfgeat*.[9] His *Hexameron* also contains similar material; although its structure is that of the six days' work, it closes with a reference to the redemption and eternal life and a passage of exhortation.[10] In the *Letter to Sigeweard* Ælfric uses two phrases which are fairly close to two in *De Corr.*

[1] See *Homilies of Ælfric*, ed. Pope II, 671–3.
[2] *De Initio*, p. 22; cf. *De Corr. Rust.* 6–7.
[3] *De Initio*, p. 28; cf. *De Corr. Rust.* 13–14.
[4] *De Initio*, pp. 26–8; cf. *Scarapsus* 9.
[5] *De Initio*, p. 24; cf. *Scarapsus* 5–6.
[6] For instance, it includes more details about the fall of the angels, and discussion of the Tower of Babel.
[7] Karl Jost, *Wulfstanstudien*, Schweizer anglistische Arbeiten 23 (Bern, 1950), 55–61.
[8] *The Old English Version of the Heptateuch, Ælfric's Treatise on the Old and New Testament and his Preface to Genesis*, ed. S. J. Crawford, EETS o.s. 160 (London, 1922), 'Ælfric: On the Old and New Testament', lines 1–126. This account goes as far as the redemption.
[9] *Angelsächsische Homilien und Heiligenleben*, ed. Bruno Assman, Bibliothek der angelsächsischen Prosa 3 (Kassel, 1889), 1: 'Ælfric's Sendschreiben an Wulfget zu Ylmandun, lines 1–79. Cf. also the two small pieces, *De Creatore et Creatura* and *De Sex Etatibus huius Seculi*, mentioned by P. A. M. Clemoes, 'The Chronology of Ælfric's Works', *The Anglo-Saxons: Studies in some Aspects of their History and Culture presented to Bruce Dickins*, ed. P. Clemoes (London, 1959), pp. 241–2.
[10] *Exameron Anglice*, ed. S. J. Crawford, Bibl. der ags. Prosa 10 (Hamburg, 1921), lines 505–42.

Rust./Scarapsus;[1] compare, in his description of the genesis of the devil's pride, '. . . gesceawode se an engel þe þær ænlicost wæs, hu fæger he silf wæs 7 hu scinende on wuldre'[2] with 'Ex quibus unus . . . videns se in tanta gloria praefulgentem'[3] and, in his allusion to Lucifer's failure to honour his creator, '7 nolde wurðian þone, þe hine geworhte'[4] with 'non dedit honorem deo creaturi suo'.[5] Ælfric's employment of expressions with *ræd*[6] to describe the conspiracy of the rebel angels may also be inspired by the phrase in *De Corr. Rust./Scarapsus* 'illi angeli, qui consentientes illi fuerunt'.[7] There is also evidence that the *Letter to Sigeweard*, the *Letter to Wulfgeat* and the *Hexameron* all lean on the *De Initio* in diction and phraseology.[8] The *De Initio* was Ælfric's most complete version; it is as if all the later accounts presuppose the existence of this basic one.[9]

Anyone who reads the *De Initio* with Augustine's instructions in mind cannot fail to be impressed by how faithfully and how brilliantly Ælfric carried out the great bishop's advice. For instance, he alludes to the redemption twice[10] in the course of his narration before actually describing it and thus follows Augustine's suggestion that the redemption should be kept in mind throughout. His selection and summary of the important events and his brief but lucid discussion of some of the theological issues which arise from them are masterly. The catechetical background explains why he chose the *De Initio* to open his *Catholic Homilies*: the catechetical sermon is the traditional introduction to Christianity. In the *Letter to Sigeweard* the *narratio* serves as an introduction to a discussion of the bible and Ælfric's various translations from it. The Augustinian background makes clear how apt this is. Augustine considered that the catechetical *narratio* should provide the essential narrative and message of the scriptures interpreted for the ignorant: the *narratio* is to lay down the guidelines for the understanding of scripture. Accordingly, before allowing his reader to proceed to what he conceived of

---

[1] Like those phrases cited in connection with Vercelli xix they are contained in a passage of the *De Corr. Rust.* (3–5) which was copied almost verbatim in the *Scarapsus* (3–4), so that it is not possible to say which of the two was being used.

[2] *Letter to Sigeweard*, lines 70–3.   [3] *De Corr. Rust.* 3; *Scarapsus* 2.

[4] *Letter to Sigeweard*, lines 81–3.   [5] *De Corr. Rust.* 3; *Scarapsus* 2.

[6] For instance, 'ac feoll sona adun mid eallum ðam englum ðe æt his ræde wæron', *Hexameron*, lines 317–18; cf. *De Initio*, p. 10, lines 27–8; *Letter to Sigeweard*, lines 94–6; and *Ælfric's Lives of Saints*, ed. Walter W. Skeat, EETS o.s. 76, 82, 94 and 114 (London, 1881–1900), I, 296, lines 182–3.

[7] *De Corr. Rust.* 3; *Scarapsus* 2.

[8] Compare, for instance, *Hexameron*, lines 324–8 with *De Initio*, p. 12, lines 25–8; *Hexameron*, lines 449–52 with *De Initio*, p. 16, lines 26–31; and *Letter to Wulfgeat*, line 30 with *De Initio*, p. 10, line 15. The *Hexameron* is written in rhythmical prose, and in it Ælfric coined some half-lines which were to do service in the other two rhythmical accounts; compare, for instance, *Hexameron*, lines 103–5, *Letter to Sigeweard*, lines 55–60, and *Letter to Wulfgeat*, lines 27–33.

[9] 'Be ðam we sædon hwilum ær swutelicor on gewrite', as Ælfric himself wrote concerning angels, *Hexameron*, line 106.

[10] *De Initio*, p. 18, lines 34–5 and p. 24, lines 13–16.

as the dangerous terrain of the bible itself,[1] Ælfric took the opportunity to clarify the correct message to be derived from it. In the *Letter to Wulfgeat* also the context of the *narratio* is clearly 'catechetical': Ælfric prefaces his advice on how to live a moral life with a brief outline of the Christian cycle, exactly as Augustine had recommended that the *narratio* be followed by exhortation.[2] In general Ælfric's production of several versions of the *narratio* – as well as his use of some similar material in the *Hexameron* – has the aim of providing a framework for the unlettered, of placing each particular point of Christian doctrine in relation to the pattern of the whole.[3] No exact sources have been discovered for any of Ælfric's versions of the *narratio*, and it seems to me possible that none existed. The catechetical context is exactly that in which Ælfric might well have decided to compose his own accounts, since this is what Augustine advised priests to do.

An example of the influence that the catechetical *narratio* had on later literature is provided, I think, by the cyclical form of the English mystery plays.[4] Of course, the structure of these varies in detail, but their general form is that of the Christian cycle. The subjects usually included the fall of Lucifer (with an introductory statement by God, defining himself and indicating his creative powers; compare the sermons), the creation and fall of man, Cain and Abel, Noah and the flood, Abraham and Isaac, sometimes Moses and the Exodus or Moses and the Law, sometimes the Prophets, the nativity, the raising of Lazarus, the passion, the resurrection and Doomsday. Hardin Craig has attempted to explain the Old Testament sequence as a development from a dramatization of the breviary lections for Lent.[5] Even if this

---

[1] See *Preface to Genesis*, ed. Crawford, p. 76, lines 8–10 and p. 77, lines 41–5.

[2] *De Cat. Rud.* 8.2; cf. Cædmon.

[3] So, in his sermon on the *Annunciatio S. Mariae*, in order to explain what made the redemption necessary, Ælfric provided a résumé of the *narratio* (*Catholic Homilies*, ed. Thorpe I, 192), a résumé which is not in his source (Bede, *Homeliarum Evangelii Libri II* 1.3 and 4, ed. D. Hurst, Corpus Christianorum Series Latina 122, 14–20, and 21–31; see M. Förster, 'Über die Quellen von Ælfrics exegetical Hom. Catholicae', *Anglia* 16 (1894), 20; and Cyril Smetana, 'Ælfric and the Early Medieval Homiliary', *Traditio* 15 (1959), 188).

[4] *The Chester Plays*, ed. Hermann Deimling, EETS e.s. 62 and 115 (London, 1893 and 1916); *The Towneley Plays*, ed. George England, EETS e.s. 71 (London, 1897); *Ludus Coventriae*, ed. K. S. Block, EETS e.s. 120 (London, 1922); *York Plays*, ed. Lucy Toulmin Smith (Oxford, 1885). The lost Beverley plays also had a cyclical structure; see Rosemary Woolf, *The English Mystery Plays* (London, 1972), p. 67. I confine my remarks here to the English cycles, but, of course, they are relevant to the development of the cycle form in general. Examples of cycles similar in structure to the English cycles are known from the continent, both from extant plays, and from descriptions of lost plays. A play from Künzelsau, *Das Künzelsauer Fronleichnamspiel*, ed. Peter K. Liebenow (Berlin, 1969), runs from the creation to the last judgement. A lost play from Regensburg is described in the *Annales Ratisponenses* (see Karl Young, *The Drama of the Medieval Church* (Oxford, 1933) II, 542) as beginning with the creation and fall of Lucifer, but it is not certain how far this play extended. The play, described as having taken place in Cividale in 1304 (*ibid.* II, 540), goes from the creation of the first parents to the last judgement. A play from Riga (*ibid.* II, 542) may also have had the structure of the Christian cycle.

[5] Hardin Craig, 'The Origin of the Old Testament Plays', *MP* 10 (1912–13), 473–87.

were correct, and there are reasons for believing that it is not,[1] we would still have the complete cycle form to explain. It is true that the first cyclical plays seem to have been associated with Septuagesima,[2] but this association, although interesting, does not in itself suggest a model on which a complete cycle could have been based. Rosemary Woolf, in her book *The English Mystery Plays*, fully considers the cycle form. She mentions several cycles of illustrations which depict Christian history[3] and suggests that these had an important influence. Earlier than any of her examples, however, are the *Versus ad Picturas Domus Domini Mogontinę of Ekkehart IV* (980–1060);[4] these follow the course of the *narratio*, and seem to have been intended as a list of possible subjects for the pictures.[5] Ekkehart was providing captions for pictures, and thus his captions and the pictures were both designed to follow the course of the catechetical *narratio*: a division between art and literature is artificial in this context.

At the end of her chapter on the development of the cycle form Miss Woolf writes:

The development of the cycle form has formerly been explained in liturgical terms: it has been thought of either as an unconsidered conjunction of plays originally distinct and closely attached to liturgical seasons or as a dramatic form specially constructed for the feast of Corpus Christi.[6] Whilst any attempt to reconstruct the historical development of the form is necessarily speculative, it seems more likely in view of the evidence set out in this chapter, that, whilst the cycles were consciously designed, the authors were not primarily moved by liturgical considerations. Far more important was the intention of instructing the unlearned . . .[7]

I agree with her, but I suggest that behind both the iconographic cycles and the mystery play cycles lies the catechetical *narratio*,[8] a version of Christian cosmology and history which every Christian ought to have had preached to him by his priest. It is worth noting that the intention of instructing the unlearned is explicitly claimed in the account of the play performed at Riga,

---

[1] See Woolf, *Plays*, p. 356, n. 13.

[2] *Ibid.* pp. 56–7.

[3] *Ibid.* pp. 57, 58 and 62.

[4] *Versus ad Picturas Domus Domini Mogontinę*, ed. Johannes Egli, *Der Liber Benedictionum Ekkeharts IV. nebst den kleinern Dichtungen aus dem Codex Sangallensis 393* (St Gall, 1909), pp. 316–68.

[5] Egli, *Der Liber Benedictionum*, p. xx.

[6] Woolf, *Plays*, pp. 70–1 argues convincingly against this.

[7] *Ibid.* p. 75.

[8] V. A. Kolvé, *The Play called Corpus Christi* (London, 1966), pp. 86–100, argues that the principle of selection in the Old Testament sequences of the English cycles was the allocation of one play to each of the figures representing the seven ages of the world. In fact, this idea does not work out in detail for all the cycles. The material which goes into an enumeration of the ages of the world overlaps with that involved in the catechetical *narratio*. Augustine's own version of the *narratio* contains an enumeration of the ages of the world, *De Cat. Rud.* 29.

and this play was performed in a missionary context identical to that in which versions of the catechetical *narratio* were preached.[1]

[1] It is said that the play was performed, 'in media Riga, ut fidei Christianae rudimenta gentilitas fide etiam disceret oculata. Cuius ludi et comoediae materia tam neophytis, quam paganis, qui aderant, per interpretem diligentissime exponebatur . . . et per doctrinam Veteris et Novi Testamenti erat instruenda, qualiter ad verum pacificum et ad vitam perveniat sempiternam' (Young, *The Drama* II, 542). Note the references to *fidei Christianae rudimenta* and to neophytes and pagans. In some of the German passion plays, which have connections in structure with the cycle form, there is a narrator figure; in a Frankfurt play this is Augustinus, see Liebenow, *Künzelsauer Fronleichnamspiel*, p. 258.

I am very grateful to Professor Clemoes for all the help which he gave me in the presentation of this material.

The concept of the hall in Old English poetry

KATHRYN HUME

The range of cultural assumptions underlying Old English poetry and the sentiments and sources which inspired it, not to mention the methods of composition – oral or written – are subjects of vigorous dispute. Much that was once considered indigenous and Germanic is now being revalued in the light of Latin analogues[1] and works accepted for a century as secular are being treated by many as Christian doctrinal discourses. Since the intellectual milieu is so uncertain a basis for interpreting controversial poems, other approaches are needed. One that suggests itself is the exploration of idea-complexes. When a theme or situation recurs in a number of poems, in widely differing contexts, patterns of association can be isolated and analysed. The theme of exile, for example, is a centre of a cluster of ideas.[2] Another is the concept of the hall: what is looked to for safety and what is feared as a threat to that security make apt points of departure for a study of a culture's major assumptions. Moreover, because the hall is the focus for conflicting attitudes, the array of associations proves useful to a more general understanding of the nature of Old English poetry.

Until fairly recently belief in the impressiveness of the halls celebrated by poets was largely an act of faith. Long-house or Warendorf-type structures were considered possibilities, but there was no firm evidence for any dwellings but sunken hovels, and poets were assumed to be exaggerating the splendour of what they described. But what Sutton Hoo did for the account

---

[1] J. E. Cross has discovered sources and analogues for many of the more memorable Anglo-Saxon topoi: see 'The Old English Poetic Theme of *The Gifts of Men*', *Neophilologus* 46 (1962), 66–70; 'On *The Wanderer* lines 80–4: a Study of a Figure and a Theme', *Årsbok Vetenskaps-Societeten i Lund* (1958–9), 77–110; and '"Ubi sunt" Passages in Old English – Sources and Relationships', *ibid.* (1956), 25–44. G. V. Smithers and Dorothy Whitelock relate the Wanderer-Seafarer personae to the religious *peregrinus*: see G. V. Smithers, 'The Meaning of *The Seafarer* and *The Wanderer*', *MÆ* 26 (1957), 137–53 and 28 (1959), 1–22, and Dorothy Whitelock, 'The Interpretation of *The Seafarer*', *The Early Cultures of North-West Europe* (H. M. Chadwick Memorial Studies), ed. B. Dickins and Sir Cyril Fox (Cambridge, 1950), pp. 261–72. *Beowulf* has frequently been studied for Christian meanings, and even figures formerly thought to be purely secular, like Byrhtnoth of *The Battle of Maldon*, are being likened to saints; see N. F. Blake, 'The Battle of Maldon', *Neophilologus* 49 (1965), 332–45.

[2] See Stanley B. Greenfield, 'The Formulaic Expression of the Theme of "Exile" in Anglo-Saxon Poetry', *Speculum* 30 (1955), 200–6. For an analysis of numerous small centres of poetic thought, see E. G. Stanley, 'Old English Poetic Diction and the Interpretation of *The Wanderer*, *The Seafarer* and *The Penitent's Prayer*', *Anglia* 73 (1956), 413–66.

of Beowulf's burial new finds have been doing for the great hall that Hrothgar built, admired so much for its size and loftiness, its strength and its shining magnificence. West Stow boasted six hall-sites during the fifth and sixth centuries. The royal hall at Cheddar was 78 feet long, and at Old Yeavering (the *villa regalis ad Gefrin* mentioned by Bede) traces of four successive great halls have been found, one of them 80 feet long and 50 wide. The Thetford great hall was a staggering 110 feet in length.[1] Some of these structures were centres for extensive social units, and certainly by the time the extant poems were written kings were surrounding themselves with administrators, henchmen, clerks and all the middlemen of a complex civilization, with the result that living conditions at court were correspondingly elaborate and the king increasingly remote, but the ideal which attracted poets was essentially a settlement that brought lord and retainers into close, personal, daily contact. The *burh* at *Merantun*, whose features are deducible from the Chronicle account of the death of King Cynewulf in 786, was such a settlement at its simplest, consisting of outer defences, a hall and small separate buildings – bowers – which provided private night quarters for those of rank and presumably housed food supplies and facilities for such operations as baking.[2] To the poets the *burh* walls, the hall and the *gifstol* are the frame for the connotations and associations of the idea-complex of the hall.

What the poems celebrate is, of course, not simply the hall as a building but the social system associated with it. Though assumptions about halls were never elaborated into an articulated social philosophy, any reader can deduce from incidental comments that the hall was pictured, for poetic purposes, as a circle of light and peace enclosed by darkness, discomfort and danger. It was the 'centre of power from which treasure is distributed':[3] the fundamental gesture was the lord's giving of treasure from the high seat. The distribution of gifts seems, from its many usages, to have been the imaginative centre of all the clustered hall associations. The phrasals *beaggyfa*, *sinces brytta* and the like are a sign of the potency of this concept. In the Finn episode in *Beowulf* the agreement drawn up between the surviving Danes and Frisians has it as a primary condition that Finn shall daily confer gifts

---

[1] Though returns are not yet complete, the current state of information is summarized (with helpful illustrations) by P. V. Addyman, 'The Anglo-Saxon House: a New Review', *ASE* 1 (1972), 273–307. Additional material is available in C. A. Ralegh Radford, 'The Saxon House: a Review and Some Parallels', *MA* 1 (1957), 27–38; Philip Rahtz, 'The Saxon and Medieval Palaces at Cheddar, Somerset – an Interim Report of Excavations in 1960–2', *ibid*. 6–7 (1962–3), 53–66; a summary description of Old Yeavering, *ibid*. 1 (1957), 148–9; and Rosemary J. Cramp, '*Beowulf* and Archaeology', *ibid*. pp. 57–77.

[2] For an analysis of the hall and hall-life covering these and other points, see Dorothy Whitelock, *The Beginnings of English Society* (Harmondsworth, 1952), pp. 88–92.

[3] Jeffrey Helterman ('*Beowulf*: the Archetype enters History', *ELH* 35 (1968), 1–20, esp. 6) analyses the archetypal significances of the hall/*gifstol* combination.

on the Danes equal to those that he gives to his own followers (1089–94). The gifts made to Beowulf by Hrothgar (1020–49) and by Wealhtheow (1192–1214a) after his defeat of Grendel are described at considerable length. When the Wanderer sums up what he has lost, he does so with heavy emphasis on treasure:

> Warað hine wræclast,   nales *wunden gold*,
> ferðloca freorig,   nalæs foldan blæd.
> Gemon he selesecgas   ond *sincþege*,
> hu hine on geoguðe   his *goldwine*
> wenede to wiste.   Wyn eal gedreas![1] (32–6)

Not only did retainers account distribution of gold as the most significant feature of their experience; lords did too. From a leader's point of view gifts were both a reward for deeds done on his behalf (e.g. *Beowulf* 1020–49) and an insurance for the future (*Beowulf* 20–4a). Hrothgar's function was 'eall gedælan / geongum ond ealdum, swylc him god sealde' (71b–2). In *The Husband's Message* (admittedly in one of the defective passages) the chance to join in dispensing gifts seems to be offered as an inducement (30–5a). The gnomic statements, famous for their power to distil a subject to its essence, display for us, as if he were a fly in amber, a king and his kingliness: 'Cyning sceal on healle / beagas dælan' (*Maxims II* 28b–9a). Among the many allusions to treasure-giving in *Beowulf* three bear witness especially clearly to the tremendous power of this idea. The *geong guma* of 20a is not necessary to the narrative; he and his generosity enter associatively as part of the joy felt over confirmation of the new ruler. The author seems to find generosity so important that he speaks didactically about it whenever the subject arises. Hrothgar also devotes much commentary to it. His 'sermon' (1700–84) touches on many issues, but he mentions dispensing treasure no less than five times. Finally, when Grendel is ironically identified as a *healþegn* (142a), he is specifically denied any benefit from the *gifstol*, the suggestion being that such benefits mattered most and were what separated reality from travesty.

    Gifts, however, are not all that hall-life had to offer. As any student of the poetry knows, they are part of a larger pattern of interwoven obligations which gave a retainer the security of a defined position in his society. His status was unambiguous, formally acknowledged by his membership of *geoguð* or *duguð* and by his place on the bench. Any action calling for thanks was given public recognition, like that bestowed on Beowulf by Hrothgar (1020–49 and 1866–7) and by Wealhtheow (1192–1231) or that recalled in *The Wanderer* (41–4). In return the retainer had to perform loyal service,

---

[1] All quotations and line references are to The Anglo-Saxon Poetic Records, ed. G. P. Krapp and E. V. K. Dobbie, 6 vols. (New York, 1931–53). The italics in this and other quotations are, of course, mine.

even if it meant certain death. The retainers at Maldon lived up to their vows; Beowulf's men, when he faced the dragon, did not. All the ceremony and ritual, all the elaborate beauty of hall-treasures and decorations, the music and the stories of past heroes impose pattern and order on hall-life, making it strikingly different from the chaos outside.

Although generosity, the loyalty that is its counterpart, and shared pleasure make the whole complex of ideas dynamic, so that the hall never becomes a mere passive symbol of retreat, the forces of opposition ranged against the *burh* and the hall as its principal building were – as one might expect from the etymology of *burh* (*beorgan*, 'to protect, shelter') – of great importance to poetic usage. The most feared agent of destruction was strife – internal or external, for either might end in the burning of the hall.[1] Fire was the only force which the builders of Heorot feared (*Beowulf* 778–82a) and it was indeed fire which destroyed it (81b–5). Attack was an ever-present threat. When Hrothgar's men lay down to sleep in the hall at night they kept their weapons close to hand to meet any emergency (*Beowulf* 1242–50). The horn of Riddle 14 sees life as an oscillation between the field of battle and the feast. Riddle 20 reduces the rich variety of life to the same elemental contrast. When there is fighting in the hall itself this confrontation of opposites is at its most intense. Hall-strife, often fostered by drink, is mentioned in *Vainglory* (13–21a), *The Fortunes of Men* (48–57) and *Juliana* (483b–90a). In the *Finnesburg Fragment* Hnæf and his men are attacked in a hall. In *Beowulf* Unferth's belligerence in Heorot is partly attributed to beer (531a), Heorot is the scene both of mortal combat between Beowulf and Grendel and of the feasting which follows it, and violent killing in a hall is climactic to both the Finn and Ingeld episodes. To come to blows before a king meant that he had failed to perform his essential rôle. Hall-violence in poetic contexts probably had more profound impact on a contemporary audience than on us because of the assumptions about kingship and the hall. Some of the earliest Anglo-Saxon laws regard violence committed in the king's presence as a very grave offence.[2]

In a world picture where the hall signifies order, social pleasure and security, that which is outside will naturally be an opposite. When strife is not

[1] Wooden and partly wooden buildings such as halls were natural targets in war. Bede (*HE* III.16 and 17) mentions two instances of fire-razing by King Penda, though Aidan's prayers frustrated his attempt to incinerate the inhabitants of Bamborough. Of the four successive halls at Old Yeavering two were destroyed by fire, probably in battle by Cadwallon in 632 and by Penda in 651. Norse records are full of such incidents: a quick glance at Snorri Sturluson's *Heimskringla* turns up various forms of hall-burning five times in *Ynglinga saga* (chs. 14, 31, 36, 39 and 40), once in *Hálfdanar saga Svarta* (ch. 5), and twice in *Haralds saga Hárfagra* (chs. 12 and 34). Sigmundr's revenge on Siggeirr in *Vǫlsunga saga* and Guðrún's on Atli later in the same story are famous instances of hall-burning, as are the smaller scale incidents of the burning of Blund-Ketill and Njáll in their homes.

[2] See, e.g., the laws of Ine (drawn up between 688 and 694), *English Historical Documents* i, ed. Dorothy Whitelock (London, 1955), 365.

the enemy of hall-life in a specific poetic context, storm often is, whether literally as wind, rain, snow, hail, thunder, cold, and darkness or figuratively as metaphor for battle. The arrows or blows of battle come in showers, the noise of battle is like the roar of a storm:

> Hie ða fromlice
> leton forð fleogan   flana *scuras*,
> hildenædran,   of hornbogan,
> strælas stedehearde;   *styrmdon hlude*
> grame guðfrecan,   garas sendon
> in heardra gemang. (*Judith* 220b–5a)

Or, again, Beowulf was a chief who '... oft gebad isernscure, / þonne stræla storm strengum gebæded / scoc ofer scildweall' (3116–18a). We still speak of storming a fortification; Satan in *Christ and Satan* was moved by the same metaphor:

> Þis is stronglic,   nu þes storm becom,
> þegen mid þreate,   þeoden engla. (385–6)

In Riddle 3 ('Storm') storm-clouds are personified as battling horsemen striking terror into *burh*-dwellers:

> Se bið swega mæst,
> breahtma ofer *burgum*,   ond gebreca hludast,
> þonne scearp cymeð   sceo wiþ oþrum,
> ecg wið ecge;   earpan gesceafte ...
> farað feohtende ...   Winnende fareð
> atol eoredþreat,   egsa astigeð,
> micel modþrea   monna cynne,
> brogan on *burgum*,   þonne blace scotiað
> scriþende scin   scearpum wæpnum.
> Dol him ne ondrædeð   ða deaðsperu,
> swylteð hwæþre,   gif him soð meotud
> on geryhtu   þurh regn ufan
> of gestune læteð   stræle fleogan,
> farende flan.   Fea þæt gedygað,
> þara þe geræceð   rynegiestes wæpen. (39b–42, 46a
>   and 48b–58)

In Riddle 1 the personification becomes even more forcefully direct when 'storm' proclaims 'fere geond foldan, folcsalo bærne, / ræced reafige' (5–6a).

    The implications of most such passages are that the hall is poetically equivalent to the *mondream* it encloses, the best feature that society could offer to its members. If the hall is destroyed, the survivor can expect only loneliness and the paths of exile. In real life no one would interpret the loss of a house as condemning one to endure winter weather without any sort of roof for years, possibly for the rest of one's life, but that is how the loss is handled in the poetic tradition. When the burning of Heorot is referred to or when the dragon fires Beowulf's hall we should not regard the destruction as a temporary and purely physical inconvenience; in poetic modes of thought, at least, the loss is far more damaging.

When chaos and violence take the form of a definite antagonist, a malignant being, its dwelling becomes an anti-hall. This may be as well constructed as a normal hall: the home of the Grendel ménage seems to be. It is a *hof*, *niðsele*, *hofsele*, *reced*; it has a *flet*, treasure and walls hung with weapons. In harmony with this style of dwelling, Grendel's mother is an *ides* as well as an *aglæcwif*; she '. . . floda begong / heorogifre beheold hund missera' (1497b–8) as if she were a queen. More often, the anti-hall is pictured as a negation of one or more normal hall characteristics, or as an internalization of the usual hall enemies. Instead of being an elaborately wrought and ornamented building, it may be a crude *beorg* or *scræf*. The *Beowulf* dragon's *beorg* (though it has *stanbogan* and is called *eorðreced*) is probably such a structure. Treasure-giving may be the element eliminated, as, with reference to hell, in *Juliana* 683–8a. Bad weather is not kept at bay by the anti-hall's walls, but is made part of the internal conditions: hell is a *windsele* or a 'windiga sele / eall inneweard atole gefylled' (*Christ and Satan*, 384a and 135b–6). Anti-halls of this sort gain poetic resonance from their affinities with the grave. The dragon inhabits a burial-mound, in *The Wanderer* a saddened survivor of a hall-*duguð* hides his friend in an *eorðscræf* (83b–4),[1] where, we can well imagine, the body will be subjected to seeping damp and worms. Holofernes is dispatched to a *wyrmsele* (*Judith* 119a), a term suggestive of both serpents in hell and the worms of the grave.

The core conceits in the hall-cluster are, then, gift-giving, loyalty and *wynn* on the one hand, and strife, storm and the anti-hall on the other. The basic connotations attaching to their literal use are plain. Halls had a positive value based on their rôle as protecting roofs and as centres for early Anglo-Saxon civilization. The glorification which the building itself and the primitive form of society it embraced underwent in later centuries is not difficult to understand. The close fellowship among men devoted to the same kind of life, the personal friendship with a lavishly munificent lord, the harp-

---

[1] That graves should be seen as dwellings is hardly unique to the Anglo-Saxons, but the range of resonances conjured up by *wyrmsele* or *eorðscræf* is far more extensive than those the author of *The Grave* was able to manipulate in his late, fragmentary poem, in so far as it can be judged. He had lost the complexities and grandeur inherent in using the hall as his unit, and only shuffles commonplaces about dwellings and houses adapted from the Soul and Body debate. Too late to be included in ASPR, this piece can be found, ed. Arnold Schröer, in *Anglia* 5 (1882), 289–90.

ing and feasts, were doubtless never as glorious in truth as in song, but, once so described, they would be attractive to men of later generations whose own times left much to be desired. The destruction of the hall was also an observable fact, given the politics of the age; hence the emphasis on its enemies in poetry, and hence too the possibility that lament over ruins was a motif spontaneously generated within the native poetic tradition.[1]

Were the poetic uses of halls nothing more than nostalgia for a glorified past, little comment would be called for. The religious changes rung on the theme, however, and the symbolic elaborations shed interesting light on how Anglo-Saxons viewed this world and on how they expressed emotions. Both in religious contexts and those not overtly so the hall, its enemies, and the anti-hall provide the vocabulary for what appear to be the principal Anglo-Saxon existential metaphors.

In a well-known passage in his Latin *Historia Ecclesiastica* Bede credits one of King Edwin's counsellors with a most effective use of the hall-idea as an image of man's life:

'Talis,' inquiens, 'mihi uidetur, rex, uita hominum praesens in terris, ad conparationem eius, quod nobis incertum est, temporis, quale cum te residente ad caenam cum ducibus ac ministris tuis tempore brumali, accenso quidem foco in medio, et calido effecto caenaculo, furentibus autem foris per omnia turbinibus heimalium pluuiarum uel niuium, adueniens unus passerum domum citissime peruolauerit; qui cum per unum ostium ingrediens, mox per aliud exierit. Ipso quidem tempore, quo intus est, hiemis tempestate non tangitur, sed tamen paruissimo spatio serenitatis ad momentum excurso, mox de hieme in hiemem regrediens, tuis oculis elabitur. Ita haec uita hominum ad modicum apparet.'[2]

The hall as a small realm of protection and warmth, within an encircling waste of winter, rain and cold, figures human life within the unknown that encompasess it, and life in its brevity is like a sparrow's flight through the hall. Bede attributes to the pagan party a use of the hall as a positive existential metaphor; it represents to them the best that life has had to offer man, at least until the coming of Christianity.

More common in vernacular poetry is the use of the ruined hall to signify

---

[1] Whether this topos has Latin or native roots is debatable, but I suggest that a distinction should be made between ruined halls and cities when that is possible, though the ambiguity of *burh* makes this difficult. P. J. Frankis's article in *ASE* 2 (1973) uncovers and analyses Latin analogues to the latter, but neither these nor the Gaulish Latin analogues cited by Nora K. Chadwick (*Poetry and Letters in Early Christian Gaul* (London, 1955), pp. 122–8) seem to me to account fully for the range of particular features found in the Anglo-Saxon treatments of halls and their destruction. Some support for the idea of an indigenous, native tradition is found in Scandinavian material such as Snorri's *Edda, Gylfaginning*, ch. 52.

[2] II.13; the edition cited is that of C. Plummer (Oxford, 1896). The Old English Bede renders *caenaculum* as 'heall'.

the transience of the social structures which gave men their chance of earthly security and happiness:

> . . . nu missenlice geond þisne middangeard
> winde bewaune weallas stondaþ,
> hrime bihrorene, hryðge þa ederas.
> Woriað þa *winsalo*, waldend licgað
> dreame bidrorene, duguþ eal gecrong,
> wlonc bi wealle.
>
> Stondeð nu on laste leofre duguþe
> weal wundrum heah, wyrmlicum fah.[1]
> Eorlas fornoman asca þryþe,
> wæpen wælgifru, wyrd seo mære,
> ond þas stanhleoþu stormas cnyssað,
> hrið hreosende hrusan bindeð,
> wintres woma, þonne won cymeð,
> nipeð nihtscua, norþan onsendeð
> hreo hæglfare hæleþum on andan.
>
>   (*The Wanderer* 75–80a and 97–105)

When giving emotional power to gloomy states of existence, the poets frequently turned to the anti-hall part of the idea-complex. The Seafarer says that he has 'gecunnad in ceole cearselda fela, / atol yþa gewealc' (5–6a). In *cearselda* we see the creation of an anti-hall: care, an enemy to be kept at bay by hall-society, is instead made the dominant trait of this hall-like structure, the wooden ship. When the Seafarer is said to be *hreo hyge*, he is internalizing storms to his mind in the same fashion. In *The Wife's Lament* it is the primitive anti-hall which is used to suggest a state of mind. The speaker is supposedly forced to dwell in an *eorðscræf, eorðsele*, a *wic wynna leas*, but these surroundings clearly correspond to mood. The longed-for friend is pictured as being in similarly deplorable circumstances in a *dreorsele*, and in the latter case it is difficult to determine whether any sense of an actual physical hall remains, for the structure seems completely transmuted into an indicator of mood. The old man's lament in *Beowulf* (2444–62a) is perhaps our most complex example of this poetic practice. I. L. Gordon wonders why the hall should be made empty by a son's death.[2] The father sees the 'winsele westne, windge reste / reote berofene' (2456–7a). In real life, a son's being

---

[1] Because of the prevalence and grandeur of Roman ruins in Britain, we sometimes find the sort of cultural combination seen here of native lord and *duguð* with what is apparently a Roman rampart. The patterning on this wall, *wyrmlicum fah*, has always been a puzzle. The most recent editors, Dunning and Bliss jointly and Leslie, agree on a probable translation of 'adorned with serpentine shapes'. Perhaps the phrase is no more than a vivid response to the effects of storm. In *Volpone* I.v Ben Jonson speaks of 'an old smoked wall, on which the rain ran down in streaks'.

[2] Introduction to *The Seafarer*, ed. I. L. Gordon (London, 1960), p. 15.

hanged would not terminate all harp-song, all 'gomen in geardum' (2459a) for ever, but declaring them missing is simply the negation of a hall feature, the creation of an anti-hall, and is as much a method of communicating sorrow as is an exiled speaker's hyperbolic assertion that he will never again have a roof between him and the elements. Similarly 'Ridend swefað, / hæleð in hoðman' (2457b–8a) is a negation of the normal, a hyperbolic observation more vivid in thought than but no different in kind from Lamartine's 'un seul être vous manque, et tout est dépeuplé' (*L'Isolement*). The similarities of diction between the old man's lament and *The Wanderer*, *The Seafarer* and *The Wife's Lament* and the extra attention lavished on its composition, as shown by the incidence of enjambed alliteration, suggest that the poet was consciously working in a traditional vein of expression, and that the tradition included not just mood but a reflex of the hall idea-complex as well.

That the Seafarer is trying to persuade his audience to renounce its emotional allegiance to the kind of secular life represented by the hall seems obvious. In his eyes hall-society has the limited outlook that he yearns to escape from. He admits gold-givers of spectacular munificence to have existed, but only in the early ages of the earth:

> næron nu cyningas   ne caseras
> ne goldgiefan   swylce iu wæron,
> þonne hi mæst mid him   mærþa gefremedon
> ond on dryhtlicestum   dome lifdon. (82–5)

In *Guthlac A* renunciation takes a different form. In this poem we are told that the saint himself felt tempted to lead a heroic secular life, and according to the Old English prose version Guthlac actually spent nine years as a plunder-seeker. Such a background makes Guthlac's later experiences all the more meaningful, for what he does in *Guthlac A* is train himself to reject earthly halls and accept in the *beorg*, fen-dwelling of devils, an anti-hall open to all unpleasant weather. When he has sufficiently subdued all ordinary responses to its miseries so that it seems pleasant to him (731–48a), he is deemed ready for heaven and his soul receives as reward from the Protector a 'setl on swegle' (785a). In more senses than one Guthlac 'gearwaþ gæstes hus' (802a). He has disciplined his body (the soul's house) with hardships, taking as an appropriate earthly house a barrow, with its discomforts and sepulchral reminders of mortality, and has thus prepared for his soul a home in heaven. Laurence K. Shook offers a good study of the manner in which the author of *Guthlac A* rang changes on the notion of the *beorg* as dwelling.[1] His observations gain in richness if the barrow is recognized as an anti-hall, for Guthlac's struggles are then placed in relation to secular halls. That heroism is being redefined in *Guthlac A* and *B* has always been apparent: it needs to

---

[1] 'The Burial Mound in *Guthlac A*', MP 58 (1960), 1–10.

be observed as well that the hall-ideal is also being transformed to accord with the new frame of values. In *Andreas*, we find total rejection of the hall-imagery. The author could not accept the compromise of transforming the secular ideal, preferring to vilify it by associating such terms as *modige maguþegnas* (1140a), *ellenrofe* (1141b), *hornsalu* (1158b) and *winræced* (1159a) with the grisly Mermedonian cannibals and their dwelling.

Clearly Christianity contributed new dimensions to the poetic handling of halls and *burga*, often disapproving. In addition to associations with pagan ethos, the earthly hall or *burh* could take on the connotations of the *civitas terrena*. Except for Jerusalem (and spiritual conceits built upon it), cities impressed post-Augustinian Christians unfavourably as a rule. The biblical use of Babylon as a city of sin, of Babel as an expression of pride and of Sodom and Gomorrah as cesspools of human degeneracy fed their imaginative responses to cities, as did the fact that the first such settlement was founded by Cain. How much, then, may this condemnation of earthly structures be deemed to have affected either the poet's response or the audience's toward halls mentioned in poetry? Was Heorot automatically equated with Babel as built out of overweening pride and is it akin to the Grendelmere rather than opposed to it? Are the remains in *The Ruin* merely marvelled at, lamented in their passing, or are they Babylon and viewed as remnants of deserved destruction?[1] Those quick to read Babel into Heorot can point to the reasons for its construction, to its impermanence, to the sorrow and destruction in store for it, to the presence of evil within the circle of light. Other critics, more moderate in their theological assumptions, merely feel that an Anglo-Saxon audience would reject the earthly hall-society because of its transient nature. According to this viewpoint the *Wanderer* poet, for example, reasons and the *Beowulf* poet teaches indirectly that hall-life is too flawed to appeal to reasonable men. This is a view that has been gaining adherents;[2] its degree of probability needs to be carefully estimated.

The Wanderer, it seems to me, shows a great deal of admiration for the hall and all that it represents. The *deorce lif* (89a) portrayed is one in which proud halls become roofless shells, men of spirit fall and ruined walls are left resisting the terror of winter. The Wanderer wonders what keeps him sane

[1] Hugh T. Keenan, '*The Ruin* as Babylon', *Tennessee Stud. in Lit.* 11 (1966), 109–17. On p. 115 he equates Heorot with the Grendelmere.

[2] Among the most interesting of the studies which posit ultimate if sometimes reluctant rejection are those by Alvin A. Lee (*The Guest-Hall of Eden* (New Haven, 1972)), Margaret E. Goldsmith (*The Mode and Meaning of 'Beowulf'* (London, 1970)) and John Leyerle ('Beowulf the Hero and the King', *MÆ* 34 (1965), 89–102, and 'The Interlace Structure of *Beowulf*', *Univ. of Toronto Quarterly* 37 (1967), 1–17). H. L. Rogers and E. G. Stanley are more forceful and vigorous in condemning the heroic. See, respectively, 'Beowulf's Three Great Fights', *RES* n.s. 6 (1955), 339–55, and 'Hæthenra Hyht in *Beowulf*', *Studies in Old English Literature in Honor of Arthur G. Brodeur*, ed. Stanley B. Greenfield (Eugene, Oregon, 1963), pp. 136–51.

when he thinks on the losses life suffers before the forces of violence and there is little of moral rejection in the tone when it is observed

> Ongietan sceal gleaw hæle   hu gæstlic bið,
> þonne ealre þisse worulde wela   weste stondeð.[1] (73–4)

God and Christian consolations are turned to because the halls of the world are fated not to last. The argument is more persuasive to some than the Seafarer's eager acceptance of hardships because it acknowledges the attractiveness of the world. I. L. Gordon makes an important distinction when she says 'there is an essential difference between the old poetic view of transience, which sees it as tragic fact, a part of the woes of men, and the Christian view which sees it as a proof of the vanity of worldly things'.[2] It is a matter of judgement: in my opinion *The Wanderer* does not exhibit the extreme form of Christian allegorisis which Smithers postulates; rather, I believe, there is relatively clear evidence for a tension between the outlook inculcated and the emotions felt.

Beowulf, to my mind, seems relatively untroubled by tensions over worldly matters – 'fighting words' in the current state of scholarly dispute. Heorot seems to me to retain most of the positive power of the kernel-material of the hall-ideal. Granted that it is ultimately doomed, and granted the presence of ambition, envy and like dangers within its circle, Heorot nonetheless emerges as very attractive. If the *Beowulf* poet had meant to persuade his audience of the hall's shortcomings (let alone of its vanity, its identity as a Castle of Pride and new Babel), he could have destroyed its claim to heroism and joy just as the *Judith* poet describes the feast of Holofernes without rousing any desire to take part simply by stressing the drunkenness of the carousal and by pointedly avoiding the usual terms *dream* and *wynn*. The manner in which grandeur and glory are stressed in *Beowulf* suggests, however, that an audience is intended to respond in warmly positive terms to a picture of lord and retainers, of gift-giving and loyalty, however ephemeral or flawed these may be as ideals from a Christian point of view. If my interpretation of the evidence is accepted, the validity of several heavily moralistic readings of *Beowulf* is called into question.

There is solid evidence that the ideal of hall-life retained a strong hold on audience-imagination in Christian times. The Wanderer's *angst*, his sense of

---

[1] Recent editors agree that *gæstlic* in this context means 'terrifying, awesome'. Smithers ('Meaning', pp. 141–2) implies that the terror is induced by the idea of the end of the world, when indeed all earthly goods will be destroyed. Possibly, though, the emotion is a response to the thought of the destruction rather than to its cause. The narrator finds ghastly to contemplate the idea that the buildings and treasures of once-great societies will stand unused, their potential wasted. (*Weste*, like *idel* in similar statements (87 and 110), can mean 'unused, wasted, deserted, empty' as well as 'useless, desolate, devastated'.) His distress may be at 'the pity of it', rather than fear of what will happen to his soul on Judgement Day.

[2] 'Traditional Themes in *The Wanderer* and *The Seafarer*', *RES* n.s. 5 (1954), 1–13, esp. 8.

the 'tears of things' crystallize about this image-centre. To the authors of *Guthlac A* and *Andreas* the lure of the heroic hall had desperately to be rejected if salvation were to be sought. To the men of Maldon it was (metonymically) the ideal for which they voluntarily sacrificed their lives, and they were Christian. Anglo-Saxon poetic treatments of heaven and hell are heavily influenced by portions of the idea-complex.[1] In *Christ and Satan* hell is an anti-hall, a *windiga sele* and *atole scref* (135b and 26b). As such, descriptions of hell had particular power to terrify. By the same token heaven became readily comprehensible as a place of shared bliss in terms of the hall-ideal: to be welcomed as a member of an earthly hall-society could mean great happiness and to be deprived of membership spelled misery and alienation; the reward of exercising certain kinds of selflessness and restraint was to belong to a community in which peace and order were to be had. The hope of the visionary in *The Dream of the Rood* was, he says, that the cross would bring him

> þær is blis mycel,
> dream on heofonum,   þær is dryhtnes folc
> geseted to symle,   þær is singal blis,
> ond me þonne asette   þær ic syþþan mot
> wunian on wuldre,   wel mid þam halgum
> dreames brucan. (139b–44a)

Ironically, of course, the earthly hall-community tended to foster just the sort of arrogance and competitive spirit most likely to destroy it.

Whatever the factors – climactic, geographic, sociological or psychological – to which it is to be attributed, the central place which the hall had in Anglo-Saxon thought is undeniable. What we should learn from seeing the many ways in which the idea-complex is used is that simple generalizations about Anglo-Saxon attitudes, whether of author or of audience, are likely to be unsound.[2] Poetic contexts suggest that halls may be positive or negative in either secular or religious terms. For example, Heorot is an earthly structure, and so may be branded with the negative religious symbolic ambience of Babel or the *civitas terrena*, but its construction may also be likened positively to the cosmogonic act, and its name hint at its being the integumen for the 'aspiring soul'. Similarly its virtues and imperfections may be cast in purely practical and secular terms. Thus we have evidence for an impressively divergent array of attitudes, and we do the people and its poetry less than justice if we assume that they can be reduced to simple formulas of consistent outlook and interpretation.

[1] The most thorough treatment of this is Alvin A. Lee's *The Guest-Hall of Eden*. He argues not just that heaven and hell are cast in terms of the hall but also that the hall is the submerged metaphor for the whole created world, as, for instance, in *Cædmon's Hymn*.

[2] The fallacy of homogeneity is well analysed by R. S. Crane in response to 'historical criticism' and by Stanley B. Greenfield. See, respectively, *The Idea of the Humanities*, 2 vols. (Chicago, 1967) II, 236–60, and *The Interpretation of Old English Poems* (London, 1972), pp. 8–11.

Second thoughts on the interpretation
of *The Seafarer*

JOHN C. POPE

My article[1] begins in true medieval fashion with a retraction. A few years ago I argued that *The Wanderer* and *The Seafarer* involved two imaginary speakers rather than one.[2] Ever since the publication of this argument I have been assailed by doubts of its validity, not only because most persons whose judgement I trust in such a matter have been either politely noncommittal or vociferously hostile, but because I myself, in returning again and again to the poems, have been less and less convinced that their texts would support my reading.[3] The decisive moment came, I think, when I read P. L. Henry's strong reinforcement,[4] from the Celtic side, of Dorothy Whitelock's view of *The Seafarer* as the monologue of a religious ascetic who had chosen exile on and beyond the sea for the love of God – a *peregrinus pro amore Dei* of a sort well known in the British Isles from before Bede's time to Alfred's wherever Celtic Christianity had taken root.[5] In thus returning to Professor Whitelock's interpretation I found myself completely convinced of its superiority. Since that time I have altogether abandoned my former view of *The Seafarer*, and with it my view of *The Wanderer* also, and I welcome the opportunity to say so.

But a mere retraction, in the case of *The Seafarer* at any rate, is not enough.

[1] This is a revised version of a paper read at a meeting of the Old English Group of the Modern Language Association in New York City, 28 December 1972.

[2] 'Dramatic Voices in *The Wanderer* and *The Seafarer*', *Franciplegius: Medieval and Linguistic Studies in Honor of Francis Peabody Magoun, Jr*, ed. Jess B. Bessinger, Jr and Robert P. Creed (New York, 1965), pp. 164–93.

[3] The doubts actually began earlier. My article was submitted to the editors of *Franciplegius* in November 1962, and a lecture based on it was delivered in Cambridge on 22 February 1963, at the invitation of Professor Whitelock, whose friendly but emphatic disagreement was the earliest warning I received, and among the most disquieting.

[4] *The Early English and Celtic Lyric* (London, 1966; New York, 1967). For an excellent and succinct survey of Irish pilgrimage, see Kathleen Hughes, 'The Changing Theory and Practice of Irish Pilgrimage', *JEH* 11 (1960), 143–51.

[5] 'The Interpretation of *The Seafarer*', in *The Early Cultures of North-West Europe* (H. M. Chadwick Memorial Studies), ed. Sir Cyril Fox and Bruce Dickins (Cambridge, 1950), pp. 259–72. Both this article and mine have been reprinted in *Essential Articles for the Study of Old English Poetry*, ed. Jess B. Bessinger, Jr and Stanley J. Kahrl (Archon Books, Hamden, Connecticut, 1968), and in *Old English Literature: Twenty-two Analytical Essays*, ed. Martin Stevens and Jerome Mandel (University of Nebraska Press, Lincoln, Nebraska, 1968).

John C. Pope

The Wanderer has been ably described by Stanley Greenfield and others who have supposed that there is only one dramatic speaker, the man who is introduced as an *eardstapa* near the beginning and is characterized at the end as one *snottor on mode*.[1] The contrast I drew between the two 'voices' is by no means without foundation in the text, but if these voices belong to the same speaker, the second voice must be allowed to subsume the first. The wanderer's personal sorrows, though their constricting effect is vividly described and may not have been altogether outlived, have been partially absorbed into the general meditation that follows. The larger view, based on the vicarious knowledge granted to the wise, deepens his conviction of the instability and waste of the world yet in some measure liberates him from the bonds of his own experience. On the whole there has been increasing agreement about this poem. There are matters still open to debate, such as the precise limits of the wanderer's speech at beginning and end, but they are of minor importance.[2]

The Seafarer is another matter. I am reluctant to abandon my erroneous interpretation of its structure without suggesting an alternative explanation for that feature of the poem which seemed to demand a change of speakers, and without attempting a partial reassessment of the poem as a whole.

Ever since the dialogue theory was broached by Rieger, the chief reason for suspecting a change of speakers in *The Seafarer* has been the occurrence of the word *sylf* in the sentence that begins in the middle of line 33.[3] This

[1] S. B. Greenfield, '*The Wanderer*: A Reconsideration of Theme and Structure', *JEGP* 50 (1951), 451–65. Essentially the same interpretation is fully elaborated by Willi Erzgräber, 'Der Wanderer: Eine Interpretation von Aufbau und Gehalt', *Festschrift zum 75. Geburtstag von Theodor Spira*, ed. H. Viebrock and W. Erzgräber (Heidelberg, 1961), pp. 57–85. See also the related references in my previous article ('Dramatic Voices', pp. 165 and 188–9), and add the two recent editions of the poem, one by R. F. Leslie (Manchester, 1966), the other by T. P. Dunning and A. J. Bliss (London, 1969).

[2] Greenfield and Erzgräber have taken lines 1–7 and 111–15 as prologue and epilogue, spoken by the poet. Leslie limits the poet's intrusion to lines 6–7 and 111, those in which the wanderer, as speaker of all else, is identified and described. Dunning and Bliss almost agree but allow the poet to intrude also at lines 88–91 in order to call attention to the wanderer's achievement of wisdom before he launches into the *ubi sunt* passage, lines 92–110. I much prefer the older view, ably defended by Erzgräber, p. 70, that the wanderer continues to speak, adding a certain objectivity and weight to his own deepest sentiments by representing them as what any wise man who thinks seriously about this life may be expected to say. As for the opening and closing lines, I agree (and have argued) that lines 1–5 are best taken as spoken by the wanderer (though the poet would necessarily concur), but I hesitate to abandon the notion that lines 112–15, with their quiet assurance and their inclusive reference to *us*, are spoken by the poet (though I think the wanderer, at least in another mood, would concur). Maintenance of the hypermetric form introduced at line 111 helps to set these lines apart as a kind of epilogue, no matter who is talking.

[3] Max Rieger's interpretation of the poem as a dialogue, and his arrangement of it as such, were included in his article, 'Über Cynewulf', *Zeitschrift für deutsche Philologie* 1 (1869), 330–2 and 334–9. F. Kluge, 'Zu altenglischen Dichtungen, 1, Der Seefahrer', *EStn* 6 (1883), 322–7, differed as to details but agreed that there was a change of speakers at line 33b. Richard Wülker, *Grundriss zur Geschichte der angelsächsischen Literatur* (Leipzig, 1885), p. 210, supported the interpretation of *sylf* in line 35 as the chief evidence for the change.

is the point where, after the opening speaker has completed his recital of the hardships, physical and mental, he has endured at sea – hardships beyond the ken, he maintains, of the prosperous landsman – he startles us, if indeed it is he and not a second speaker, by announcing that he is now strongly impelled to undertake a voyage:

> Forþon cnyssað nu
> heortan geþohtas   þæt ic hean streamas,
> sealtyþa gelac   sylf cunnige.[1]

If *sylf* in this passage has to mean 'I myself', as, following Rieger and others, I had supposed, it must imply that the speaker is not the experienced seafarer who has been speaking up to this point. I am now convinced that it does not have to mean 'I myself', that there is a sound alternative meaning; but what that meaning is requires further consideration.

Stanley Greenfield, in a recent attack on my article, very properly faced the problem of *sylf* and put forward as a satisfactory alternative to 'I myself' the meaning 'of my own accord'.[2] He had found this meaning offered without comment by P. L. Henry in his translation of the passage,[3] and he discovered that it was supported in the Bosworth–Toller dictionary under *self*, section IV, headed 'denoting voluntary or independent action'. 'If', he said, '*sylf* can mean "of my own accord", we are not confronted with "the implication that the speaker has not been to sea before" [as I had maintained] but rather with the right dictional pivot for the change in figural stance from the endurance of involuntary exile in lines 1–33a to the eagerness for voluntary exile in what follows.'[4]

With Professor Greenfield's main conclusion, that the poem is a monologue, I am more than ready to agree; but I am troubled by the meaning he assigns to *sylf* and still more by the inference he draws from it.

There is indeed not the slightest doubt that the exile the speaker now

---

1 'Truly [or possibly 'And yet'] my heart's thoughts are now urging that I *sylf* make trial of the high [or 'deep'] streams, the tossing of the salt waves.' The minor uncertainties of this sentence (the precise meaning of *forþon* and *hean*, and the grammatical construction of *heortan geþohtas*) have no bearing on the present argument. An adversative sense of *forþon* ('and yet'), though not essential, seems logically somewhat superior. See the references in my previous article, 'Dramatic Voices', pp. 189, n. 11 and 191, n. 28, and especially, for the adversative sense, Marjorie Daunt, 'Some Difficulties of *The Seafarer*', *MLR* 13 (1918), 474ff. A later article by S. B. Liljegren, 'Some Notes on the Old English Poem *The Seafarer*', *SN* 14 (1941–2), treats *forþon* on pp. 152–5, and though not very clear lends some support to the adversative sense. My quotations from *The Seafarer* are from the edition of Mrs. I. L. Gordon (London, 1960), though I have preferred to print *forþon* as one word. I also take *heortan* as a genitive modifying *geþohtas*, as suggested by the alliteration and the occurrence of the same phrase in other poems, rather than as the object of *cnyssað*, as Mrs Gordon recommends.
2 '*Mīn, Sylf*, and "Dramatic Voices in *The Wanderer* and *The Seafarer*"', *JEGP* 68 (1969), 212–20. On *sylf*, pp. 217–19. Shortly after he had submitted this article, Greenfield learned that I had already abandoned the dialogue idea. He generously suggested that I add my own comment to his article, but it turned out that the editors had sent the article to press and would not accept an addition.   3 *Early English and Celtic Lyric*, p. 154.   4 '*Mīn, Sylf*', p. 219.

contemplates is altogether voluntary. His own heart's thoughts are urging him on in the passage I have quoted, and subsequent lines increase the impression of eagerness. Merely to establish this point there is no need for a *sylf* meaning 'of my own accord'. What is disturbing, apart from my belief that *sylf* can more naturally, in this context, have a slightly different meaning, is Greenfield's inference that *sylf* in his sense should be taken as a pivotal word, establishing a change from involuntary to voluntary exile. It is conceivable, certainly, that the seafarer's earlier voyages have been imposed by his confessor as a penance for some deadly sin, and that he is now so far purified by his sufferings that he is eager for a more positive, self-imposed voyage inspired by the love of God. But I can find nothing in the first thirty-three lines of the poem to assure us that the previous voyages have been imposed as a penance, or have been involuntary. For all we know the previous voyages, if they had a religious motive, may have been self-imposed acts of mortification, whether for some specific sin or as a means of overcoming the normal lusts of the flesh. It is noteworthy that the speaker never refers to himself as a sinner. Whatever unruly desires may once have disturbed him have been, not suppressed, but redirected towards the spiritual joys he now intensely craves.[1] If the voyage he is contemplating differs from earlier voyages, as it seems to do merely by the emphasis placed upon it, the difference may lie mainly in a freshly defined objective combined with a clarification and enlargement of purpose. He still expects voyaging to involve suffering.

Furthermore, I do not think that *sylf*, as it occurs in the passage under discussion, very readily invites the sense 'of my own accord'. The alliterative line, 'sealtyþa gelac sylf cunnige', calls up most readily an image of confrontation between the tumultuous sea and the individual *sylf* that would make trial of it. The meaning 'independently', 'by myself', hence 'alone' comes to mind more readily, I think, than 'of my own accord', and can be supported even more strongly by the group of quotations in Bosworth–Toller on which Greenfield has relied to justify 'of my own accord'. The very passage in which the dictionary inserts Greenfield's translation, 'Ðonne wearp seo eorþe hit sona sylf ('of its own accord') of hire', though the translation is apt, suggests independent action ('of itself' or 'by itself') as much as volition. The passage is from Blickling Homily XI, on Ascension Day,[2] and the homilist is attributing to the earth where Christ left his footprints at his departure a miraculous response to his divinity. It rejects whatever ornaments, gold or silver, anyone tries to lay upon the footprints, just as if it were an

---

[1] I agree with Morton Bloomfield, 'Understanding Old English Poetry', *Annuale Mediaevale* 9 (1968), 25, n. 37, that Henry should not have classified *The Seafarer* as a penitential poem, still less *The Wanderer*. Only *Resignation* contains definitely penitential elements.

[2] *The Blickling Homilies*, ed. R. Morris, Early English Text Society o.s. 58, 63 and 73 (London, 1874–80; reprinted as one volume, 1967), p. 127, lines 1–2.

animate being. But among the passages cited in the dictionary, perhaps the closest approximation to the use of *sylf* in *The Seafarer* occurs in a negative clause in *Elene*, lines 466–7, where the true name of God is spoken of as a mystery 'þone sylf ne mæg . . . man aspyrigean' 'which man of himself [or 'by himself'] cannot search out'.[1]

A few years ago, when I was suggesting the sense 'by myself' to a younger colleague, Traugott Lawler, he said, 'Why yes, I always thought it meant "alone".' To my mind this interpretation is not only more natural in the immediate context than 'of my own accord', but more completely in harmony with the rest of the poem. On the one hand it confirms what has been clearly implied about the earlier voyages. The seafarer's anxiety and loneliness, as described in the first section of the poem, depend, like the wanderer's visions of his deceased lord and comrades, on the absence of any human companions. On the other hand this interpretation tells us what we might have expected but do not otherwise know for certain about the prospective voyage, that once more he proposes to set forth unaccompanied. I had been ready to give Professor Lawler sole credit for taking *sylf* as 'alone' when, as I was preparing this article, I found to my surprise that Ezra Pound had anticipated us both. Pound's well-known version of *The Seafarer* is a spirited poem in its own right, though not a reliable translation, but in this passage he stays close to the original and his poet's intuition would seem to have served him well. It is obvious that in the following sentence, corresponding to lines 33b to 35 of the original, he takes *sylf* as implying 'alone':

> Nathless there knocketh now
> The heart's thought that I on high streams
> The salt-wavy tumult traverse alone.[2]

---

[1] I should include here the *sylf* in *Resignation* (or *The Penitent's Prayer*), line 73, 'ic . . . wylle . . . fundian / sylf to þam siþe', which Greenfield (p. 218) tentatively includes under the meaning 'of my own accord'. The speaker certainly wishes to put to sea by himself, though he has no money to buy a boat. In several other passages in the poetry the word suggests independent action or decision. In *Genesis A* 1572, it is said that the drunken Noah could not 'hine handum self mid hrægle wryon' (an example cited by J. Bosworth and T. N. Toller, *An Anglo-Saxon Dictionary* (Oxford, 1898)). In *Christ III* 1140, we read that the veil of the temple 'sylf slat on tu'. In Riddle 62, 3–4, the subject (a poker?) says, '[ic] me weg sylfa / ryhtne geryme'. Compare also *selfes mihtum* (*Beowulf* 700), *selfes dome* (*Beowulf* 895), and several of the compounds of *self* in the dictionary: e.g. *selfdema*, *selfsceaft*, *selfwilles*. One text actually certifies the sense 'alone'. T. N. Toller, *Supplement* to BT (Oxford, 1921) calls attention to three instances in the Old English gloss to Defensor's *Liber Scintillarum* (ed. E. W. Rhodes, EETS o.s. 93 (London, 1889)) where *solus* is glossed by *self*, and I have found ten additional instances in the same text, making thirteen in all, which occur (by page and line) at 7,5; 32,9 and 16; 61,1; 62,13; 121,14; 139,7; 141,2; 144,11; 183,11; 216,8; and 235,6 and 10. I have not found this correspondence in any other glosses.

[2] The first edition, from which I quote, appeared in *Ripostes of Ezra Pound* (London, 1912), pp. 25–30. There is a convenient reprint in *Selected Poems of Ezra Pound* (New York, 1957), pp. 18–21. For a comparison of the printed text with an oral version by Pound, a review of critical opinion and a judicious appraisal of the piece in relation to the original, see J. B. Bessinger, 'The Oral Text of Ezra Pound's *The Seafarer*', *Quarterly Jnl of Speech* 47 (1961), 173–7.

The emphasis on solitary voyaging tends to support other indications that set the speaker apart from ordinary seafarers. Dr Henry, concluding from an earlier passage that the previous voyages had been undertaken alone, says, 'From medieval Irish sources we learn that it was common practice for a small group of *peregrini* to travel together, as it was also to fare forth alone.'[1] An unaccompanied voyage seems to be contemplated in each of the two poems attributed to Cormac which Henry quotes earlier in his book.[2] The seafarer's references in the first few lines to exile, whether self-imposed or not, and to the hot sorrow that combined with hunger to torment him while his feet were numb with frost further differentiate him from the ordinary sailor, as does his metaphorical reference to the halls of care he has visited. Dr Henry has called attention to the fact that the seafarer never mentions the pleasanter aspects of the sea even when he is looking forward to another voyage.[3] From beginning to end of the seafaring half of the poem, along with the realistic vividness of detail, there is a consistent attitude towards the sea as a test of endurance, a place of trial and suffering. Voyaging is not presented as an end in itself, but as a means to something beyond.

It goes without saying that my acceptance of Professor Whitelock's interpretation of the seafarer's character entails a literal interpretation of his voyages. Yet Dr Henry, who agrees, nevertheless argues that 'a *second* religious and allegorical level may be and even must be assumed. It is implicit', he says, 'in the *peregrinatio* project.' And he adds, 'There is absolutely no conflict between the two levels, actual and figurative.'[4] With this way of settling a much-disputed question I am at least partially in agreement; yet there is some danger of accepting the notion of allegory in too relaxed a fashion and so lapsing into a vaguely general and ultimately confusing reading of the poem.

It is true that the '*peregrinatio* project' involves both literal and figurative meanings. One can see the two kinds of meaning intertwined in one of the seminal passages of the bible, the eleventh chapter of the Epistle to the Hebrews, where Abraham is introduced as a type of the man of faith, a prime example being his obedience to the Lord's command to leave country and kindred and his father's home for a land the Lord would show him.[5] And presently, in verses 13–16 of the same chapter, Abraham is included with others of true faith as a stranger and pilgrim on the earth, seeking another country. That country now becomes the heavenly country from which (though it is not said in this passage) mankind had been estranged by Adam's sin. To heaven, as to his proper home, the exiled Christian must seek, as a pilgrim, to return. In thus treating the actual pilgrimage of Abraham as a type, prefiguring a spiritual pilgrimage, the biblical passage moves from the

---

[1] *Early English and Celtic Lyric*, p. 134.　　[2] *Ibid.* pp. 58–65.
[3] *Ibid.* p. 156.　　[4] *Ibid.* p. 134.　　[5] Genesis XII. 1.

literal to the allegorical level, whereas the Celtic and Anglo-Saxon *peregrini*, reversing this direction, as it were, chose to imitate the example of Abraham literally, leaving their earthly homes to seek a land of strangers. Nevertheless theirs was a spiritual quest and their ultimate objective was the same as that of the allegorical pilgrims, so that the two kinds of pilgrimage might almost be regarded as but two sides of the same coin. Both are included, along with the example of Abraham, in an illuminating preamble to a life of St Columba that is quoted at length by Dr Henry.[1]

Thus it is no wonder if, in *The Seafarer*, a discourse that begins with talk of actual voyaging, past and prospective, should attach a figurative meaning to some of its terms, and at its conclusion should allow the literally conceived pilgrimage of the speaker to suggest the broader idea of allegorical pilgrimage. A figurative extension of meaning, though prepared for by the spiritual intensity and the sense of portentous issues in the talk about the projected voyage,[2] first comes unmistakably to the surface in the explosive declaration that climaxes the first half of the poem and introduces the second:

> forþon me hatran sind
> Dryhtnes dreamas   þonne þis deade lif
> læne on londe.[3]

The earlier contrast between life at sea and life on land has established the land as the secure habitat of the prosperous nobleman or loyal young retainer, where a life of ease and luxury or of pleasurable excitement among congenial companions is to be expected. Now suddenly, as the images of hardship in the life at sea are replaced in the comparison by the joys of the Lord, life on land begins to shift its meaning. In relation to what has preceded, it is still literally life on land; but the adjectives *dead* and *læne* and the contrast to eternity point towards a wider, figurative meaning that embraces all worldly life and its supposed satisfactions, whether on land or sea. As the

---

[1] *Early English and Celtic Lyric*, pp. 29–32, quoted from *Lives of Saints from the Book of Lismore*, ed. Whitley Stokes (Oxford, 1890), pp. 168ff.; the Irish text is on pp. 20ff.

[2] Line 49b, 'woruld onetteð', 'the world hastens on', makes reasonable sense even if it is not interpreted as an allusion to the impending end of the world, as G. V. Smithers and J. E. Cross have independently argued that it should be. (See respectively 'The Meaning of *The Seafarer* and *The Wanderer*', *MÆ* 28 (1959), 7 and 'On the Allegory in *The Seafarer*', *ibid.* 104–5.) Cross's argument, based on Gregory the Great's commentary on the similitude of the fig tree of Luke XXI. 25–32, is particularly interesting and would be persuasive if one could be sure that the poet had encountered this commentary, either directly or indirectly, for it is appropriate enough.

[3] 'Because the joys of the Lord are hotter to me than this dead life, passing away, on land' (64b–66a). Mrs Gordon puts a mere comma before this clause and, following Professor Whitelock, takes *forþon* as correlative with the *forþon* of line 58. I prefer a looser connection, with at least a semicolon preceding the clause, because to anticipate the explanation as early as line 58 is to weaken the immediacy of the vividly imagined passage in lines 58–64a, on which I comment below. The clause beginning at line 64b should come, I think, as an explanation not fully preconceived, but evoked by the intensity of desire that has just found expression.

thought moves forward, the previously contrasted images of land and sea are no longer of service. The sea is never mentioned again, and even the land as a distinctive image disappears. The reasoned discourse that follows accepts the figurative extension of meaning and deals directly with the relative values of this world and the next. Finally, in the conclusion, the erstwhile strenuous seafarer and earnest philosopher, having faded into a still earnest but conventional preacher, includes his congregation in a pastoral first person plural as he begins his closing exhortation:

> Uton we hycgan   hwær we ham agen,
> ond þonne geþencan   hu we þider cumen.[1]

Here at last is the allegorical pilgrimage of all good Christians towards the heavenly home.[2] Literal pilgrimage and voyaging as a form of it are no longer in the foreground, and the allegorical idea as here expressed is a poor substitute, a mere unpoetical commonplace. As we look back, however, from this point of vantage, we can see the seafarer's voyaging, not as in itself an allegory, but as something more than a supposedly practical means of salvation. It becomes in addition a pregnant example, typifying the whole range of possibilities in the idea of pilgrimage for the love of God.

This double view is but one of the ways in which the poem can surprise and fascinate us by its imaginative complexity. In spite of its disappointingly tame conclusion, the greater part of it challenges us by the sensitivity and vividness of its psychologically arresting images, which dominate the first, seafaring half, and by the vigorously expressed thought that dominates the second half and illuminates the whole. Like *The Dream of the Rood* and *The Wanderer*, it moves from vivid personal experience to didactic reflection, and though it does so less successfully than these other poems from the standpoint of artistic coherence and unity, the interaction of the two halves is by no means lacking in cogency. Professor Greenfield has rightly emphasized the unusual complexity of feelings and attitudes in the poem as one of its chief attractions.[3] In particular he has called attention to the verbal play, in both

---

[1] 'Let us consider where we have our home, and then think how we may come thither' (117–18). My earlier attempt ('Dramatic Voices', pp. 179–80) to treat lines 103–24 as an epilogue spoken by the poet, on the analogy of lines 111–15 of *The Wanderer* (see above, p. 76, n. 2), must be abandoned for lack of a sufficiently decisive indication of the shift. Line 102 concludes the seafarer's disparagement of the world and its values, and line 103, in hypermetric form, introduces a series of gnomic admonitions before the homiletic close; but there is no 'swa cwæð' to mark the boundary, and the passage ending at line 102 lacks the sort of finality that is reached at line 110 of *The Wanderer*. A similar view of the ending as involving a fading away of the speaker's vigorous individuality is set forth by Daniel G. Calder, 'Setting and Mode in *The Seafarer* and *The Wanderer*', *NM* 72 (1971), 267.

[2] There may be a passing allusion to allegorical voyaging much earlier, in lines 39–43, where the speaker seems to imply that every serious-minded man has a voyage to make, but the negative form of the sentence makes this implication uncertain.

[3] 'Attitudes and Values in *The Seafarer*', *SP* 51 (1954), 15–20.

halves of the poem, on the contrast between earthly and heavenly values – the earthly *dryhten* being juxtaposed with the heavenly *Dryhten*, earthly with heavenly warfare, reputation and, above all, joys – the *dreamas* that, as anticipated in their heavenly form, render nugatory the traditional *dreamas* of the great chieftain's hall and lead the seafarer to call life on land dead. One might say that the verbal complexity springs from and reflects the finely imagined complexity attributed by the poet to his seafaring speaker. There is to me something refreshingly human in this rigorous ascetic's sensitivity to the aristocratic values and social satisfactions he is determined to leave behind. For the most part he has repressed all outward regret. He is fortified, as a recent article reminds us, by the 'glory in tribulations' that belongs to the ascetic tradition.[1] Yet just here one may detect a lingering fondness for the heroic values of the secular tradition. In his scorn for the prosperous landsman is there not a touch of pride in his ability to endure affliction? He wants the praise of the angels, but also that of his successors on earth. And when he disparages the rulers of his own day, it is not so much because they represent a false ideal as because they are not the equals of the kings and caesars of old. We might imagine that, like Guthlac, he had been attracted to the aristocratic, would-be heroic life of the warrior in his youth, only to find the times, in this degenerate sixth age of the world, out of joint, and the spiritual struggle, under the circumstances, a worthier and more challenging alternative.

A complexity of imagery rather than of character enlivens the daringly imagined passage that precedes the climactic declaration at the centre of the poem and prepares us for it by placing renewed and heightened emphasis on the urgency of the intended voyage. This is the much-discussed passage describing the bird-like flight of the seafarer's mind or soul as it leaves his body, soars out over sea and earth's expanse, and comes back to him filled with an insatiable desire for what it has seen:

> Forþon nu min hyge hweorfeð   ofer hreþerlocan,
> min modsefa   mid mereflode
> ofer hwæles eþel   hweorfeð wide,
> eorþan sceatas,   cymeð eft to me
> gifre ond grædig;   gielleð anfloga,
> hweteð on [h]wælweg   hreþer unwearnum
> ofer holma gelagu.[2]

[1] F. N. M. Diekstra, '*The Seafarer* 58–66a: The Flight of the Exile's Soul to its Fatherland', *Neophilologus* 55 (1971), 433–46.

[2] 'Indeed now my mind ranges out over the confines of my breast, my soul ranges widely with the sea's current over the whale's home, over the reaches of earth, comes back to me ravenous and greedy; the lone flier screams, whets my heart irresistibly onto the whale's way over the swelling concourse of waters' (58–64a). The bracketed *h* in line 63 is not in the manuscript, but the emendation, first made by Thorpe, appears to me right beyond reasonable doubt.

The idea that the mind or soul can fly out to distant regions, leaving the body behind, rests on simple observation available to any introspective person, but it could have been suggested in this instance by an account of the soul's intellectual and imaginative powers in Alcuin or Lactantius,[1] together with popular superstitions concerning the soul's power to leave the body in the form of an animal, especially a bird.[2] What makes the passage so brilliantly effective in this context, however, has little to do with its sources and much with its expression. Not only is the sense of motion and excitement enhanced by a deft choice and deployment of the verbs (*hweorfeð – hweorfeð – cymeð eft – gielleð – hweteð*), but also, and especially, the mood of the man and the character of the bird are startlingly combined in the pair of verses, 'gifre ond grædig' and 'gielleð anfloga' – so startlingly, in fact, that some readers have been led far astray and even Professor Greenfield, normally an astute critic, has recently professed bewilderment.[3] The bird to which the soul is likened, being a lone flier (*anfloga*) that screams (*gielleð*) and is ravenous with hunger (*gifre ond grædig*) for something it has sighted far off has plainly the characteristics of a bird of prey. The verb *giellan* is applied to a jay's imitation of a hawk in Riddle 24,3 ('ic gielle swa hafoc'); and *bigiellan* refers to the screams of an eagle earlier in *The Seafarer* itself ('ful oft þæt earn bigeal', 24). A raven is *wælgifre* at *Judith* 207 (as is a sea-gull, otherwise an inappropriate model, at *Andreas* 372); and at *Brunanburh* 64 the *guðhafoc*, probably a kenning used as a variation for the eagle of the preceding line, is *grædig*. As I suggested in my previous article,[4] the eagle seems to supply the greatest number of relevant characteristics for this metaphorical bird, since he not only flies alone, screams, and has a voracious appetite, but is noted for his powerful flight and his sharp eyes. There is no need, however, to insist on

[1] For Alcuin, see Peter Clemoes, '*Mens absentia cogitans* in *The Seafarer* and *The Wanderer*', *Medieval Literature and Civilization: Studies in Memory of G. N. Garmonsway*, ed. D. A. Pearsall and R. A. Waldron (London, 1969), pp. 62–77. The quotations from Alcuin's *Animae ratione liber*, in prose and verse, on pp. 63–4, are remarkably close in substance to the basic idea of this passage. Diekstra, however ('*The Seafarer* 58–66a', p. 434) quotes a passage from Lactantius, *De opificio Dei*, cap. 16, which Alcuin's prose version merely repeats, essentially word for word. Clemoes points out that Alcuin's treatise was later used by Ælfric, and it may have been more readily available than Lactantius to the author of *The Seafarer*, if, as is likely but not certain, the poem postdates Alcuin's treatise. I do not think Alcuin's verse rendering of the idea is sufficiently closer to the poem than his prose to settle the matter; and it is possible, as I have intimated, that the poet came by the idea independently of either of these authors.

[2] See the discussion of the possible sources of this passage in Vivian Salmon, '*The Wanderer* and *The Seafarer*, and the Old English Conception of the Soul', *MLR* 55 (1960), 1–7.

[3] Stanley B. Greenfield, *The Interpretation of Old English Poems* (London, 1972), pp. 43–5. He is inclined to interpret the passage rightly but is puzzled by 'gifre ond grædig'. Mrs Gordon in her edition has revived the unfortunate notion of Sieper that the *anfloga*, instead of describing the bird-soul, refers to the cuckoo of line 53. Sieper was misled by the vague resemblance between the singing cuckoo's warning and mournful foreboding and the screaming *anfloga's* incitement. This unsound and hopelessly confusing identification should be consigned to oblivion.

[4] 'Dramatic Voices', p. 192, n. 39.

so positive an identification where all is imaginary. More significant for the poem is the application of these terms to the speaker's soul. So applied they are certainly startling. One does not normally associate immoderate appetite or the screams of irresistible desire with the rigorously disciplined ascetic. Professor Greenfield rightly observes that the poetic formula 'gifre ond grædig' is elsewhere used of evil or dangerous things and persons. It is associated with the rapacity of devils (*Christ and Satan* 32 and 191), the all-consuming voracity of fire (*Phoenix* 507), and the gluttonous maw of hell (*Genesis B* 793). Yet the inordinate desire that these words convey ceases to be regarded as evil when it is directed towards a spiritual good. Thus we find King Alfred using *gifre* to characterize a virtuous appetite for instruction;[1] and Ælfric approves of receiving the word of life with *grædignysse*.[2] According to the beatitude, 'Blessed are they which do hunger and thirst after righteousness'. Surely, then, the application of 'gifre ond grædig' to the seafarer's soul, though startling, is no cause for bewilderment. On the contrary it conveys precisely the overwhelming desire, comparable to the fierce greediness of a bird of prey but purified by its object, that the seafarer feels for what he is about to name as 'Dryhtnes dreamas', 'the joys of the Lord'. What the bird-soul has seen on its brilliantly imagined flight is not merely some foreign country across the sea, the 'elþeodigra eard' that is the seafaring pilgrim's immediate destination, but, somehow, those ultimate and eternal joys.[3]

At the beginning of this century a distinguished critic, W. W. Lawrence, in the belief that the poem had originally ended with the passage just quoted, and that all else (lines 64b–124) was a homiletic addition, was able to persuade himself that *The Seafarer* was a wholly secular poem revealing the mixed emotions of an adventurous seaman who could not but yield to the irresistible fascination of the sea in spite of his knowledge of its perils and hardships.[4] In the light of what has subsequently been revealed to us, especially by Professor Whitelock, this romantically biased interpretation is seen to be mistaken. Even lines 1–64a contain the seeds of a religious orientation that

---

[1] *King Alfred's Old English Version of Boethius's De consolatione philosophiae*, ed. W. J. Sedgefield (Oxford, 1899), cap. xxii, line 24, p. 50.

[2] *The Homilies of the Anglo-Saxon Church: the First Part containing the Sermones Catholici or Homilies of Ælfric*, ed. B. Thorpe 2 vols. (London, 1844–6) ii, 280, line 16.

[3] The notion advanced by G. V. Smithers, *MÆ*, 26 (1957), 151, that '*elþeodigra eard*' should be taken to mean 'the heavenly home (*patria*) of good Christians (*peregrini*)' must be rejected as a primary meaning in view of the general interpretation here adopted. It would not be inappropriate as a secondary meaning, since the heavenly home is certainly the seafarer's ultimate destination; but this becomes clear enough later and to anticipate it now may involve too complicated a mental exercise, since to accept the secondary meaning is to alter drastically the primary meaning already attached to each of the two words.

[4] '*The Wanderer* and *The Seafarer*', *JEGP* 4 (1902), 466–7. Lawrence even thought that lines 103–24 might be a fragment of an unrelated poem.

Lawrence did not allow for. Yet his impressions were not entirely false. The speaker is indeed an ardent adventurer even though a religious one, and his responses to the world he wants to reject are as keen as his desire for the world to come. I said earlier that voyaging is not presented as an end in itself but as a means to something beyond, yet there is no denying the excitement he feels in pitting his strength and his spirit against the sea, or the lively response of his senses to the pleasures and pains of existence in this world. The first half of the poem especially strikes home to our feelings and our imagination no matter what our creeds. In its manifold sensitivity and awareness, as in its singing quality, its subtle manipulation of sound and movement, its nuances of feeling and tone, and the passionate energy that animates and directs it, it is as broadly intelligible and as unfathomable as one could wish poetry to be. What begins as a song ends as a sermon, and they are necessary to each other, but the song as illuminated by the sermon is what places *The Seafarer* high among the lyric and dramatic achievements of Old English poetry.

God's presence through grace as the theme of Cynewulf's *Christ II* and the relationship of this theme to *Christ I* and *Christ III*

COLIN CHASE

Cynewulf's dependence on Gregory the Great's Ascension Day homily[1] for the structure and much of the subject matter of *Christ II* has been acknowledged since 1853.[2] After commenting in some detail on the gospel text for the day (Mark XVI. 14–20) Gregory devotes the final third of his homily to more general reflections – 'ut aliquid de ipsa tantae solemnitatis consideratione dicamus'[3] – on the theme of the elevation of human nature in the Lord's ascension: 'Ascendente vero Domino, est humanitas exaltata.'[4] Though Cynewulf takes his lead from these general reflections of Gregory at every point, a comparison of poem and homily shows that in doing so he substitutes his own theme of God's continuing presence with man since the ascension in his gifts of grace. This article concerns this thematic change and its implications for the relationship of *Christ II* to *Christ I* and *Christ III*.[5]

Both Gregory and Cynewulf begin with variations of the same question: 'Why did the angels not wear white at the Lord's birth, while they did wear white at his ascension?' Their answers are to a degree similar. 'Quid est', says Gregory, 'nisi quod tunc magna solemnitas angelis facta est?'[6] and Cynewulf says:

> Hwite cwoman
> eorla eadgiefan   englas togeanes.
> Ðæt is wel cweden,   swa gewritu secgað,
> þæt him albeorhte   englas togeanes
> in þa halgan tid   heapum cwoman,
> sigan on swegle.   Þa wæs symbla mæst
> geworden in wuldre. (545b–51a)

---

[1] *In Evangelia XXIX*, Migne, Patrologia Latina 76, cols. 1213–19.

[2] Friedrich Dietrich, 'Cynevulfs *Crist*', *ZDA* 9 (1853), 204; Albert S. Cook provides a detailed analysis of the relation of the poem to the homily, *The Christ of Cynewulf*, 2nd ed. (Boston, 1909; repr. with preface by John C. Pope, Hamden, Connecticut, 1964), pp. 115–16. Cook's edition has the most complete commentary. The text quoted in this article is that of *The Exeter Book*, ed. George Philip Krapp and Elliott Van Kirk Dobbie, Anglo-Saxon Poetic Records 3 (New York, 1936), 15–27.

[3] 'To say something about the very thought of so great a feast' (PL 76, col. 1218).

[4] 'But when the Lord ascended, humanity was exalted' (*ibid.*).

[5] I wish to express my thanks to Professor P. A. M. Clemoes and Professor John F. Leyerle for their care in helping me to prepare this article.

[6] 'Why is it . . . if not because there was a great feast day for the angels then?' (*ibid.*).

For both homilist and poet white is worn as a sign of celebration. Each goes on to describe the event the angels are celebrating. For Gregory the celebration commemorates the day 'cum coelum Deus homo penetravit. Quia nascente Domino videbatur divinitas humiliata; ascendente vero Domino, est humanitas exaltata. Albae etenim vestes exaltationi magis congruunt quam humiliationi.'[1] Gregory focuses on the idea that in virtue of the hypostatic union of divine and human natures in Christ man first achieved heaven in the ascension. Cynewulf's focus, however, is different. In the poem the angels are celebrating the saviour's victory over Satan and the establishment of peace between God and man. Their spokesman expresses this as the triumphant Lord 'mid þas bliðan gedryht' approaches the gates of heaven:[2]

> 'Hafað nu se halga   helle bireafod
> ealles þæs gafoles   þe hi geardagum
> in þæt orlege   unryhte swealg.
> Nu sind forcumene   ond in cwicsusle
> gehynde ond gehæfte,   in helle grund
> duguþum bidæled,   deofla cempan.
>
> Sib sceal gemæne
> englum ond ældum   a forð heonan
> wesan wideferh.   Wær is ætsomne
> godes ond monna,   gæsthalig treow,
> lufu, lifes hyht,   ond ealles leohtes gefea.' (558–63
> and 581b–5)

The victory has been won. Peace has been established. Now Christ has returned to his heavenly kingdom to distribute wealth from his gift-throne:

> Wile nu gesecan   sawla nergend
> gæsta giefstol,   godes agen bearn,
> æfter guðplegan. (571–3a)

He is described as 'folca feorhgiefa' (556a), a treasure-giver whose treasure is eternal life.

This pattern of battle, peace and gift-giving is reminiscent of, for instance, events at *Finnsburh*, where:

---

[1] '. . . when God as man penetrated heaven. Because at the Lord's birth the divinity appeared lowered; but at the Lord's ascension mankind was raised high. For white clothes suit exaltation more than humiliation' (*ibid.*).

[2] As Cook pointed out (*Christ*, pp. 116–18), this speech is based on part of Bede's Ascension Day hymn, which is to some extent modelled on (Vulgate) ps. XXIII. 7 and 10; though there is a leaf missing from the Exeter Book just prior to the speech quoted (following *frætwum* 556b), the general character of the celebration is clear. See J. C. Pope, 'The Lacuna in the Text of Cynewulf's *Ascension* (*Christ II*, 556b)', *Studies in Language, Literature and Culture of the Middle Ages and Later*, ed. E. B. Atwood and A. A. Hill (Austin, Texas, 1969), pp. 210–19.

   ...æt feohgyftum   Folcwaldan sunu
dogra gehwylce   Dene weorþode,
Hengestes heap   hringum wenede
efne swa swiðe   sincgestreonum
fættan goldes,   swa he Fresena cyn
on beorsele   byldan wolde. (*Beowulf* 1089–94)[1]

Christ, bestowing gifts on loyal angels and newly reconciled man, can be compared with Finn, treating Danes and Frisians alike. The pattern is repeated in ninth-century[2] history when King Alfred defeats Guthrum at Eddington in 878 and confirms the peace treaty with generous gifts:

7 þæs ymb iii wiecan com se cyning to him Godrum þritiga sum þara monna, þe in þam here weorþuste wæron, æt Alre, 7 þæt is wiþ Æþelinggaeige; 7 his se cyning þær onfeng æt fulwihte 7 his crismlising was æt Weþmor 7 he was xii niht mid þam cyninge 7 he hine miclum 7 his geferan mid feo weorðude.[3]

Besides the gift-giving a more particular similarity between the twelve days of rejoicing in Somerset and the angelic banquet in heaven sheds light on Cynewulf's symbolism: both Guthrum and the angels wear white.[4] For Guthrum this expresses his acceptance of the baptism that has been conferred upon him and the purification which is its result; for the angels it is an external sign of what baptism also conveys – the greatest of the gifts which Christ the conqueror gives to man – salvation itself. The image is picked up again at the end of the poem, immediately before the concluding sea metaphor:

               Is us þearf micel
þæt we gæstes wlite   ær þam gryrebrogan
on þas gæsnan tid   georne biþencen. (847b–9)

The angels' white clothing is like the spiritual beauty which must adorn us on Judgement Day. Cynewulf's summary expression of all this, his inclusive answer to the question with which he begins, focuses on the gift of redemption, and on the freedom, peace and protection given to man through the redemption, as the meaning of Christ's ascension:

[1] *Beowulf and the Fight at Finnsburg*, ed. Fr. Klaeber, 3rd ed. (Boston, 1950).

[2] For evidence that Cynewulf wrote in the ninth century, see Kenneth Sisam, 'Cynewulf and his Poetry', *Proc. of the Brit. Acad.* 18 (1932), 303–8.

[3] *The Parker Chronicle*, ed. A. H. Smith (London, 1951), p. 33, *s.a.* 878. Between the reigns of Alfred and Æthelred the concept of *frið* was defined in increasing detail, ordinarily including the relinquishment of hostilities and rights of revenge, the giving of royal gifts, special rights of royal protection for any party to the peace (*friðmann*) and specific penalties for those breaking the terms of the peace. Each of these elements is present in the poem. See *Die Gesetze der Angelsachsen*, ed. F. Liebermann (Halle, 1903–16; repr. Aalen, 1960) I, 126–35 (on Alfred) and 220–4 (on Æthelred).

[4] On the custom of wearing white garments and a linen fillet (chrismale) until the Sunday after baptism (*crismlising*), see *Venerabilis Baedae Opera Historica*, ed. C. Plummer (Oxford, 1896) II, 280–1.

> Hwæt, we nu gehyrdan   hu þæt hælubearn
> þurh his hydercyme   hals eft forgeaf,
> gefreode ond gefreoþade   folc under wolcnum,
> mære meotudes sunu. (586–9a)

By answering his opening question as he does, Cynewulf shifts the thematic direction of his work away from Gregory's anagogic emphasis ('ascendente vero Domino, est humanitas exaltata') towards a more this-worldly, present concern with the coming of the peace of Christ to people on earth, to 'folc under wolcnum' (588b).[1]

Similar shifts in thematic emphasis occur throughout the rest of the poem. The first comes at the beginning of the narrative section, in Christ's final discourse to the apostles just before he ascends. Half of this speech (481–8a) is based on a section of the Ascension Day gospel text (Mark XVI. 15–18) which inspires the first two-thirds of Gregory's homily. The rest has no basis in Cynewulf's source but appears to be an expansion of the last verse of Matthew (XXVIII. 20: 'Et ecce ego vobiscum sum omnibus diebus usque ad consummationem saeculi'[2]):

> Gefeoð ge on ferððe.   Næfre ic from hweorfe,
> ac ic lufan symle   læste wið eowic,
> ond eow meaht giefe   ond mid wunige,
> awo to ealdre,   þæt eow æfre ne bið
> þurh gife mine   godes onsien. (476–80)

The idea that Christ remains with his disciples is not mentioned by Gregory, who concentrates on the physical ascension as a figure of man's destiny in heaven, 'Desideria terrena fugiamus, nihil nos jam delectet in infimis, qui patrem habemus in coelis.'[3] Cynewulf gives the idea some prominence, repeating it at the end of the farewell discourse:

> Ic eow mid wunige,
> forð on frofre,   ond eow friðe healde
> strengðu staþolfæstre   on stowa gehware. (488b–90)

Much of the remainder of the poem shows how Christ remains with his followers.

The next passage from Gregory's homily directly paraphrased by Cynewulf has to do with Christ's reversal of the curse incurred by Adam's fall:

[1] Peter Clemoes ('Cynewulf's Image of the Ascension', *England Before the Conquest: Studies in Primary Sources presented to Dorothy Whitelock*, ed. Peter Clemoes and Kathleen Hughes (Cambridge, 1971), p. 295, n. 4) comments on the opening passage and on several others to show the way in which 'Cynewulf uses the ideas he derives from Gregory as starting-points for imagistic writing throughout the poem'. In developing his images Cynewulf radically alters their significance.

[2] 'And behold I am with you all days even to the end of time.'

[3] 'Let us flee earthly desires, let nothing in the lower regions delight us, who have a father in the heavens' (PL 76, col. 1219).

Sed hoc nobis magnopere, fratres charissimi, in hac solemnitate pensandum est, quia deletum est hodierna die chirographum damnationis nostrae, mutata est sententia corruptionis nostrae. Illa enim natura cui dictum est: 'Terra es, et in terram ibis' [Genesis III. 19], hodie in coelum ivit.[1]

Because of Christ's ascension, man is no longer earthbound but heavenbound. Cynewulf expands his source by adding further details from Genesis:

> Cwide eft onhwearf
> saulum to sibbe, se þe ær sungen wæs
> þurh yrne hyge ældum to sorge:
> 'Ic þec ofer eorðan geworhte, on þære þu scealt yrmþum lifgan,
> wunian in gewinne ond wræce dreogan,
> feondum to hroþor fusleoð galan,
> ond to þære ilcan scealt eft geweorþan . . .' (618b–24)

Where Gregory's text refers only to the sentence of death, Cynewulf's paraphrase includes the other trials and difficulties of life on earth which were also part of Adam's curse.[2] The implication is that this part of the curse has in some sense been reversed as well. Cynewulf prepares for this idea by inserting between the narrative section and the paraphrase in question a passage (586–611a) enumerating the natural and supernatural gifts God has given us. First there is the gift of salvation, creating for man the possibility of choice between heaven and hell, glory and punishment:

> swa lif swa deað, swa him leofre bið
> to gefremmanne, þenden flæsc ond gæst
> wuniað in worulde. (596–8a)

Then there are the natural gifts for which it is fitting 'þætte werþeode / secgen dryhtne þonc' (600b–1a), things such as 'æt', 'weder liþe', 'sunne ond mona' and 'deaw and ren'. For all these things we ought to be thankful,

> ond huru þære hælo þe he us to hyhte forgeaf,
> ða he þa yrmþu eft oncyrde
> æt his upstige þe we ær drugon,
> ond geþingade þeodbuendum
> wið fæder swæsne fæhþa mæste,
> cyning anboren. (613–18a)

---

1 'But on this feast day, dearly beloved brethren, we ought chiefly to reflect that today the decree of our condemnation has been wiped out, the sentence of our destruction commuted. For that nature to whom it was said: "You are earth and into the earth you will go", has today gone to heaven' (*ibid.* col. 1218). Gregory quotes from the Old Latin Genesis. See *Vetus Latina: Die Reste der Altlateinischen Bibel* II: Genesis, ed B. Fischer (Freisburg, 1951–4), p. 74.

2 'Maledicta terra in opere tuo: in laboribus comede ex ea cunctis diebus vitae tuae. Spinas et tribulos germinabit tibi, et comedes herbam terrae. In sudore uultus tui vesceris pane, donec revertaris in terram de qua sumptus es; quia pulvis es et in pulverem reverteris' (Genesis III. 17–19).

For Cynewulf the gifts both of nature and of grace that are ours are part of the peace settlement which Christ won when he conquered Satan and 'æt his upstige' reconciled us to the Father. By treating in this way the idea of the reversal of Adam's curse Cynewulf has again replaced an original focus on man's heavenly destiny with a thematic emphasis on God's present dealings with man in this world.

The next figure which Cynewulf derives from Gregory is the figure of Job's bird: 'Pro hac ipsa namque carnis nostrae sublevatione per figuram beatus Job Dominum avem vocat',[1] an idea to which he gives further emphasis a sentence later: 'Avis enim recte appellatus est Dominus, quia corpus carneum ad aethera libravit.'[2] Cynewulf develops this figure over several lines (633–58) but he suppresses any reference to Gregory's central point, that the bird is a figure for Christ's raising up of human nature in his ascension. At the same time he makes an addition which changes the implicit meaning of the image, for where Gregory speaks only of the bird's upward flight, Cynewulf refers also to a return journey:

> Swa se fæla fugel   flyges cunnode;
> hwilum engla eard   up gesohte,
> modig meahtum strang,   þone maran ham,
> hwilum he to eorþan   eft gestylde,
> þurh gæstes giefe   grundsceat sohte,
> wende to worulde. (645–50a)

In Cynewulf's treatment the image of Job's bird expresses once more the way in which Christ fulfilled his promise to remain with his disciples by returning in the gifts of the Holy Spirit.

The passage in *Christ II* immediately following (659–91a) goes on to list ten gifts God has bestowed on man. Five of these are gifts of the mind (e.g. 'Sum mæg searolice / wordcwide writan', 672b–3a) and five are gifts of physical skill (e.g. 'Sum mæg fromlice / ofer sealtne sæ sundwudu drifan', 676b–7).[3] This list corresponds to the list of the gifts of the Holy Spirit which Gregory gives as part of his commentary on (Vulgate) ps. LXVII. 19, 'Ascendens in altum captivam duxit captivitatem, dedit dona hominibus.'[4] Having explained the first part of the verse ('corruptionem nostram virtute suae incorruptionis absorbuit'[5]), Gregory explains the second by mentioning six spiritual gifts of the kind referred to by St Paul (I Corinthians XII. 8–10).

---

[1] 'On account of this same raising up of our flesh blessed Job figuratively calls the Lord a bird' (PL 76, col. 1218).
[2] 'For the Lord is rightly called a bird since he flew a fleshly body to the heavens' (*ibid.*).
[3] See the discussion of this passage by Peter Clemoes *Rhythm and Cosmic Order in Old English Christian Literature*, an Inaugural Lecture (Cambridge, 1970), pp. 12–13.
[4] 'Ascending on high he led captivity captive, gave gifts to men' (PL 76, col. 1218).
[5] 'Our corruption he absorbed by the power of his incorruption' (*ibid.*).

In order to get to this reference in his source Cynewulf passes over two intervening allusions ('Elevata est magnificentia tua super coelos' (ps. VIII. 2) and 'Ascendit Deus in jubilatione, et Dominus in voce tubae' (ps. XLVI. 6)[1]) and eliminates the first half of the third, the part which connects it to Gregory's Ascension Day theme ('Ascendens in altum . . .'). In dealing with the allusion to gifts Cynewulf makes his list more secular than that of his source, increases the number of gifts from six to ten and expands his treatment considerably.[2] The effect is once again to shift thematic emphasis away from the ascension as a physical event signifying the elevation of human nature and towards the continuing concern of God for man, shown in his gifts. Here, as before, even the natural gifts of God are treated as part of the salvation won by Christ. Both at the beginning and the end of this passage they are mentioned in conjunction with the happiness reserved for the blessed in heaven:

> Đa us geweorðade   se þas world gescop,
> godes gæstsunu,   ond us giefe sealde,
> uppe mid englum   ece staþelas,
> ond eac monigfealde   modes snyttru
> seow ond sette   geond sefan monna.

> Đus god meahtig   geofum unhneawum,
> cyning alwihta,   cræftum weorðaþ
> eorþan tuddor;   swylce eadgum blæd
> seleð on swegle,   sibbe ræreþ
> ece to ealdre   engla ond monna. (659–63 and 686–90)

In both poem and homily the next reference is to Habakkuk. Gregory has, 'De hac Ascensionis ejus gloria etiam Habacuc ait: "Elevatus est sol, et luna stetit in ordine suo."'[3] Cynewulf's translation is close to this, but by changing the demonstrative adjective *hac* to a demonstrative pronoun (*þon*) he shifts the reference of the passage:

> Bi þon se witga cwæð
> þæt ahæfen wæren   halge gimmas,
> hædre heofontungol,   healice upp,
> sunne ond mona. (691b–4a)

In this sentence *bi þon* cannot refer to the ascension (as *hac* does) for the ascension has not been mentioned for over thirty lines. Instead it has to refer to the subject of the immediately preceding passage – the gifts of

---

[1] 'Your magnificence is raised up above the heavens'; 'God ascended in the midst of rejoicing, the Lord in the sound of the trumpet' (*ibid.*).

[2] Thirty-three and a half lines in Cynewulf's version, three and a half in Gregory's.

[3] 'Concerning this glory of his Ascension Habacuc also speaks: "the sun is raised up and the moon has stood in its rank"' (PL 76, col. 1218). As before, Gregory quotes from the Old Latin (Habakkuk III. 4), based on the Septuagint version. See above, p. 91, n. 1.

God both in heaven and on earth – and the sun and moon become expressions for God and the church as ultimate and mediate sources of those gifts. Gregory explains the expression from Habakkuk, 'Elevatus est sol, et luna stetit in ordine suo', with reference to the ideas of elevation and stasis as images of the ascension and of the fortitude of the apostolic church:

> Quousque enim Dominus ascendit ad coelos, sancta ejus Ecclesia adversa mundi omnimodo formidavit; at postquam ejus Ascensione roborata est, aperte praedicavit quod occulte credidit. 'Elevatus est ergo sol, et luna stetit in ordine suo', quia cum Dominus coelum petiit, sancta ejus Ecclesia in auctoritate praedicationis excrevit.[1]

Cynewulf exploits another facet of the images, treating both God and church as sources of light and strength. The sun and moon are raised up above the earth and shed their beneficent rays on men below:

> Hwæt sindan þa
> gimmas swa scyne   buton god sylfa?
> He is se soðfæsta   sunnan leoma,
> englum ond eorðwarum   æþele scima.
> Ofer middangeard   mona lixeð,
> gæstlic tungol,   swa seo godes circe
> þurh gesomninga   soðes ond ryhtes
> beorhte bliceð. (694b–701a)

Here again the upward movement dominating Gregory's imagery has been replaced by an emphasis on the downward movement of gifts from above. The passage echoes the earlier lines inserted by Cynewulf describing some of the natural gifts for which we should be thankful:

> Sunne ond mona,
> æþelast tungla   eallum scinað,
> heofoncondelle,   hæleþum on eorðan. (606b–8)

The echo strengthens the figural sense at the heart of Cynewulf's poem, according to which the natural order is so often a semi-sacramental expression of the life of grace. Both Cynewulf and Gregory refer to the courage of the early Christians in the face of persecution, but while for Gregory this fortitude is attributed directly to the ascension ('at postquam ejus Ascensione roborata est, aperte praedicavit quod occulte credidit') for Cynewulf it is a gift of the Spirit:

---

[1] 'For until the Lord ascended to heaven, his holy church was completely afraid of the adversities of the world; but after she was strengthened by his ascension, she openly preached what she secretly believed. "The sun is raised up and the moon has stood in its rank", because when the Lord sought heaven, his holy church increased in the authority of her preaching' (PL 76, col. 1219).

Þær ða synsceaðan   soþes ne giemdon,
gæstes þearfe,   ac hi godes tempel
bræcan ond bærndon,   blodgyte worhtan,
feodan ond fyldon.   Hwæþre forð bicwom
þurh gæstes giefe   godes þegna blæd
æfter upstige   ecan dryhtnes. (706–11)

The next scriptural image expounded by Gregory is that of the leaping figure mentioned in the Song of Songs: 'Ecce iste venit saliens in montibus, et transiliens colles' (ii. 8).[1] Considering the mountains as 'tantorum operum culmina', he connects the leaps with five moments of transition in the life of Christ: 'Vultis, fratres charissimi, ipsos ejus saltus agnoscere? De coelo venit in uterum, de utero venit in praesepe, de praesepe venit in crucem, de cruce venit in sepulcrum, de sepulcro rediit in coelum.'[2] The ascension includes the resurrection and is the heavenly culmination of a series of leaps which led up to it. The practical moral is drawn at once: 'Unde, fratres charissimi, oportet ut illuc sequamur corde, ubi eum corpore ascendisse credimus.'[3] The example of Christ in the ascension should lead us to raise our minds heavenward. Cynewulf's emphasis is more directly on Christ's mission of salvation. First in quoting the Song of Songs he attributes to Solomon knowledge that his leaping figure 'woruld alyseð, / ealle eorðbuend, þurh þone æþelan styll' (718b–19). The leaps are not taken as a series but individually, some with their own particular emphasis. For example, the first leap emphasizes the saving mission:

... þær mennisc hiw
onfeng butan firenum   þæt to frofre gewearð
eallum eorðwarum. (721b–3a)

Cynewulf increases the number of *hlypas* from five to six, adding a six-line description of the harrowing of hell (730b–6a) with stress on Christ's victory over Satan and the devil's imprisonment in the underworld:

þær he gen ligeð
in carcerne   clommum gefæstnad,
synnum gesæled. (734b–6a)

Finally, after an exhortational conclusion (744–57) like Gregory's quoted above, Cynewulf adds a long passage (758–82b) considering the help God

---

[1] 'Behold he comes dancing on the mountains, leaping over the hills' (*ibid.*).
[2] 'Beloved brethren, do you wish to know those leaps of his? From heaven he came into the womb, from the womb he came into the crib, from the crib he came onto the cross, from the cross he came into the tomb, from the tomb he went back to heaven' (*ibid.*).
[3] 'Wherefore, beloved brethren, it behoves us to follow in our hearts where we believe he has ascended in the flesh' (*ibid.*).

provides against the attacks of the devil, first in this life and then at the Last Judgement:

> Habbað we us to frofre   fæder on roderum
> ælmeahtigne.   He his aras þonan,
> halig of heahðu,   hider onsendeð,
> þa us gescildaþ   wið sceþþendra
> eglum earhfarum . . .
>
> Ne þearf him ondrædan   deofla strælas
> ænig on eorðan   ælda cynnes,
> gromra garfare,   gif hine god scildeþ,
> duguða dryhten. (758–62a and 779–82a)

Through most of this section (712–78) Cynewulf's added material shifts the focus of attention towards the gifts of God's grace, first in Christ's original mission of salvation and then in present everyday help against the attacks of the devil. At line 779, where the poet's consideration turns directly to the Last Judgement, his theme is more closely aligned with that in Gregory's homily, so that the many changes and expansions he effects in urging his audience to fear God's judgement are not pertinent to my present inquiry.

At the end of the poem Cynewulf returns to the theme of the whole work in the famous image of life as a voyage, so reminiscent of *The Wanderer* and *The Seafarer*. The foundation for this in Gregory's homily is the barest hint of a nautical metaphor in a sentence which opposes the peace and calm of heaven to the turbulence of life lived below: 'Quamvis adhuc rerum perturbationibus animus fluctuet, jam tamen spei vestrae anchoram in aeternam patriam figite, intentionem mentis in vera luce solidate.'[1] Consistent with his theme throughout the rest of the poem, Cynewulf develops the metaphor by considering how our course was set by Christ and how his gifts help us to a smoother passage:

> Wæs se drohtað strong
> ærþon we to londe   geliden hæfdon
> ofer hreone hrycg.   Þa us help bicwom,
> þæt us to hælo   hyþe gelædde,
> godes gæstsunu,   ond us giefe sealde
> þæt we oncnawan magun   ofer ceoles bord
> hwær we sælan sceolon   sundhengestas,
> ealde yðmearas,   ancrum fæste. (856b–63)

By introducing at the end the image of Christ as pilot and captain Cynewulf gives a final emphasis to the theme which has preoccupied him throughout: Christ's continuing presence among mankind in the gifts of his grace.

---

[1] 'Although your heart is still tossed about by the disturbances of [your] affairs, nevertheless put the anchor of your hope now in the eternal fatherland, fix your mind's direction on the true light' (*ibid.*).

Once due account has been taken of the internal evidence that Cynewulf systematically altered the theme of Gregory's homily in this way, a further question arises, for in the Exeter Book *Christ II* is flanked by two poems treating other ways in which Christ approaches mankind, *Christ I* dealing with his coming in the incarnation and *Christ III* with his coming in judgement. However they came to be joined in this way these three poems collectively have the appearance of a triptych of pictures contrasting in their styles and colours but united in their development of a common theme.

Thoughts of this kind have been expressed more than once,[1] though without the foundation of the foregoing analysis of *Christ II*. The argument most nearly related to the present discussion is Smithson's.[2] He saw in the three poems a unity corresponding to St Bernard's description of Christ's advent 'ad homines, in homines, contra homines', but his interpretation has been rejected because of the three-century gap between the probable date of the poem's composition and the proposed cultural background.[3] This was unfortunate, because evidence exists indicating that the idea of a threefold coming of Christ, past, present and future, was a conventional motif of later Anglo-Saxon spirituality. This evidence is taken from two sources in modern edited form: a sacramentary attributed to Gregory based on continental manuscripts of the ninth and tenth centuries[4] and the early-

---

[1] See Dietrich, '*Crist*', pp. 193–214, esp. 194 and 209; Samuel Moore, 'The Old English *Christ*: Is it a Unit?', *JEGP* 14 (1915), 550–67, esp. 556ff.; and Kenneth Mildenberger, 'The Unity of Cynewulf's *Christ* in the Light of Iconography', *Speculum* 23 (1948), 426–32. All these critics argue for unity among the poems but without adverting to Cynewulf's preoccupation with Christ's presence with mankind after his physical departure. Thus Dietrich's threefold coming includes Christ's arrival in heaven as the 'advent' depicted in *Christ II* and Moore adduces patristic references to the advent, ascension and Last Judgement to show that they were associated in the tradition. Mildenberger's iconographic evidence for the same interpretation is unconvincing: three of his seven examples are from a single Coptic monastery, Mary without the infant is taken three times to stand for the advent there and only one example from Anglo-Saxon England is adduced. A summary of the history of the controversy is available in Claes Schaar, *Critical Studies in the Cynewulf Group* (Lund, 1949), pp. 104–7. See also George A. Smithson, *The Old English Christian Epic*, Univ. of California Publ. in Mod. Philol. 1, no. 4 (1909–10), 303–400.

[2] *Ibid.* James F. Burke ('The Four "Comings of Christ" in Gonzalo de Berceo's Vida de Santa Oria', *Speculum* 48 (1973), 294, n. 7) cites many references to Christ's multiple comings from the twelfth century and later. Some distinguish between the last general judgement and the personal judgement at death, adding a fourth coming.

[3] Dom Edward Burgert, O.S.B., *The Dependence of Part I of Cynewulf's Christ upon the Antiphonary* (Washington, 1921), pp. 9–10.

[4] 'Liber Sacramentorum', ed H. Menard in *Opera Omnia Sancti Gregorii* (Paris, 1705) III, 1–616; repr. PL 78, cols. 25–582 (cited hereafter for convenience). The firmest dating is the manuscript written by 'Rodradus' who was ordained in 853 (PL 78, cols. 17–20). Menard believed the 'Saint Eligius' manuscript to have been earlier but gives no solid evidence (*ibid.* cols. 15–18). His statement that it is palaeographically very close to Rodradus makes it unlikely that it is later (*ibid.* cols. 15–16). His third manuscript, written by Abbot Ratoldus, is dated by his death in 986 (*ibid.* cols. 19–20). The fourth manuscript is probably later. Menard's notes (*ibid.* col. 435) show that the blessings cited here occur in all manuscripts without significant variation.

eleventh-century *Benedictional of Archbishop Robert* (so-called after its later Norman owner).[1] The conventional nature of this evidence is guaranteed by the liturgical character of the documents and by the frequent recurrence of the same blessings in other benedictionals, pontificals and missals.[2] The argument here depends on the likelihood that what was done on the continent in the days of Alcuin and his successors and in England in the time of Ælfric can give us some impression of liturgical attitudes in England in the reign of Alfred and before. For each of the four weeks of Advent a choice of three blessings is provided, many of them emphasizing a connection between the first and second coming,[3] others with a slightly different emphasis. Relevant to our discussion is a series of blessings, one for each Sunday of Advent, which includes a present coming in grace along with those of the incarnation and judgement:

First Sunday: Deus cuius unigeniti aduentum et preteritum creditis et futurum expectatis eiusdem aduentus uos inlustratione sua sanctificet et sua benedictione locupletet. Amen.

Second Sunday: Omnipotens deus cuius aduentus incarnatione preteritus creditur et iudicii uenturus expectatur uos antequam ueniat expiet ab omni contagione delicti. Amen.

Third Sunday: Et qui hos dies incarnatione unigeniti sui fecit esse sollempnes a cunctis presentis et futurae uitae aduersitatibus uos reddat indempnes. Amen.

Fourth Sunday: Deus qui uos et prioris aduentus gratia reparauit et in secundo daturum se uobis regnum cum sanctis angelis repromisit aduentus sui uos inlustratione sanctificet. Amen.[4]

---

[1] *The Benedictional of Archbishop Robert*, ed. H. A. Wilson, Henry Bradshaw Soc. 24 (London, 1903), 29–30. Wilson argues for a late-tenth-century dating (*ibid*. pp. xi–xiii), but the manuscript (Rouen, Bibliothèque Municipale Y.6) is at present considered to date from the early eleventh century; see N. R. Ker, *Catalogue of Manuscripts Containing Anglo-Saxon* (Oxford, 1957), pp. 447–8.

[2] Wilson collated his text with a selected set of fourteen similar documents, most of them English and of about the same period or later, some of them earlier continental examples. Ten of these have the blessings without significant variation. See *The Benedictional of Archbishop Robert*, pp. 169–70.

[3] E.g. 'Et qui de aduentu **redemptoris** nostri secundum carnem deuota mente letamini in secundo cum in maiestate sua uenerit premiis aeternae uitae ditemini' ('And may you who rejoice with devoted heart over the coming of our redeemer according to the flesh, be enriched with the rewards of eternal life when he comes in his majesty in the second [coming]'; *ibid*. p. 29).

[4] '*First Sunday*: "May God, the advent of whose only begotten son you both believe to have happened and expect to occur again, sanctify you by the illumination of the same [son's] coming and enrich you with his blessing. Amen." *Second Sunday*: "May almighty God, whose past coming in the incarnation is believed and whose future coming for judgement is awaited, cleanse you from all infection of sin before he comes. Amen." *Third Sunday*: "And may he who has made these days festive by the incarnation of his only-begotten son render you free of all adversities of the present and future life. Amen." *Fourth Sunday*: "May God, who restored you through the grace of his previous coming and in the second has promised to give you his kingdom with the holy angels, sanctify you by the illumination of his advent. Amen"' (*ibid*. pp. 29–30).

These blessings provide a parallel in pre-Conquest liturgy for a theme of threefold coming in which Christ can come to man at present by external enrichment ('sua benedictione locupletet'), by protection from evil ('a cunctis presentis et futurae uitae aduersitatibus uos reddat indempnes') or by interior enlightenment ('aduentus sui uos inlustratione sanctificet'). A similar pattern of thought is present in Ælfric's homily for the first Sunday of Advent:

Crist com on ðam timan to mancynne gesewenlice, ac he bið æfre ungesewenlice mid his gecorenum þeowum, swa swa he sylf behet, þus cweðende, 'Efne ic beo mid eow eallum dagum, oð þissere worulde gefyllednysse.' Mid ðisum wordum he geswutelode þæt æfre beoð, oð middangeardes geendunge, him gecorene menn, ðe þæs wyrðe beoð þæt hi Godes wununge mid him habban moton.

Þa halgan witegan witegodon ægðer ge ðone ærran tocyme on ðære acennednysse, and eac ðone æftran æt ðam micclum dome. We eac, Godes ðeawas, getrymmað urne geleafan mid þyssere tide þenungum, forðan ðe we on urum lofsangum geandettað ure alysednysse þurh his ærran tocyme, and we us sylfe maniað þæt we on his æftran tocyme gearwe beon, þæt we moton fram ðam dome him folgian to ðam ecan life, swa swa he us behet.[1]

To summarize the argument so far: a close comparison of *Christ II* with its source in Gregory the Great's twenty-ninth homily has shown that Cynewulf systematically altered the theme of his model; the alterations are such that they seem, for the modern reader at least, to establish an implicit relationship between the three *Christ* poems, each of which develops one mode of Christ's presence with man, incarnation, grace and judgement; evidence from pre-Conquest liturgy shows that at least the scribe of the Exeter Book would have found such a theme meaningful (and continental sources suggest that Cynewulf would have done too). Beyond this point any theory necessarily becomes speculative, but there is evidence worth considering which suggests as yet uninvestigated possibilities.

Cynewulf's runic signature woven into the closing lines of *Christ II* makes it unlikely that he is to be taken as author of a long three-part poem on the 'three comings of Christ':[2] his signature lays claim only to the second of the

---

[1] *The Homilies of the Anglo-Saxon Church: the First Part, Containing the Sermones Catholici or Homilies of Ælfric*, ed. Benjamin Thorpe (London, 1844) I, 600.

[2] Brother Augustine Philip ('The Exeter Scribe and the Unity of the *Christ*', *PMLA* 55 (1940), 903–9) examined the manuscript for evidence pertinent to the unity question. His conclusion that the scribe 'reserved one set of symbols to designate the separate selections and used another set to show secondary parts within a given selection' (p. 908) seems over-refined. Nine of the collection's 127 poems begin with the ornamented large initial and line of small capitals which introduce *Christ II* and *Christ III* (the beginning of *Christ I* is missing). The rest of the poems and the internal divisions of longer works begin with a small capital, the degree of ornamentation varying with the length of the succeeding poem or division. This practice is not consistent enough to tell us whether the scribe distinguished clearly between three poems developing closely related themes and one poem incorporating a variety of styles and conventions. See *The Exeter Book of Old English Poetry* (photographic facsimile), with introductory chapters by

three poems. Does the evidence suggest rather that Cynewulf composed *Christ II* in order to join together two poems already in existence, according to the liturgical theme noted above? Such an hypothesis would explain his emphasis at the beginning on the nativity, of which he provides a relatively independent fifteen-line resumé (440–55a) before mentioning the ascension. It would also explain the emphasis on the Last Judgement at the end of the poem (779–849) contrasting with Cynewulf's previous focus on the present life of man. And it would give added point to some of his more resonant uses of language: 'Hyht wæs geniwad, / blis in burgum, þurh þæs beornes cyme' (529b–30); 'Hwæt, we nu gehyrdan hu þæt hælubearn / þurh his hydercyme hals eft forgeaf' (586–7). In these verses *cyme* and *hydercyme* refer to Christ's ascension but imbue the ascension with the character of a repetition and a fulfilment of the promise of the incarnation. As it stands *Christ II* seems a much less independent poem than either of the other two.[1] First its source is not a whole work but the last third of a homily whose main purpose is to consider the day's gospel. The thematic changes which Cynewulf works makes his poem reliant on ideas outside itself, for Christ's coming in grace implies that he has come in the flesh and that he will come again to judge. And then *Christ II* has a mixed style: its combination of a narrative section of 146 lines (440–585)[2] with a symbolic sequence of 281 lines (586–866) weakens its internal consistency. This could suit the hypothesis that it was composed to join the symbolic *Christ I* with the more straightforwardly narrative *Christ III*. Such a method of composition would suit an era concerned less with authorship and more with *auctoritas* than our own. The patchwork poetry of the *cento* was still being written.[3] And the

R. W. Chambers, Max Förster and Robin Flower (London, 1933). Current opinion generally rejects the idea that *Christ I*, *Christ II* and *Christ III* form a unified work. See, e.g., *The Advent Lyrics of the Exeter Book*, ed. Jackson J. Campbell (Princeton, 1959), p. viii; Rosemary Woolf, 'Review of Jackson J. Campbell, *The Advent Lyrics of the Exeter Book*', *MÆ* 29 (1960), 125; Stanley B. Greenfield, *A Critical History of Old English Literature* (New York, 1965), p. 124; and Robert B. Burlin, *The Old English Advent: a Typological Commentary* (New Haven, 1968), p. 38. For the most part these critics offer unelaborated opinions reflecting the current consensus.

[1] Recent editions and critical commentary regarding *Christ I* are indicative of the poem's independent nature. See Burlin, *Old English Advent*; Campbell, *Advent Lyrics*; and Thomas D. Hill, 'Notes on the Imagery and Structure of the Old English *Christ I*', *N & Q* 19 (1972), 84–9. The existence of two other Judgement Day poems in Old English shows the independent significance of that theme for the Anglo-Saxons.

[2] Or about 200 lines if the leaf missing after *frætwum* (556b) is taken into account; see above, p. 88, n. 2.

[3] *Centos* (Gk 'patchwork cloak'): this practice of stitching together verses or passages from well-known authors for one's own purposes went back to classical times. In Latin literature Vergil was most often used, and Proba's versification of the gospel made from Vergil's hexameters is one of the better known *centos*. A ninth-century example is a poem attributed to Waldram ('Salomonis et Waldrammi Carmina', ed. Karl Strecker, Monumenta Germaniae Historica, Poetae 4, 296–310), in which passages from the bible and from Boethius, Jerome and Gregory are spliced together for elegiac purposes. See Max Manitius, *Geschichte der lateinischen Literatur des Mittelalters* (Munich, 1911) I, 596–7.

ordinary mode of poetic composition was more often a reworking than a fresh creation, as the three *Christ* poems individually bear witness.[1]

Such 'bridge' composition is widespread in Old English homilies. J. C. Pope's edition of homilies by Ælfric contains several examples, one of which might be cited here.[2] In two manuscripts of Ælfric's sermon 'De Auguriis' two stories have been added, both composed by Ælfric. To join 'De Auguriis' and these added stories a short link has been specially composed, not, in Pope's view, by Ælfric himself. If Cynewulf composed *Christ II* to join together *Christ I* and *Christ III* he would have been doing something akin to this but on a larger scale.

Other hypotheses are possible. Cynewulf lived at a time when authors almost never signed their work: his signature might not mean that he composed only the second of the three poems. Or a compiler may have seen the thematic affinity of these three poems, none of them his own composition, and have joined them together with or without alteration. For the purposes of this study the question must remain open. What we can be reasonably sure of is that an alert Christian reading the first three poems in the Exeter Book in the early eleventh century would have recognized their thematic unity.

[1] The author of *Christ I* began with a series of liturgical antiphons, including four of the 'Great O' antiphons of the Christmas season and eight others from other liturgical sources; Cynewulf, as we have seen, exploited Gregory's twenty-ninth homily for his purposes; and the poet of *Christ III* relied very heavily on Bede's Judgement Day hymn, 'Apparebit repentina dies magna Domini'. See Cook, *Christ*, pp. 71–3, 115–16 and 171–7.

[2] *Homilies of Ælfric: a Supplementary Collection*, Early Eng. Text Soc. 259 and 260 (London, 1967–8), II, 786–98.

King Alfred's *æstel*

BRUCE HARBERT

King Alfred's preface to the Old English *Pastoral Care*, explaining how and why he made this translation from the original of Gregory the Great, ends thus:

Siððan ic hie geliornod hæfde, swæ swæ ic hie forstod, ond swæ ic hie andgitfullicost areccean meahte, ic hie on Englisc awende; ond to ælcum biscepstole on minum rice wille ane onsendan; ond on ælcre bið an æstel, se bið on fiftegum mancessa. Ond ic bebiode on Godes naman ðæt nan mon ðone æstel from ðære bec ne do, ne ða boc from ðæm mynstre; uncuð hu longe ðær swæ gelærede biscepas sien, swæ swæ nu Gode ðonc welhwær siendon: forðy ic wolde ðætte hie ealneg æt ðære stowe wæren, buton se biscep hie mid him habban wille, oððe hio hwær to læne sie, oððe hwa oðre bi write.[1]

The interpretation of *æstel* has been much discussed. Our earliest evidence for its meaning comes in Ælfric's *Glossary*, where *æstel* occurs as a gloss on Latin *indicatorium*:[2] this is the only occurrence of the word in Old English outside Alfred's preface. Secondly, the thirteenth-century Worcester 'tremulous hand' has glossed *æstel* with Latin *festuca* in the D manuscript of the *Pastoral Care* (Cambridge, Corpus Christi College 12). Before we can interpret *æstel*, we must inspect these two glosses.

I have not found *indicatorium* in any Latin dictionary or in any text other than Ælfric's *Glossary*. We have therefore no parallel uses to help determine its meaning. It is likely to mean some object whose function is to indicate (*indicare*), and scholars have probably been right in assuming that it means 'pointer' or 'bookmark'.[3] In Ælfric's *Glossary* it occurs in a list of articles of church furniture and probably means a ceremonial pointer for showing the place in liturgical texts. This fits *æstel* well if it is derived, as has usually been supposed, from Latin *(h)astula*, 'small spear'. *Festuca* is common in classical and medieval Latin and means basically 'small piece of wood or straw'. In classical Latin it has the specialized meaning 'rod with which slaves were

---

[1] Text from Oxford, Bodleian Library, Hatton 20. The publication of the *Pastoral Care* is authoritatively discussed by Kenneth Sisam, *Studies in the History of Old English Literature* (Oxford, 1953), pp. 140–7.

[2] *Ælfrics Grammatik und Glossar*, ed. J. Zupitza (Berlin, 1880), p. 314.

[3] E.g. M. Förster, 'Zur Geschichte des Reliquienkultus in Altengland', *Sitzungsberichte der Bayer. Akademie der Wissenschaften, Phil. hist. Abt.* (1943), Heft 8, p. 11. A convenient list of earlier interpretations is given in A. J. Wyatt, *An Anglo-Saxon Reader* (Cambridge, 1919), p. 214.

touched during the ceremony of manumission'. This use was extended in the Middle Ages and *festuca* was the name given to many ceremonial rods of office.[1] I know no instance where it refers to an instrument used for pointing at books. It seems probable that *indicatorium* and *festuca* cannot be synonymous and that the two glossators were thinking of different meanings of *æstel* when they equated it with these two Latin words.

Modern scholars have most frequently interpreted *æstel* as a 'bookmark' or 'pointer' worth fifty mancuses ('on fiftegum mancessa'). It would have to be made at least partly of precious metal to be worth so much. Etymological evidence, however, and the uses in Middle English of *astel*,[2] a possible reflex of OE *æstel*, suggest that it must be made of wood. This difficulty can be circumvented if we conceive of a bookmark or pointer of wood set in a precious mount, the word *æstel* being used, by a slight semantic shift, to mean not only the wooden part, but the whole assembly. Hence we can see how *indicatorium* and *festuca* might be used as equivalents for one Old English word: *indicatorium* would refer to the whole object, *festuca*, meaning 'small piece of wood', to its most important functional part, the piece of wood that marks the place in the book. Thus Förster's view[3] that *æstel* is related to OIr *astal*, glossed by Cormac as 'slisin nó gai liub(air)', 'a chip or spear of a book', would be confirmed: an *æstel* would be a piece of wood used for marking places, and Alfred's *æstel* would be an especially splendid one. It has been suggested that the Alfred Jewel in the Ashmolean Museum at Oxford is an *æstel* and originally had a wooden rod projecting from its pointed end.[4]

This interpretation, however, is made less plausible by Alfred's words 'on ælcre bið an æstel'. The preposition *on* here must mean that the *æstel* was 'on' the book in some way or was 'in' it. If it were a bookmark it must have been between the pages of the book when it was closed. If the bookmark were made as suggested above, this would have been dangerous, since the precious mount would project outside the pages and could easily be broken. Moreover, no parallels to a bookmark of this kind have been suggested: the medieval bookmarks that survive from the twelfth century onwards are leather thongs or pieces of twine, passed through a hole in the top flap of the binding, secured by a knot, and resting between the pages.[5] If the *æstel*

---

[1] E.g. see *s.v. festuca* in C. Du Cange, *Glossarium Mediae et Infimae Latinitatis*, ed. L. Favre (Paris, 1883–7), and J. F. Niermeyer, *Mediae Latinitatis Lexicon Minus* (Leiden, 1954–).

[2] See *Middle English Dictionary*, ed. H. Kurath, S. M. Kuhn *et al.* (Ann Arbor, 1952–), *s.v.*

[3] See above, p. 103, n. 3.

[4] J. R. Clarke and D. A. Hinton, *The Alfred and Minster Lovell Jewels* (Oxford, 1971), pp. 8–9. T. D. Kendrick's suggestion (*Anglo-Saxon Art to A.D. 900* (London, 1938), p. 216) that an *æstel* was a page-weight and that the Alfred Jewel is an example, is not reconcilable with the glosses or the etymological evidence.

[5] See G. Pollard, 'The Construction of English Twelfth-Century Bindings', *The Library* 5th ser., 17 (1962), 16–17.

were used only as a pointer, it could have been fixed to the outside of the book by some device incorporated in the binding, but again no parallels have been suggested. The purpose of this article is to suggest a new interpretation, that an *æstel* may be a fragment of the true cross.

Etymological evidence accords with this interpretation. *Æstel* is usually derived from Latin (*h*)*astula*, a diminutive of *hasta*.[1] (*H*)*astula* is used for wooden objects of various kinds: 'small spear', 'twig', 'firewood'. Paulinus of Nola uses it three times to refer to a relic of the cross, e.g.: 'Nam crucis e ligno magnum breuis hastula pignus, / totaque in exiguo segmine uis crucis est.'[2] Gregory of Tours also uses *hastula* to refer to a wooden relic, though not of the cross. Splinters from the wooden shrine of St Medard, after it had been destroyed to make room for a stone church, were used to cure toothache: 'Nam saepius de eo hastulae factae parumper acutae dolori dentium remedia contulerunt.'[3] Bede uses *hastula* for the fragments of the wooden cross that Oswald had set up on the battlefield of *Maserfeld*, which had miraculous properties: 'Nam et usque hodie multi de ipso ligno sacrosanctae crucis hastulas excidere solent, quas cum in aquas miserint, eisque languentes homines aut pecudes potauerint siue asperserint, mox sanitati restituuntur.'[4] *Æstel* may, however, come from Latin (*h*)*astella*, another diminutive of *hasta*. This is used for 'wooden relic' by Adamnan when describing the oak of Abraham at Mambre: '. . . de quo uidelicet conroso spurio et ex omni parte securibus circumciso astellarum ad diuersas orbis prouincias particulae asportantur ob eiusdem quercus uenerationem et recordationem.'[5] In none of these passages does (*h*)*astula* or (*h*)*astella* mean 'wooden relic' alone: its meaning is always made clear by context. So if OE *æstel* in the preface to the *Pastoral Care* means 'fragment of the cross', it must bear this meaning independently of context. To accept this interpretation, we must assume a semantic shift between the Latin uses of (*h*)*astula* and (*h*)*astella* and Alfred's use of *æstel*.[6]

It is possible, however, that *æstel* is not of Latin derivation, but is related

---

[1] E.g. F. Holthausen, *Altenglisches etymologisches Wörterbuch* (Heidelberg, 1934), *s.v.*

[2] *Epistula* 32, ch. 11, ed. G. de Hartel, Corpus Scriptorum Ecclesiasticorum Latinorum 29 and 30. Cf. *Epistula* 31, ch. 1 and *Carmen* 28, 137.

[3] *Gloria Confessorum* 93, ed. B. Krusch, Monumenta Germaniae Historica, Script. Rer. Merov. I.2, 808.

[4] *Bede's Ecclesiastical History of the English People*, ed. B. Colgrave and R. B. Mynors (Oxford, 1969) III.2. *The Old English Bede* (ed. T. Miller, Early Eng. Text Soc. o.s. 95, 96, 110 and 111 (London, 1890–8)) translates *hastulas* here by *sponas 7 sceffon*. The translator may have avoided *æstel* because he knew it in the sense of 'relic of the cross' and not in the more general sense 'splinter, chip'. Cf. *HE* III.13, where the Old English has *scæfpan* for *hastulam*.

[5] *De Locis Sanctis*, ed. D. Meehan, Scriptores Latini Hiberniae 3 (Dublin, 1958), II, 11, 5.

[6] Probable derivatives of Latin (*h*)*astella* retain the meaning 'piece of wood': OF *astelle*, 'splinter, chip'; Modern Welsh *astell*, 'board, plank'; and Cornwall dialect *astel*, 'board, plank' (for which see J. Wright, *English Dialect Dictionary* (London, 1898–1905)). Similarly OIr *astal* < Latin (*h*)*astula* means 'splinter, chip'.

to Goth. *asts* and OHG, MHG and MDu *ast*, 'branch'. MHG and MDu *ast* is occasionally used of the crossbeam of the cross, as in *Barlaam und Josaphat*:

> Krist wart an der selben stunt
> genagelet vil vaste
> zuo des kriuzes aste.[1]

And as in:

> Op des cruces aste
> daer bloeyet die rode wijn[2]

We should expect the Old English cognate of Goth. *asts* and OHG, MHG and MDu *ast* to be **æst*, but this does not occur. *Æstel* may, however, be a diminutive of this unrecorded form.[3] It would be likely to mean 'small branch', and since MHG and MDu *ast* is used for a part of the cross, it could have the special meaning 'fragment of the cross'.

To the etymological evidence must be added that provided by ME *astel*, recorded in the fifteenth century with reference to pieces of wood, either broken haphazardly or broken and shaped for a purpose, such as to make planks or splints. This may be from OF *astele*, as suggested by the *Middle English Dictionary*,[4] and hence unrelated, or only distantly related, to OE *æstel*. It may, however, be descended from OE *æstel*, and so lend strength to the view that the Old English word meant 'piece of wood'. If it remained in the language from the ninth century to the fifteenth, although not recorded in writing, the thirteenth-century scribe of the 'tremulous hand' may have known it as a living word. His testimony is especially valuable since he knew and glossed Hatton 20 and may actually have seen the *æstel*. Since Latin has no single word for 'relic of the cross', he may have chosen *festuca* as the best word he could find to convey this meaning.

The clue to the way in which the *æstel* was attached to the book is given by Alfred's words 'on ælcre bið an æstel, se bið on fiftegum mancessa'. The second clause is usually translated 'which is worth fifty mancuses', which obliges us to assume, in spite of the etymological evidence, that *æstel* can be used for objects made at least partially of substances other than wood. I suggest that the clause should be translated 'which is set in fifty mancuses of gold'. That is, the relic was enclosed in a golden reliquary.

Mancus, as Grierson has shown,[5] can mean a coin or the weight in gold of this coin or the value of this coin in silver currency. This last sense is used, to my knowledge, only once in Old English, in the will of Ælfwold of

---

[1] Ed. F. Pfeiffer, *Dichtungen des deutschen Mittelalters* III (Leipzig, 1843), col. 74.

[2] *Horae Belgicae*, ed. H. v. Fallersleben, pt 10 (Hanover, 1854), p. 204, no. 103, stanza 2.

[3] For *-el* as a diminutive suffix in Old English, see E. Eckhardt, 'Die angelsächsische Deminutiv-bildungen', *EStn* 32 (1903), 334–8.

[4] See above, p. 104, n. 2.

[5] P. Grierson, 'Carolingian Europe and the Arabs: the Myth of the Mancus', *Revue Belge de Philologie et d'Histoire* 32 (1954), 1066.

Crediton: *v manc̄ pē*, 'five mancuses of pennies'.[1] Much more commonly, *mancus* in Old English is followed by the defining genitive *goldes*.[2] Except for the one use in Ælfwold's will, it does not occur with the specification of any substance other than gold. It seems, then, that *mancus* in Old English is closely linked with the idea of gold, and when it occurs without *goldes*, we should assume that gold, and not any other substance, is being measured. In many of the uses without *goldes* one cannot tell whether the writer has in mind gold in coin form or gold measured by weight, e.g. 'he eac me gesealde feowertig mancesa'.[3] When *mancus* occurs in a prepositional phrase governed by *on*, as in the preface to the *Pastoral Care*, the gold cannot be in coin form, but it is often not possible to tell whether the value of the object in question is being specified, or the amount of gold that it contains, e.g. 'ænne sweorbeah on XL mancysen'[4] could mean 'a sword-ring worth forty mancuses' or 'a sword-ring made of forty mancuses'. An *æstel*, if it consisted entirely of wood, could not be worth fifty mancuses. If it were a relic of the cross it would have been regarded as priceless. When, therefore, Alfred talks of 'an æstel se bið on fiftegum mancessa', probably he is giving the value of the gold surrounding the relic, 'a fragment of the cross in fifty mancuses of gold'.[5]

In enclosing a relic of the cross in precious metal, Alfred would have been following common medieval practice. The relic at Jerusalem was enclosed in silver-gilt, as the *Itinerarium Egeriae* records, telling of a 'loculus argenteus deauratus, in quo est lignum sanctae crucis'.[6] Medieval references to relics

---

[1] *The Crawford Collection of Early Charters and Documents*, ed. A. S. Napier and W. H. Stevenson (Oxford, 1895), p. 23, line 22.

[2] E.g. *ibid.* p. 23, *passim*; *Select English Documents of the Ninth and Tenth Centuries*, ed. F. E. Harmer (Cambridge, 1914), p. 4, lines 7–8, p. 20, line 24 and p. 35, *passim*; *Anglo-Saxon Wills*, ed. D. Whitelock (Cambridge, 1930), p. 10, line 4, p. 12, lines 20–1, p. 20, lines 11–12, p. 22, lines 17, 19 and 23–4, p. 24, lines 16–17, 20 and 25, p. 26, lines 2, 7, 17, 21 and 24, p. 28, lines 1, 4 and 23, p. 30, lines 5, 6, 12 and 18, p. 32, line 17, p. 34, line 15, p. 42, line 8, p. 46, lines 9–10 and 12, p. 52, line 17, p. 56, lines 5, 17 and 19–20, p. 60, line 6, p. 62, lines 18–19, and p. 64, lines 7–8 and 21; and *Anglo-Saxon Charters*, ed. A. J. Robertson, 2nd ed. (Cambridge, 1956), p. 80, lines 7 and 23, p. 84, line 6, p. 92, line 14, p. 94, lines 9 and 11, p. 104, lines 2–3, p. 106, lines 16–17, p. 112, line 12, p. 122, line 19, p. 148, line 22, and p. 254, lines 7, 8, 11 and 19.

[3] Harmer, *Documents*, p. 26, lines 35–6. Cf. *ibid.* p. 6, lines 2–3, and p. 18, *passim* and Whitelock, *Wills*, p. 14, line 13. King Eadred's will (Harmer, *Documents*, p. 35) has 'þanne nime man twentig hund mancusa goldes and gemynetige to mancusan', where the first use of *mancus* must refer to gold by weight and the second to coins.

[4] Whitelock, *Wills*, p. 26, line 25. Cf. *ibid.* p. 14, line 12, p. 20, lines 18 and 21–3, p. 28, line 2, and p. 30, line 8 and Harmer, *Documents*, p. 33, lines 16–17.

[5] William of Malmesbury's summary of Alfred's preface in *De Gestis Regum Anglorum* II, 123 (ed. W. Stubbs, Rolls Series (1887)), says that Alfred ordered the copies of the *Pastoral Care* to be sent to his bishops 'cum pugillari aureo in quo esset manca auri'. He has misread *mancus* as *manca*, 'handle', or may have known a currupt text of the preface. His interpretation of *æstel* as 'pugillaris aureus' is probably a guess.

[6] *Itinerarium Egeriae* I, p. 37, ed. A. Franceschini and R. Weber in Itinera et alia Geographica, Corpus Christianorum Series Latina 175.

of the cross have been collected by Frolow, and many of these were enclosed in gold, for example those recorded in the period before Alfred at Tours, Poitiers, Rome, Naples and St Wandrille.[1] Two Anglo-Saxon reliquaries made from precious metal to contain pieces of the cross survive: the Brussels Cross and the gold cross in the Victoria and Albert Museum.[2]

Alfred's reliquary was probably fixed to the binding of the book. This gives a satisfactory sense to *on* in 'on ælcre bið an æstel'. The reliquary may have been a gold medallion fixed on to a top board of wood (or of leather on wood), or gold may have covered the whole top board of the book, and perhaps the bottom board and spine as well. Examples of bindings containing relics, both of the cross and of saints, are given by Frolow and Braun.[3] Most of those that survive are from the later Middle Ages, but one example from the ninth century or the tenth is the evangeliary of the Abbey of Morienval, now in the cathedral at Noyon.[4] The binding of this book, made of horn and ivory, had relics set in its top board. In England no examples of this practice are recorded in the Anglo-Saxon period. However, the inventory of the possessions of St Albans Abbey, compiled in the reign of Henry IV, records a book covered in silver-gilt with a crucifix on the cover.[5] At the feet of the figure of Christ was set a fragment of the cross. York Minster and Lincoln Cathedral both had books with relics set in their bindings, as we know from early-fifteenth-century inventories.[6] That at Lincoln is described as 'the pontificall of Seint Hugh' and, if it belonged to the saint, must date from the twelfth century. Those at St Albans and York, though only recorded in the late Middle Ages, may date from an earlier time.

In 883, some seven to nine years before the publication of the *Pastoral Care*, Alfred received a relic of the cross from Pope Marinus. It may have been fragments of this relic that he sent to his bishops. Asser tells us that it was a sizeable piece ('non paruam partem').[7] In sending this relic to Alfred, the pope was adopting a common method of promoting goodwill between a

---

[1] A Frolow, *La Rélique de la Vraie Croix*, Archives de l'Orient Chrétien 7 (Paris, 1961), nos. 31, 33, 34, 63 and 91.

[2] S. R. T. O. D'Ardenne, 'The Old English Inscription on the Brussels Cross', *ESts* 21 (1939), 145–64, and H. P. Mitchell, 'English or German: a Pre-Conquest Gold Cross', *Burlington Mag.* 47 (1925), 324–30.

[3] A. Frolow, *Les Réliquaires de la Vraie Croix*, Archives de l'Orient Chrétien 8 (Paris, 1965), nos. 71–2, and J. Braun, *Die Reliquiare des Christlichen Kultes und ihre Entwicklung* (Freiburg im Breisgau, 1940), p. 47.

[4] Illustrated in A. Goldschmidt, *Die Elfbeinskulpturen* (Berlin, 1914–26) I, pl. 52, no. 119, and E. Molinier, 'L'Evangeliaire de l'Abbaye de Morienval', *Monuments et Mémoires*, ed. G. Perrot and R. de Lasteyrie (Paris, 1895) XII, 215–26, and pls. 26 and 27.

[5] *Annales Monasterii S. Albani*, ed. H. T. Riley, Rolls Series 28 (1871), II, 322.

[6] *The Fabric Rolls of York Minster*, ed. J. Raine, Surtees Soc. 35 (1859), 224, and C. Wordsworth, 'Inventories of Plate, Vestments, etc., Belonging to the Cathedral . . . of Lincoln', *Archaeologia* 53 (1892), 11.

[7] *Asser's Life of King Alfred*, ed. W. H. Stevenson (Oxford, 1904), ch. 71.

ruler and his subjects. Gregory the Great had in 599 sent a piece of the cross to the Visigothic king Reccared and another in 603 to Monza for Adulouvald, son of Queen Theudulinda, on his baptism.[1] Secular rulers also sent fragments of the cross to their subjects. There are many accounts of such donations by Charlemagne, not all of them factually reliable, but showing by their very existence that it was considered proper for a secular ruler to make such gifts. The cathedral at Sens, the baptistry at Florence, and Roger, Count of Limoges, were among the recipients of these gifts, and the twelfth-century Pseudo-Turpin *Historia Caroli Magni* boasts that Charlemagne 'multas ecclesias dotauit' with particles of a relic of the cross that he had brought from the Holy Sepulchre.[2] In England, King Ine of Wessex is recorded as having sent relics of saints to Glastonbury.[3] After Alfred's time, Athelstan is recorded as having given relics of the cross to Malmesbury and Exeter.[4] He himself received many relics from Hugh the Great, duke of the Franks.[5] It would have been natural for Alfred to adopt this practice, dividing the pope's gift into smaller fragments to send to his bishops. The fact that Alfred uses the single word *æstel* for his gift, without further explanation, implies that the object referred to was well known to his bishops. This would not be surprising if it came from the pope.

The giving of relics was not simply an act of piety. It is clear that Pope Vitalian's gift in 667 of relics of Roman saints to King Oswiu was intended to strengthen the king's loyalty to the Roman church,[6] and Gregory I's and Marinus's gifts may have been sent with a similar intention. Relics of the cross were seen as a potent protection in times of war. During the siege of Rome by the Lombards in 756 a procession of supplication was held in which a relic of the cross was carried round the city with the treaty that the Lombards had violated fixed to it. When the emperor Mauritius made his expedition to Thrace in 593, the Byzantine army set out led by a golden lance in which was set a piece of the cross. In 622, Heraclius took a relic of the cross with him when he set out on a military expedition against Persia. In 864 Pope Nicholas I took with him a relic of the cross when he went out to confront the troops of Louis II. Charlemagne used to carry with him into war a reliquary containing a fragment of the cross which was later given to the Abbey of St Corneille in Compiègne by Charles the Bald.[7] Asser tells us that Alfred himself took relics with him wherever he went.[8] The possession

---

[1] Frolow, *La Rélique*, nos. 41 and 48.
[2] *Ibid.* no. 75.
[3] William of Malmesbury, *De Gestis* I, 35.
[4] Frolow, *La Rélique*, nos. 137 and 220.
[5] William of Malmesbury, *De Gestis* II, 135.
[6] See J. M. Wallace-Hadrill, *Early Germanic Kingship* (Oxford, 1971), p. 68.
[7] Frolow, *La Rélique*, nos. 72, 38, 53, 104 and 75.
[8] *Life*, ch. 104.

of a relic of the cross seems to have been seen almost as a sign of royal power. Constantine had a crown containing a relic of the cross which had been given him by his mother Helena, and Charlemagne was buried wearing such a crown.[1] A relic of the cross was accounted one of the greatest treasures that one could possess, as we see from the numerous medieval inventories where such relics are given pride of place. William of Malmesbury gives us an example of this attitude when he calls Marinus's gift to Alfred 'munus omni obrizo pretiosius'.[2]

The fact that Alfred directs that the *æstel* shall not be removed from the book before he directs that the book shall not be removed from the minster seems to imply the great importance that the *æstel* had in his eyes. A copy of Gregory's *Pastoral Care* with a relic of the cross set in gold incorporated in its binding would have been a gift highly valued by its recipients and inter-preted as a sign of Alfred's royal power, of his favour towards his bishops and of his desire to secure their goodwill and co-operation in his programme of educational reform.

[1] Ambrose, *De Obitu Theodosii*, ed. Otto Faller, Corpus Scriptorum Ecclesiasticorum Latinorum 73, 47, and Ademar of Chabannes, *Chronicon*, ed. J. Chavanon (Paris, 1897), p. 105.
[2] *De Gestis* II, 122.

Laurence Nowell's transcript of
BM Cotton Otho B. xi

RAYMOND J. S. GRANT

Madden's note on the flyleaf of BM Cotton Otho B. xi introduces the scholar to the remnants of a most interesting manuscript: 'Previous to the fire of 1731 this MS. consisted of 231 leaves. In 1734 Oxley reported it as "burned", and Planta says "Desideratur". A description of its contents when perfect is given by Dr. Smith in his Catalogue 1696 and more in detail by Wanley in his Cat. libb. Septentr. apud Hickes, p. 219.'[1]

Otho B. xi was written at Winchester partly in the middle of the tenth century and partly about the middle of the first half of the eleventh century according to Ker.[2] It belonged in the thirteenth century to the Augustinian priory of Southwick, Hampshire, and the Bede section was seen there by the historian Thomas Rudborne (*fl.* 1460). In 1562 the manuscript was available to Laurence Nowell in the house of Sir William Cecil (Lord Burleigh),[3] and it came into the possession of Sir Robert Cotton early in the seventeenth century, certainly before 23 April 1621 when he lent it to William L'isle.[4] A leaf was detached in the seventeenth century and, undamaged, is now

---

[1] I am indebted to Mr W. H. Kelliher, Assistant Keeper of Manuscripts at the British Museum, for the following information on the note on the flyleaf: 'It is in the hand of Sir Frederick Madden, Assistant Keeper of Manuscripts at the Museum in 1828 and Keeper from 1832 until his death in 1873. Despite the certificate of foliation entered in March 1884 at the back of the manuscript, the flyleaf upon which Madden wrote appears to belong to a binding added in August 1866. This then is the probable *terminus a quo* for Madden's note.'

[2] N. R. Ker, *Catalogue of Manuscripts Containing Anglo-Saxon* (Oxford, 1957), pp. 230–4, MS 180. Ker considers that the statement in Madden's note that before the fire of 1731 the manuscript had 231 leaves is inaccurate since Wanley (see below, p. 112, n. 3) says that *The Seasons for Fasting* began on p. 351 and the poem is not long.

[3] See Add. 43703 264v: 'Haec scripsit Laurentius Nowellus propria manu in aedibus Cecillianis anno dni. 1562. Londini.' 'Haec . . . Cecillianis' has been deleted and rewritten above the original note, which seems to have been identical. A reduced facsimile of this page appears in C. E. Wright, 'The Dispersal of the Monastic Libraries and the Beginnings of Anglo-Saxon Studies', *Trans. of the Cambridge Bibliographical Soc.* 1 (1949–53), 235. In 1562 Nowell was resident in Cecil's house as tutor to the young earl of Oxford. For further information about Sir William Cecil (later Lord Burleigh or Burghley), his manuscripts and his relations with Nowell and Parker, see *The Peterborough Chronicle*, ed. Dorothy Whitelock, EEMF 4 (1954), 25–6.

[4] BM Harley 6018 records Cotton's book loans, and note 161 (148v) states that Otho B. xi was lent to 'Mr Lill' before 23 April 1621. See *Brit. Museum Quarterly* 14 (1939–40), 81–2. For further information about William L'isle (1569?–1637), see Whitelock, *Peterborough Chronicle*, pp. 24–5.

BM Add. 34652, fol. 2.[1] A collection of medicinal recipes and leechdoms was at the end of the manuscript in Nowell's time but not when the manuscript was used by Wheloc in 1643–4[2] and Wanley in 1705;[3] nothing more has been heard of this collection and it must be presumed lost.[4] Otho B. xi in its original state was a primary source of main importance in that it contained a Winchester text, fairly closely dated and comparatively early, of the Old English Bede, a version of the Anglo-Saxon Chronicle taken from the Parker Chronicle before it underwent addition and alteration at Canterbury, a collection of laws, the Burghal Hidage and a poem on fasting which is not otherwise extant.

Before the Cottonian fire of 1731, which largely destroyed it, the manuscript, fortunately, had been transcribed practically in its entirety by Nowell.[5] Also before the fire Wheloc had made limited use of its Bede text and main use of its Chronicle text for his printed edition, Wanley had described its contents and John Smith had printed some readings from its Bede text in 1722.[6] Since the fire the surviving fragments have become disordered, and some tiny, charred ones have become separated from the main manuscript and are now BM Cotton Otho B. x, fols. 55, 58 and 62. There is a further scrap in a box of fragments marked as coming from burnt Cotton manuscripts. Add. 34652, fol. 2, is the only undamaged leaf. Much the most extensive evidence for the contents of the manuscript before the disaster of 1731 is thus Nowell's transcript.

Laurence Nowell[7] was a protestant clergyman (Dean of Lichfield 1559, d. 1576) who did a lot of valuable work in London in the 1560s on the manuscript collections being assembled there. He associated with the circle

---

[1] See *BMQ* 14 (1939–40), 81–2, for notes on Otho B. x and Otho B. xi and a full account of Add. 34652. It would appear that L'isle detached this leaf when he borrowed Otho B. xi from Cotton and collated its Chronicle text with the Peterborough Chronicle.

[2] *Historiæ Ecclesiasticæ Gentis Anglorum Libri V*, ed. Abraham Wheloc (Cambridge, 1643–4).

[3] Humfrey Wanley's catalogue was published as the second volume of G. Hicke's *Linguarum Vett. Septentrionalium Thesaurus Grammatico-Criticus et Archæologicus* (Oxford, 1705). The contents of Otho B. xi are described on p. 219.

[4] Without Nowell's transcript we would not suspect that Otho B. xi had ever contained any recipes or leechdoms, for Wheloc places *The Seasons for Fasting* 'ad finem Bedae Sax. MS. Cot.' while Wanley states that the poem was 'truncatum etiam in fine' and lists no further contents.

[5] He omitted all the preliminary matter and began with 1.1 of the Bede. He also omitted 23v and 24r, corresponding to *hiowesclice cuðon – ongunne hliapettan* (*The Old English Version of Bede's Ecclesiastical History of the English People*, ed. Thomas Miller, Early Eng. Text Soc. o.s. 95, 96, 110 and 111 (London, 1890–1 and 1898, repr. 1959 and 1963), 1, 386.30 – 390.9).

[6] *Historiae Ecclesiasticae Gentis Anglorum Libri Quinque*, ed. John Smith (Cambridge, 1722). I hope to investigate in a future article the possibility that Otho B. xi was also used by William Lambarde and William Somner before the Cottonian fire.

[7] See Robin Flower, 'Laurence Nowell and the Discovery of England in Tudor Times', *Proc. of the Brit. Acad.* 21 (1935), 47–73. London, Lambeth Palace 692, fol. 32, contains a word-list compiled from Otho B. xi by Nowell. On his dictionary of Anglo-Saxon in Oxford, Bodleian Library, Selden supra 63, see *Laurence Nowell's Vocabularium Saxonicum*, ed. Albert H. Marckwardt (Ann Arbor, 1952).

of Archbishop Parker in seeking to preserve England's literary, historical and linguistic past, and may have met John Leland, although there is no direct evidence that he did. With his friend and pupil William Lambarde (1536–1601), Nowell was responsible for several important transcripts of Old English manuscripts, and his importance as a pioneer in Anglo-Saxon studies is second only to that of Joscelin. At one time or another, both BM Cotton Vitellius A. xv (the *Beowulf* manuscript) and the *Codex Exoniensis*, containing between them about half the corpus of surviving Old English verse, passed through his hands. Nowell's transcript of our manuscript was one of eight by him given to the British Museum in 1934 by Lord Howard de Walden and is now BM Add. 43703.[1] Until it was given to the Museum it was not known to exist.

The following brings together the relevant information about the original contents of the manuscript, the surviving fragments, the transcript and modern secondary sources. Ker distinguishes three hands: scribe no. 1, of the middle of the tenth century, wrote B. xi 1–34 and 37–8 and B. x 55, 58 and 62; scribe no. 2, of the first half of the eleventh century, wrote B. xi 35–6, 39–47, 49, 50 and 52–3 and Add. 34652 2; scribe no. 3, also of the first half of the eleventh century but probably later than scribe no. 2, wrote B. xi 48 and 51.

1. *The Old English Bede*

B. xi 38 + B. x 62, B. xi 1–3, B. x 55, B. xi 4–13, B. x 58 and B. xi 14–24, 37 and 25–36 (B. xi 38, B. x 62, B. xi 3 and B. x 55 and 58 bound the wrong way round); Add. 43703 7–198

Originally there were probably 115 leaves of the Old English translation of the *Historia Ecclesiastica*. In several places there are alterations and marginalia which are believed to be by L'isle. Wheloc and John Smith had access to the entire text before the Cotton fire and occasionally collated it in their editions.[2] The text in its present state has been collated (except for the leaves in B. x) by Miller and Schipper;[3] they refer to it as C.

---

[1] 2r bears the inscription, 'Laurence Nowell the owner 1562'. On the gift by de Walden, see Robin Flower, 'Laurence Nowell and a Recovered Anglo-Saxon Poem', *BMQ* 8 (1934), 130–2. On the contents of the transcript, see Robin Flower, 'The Text of the Burghal Hidage', *London Med. Stud.* 1 (1937), 60–4; Ker, *Catalogue*, pp. 230–4; and *The British Museum Catalogue of Additions to the Manuscripts 1931–1935* (London, 1967), pp. 196–7.

[2] Wheloc prints from Cambridge, University Library, Kk. 3.18, with a few readings from the other manuscripts. Where his main manuscript is in lacuna in II.5–7 (Miller 110.30–118.16), Wheloc prints from Otho, giving us a check on Nowell for these pages and showing that he was guilty of omission by homoeoteleuton; for instance *forhycgað . . . in þæt bæð* (Miller 112.15–17 and *geclæsnunge fulwihtes bæðes þæm halgan* (112.20–1) are in Wheloc but not in Nowell. Smith prints only a few variants from Otho.

[3] *König Alfreds Übersetzung von Bedas Kirchengeschichte*, ed. Jacob Schipper, Bibliothek der angelsächsischen Prosa 4 (Leipzig, 1897 and 1899). Schipper's attempt to print from five manuscripts at once proved disastrous and his edition cannot be used with any confidence.
Miller used C for his main text in two places: with Oxford, Corpus Christi College 279 for

Nowell's transcript of the Bede is virtually complete.[1] Throughout, Nowell has marginal and interlinear notes in Latin which are very short.[2] There are also in many places in the margins proper names and single words written out again in pencil; they are not in Nowell's hand and look modern. Of great interest are passages of Old English added to bk 1, ch. 15, which are not taken from any other surviving manuscript but are in fact translations from the Latin original made by Nowell himself.[3]

2. *The West-Saxon Genealogy*

Add. 34652 2

This list of the West Saxon kings, which ended with Alfred, was a direct copy of the one in the Parker Chronicle, although it has some spelling errors paralleled elsewhere in Otho and has introduced some errors in rendering the regnal years in words instead of figures. Wanley makes no mention of the genealogy, of course, because the leaf had been detached many years earlier.[4] The separate leaf was later in the possession of Thomas Astle (d. 1803) and was purchased for the British Museum in 1894.[5] It has been printed by Napier.[6]

Nowell did not transcribe this copy of the genealogy, preferring the longer one in BM Cotton Tiberius A. iii (fol. 178; Add. 43703 5).

304.9–306.19; and for 472.27–486.15. Otherwise he prints C as variants in his part II. A comparison of the readings of burnt C with Miller reveals over 200 differences. It is likely that Miller saw C in a better condition than it is in now and this supposition is supported when Nowell agrees with Miller, as he often does. When Miller and Nowell disagree, either may be correct, but Nowell is to be preferred only when C remains clear today and agrees with Nowell's transcript or when other manuscripts support Nowell's reading against that of Miller. Nevertheless it seems that Miller made errors where burnt C is quite legible. Although he does not have nearly the number of mistakes shown by Nowell, his errors are in the main of the same types: for example, like Nowell, he has difficulty over *e* and *æ*, *i* and *y*, *a* and *o* and other vowels and diphthongs, he adds and omits unaccented vowels, final *-e*, initial *ge*, various consonants and accent markings and does not distinguish *þ* and *ð*, single and double consonants, or contractions all of the time. He omits a considerable number of words.

[1] See above, p. 112, n. 5.

[2] For instance on 8v *dalreadingas* is glossed in the margin *Dalreudini* (Miller 28.29).

[3] These pseudo-Anglo-Saxon passages are added between the lines and in the margins of 19v, 20r and v and 21r. They have been printed by Flower, 'Nowell and the Discovery of England', p. 73, n. 16. There are two errors in Flower: Nowell *of ʒslægæne* and *ʒflitis*; Flower *ofgeslógene* and *geflites* (Miller 52.11 and 52.20). Flower (*ibid.*) points out that these passages confirm Sisam's theories ('The Authenticity of Certain Texts in Lambard's *Archaionomia*, 1568', *Studies in the History of Old English Literature* (Oxford, 1953), pp. 232–58) that the 'ghost' manuscript of the laws of Athelstan used by Lambarde was in fact a translation by Nowell.

[4] See above, p. 112, n. 1. See also Ker, *Catalogue*, pp. 424–6, no. 346, and Whitelock, *Peterborough Chronicle*, p. 24 and 29v and 34v.

[5] See *BMQ* 14 (1939–40), 81–2.

[6] A. S. Napier, 'Two Old English Fragments', *MLN* 12 (1897), 53–6.

3. *The Anglo-Saxon Chronicle*

B. xi 39–43, 44+45 and 46+47 (40 bound the wrong way round); Add.
43703 199–232 and Dublin, Trinity College E. 5. 19

Otho originally contained, on thirty-four leaves, a version of the Chronicle
which appears to be an eleventh-century Winchester copy of the Parker
Chronicle up to the year 1001;[1] the Winchester portion of the Parker Chronicle
also ends at this point. L'isle collated Otho with the Peterborough Chronicle
in the early seventeenth century and Otho, while still complete, was the
basis of Wheloc's first-ever edition of the Chronicle, printed as an appendix
to his edition of the Bede.[2] The fragments of Otho remaining today have
been printed by Thorpe and Horst,[3] and Plummer notes variants from
them.[4]

Nowell copied the Chronicle from Otho in 1562 and later revised his
transcript, collating it with three other manuscripts (B, C and D) and adding
their variants in the margins. In 1564, before Nowell carried out his revision,
Lambarde copied the transcript into a manuscript which is today Dublin,
Trinity College E. 5. 19. In an appendix to his edition of *The Battle of
Brunanburh* from the Chronicle, Campbell uses Lambarde's text to establish
which readings in Nowell's transcript are original and then compares these
original readings of Nowell's with Wheloc's printed text to decide on the
probable readings of Otho.[5]

4. *List of Popes etc.*

B. xi now lost; Add. 43703 3v–4r

The Chronicle was originally followed in Otho by a list of popes, arch-
bishops of Canterbury and bishops of various English sees, copied from the
Parker Chronicle.[6] Thomas Smith[7] and Wanley provide the evidence for
the existence of this list, as does Nowell's transcript.

---

[1] The view expressed by M. Kupferschmidt, 'Über das Handschriftenverhältniss der Winchester
Annalen', *EStn* 13 (1889), 165–87, esp. 182, that this is not a copy of the Parker Chronicle and
that a more elaborate relationship must be postulated, has been refuted by Horst, *EStn* 24
(1898), 8–9, and is to be disregarded.

[2] Wheloc corrects freely, his source often being the Parker Chronicle.

[3] *The Anglo-Saxon Chronicle*, ed. Benjamin Thorpe, Rolls Series (1861), I, xx (his G). The text is
printed at the foot of pp. 110–41. K. Horst, 'Die Reste der Handschrift G der Altenglischen
Annalen', *EStn* 22 (1896), 447–50.

[4] *Two of the Saxon Chronicles Parallel*, ed. C. Plummer (Oxford, 1892–9, repr. 1952 with additions
by D. Whitelock); his A.

[5] *The Battle of Brunanburh*, ed. Alistair Campbell (London, 1938), pp. 133–44.

[6] See Ker, *Catalogue*, pp. 58 and 232. The list was compiled after 984 and probably before 988.
Ker does not point out Nowell's transcript of this item.

[7] *Catalogus Librorum Manuscriptorum Bibliothecæ Cottonianæ* (Oxford, 1696).

5. The *Anglo-Saxon Laws* (*Athelstan*)

B. xi 48, 51; Add. 43703 233–6r and 265–7

There were originally four leaves containing laws. As transcribed in Add. 43703 they are as follows:

(a) 233–6r and 265r – II Athelstan (Liebermann 150–64);

(b) 265r–6r – V Athelstan (Liebermann 166–8);

(c) 266r–7 – Iudex (Liebermann 474–6).[1]

6. The *Anglo-Saxon Laws* (*Alfred and Ine*)

B. xi 49, 50 and 52 + 53 (all bound the wrong way round); Add. 43703 236v–55r

Otho originally contained, on probably nineteen leaves, the laws of Alfred and Ine. Nowell has transcribed them *in toto*, while Liebermann has printed the fragments remaining (16–20, 72–8 and 118–22). The text is close to that of the Parker Chronicle.

7. The *Penalties for Adultery*

B. xi now lost; Add. 43703 255r

This is a further legal section on the penalties for adultery to be imposed on both the man and the woman involved, and seems to be a fragment of a letter rather than a law code. Nowell's text has been printed by Flower[2] and is important inasmuch as this piece is not extant elsewhere.

8. The *Burghal Hidage*

B. xi now lost; Add. 43703 255r–v

The Burghal Hidage, compiled between 911 and 919, survives in a manuscript of the early thirteenth century and three manuscripts of the early fourteenth. Nowell's transcript of Otho's early-eleventh-century text is therefore valuable, and it has been printed by Flower and Robertson.[3]

9. Further Note on Hides and Defence

B. xi now lost; Add. 43703 255v–6

A further note with regard to the requirements for the maintenance and defence of certain lengths of wall calculated on the basis of one man per hide. It has been printed by Hickes[4] and Robertson.[5]

---

[1] *Die Gesetze der Angelsachsen*, ed. F. Liebermann (Halle, 1903–16) I.

[2] *LMS* I (1937), 60–4.

[3] *Ibid.* and *Anglo-Saxon Charters*, ed. A. J. Robertson, 2nd ed. (Cambridge, 1956), p. 246.

[4] *Linguarum Veterum Septentrionalium Thesaurus* I, 109.

[5] *Charters*, pp. 246 and 248.

10. *The Seasons for Fasting*

B. xi now lost; Add. 43703 257–60

Wheloc printed lines 87–94 of the poem from Otho before the fire[1] while Wanley recorded the *incipit* (1–7a) and noted that the poem was incomplete even in the undamaged manuscript.

The Nowell transcript offers the whole of what survived of the poem in Otho. It concerns the fasts of the church, especially those at Lent and on Ember days, and is incomplete, of course, breaking off after a picture of priestly non-observers of fasts. Flower's death robbed us of the edition he planned[2] and the first printed edition was that of Dobbie in 1942;[3] Dobbie prints very conservatively, leaving it to Sisam later to suggest readings of greater merit.[4]

11. *Herb Recipes*

B. xi now lost; Add. 43703 261–4

The evidence of Wheloc and Wanley shows that the recipes and leechdoms had been lost from Otho well before the Cotton fire.[5] Nowell offers a series of medicinal recipes and leechdoms, most of which occur also in the 'Læceboc', Royal 12 D. xvii. Cockayne has printed the Royal texts,[6] and Ker gives a list of those items which correspond to the ones in Nowell's transcript. Ker also gives a description of four items which occur in Nowell but not in the Royal manuscript.

We have thus to rely upon Nowell's transcript for the greater part of the Bede, (together with Wheloc's printed text) for the greater part of the Chronicle and for the greater part of the laws, almost completely for the poem, and entirely for articles 4, 7–9 and 11. Before extensive use can be made of readings gleaned from Nowell's work, however, comparison must be made with the surviving portions of Otho in order to judge the accuracy and usefulness of the transcript. I have elected the Bede text as long enough to be representative and have compared Otho B. xi 1–36 with the corresponding passages in Add. 43703; Otho B. xi 2–3 and 11–12 are rather fragmentary and have been used for their legible portions only. Otho B. xi 38, B. x 62, 55 and 58 and B. xi 37 are too fragmentary to use at all.

[1] See R. J. S. Grant, 'A Note on *The Seasons for Fasting*', RES n.s. 23 (1972), 302–4.
[2] 'Nowell and the Discovery of England', p. 73, n. 20.
[3] *The Anglo-Saxon Minor Poems*, ed. E. van K. Dobbie (New York, 1942), pp. xcii–xciv, clxx, 98–104 and 194–8.
[4] *Studies*, pp. 45–60; see also Roy F. Leslie, 'Textual Notes on *The Seasons for Fasting*', JEGP 52 (1953), 555–8. [5] See above, p. 112 and n. 4.
[6] *Leechdoms, Wortcunning, and Starcraft of Early England*, ed. O. Cockayne, Rolls Series (1864–6).

For the comparison which follows I have worked direct from the manuscript and transcript, but give page and line references to Miller's edition. I cite Otho B. xi as C, Add. 43703 as CN. The first figure in the second column is the number of occurrences of the specified change; the second figure in this column, in parentheses, is a percentage number expressing the proportion which the first figure has to the total number of occurrences of the feature concerned, wherever that proportion is meaningful. I list the changes which take place twice or more, not those which occur only once.

Change	Number of occurrences			Example
æ > a	37 (1·85)	168. 22	C	soþfæstnesse
			CN	soðfastnesse
æ > e	15 (0·75)	168. 24	C	gesælig
			CN	geselig
æ > ea	3 (0·15)	386. 7	C	sæs
			CN	seas
a > æ	60 (3·00)	246. 24	C	lare
			CN	lære
e > æ	27 (0·75)	236. 9	C	eþle
			CN	æþle
a > o	7 (0·28)	246. 17	C	gehalgad
			CN	gehalgod
o > a	8 (1·6)	308. 4	C	þegnode
			CN	þenade
a > u	3 (0·14)	238. 33	C	suna
			CN	sunu
e > a	20 (0·55)	300. 7	C	mægðe
			CN	mægða
a > e	17 (0·85)	240. 17	C	bisceophada
			CN	bisceophade
e > i	14 (0·38)	246. 22	C	ciriclecan
			CN	ciriclican
i > e	8 (0·26)	468. 8	C	ærist
			CN	æreste
e > o	3 (0·07)	296. 3	C	frefrende
			CN	frofrende
o > e	4 (0·80)	240. 5	C	Eastorlican
			CN	Easterlican
e > y	2 (0·05)	168. 10	C	gecerde
			CN	gecyrde
i > y	6 (0·2)	236. 33	C	getimbrede
			CN	getymbrede
y > i	27 (3·9)	168. 9	C	cyricean
			CN	ciricean
o > u	7 (1·4)	296. 8	C	comon
			CN	cuman
u > o	8 (1·6)	308. 14	C	abbud
			CN	abbod
y > u	4 (0·57)	344. 20	C	cyþde
			CN	cuþde

Change	Number of occurrences		Example	
a > ea	4 (0·16)	374. 5	C	lindesfarona
			CN	lindesfearona
e > ea	2 (0·05)	306. 4	C	onleasde
			CN	onleasde
e > ie	2 (0·05)	300. 1	C	uhttide
			CN	uhttidie
i > ea	3 (0·09)	480. 22	C	mihte
			CN	meahte
o > eo	5 (1·00)	236. 8	C	scolde
			CN	sceolde
y > eo	2 (0·29)	224. 8	C	gyrnfulnesse
			CN	geornfulnesse
y > ie	4 (0·57)	296. 20	C	þa gyt
			CN	þa giet
ea > e	5 (0·52)	238. 13	C	lindesfearona
			CN	lindesferona
ea > eo	4 (0·41)	246. 27	C	þeawū
			CN	þeowū
eo > ea	10 (1·3)	240. 9	C	heoldon
			CN	healdon
eo > e	4 (0·52)	478. 8	C	teoþan
			CN	tweðan
eo > io	8 (1·04)	478. 33	C	heora
			CN	hiora
ie > e	3 (3·00)	248. 11	C	hie
			CN	he
io > eo	8 (4·00)	480. 20	C	ongelþiode
			CN	ongelþeode
-an > -en	2 (0·16)	376. 26	C	heortan
			CN	heorten
-an > -on	7 (1·12)	304. 2	C	ealdan
			CN	ealdon
-on > -an	9 (2·4)	296. 8	C	comon
			CN	cuman
-an > -u	3 (0·25)	304. 16	C	in his lufan
			CN	7 his lufu
-en > -on	3 (2·3)	398. 4	C	gedruncen
			CN	gedroncon
-e > -on	2 (0·05)	222. 23	C	wære
			CN	wæron
-e > -	93	168. 10	C	gecyrde
			CN	gecyrd
- > -e	108	168. 15	C	se cyning
			CN	se cyninge
metathesis	24	168. 28	C	ægelberht
			CN	ægelbriht
þ > ð	55 (4·6)	168. 22	C	soþfæstnesse
			CN	soðfastnesse
ð > þ	93 (8·5)	168. 20	C	ða
			CN	þa
þ > h	5	476. 19	C	þrowedon
			CN	hroþedon

Change	Number of occurrences		Example	
þ > w	7	238. 27	C	þæs þe
			CN	wæs þe
th > þ	2	298. 5	C	eleutherius
			CN	eleuþerius
n > r	5	366. 31	C	ealne
			CN	ealra
r > n	2	298. 23	C	þær
			CN	þæn
r > s	2	384. 18	C	gereted
			CN	geseted
ð > d	3	302. 15	C	mægð
			CN	mægd
w > f	5	390. 23	C	wræce
			CN	fꝼæce
w > g	2	302. 25	C	hwilwendlicre
			CN	wilgendlicre
w > þ	7	404. 3	C	wriðe
			CN	þriðe
reduction	18	246. 27	C	ceaddes
			CN	ceades
doubling	23	296. 28	C	gemeted
			CN	gemetted
ꝥ > ꝥte	3 (2·00)	398. 18	C	ꝥ
			CN	ꝥte
ꝥte > ꝥ	6 (16·66)	246. 31	C	ꝥte
			CN	ꝥ
ꝥ > þæt	5 (3·12)	380. 18	C	ꝥ
			CN	þæt
þæt > ꝥ	9 (23·1)	296. 24	C	þæt
			CN	ꝥ
ge > ḡ	12 (1·2)	236. 31	C	gebohte
			CN	ḡbohte
ḡ > ge	12 (50·00)	170. 11	C	ḡwat
			CN	gewat
-æm > -ǣ	120	346. 15	C	þæm
			CN	þǣ
-am > -ā	14	344. 24	C	fram
			CN	frā
-em > -ē	3	396. 29	C	orationem
			CN	orationē
-im > -ī	109	168. 33	C	him
			CN	hī
-om > -ō	51	302. 27	C	com
			CN	cō
-um > -ū	470	168. 12	C	monigum gearum
			CN	monigū gearū
suspension	75	236. 19	C	adranc
			CN	adrāc
expansion	9	168. 8	C	ꝥisp
			CN	bisceop
abbreviation omitted	7	236. 7	C	ðoñ
			CN	ðon

Change	Number of occurrences	Example		
accent added	44	168. 8	C	on
			CN	ón
accent omitted	285	168. 20	C	wíf
			CN	wife
vowel added	38	180. 27	C	druncne
			CN	druncene
vowel omitted	42	296. 21	C	unæþelicnes
			CN	unæþlicnesse
consonant added	33	380. 3	C	gif him þ selre wære
			CN	gif hī þ selfre wære
consonant omitted	54	236. 14	C	ordfruma
			CN	ordfuma
		238. 22	C	hís
			CN	ís
word added	16	478. 32	C	Scottas þa þe breotone eardiað
			CN	Scottas þa þe in breotone eardiað
word omitted	24[1]	298. 3	C	se cyning forþferde
			CN	se cyning ferde
homoeoteleuton	4	478. 7–8	C	Ond aldwine wiccetfelda bisceope. Ond aldwulfe hrofesceastre bisceope.
			CN	Ond aldwine wiccetfelda bisceope
word-order changed	2	402. 22	C	mid þa godcundan inbryrdnesse
			CN	þa mid godcundan inbryrdnesse

It is clear that Nowell either did not know or did not care about the value of *æ*, which he often confuses with *a, e* and *ea*. This means that a phonologist might be misled by CN's *e* for C's *æ* into thinking that C shows Mercian second fronting of the short sound and at least non-West Saxon origin of the long sound. Similarly CN's *ea* for C's *æ* might misleadingly suggest back mutation, especially since the occurence of forms with this feature in the Old English Bede manuscripts is one of the reasons for assuming a Mercian original.[2] CN's *lindesfearona* for C's *lindesfarona* at 374.5 also contains a false suggestion of non-West Saxon back mutation, while the opposite change obscures genuine examples at 238.13, 300.20 and 440.10. CN's *tweodes* for C's *twides* at 360.29 seems to suggest Northumbrian tenth-century rounding of *ĕ* to *ă* after *w*, whereas it is either an attempt to 'correct' to a more acceptable Elizabethan spelling for 'the Tweed' or a form taken from another manuscript.[3] As for inflexional endings confusion of *-en, -an* and *-on* means that distinctions between indicative and subjunctive, infinitive and preterite plural and so on have been undermined. Clearly Nowell was influenced by the spelling conventions of his own time. For instance, *i* and *y*

---

[1] In one of these instances two words are omitted.
[2] See D. Whitelock, 'The Old English Bede', *Proc. of the Brit. Acad.* 48 (1962), 79, n. 6.
[3] See further E. Ekwall, *English River Names* (Oxford, 1928), pp. 421–3, *s.v.* 'Tweed'.

were interchangeable in his day, printers being particularly likely to use *y* near minims, and *ís* at 238.22 is a reflection of his pronunciation, since the *h* now pronounced in Modern English in *he*, *her*, *his* and *him* is a spelling pronunciation only, not shown in *it*.

Otho B. xi is difficult to read now after the fire, but some of the almost undamaged leaves suggest that the hands could well have caused an Elizabethan to err; for example, when Nowell reads *andan* for C's *aidan* (472.29), no one could altogether blame him. His omissions are not very many and when he failed to copy 23v–24r he acknowledged the omission in the margin. His additions are usually careless, but *in* at 478.32 (see list) may be a 'correction': how far was *eardian* transitive in Old English?

The following are examples of confusion:

304. 16	C	in his lufan	(there are three such examples)
	CN	7 his lufu	
304. 14	C	hundteontig	(three examples)
	CN	hundtweontig	
	Latin	C	
374. 14	C	teoþan	(two examples)
	CN	tweoþan	
	Latin	decimam	
364. 19	C	eowde	(two examples)
	CN	eode	
298. 1	C	Se feorða bisceop	
	CN	se wæs ða bisceop	
302. 6	C	Ond meanwara mægðe	
	CN	Ond mean þære mægðe	
302. 18	C	medmicel mynster	
	CN	mid micel mynster	
362. 18–19	C	ut of þæm mynstre gongende	
	CN	ut of þǽ mynstre godgende	
376. 9	C	begyrded	
	CN	bebyrged	
378. 19	C	ham hwearf þa wearþ he	
	CN	hā hwearf þa hwearf he	
378. 24	C	we cweþað lyftadl	
	CN	we cwelað lyʒ̵ lyftadl	
384. 21	C	Ond swa micel winter ús onhreas	
	CN	Ond swa micle winter hus onreas	
400. 2–3	C	hwylc heora swiftost hors hæfde	
	CN	hwilc heora swiþust hors hæfde	
484. 8	C	confes . . . lifes bóc	
	CN	confessor liber boc.	

Obviously Nowell is unhappy about derivatives of *teon*, such as *hundteontig* used in C to emphasize that 100 is meant and not the 'long hundred' of 120 which Nowell substitutes. *Eowan*, *eowian* and compounds also cause him difficulty, and he regularly substitutes the preterite of *gan* for their preterites. 302.18 suggests that he did not know *medmicel*.

Throughout there are changes in which Nowell seems to be trying to correct C to what he thought was standard Old English. In some instances he may have been taking other sources into account; one must remember his knowledge of a large number of texts. Some examples are:

236. 28	C	hundtwelftig hida
		twentig
	CN	hundtwelftig hida
240. 16	C	cendda
	CN	ceadda
296. 24	C	wundurlicwise
	CN	wundurlicre wise
300. 7	C	þære mægðe ᵈᵉⁱʳᵃ
	CN	ᵈᵉᵃʳᵃ þare mægða
300. 10	C	eac aedhleð
	CN	eac eadhæð
347. 7	C	wilferð
	CN	wilfrið
360. 29	C	twides streames
	CN	tweodes streames
384. 23–4	C	swiðe longe wiþ þæm winde
	CN	swið longe mid þǣ winde
474. 27–8	C	feower 7 þritig wintra
	CN	feower 7 twentig wintra

Hundtwelftig is perfectly clear in C and is clear in all the Old English Bede manuscripts and in the Latin *CXX*. Nowell may have thought it meant 112 and has 'corrected'. At 240.16 he is giving the more usual form of the name *Chad* (other MSS *Ceadda*, Latin *ceaddan*), while at 296.24 he has split a compound into its parts and has inflected the adjective quite correctly. 300.7 does not seem to me a change of word-order so much as an independent addition of information from either outside knowledge or one of the other manuscripts (T *Dera*, O *Dære*, Ca *ðære*, Latin *Derorum*); the *deira* in C is probably in L'isle's hand and thus was added after Nowell copied C. Similarly at 300.10 *Eadhæd* is the usual form in the other Old English Bede manuscripts and the Latin version. 347.7 *wilfrið* is a similar case. 384.23–4 is a false correction; all other manuscripts have *wið*. At 360.29 *Tweodes*, as I have suggested before, may reflect an Elizabethan spelling or have been taken from another manuscript (Cambridge, University Library, Kk.3.18, Miller's Ca, *tweode*). That Nowell may have consulted Ca is also suggested by 474.27–8, where B, like C, has *þrittig* but Ca reads *XXIIII* (Latin *XXXIIII*). The freedom with which manuscripts were lent and borrowed in his time would have made it perfectly possible for him to have looked at Ca, but the only other indication I have found that he may have done so is the addition of *butan* above *nemne* at 52.22; at this point Ca too has *butan* above *nemne*, while B has *butan* alone. This addition occurs on a page of CN on which some of Nowell's fake Old English passages (see above) also occur and the similarity of the ink suggests that it and they were written at the same time. Since Nowell collated his version of the Chronicle with other manuscripts, it is just possible that he at one time considered doing the same with the Bede.

On the evidence presented above it is clear that Nowell's transcript of the Bede is of no use to the student of spellings, phonology or inflections and no dialect indications can be drawn from it. C alone must be used for these purposes, fragmentary as it is. I join Sisam in lamenting Nowell's inaccuracy in these fields.[1] Yet we can reflect that very few words are omitted, homoeoteleuta are very rare and changes of word-order are few. The transcript can therefore be used as evidence for the contents and word-order of C. It shows, for example, that C did not contain the story of Furseus in book III, which is omitted also in manuscripts O and Ca. CN can indeed be used to show the relationship of the C text to the other texts of the Old English Bede.[2] On a more minor matter, we can discriminate between the interlinear and marginal additions in C which are original (copied by Nowell) and those which are by L'isle (not copied by Nowell); a check is provided on the work of the palaeographers. For instance, Nowell copies the additions at 236.12 (*þæm cyninge to fultum^e comón*), 378.2–3 (*wæron gese^{t}tende*) and 378.9 (*e^{a}can*) but not that at 378.28 (*oððe gangan ^{ne} meahte*, where *ne* is above the line, in red and in a later hand). 484.6 is interesting: C has *efenm$\not$dhte*, with *mea* corrected into *ni* with a dot over *i*, and CN has *efenmeahte*, agreeing with uncorrected C.

It can be safely assumed that Nowell brought a similar attitude to bear on the other texts he copied. This makes it possible, for instance, to resolve Dobbie's uncertainty with regard to *The Seasons for Fasting*.[3] Far from reliable in detail as Nowell is, we are ever in his debt for substantially preserving texts that otherwise would be lost.

[1] *Studies*, p. 58 and n. and p. 60.
[2] It confirms the closer connection of C with Miller's O and Ca than with his B or T. The current view of the relations between the manuscripts is given by Whitelock, 'The Old English Bede', p. 81, n. 22. Professor Whitelock tells me that she is no longer satisfied with the stemma offered in her article and intends to publish a revision which will take into account the contamination to which she refers and may no longer maintain the close relationship between T and B which is normally assumed.
[3] *Minor Poems*, p. xciv, n. 1.

Æthelwold's translation of the *Regula Sancti Benedicti* and its Latin exemplar

MECHTHILD GRETSCH

St Benedict wrote his Rule for monastic communities in the first half of the sixth century. It must have reached England in the course of the seventh century[1] and was translated into Old English prose by Æthelwold, bishop of Winchester, in about 970 at the request of King Edgar and Queen Ælfthryth.[2] Æthelwold was one of the leaders of the tenth-century Benedictine reform in England and his translation of the Rule is among his major contributions to the reform movement. Moreover the Old English Rule holds a key position in the history of the development of Old English language and literature. Manuscripts of the text must have been numerous from the tenth century to the twelfth century and even the thirteenth. Scholars like William of Malmesbury, Lawrence Nowell, John Jocelyn and Francis Junius took an interest in the Old English Rule, but, except for a chapter printed from BM Cotton Faustina A.x by Thomas Wright in 1842,[3] the text was not easily accessible until Arnold Schröer published his edition in 1885, followed in 1888 by his introduction discussing date and authorship, the relationship between the manuscripts and some linguistic points. Comparatively little work seems to have been done on the Old English Rule since then except for Rohr's Bonn Dissertation of 1912[4] and Professor Gneuss's supplement to the 1964 reprint of Schröer's edition. Rohr, in an investigation of the phonology and the inflexional morphology of the manuscripts of the Old English Rule, was able to show that the language of all of them is basically late West Saxon, while Gneuss gave a survey of what is known about the Old English Rule and the Latin Rule in Anglo-Saxon England; he also pointed out the difficulties involved in an attempt to identify or reconstruct the Latin exemplar which Æthelwold used. In this article I shall consider

---

[1] See Gneuss, 'Benediktinerregel' (for full reference, see below), pp. 264–7, and P. Hunter Blair, *The World of Bede* (London, 1970), pp. 125, 153 and 197–200.

[2] For a discussion of Æthelwold's authorship and the date of the translation, see M. Gretsch, *Die Regula Sancti Benedicti in England und ihre altenglische Übersetzung* (Ph.D. thesis, Munich, 1973), pp. 9–11.

[3] *Biographia Britannica Literaria* I (London, 1842), 441.

[4] G. W. Rohr, *Die Sprache der altenglischen Prosabearbeitungen der Benediktinerregel* (Ph.D. thesis, Bonn, 1912).

four topics which seem to me essential for our understanding of the Old English Rule:[1] the question of Æthelwold's exemplar; the relationship between the manuscripts of the Old English Rule; Æthelwold's aims and techniques in his translation; and the vocabulary of the Old English Rule, with special reference to recent research in Old English word geography.

The following are the manuscripts of the *Regula Sancti Benedicti* (RSB) in Anglo-Saxon England and of its Old English translation (OE Rule) listed chronologically and the sigla used in this article:

O   Oxford, Bodleian Library, Hatton 48
      s. viii[1]. At Worcester in the later Middle Ages. *RSB*

k   Cambridge, Trinity College o.2.30 (1134), 130r–168v
      s. x med. Probably from St Augustine's, Canterbury. *RSB*

x   Oxford, Corpus Christi College 197, 1r–105r
      s. x[2]. In Bury St Edmunds by the middle of the eleventh century but not written there. *RSB* and OE Rule

h   BM Harley 5431, 6v–106v
      c. 1000. From St Augustine's, Canterbury. *RSB*

g   Cambridge, Corpus Christi College 57, 2r–32v
      s. x/xi. From Abingdon. *RSB*

q   Cambridge, Corpus Christi College 368
      s. x/xi. Now incomplete (and misbound); ends in ch. 61. 7. *RSB*

w   Cambridge, Corpus Christi College 178, pp. 287–457
      s. xi[1]. From Worcester. *RSB* and OE Rule

i   BM Cotton Tiberius A. iii, 118r–163v
      s. xi med. From Christ Church, Canterbury. *RSB* with continuous Old English interlinear gloss

i*   BM Cotton Tiberius A. iii, 103r–105r
      (cf. *i*). Ch. 4 only of *RSB* and OE Rule

j   BM Cotton Titus A. iv, 2r–107r
      s. xi med. From Winchester? *RSB* and OE Rule

u   Wells, Cathedral Library, *s. n.*
      s. xi med. *RSB* and OE Rule; fragmentary, ch. 49–65 only, some gaps

c   Cambridge, University Library, Ll.1.14, 70r–100v
      s. xi[2]. *RSB*

s   Durham, Cathedral Library, B.IV.24, 74v–123v
      s. xi[2]. In Durham since *c.* 1100. From Christ Church, Canterbury? *RSB* and OE Rule

G   Gloucester, Cathedral Library, 35, 6v
      s. xi[2]. Fragment of ch. 4 of OE Rule

F   BM Cotton Faustina A. x, 102r–148v
      s. xii[1]. OE Rule

---

[1] This article is an attempt to draw some general conclusions from the detailed evidence presented in my Ph.D. thesis; see above, p. 125, n. 2.

WV BM Cotton Claudius D. iii

s. xiii[1]. From Wintney, Hampshire. *RSB* and early Middle English adaptation
of OE Rule

S Cambridge, University Library, Ee.2.4

s. x med. From Glastonbury? Smaragdus of St Mihiel, *Expositio in Regulam
S. Benedicti*. Now incomplete: three leaves from it are in the Bodleian Library
(Lat. th. 3)

The following editions are referred to in this article:

Die angelsächsischen Prosabearbeitungen der Benediktinerregel, ed. A. Schröer, Biblio-
thek der angelsächsischen Prosa 2, 2nd. ed. with supplement by H. Gneuss
(Darmstadt, 1964); prints OE Rule from *w u*, collates *x j F*; (cited as Schröer,
Benediktinerregel; supplement cited as Gneuss, 'Benediktinerregel')

G. Caro, 'Die Varianten der Durhamer HS. und des Tiberius-Fragments der ae.
Prosa-Version der Benediktinerregel und ihr Verhältnis zu den übrigen HSS.',
EStn 24 (1898), 161–76; collates OE Rule in *s i** with Schröer's text (in-
complete, unreliable)

Gloucester Fragments, ed. J. Earle (London, 1861); prints OE Rule from *G*

The Rule of S. Benet. Latin and Anglo-Saxon Interlinear Version, ed. H. Logeman,
Early Eng. Text Soc. o.s. 90 (London, 1888); prints *RSB* and Old English
interlinear gloss from *i*

Die Winteney-Version der Regula S. Benedicti ed. A. Schröer (Halle, 1888); prints
Middle English adaptation of OE Rule from *WV* and collates *RSB* in
x w j u with Latin text printed from *WV*

Benedicti Regula, ed. R. Hanslik, Corpus Scriptorum Ecclesiasticorum Latinorum
75; collates *RSB* in *O x h g j i* with Latin text from St Gall 914 (not always
reliable)

My study is based on Schröer's edition for the Old English text of *x w j u F*
and on the manuscripts or photographs (not on Hanslik's edition) for the
Latin text of *O k x h g q w i i* j u s c S* and for the Old English text of *i* s*.
I shall not deal with the continuous interlinear Old English gloss in *i*, which
is later than the Old English prose version and independent of it. Nor shall I
consider the few scattered Old English glosses in *k* and *g*.[1] I have adopted
the sigla used by Hanslik and have supplied the sigla for those manuscripts
not collated by him. All references to chapter and paragraph of *RSB* follow
Hanslik's numbering. Quotations from *RSB* follow *x*, the oldest extant
bilingual copy of the Rule (see below, p. 136). References to OE Rule give
page and line of Schröer's edition.

---

[1] Edited by A. S. Napier (*Old English Glosses*, Anecdota Oxoniensia Med. and Mod. Ser. 11
(Oxford, 1900), 231–2).

ÆTHELWOLD'S EXEMPLAR

In order to determine the type of text of *RSB* on which the Old English Rule is based, we have to examine the history of the Latin text. This history was more or less obscure until the publication of Ludwig Traube's pioneer study.[1] Traube distinguished three types of text:[2]

(1) The *textus purus*. This is thought to derive from Benedict's original. In 787 Charlemagne saw a manuscript at Monto Cassino which – rightly or wrongly – was considered to be Benedict's autograph[3] and asked for a copy of it. The Cassinese manuscript was later destroyed in a fire and the so-called *Aachener Normalexemplar*, which had been copied from it, is now also lost, but a copy of a transcript taken from the Aachen manuscript by two monks from Reichenau, *c*. 817, is still extant. This is St Gall, Stiftsbibliothek, 914 (*A*). Traube was the first to recognize the importance of this manuscript, and all critical editions of *RSB* which have appeared since his *Textgeschichte* are based on it. As far as we know, the *textus purus* may never have reached England during the Middle Ages.

2. The *textus interpolatus*. This recension differs considerably from the *textus purus*. It exhibits numerous omissions, additions and – what seems more important – normalizations of Benedict's Vulgar Latin forms. In all probability this recension originated in Rome around 600. It was the prevailing type of text on the continent and in England during the seventh and eighth centuries before the *textus purus* spread from Aachen. Among the English manuscripts still extant Oxford, Bodleian Library, Hatton 48 (*O*) – the oldest of all the surviving manuscripts of *RSB* – belongs to this textual tradition. There are numerous corrections in *O* which point to a second exemplar used by the Anglo-Saxon corrector and now lost. This exemplar, too, must have been a member of the *interpolatus* recension.[4] Another manuscript belonging to this textual tradition is Würzburg Mp.th.q.22, which was probably copied on the continent from an Anglo-Saxon exemplar. As we shall see, the *textus interpolatus* seems to have survived in England – although not in its original form – long after the introduction and dissemination of the *receptus* tradition.

---

[1] 'Textgeschichte des Regula S. Benedicti', *Abhandlungen der königlich bayerischen Akademie der Wissenschaften, philosophisch-philologische und historische Klasse* 21 (Munich, 1898), 601–731; 2nd ed., ed. H. Plenkers, *ibid.* 25 (1910).

[2] The essentials of Traube's findings are still accepted by most scholars, although it has since been realized that the textual history of *RSB* is even more complex than he had thought. Hanslik, in his critical edition, distinguishes four groups of texts in addition to Traube's three recensions, whereas P. Meyvaert ('Towards a History of the Textual Transmission of the *Regula S.Benedicti*', *Scriptorium* 17 (1963), 105, n. 86) advocates considering the *interpolatus* and the *receptus* recensions as one group which he calls 'contaminated'.

[3] On the question of whether this manuscript was Benedict's autograph or not, see Hanslik, *Benedicti Regula*, pp. xix–xx and Meyvaert, 'Textual Transmission', p. 87, n. 28; cf. also Meyvaert, 'Problems Concerning the Autograph Manuscript of Saint Benedict's Rule', *RB* 69 (1959), 3–21. According to both authors it is rather improbable that the Monte Cassino manuscript vas written by Benedict himself.

[4] Cf. Meyvaert, 'Textual Transmission', pp. 97–8.

3. The *textus receptus* or 'mixed' recension. This type predominated all over Europe from the middle of the ninth century down to the end of the nineteenth. It originated when, as a result of Benedict of Aniane's reform, the *textus purus* was introduced as the authoritative model in many Carolingian monasteries. It came about, we may suppose, in either or both of two ways: scribes – deliberately or inadvertantly – could have introduced readings from their accustomed text, the *interpolatus*, into the *purus* when they were copying it, or they could have corrected older *interpolatus* manuscripts with variants from the *Normalexemplar*. It is obvious that we cannot expect a uniform textual tradition in this 'mixed' recension under these circumstances, and the numerous *receptus* manuscripts do indeed show largely different mixtures of variants from the *purus* and the *interpolatus* as well as independent readings. Except for O all the extant manuscripts which were written before 1100 in England belong to the *receptus* tradition: *k x h g q w i j u c s*. They must therefore derive from exemplars which had been imported from the continent during or after the ninth century, but it is impossible to decide whether any such exemplars reached England before the Benedictine reform of the second half of the tenth century.[1]

Thus in order to determine, or reconstruct, the kind of exemplar Æthelwold used for his translation we need to know which type of text it belonged to and whether it was related to any particular extant manuscript or group of manuscripts within the type.

It is comparatively easy to answer the first question. I have examined about 150 cases[2] in which the text of *RSB* has variant readings that affect the sense and therefore ought to produce the clues we are looking for. Two examples are sufficient:

Schröer 4, 24–5   we weorðaþ heofena rices yrfeweardes
RSB Prol. 39   erimus heredes regni caelorum: *O k x h g i j c s*
        (passage omitted): *A*

Therefore *A* (representing the *textus purus*) cannot be the exemplar.

Schröer 34, 1   gemyndelice butan bec
RSB 9.10   ex corde: *A k x h g q w i j c s S*
        exinde: *O*

Therefore *O* (representing the *textus interpolatus*) cannot be the exemplar. The general result is that in about 50 per cent of all cases examined neither *A* nor *O* exhibits the Latin variant reading that was translated by Æthelwold, whereas this can always be found in one or more of the English manuscripts of the *receptus* tradition. As for the rest, the required reading is in either *A* or *O* or both, but in each case the same reading is in one or more of the

---

[1] Meyvaert (*ibid.* pp. 102–3) thinks that manuscripts of this textual tradition might have reached England as early as the ninth century.

[2] For a list of these passages, see Gretsch, *Regula*, pp. 129–56, 162–3 and 167–9.

English *receptus* manuscripts as well. Consequently Æthelwold's exemplar (or exemplars) must be sought in the *receptus* tradition.

This agrees with what we know about the textual history of *RSB*. As was mentioned above, the *textus purus* never seems to have reached medieval England. The commentary on the Rule, written by Smaragdus, abbot of St Mihiel, before 820, need not be taken into account here. Although it has been alleged that it contains the Rule in its 'pure' type,[1] an examination of Cambridge University Library, Ee.2.4 (*S*), written in England in the tenth century, shows that the text of the Rule in this manuscript differs in a striking number of cases from that of *A*, whereas it shows definite links with the English *receptus* manuscripts.[2] But on the continent, too, the *purus* recension in its uncontaminated form had only a very restricted circulation during the Middle Ages.[3] As early as the middle of the ninth century the *receptus* recension began to replace the *textus purus*. Moreover, when it would have been possible to obtain an exact copy of the *Aachener Normalexemplar* there was hardly a monastic community in England which would have been interested in one since monastic life had almost completely extinguished by the Scandinavian raids during the ninth century. Unlike the *textus purus*, the *interpolatus* recension was available in tenth-century England. But, in view of the close links between the English Benedictine reform and the continental monastic movement radiating from centres like Cluny/Fleury and Gorze/Gent, it seems improbable that Æthelwold should have based his translation on the *interpolatus* recension when the *receptus* had become the common type on the continent and had undoubtedly reached England in one or more manuscript copies. We shall return later to the *interpolatus*.

If we now look for the type of *receptus* text that Æthelwold had before him, it seems reasonable to begin with the twelve extant manuscripts written in England in the tenth and eleventh centuries. In his critical edition Hanslik reconstructs a stemma comprising all the manuscripts he used; this includes the six English manuscripts (including *O*) collated by him. He divides the five English *receptus* manuscripts into two groups, *g h i* and *j x*, believing that *w*, which is mentioned briefly but not collated, also belongs in the second group.[4] In the stemma these two groups derive from quite different lines of transmission, but within each group the manuscripts, according to Hanslik, are closely related, going back to a common ancestor for each group. For at least three reasons, however, it seems improbable that the textual relationships of the Anglo-Saxon manuscripts of *RSB* can be represented by

---

[1] Cf. Hanslik, *Benedicti Regula*, p. xxxiii.   [2] Cf. Gretsch, *Regula*, pp. 114–16.

[3] Cf. Hanslik's stemma, *Benedicti Regula*, opposite p. lxxiv.

[4] Cf. Hanslik's stemma and his introduction, *ibid.* pp. lxv–lxix. For a more detailed critical discussion of Hanslik's grouping of the English *receptus* manuscripts, see Meyvaert, 'Textual Transmission', pp. 100–3 and 110, and Gretsch, *Regula*, pp. 104–11.

means of a stemma. Firstly, only two manuscripts written before the end of the tenth century have been preserved, although *RSB* must have been extant fairly early in at least one copy in each of the approximately forty-six monasteries which existed in England after the Benedictine reform and before the Norman Conquest. Secondly, an extremely high degree of contamination by memory is to be expected in a text like *RSB*. A passage from the Rule was read aloud daily in the monasteries[1] so that probably nearly every monk knew at least parts of it by heart. Consequently a copyist might well introduce variant readings from memory into the text. Thirdly Anglo-Saxon manuscripts of *RSB* frequently exhibit alternative readings; for instance we find variants belonging to a different textual tradition written above the line.[2] This indicates that a scribe may have used more than one exemplar to copy or correct his text. Accordingly a critical examination of the texts of the Anglo-Saxon manuscripts of *RSB* reveals a considerably greater extent of contamination than Hanslik's stemma and introduction indicate. A close investigation makes it clear that, owing to the degree of contamination, it is impossible to isolate any 'family' of manuscripts or to relate such families to each other with any precision. There is an almost infinite variety of groupings, and I have not the slightest doubt that neither the stemmatic nor any other method of textual criticism can produce anything like the pattern of transmission that Hanslik envisages. Thus we have manuscript groupings with different variants like the following: O against $x\,g\,w\,j\,s$ against $k\,h\,i\,c$; $O\,g\,s$ against $k\,x\,h\,w\,i\,j\,c$; $O\,x\,g$ against $k\,h\,w\,i\,j\,u\,c\,s$; $O\,h\,g\,j\,c\,s$ against $k\,x\,w\,i$; $O\,k\,x\,w$ against $h\,q\,j\,c\,s$ against g against i; $O\,k\,x\,s$ against $h\,g\,q\,w\,i\,j\,c\,S$; and $O\,g\,q$ against $k\,x\,h\,w\,j\,c\,s$ against $i\,S$. The picture becomes even more complicated when one considers original and altered readings. However, there seem to be certain combinations of manuscripts that occur more often than others. Since a stemma could not possibly solve the problem, I have had recourse to a method of textual criticism which may seem somewhat mechanical but which, I believe, has produced some useful results. My investigation has been based on about 160 passages throughout *RSB* in which two or more Anglo-Saxon *receptus* manuscripts show variant readings that affect the sense of a sentence and on all cases of variant readings (sixty-three, excluding spelling variants) in two or more Anglo-Saxon manuscripts in chs. 5, 27–30 and 58.[3]

---

[1] Cf. *Regularis Concordia*, ed. Dom Th. Symons (London, 1953), pp. xl and 17, and J. B. L. Tolhurst, 'Introduction to the English Monastic Breviaries', *The Monastic Breviary of Hyde Abbey, Winchester VI*, Henry Bradshaw Soc. 80 (1942), 53.

[2] E.g. *RSB* 4.76 ille $x\,w\,j^0$:ipse $O\,k\,h\,g\,q\,i\,i^*\,j^1\,s$; *RSB* 7.65 caelos $O\,g\,s^0$:caelum $k\,x\,h\,q\,w\,i\,j\,s^1\,S$; and *RSB* 59.3 suspectam $k^0\,x\,h^1\,q\,w\,j\,u^1\,s$:suffectam $k^1\,h^0\,g\,i\,u^0\,S$ (^{0} = an original reading; ^{1} = a variant which was added later, but not after *c*. 1100).

[3] See above, p. 129, n. 2; the variants in chs. 5, 27–30 and 58 were taken from a critical edition of these chapters in Gretsch, *Regula*, pp. 68–87.

TABLE I. *Percentage of shared readings for all possible combinations of two manuscripts of* RSB

O g	*O s*	*O k*	*O q*	*O S*	*O j*	*O c*	*O h*	*O x*	*O i*	*O w*
64	58	57	53	49	44	43	39	36	35	34
k c	*k s*	*k q*	*k h*	*k j*	*k S*	*k w*	*k O*	*k x*	*k i*	*k g*
76	75	73	68	67	59	59	57	55	54	48
x w	*x j*	*x q*	*x k*	*x c*	*x s*	*x h*	*x S*	*x i*	*x g*	*x O*
85	73	58	55	52	52	46	40	36	36	36
h c	*h i*	*h j*	*h k*	*h s*	*h q*	*h w*	*h g*	*h x*	*h S*	*h O*
85	73	70	68	64	62	51	49	46	45	39
g O	*g s*	*g q*	*g c*	*g h*	*g k*	*g S*	*g j*	*g i*	*g w*	*g x*
64	57	52	50	49	48	46	45	45	37	36
q k	*q c*	*q j*	*q s*	*q h*	*q w*	*q x*	*q S*	*q O*	*q g*	*q i*
73	71	69	67	62	60	58	57	53	52	50
w x	*w j*	*w q*	*w k*	*w c*	*w s*	*w h*	*w S*	*w i*	*w g*	*w O*
85	77	60	59	57	54	51	45	42	37	34
i h	*i c*	*i j*	*i k*	*i s*	*i q*	*i g*	*i w*	*i S*	*i x*	*i O*
73	66	56	54	53	50	45	42	37	36	35
j w	*j c*	*j x*	*j h*	*j q*	*j k*	*j s*	*j S*	*j i*	*j g*	*j O*
77	76	73	70	69	67	65	56	56	45	44
s k	*s c*	*s q*	*s j*	*s h*	*s O*	*s g*	*s S*	*s w*	*s i*	*s x*
75	70	67	65	64	58	57	55	54	53	52
c h	*c k*	*c j*	*c q*	*c s*	*c i*	*c S*	*c w*	*c x*	*c g*	*c O*
85	76	76	71	70	66	60	57	52	50	43
S c	*S k*	*S q*	*S j*	*S s*	*S O*	*S g*	*S h*	*S w*	*S x*	*S i*
60	59	57	56	55	49	46	45	45	40	37

When I calculated the percentage of readings that each of the Anglo-Saxon manuscripts has in common with every other manuscript, I arrived at the results listed in table I.[1] From this table, as well as from the number of shared readings found only in two manuscripts and nowhere else, certain conclusions can be drawn. A close relationship is found in the groups *x w* (85 per cent of readings in common), *h c* (85 per cent) and *h i* (73 per cent). The connection between *h* and *i* is not surprising, as both come from Canterbury (*h* from St Augustine's, *i* from Christ Church). The two other manuscripts which are or may be from Canterbury, *k* and *s*, can only be joined to this 'Canterbury group' with certain reservations. Their mutual

---

[1] The two fragments *i** and *u* have not been included in table I, as the number of their comparable variant readings is considerably smaller than that of the other manuscripts, so that no reliable percentages can be calculated. Fragment *i** is too short for anything to be said about its relationship with the other manuscripts, whereas *u* seems to be linked with *j* and *g*. *S* (the Smaragdus commentary) has been included because of its definite connection with the English *receptus* manuscripts (cf. above, p. 130). Although the *textus interpolatus* cannot have been the exemplar of the translation, *O* has been included because of its interesting relationship with some of the English *receptus* manuscripts. This will be discussed later on.

relationship seems to be quite intimate (75 per cent of readings in common) but their links with *h* and *i* are not as close as those within the *h i* group. Manuscript *c* is of unknown provenance; it is therefore impossible to decide whether the intimate relationship between *h* and *c* has anything to do with a common place of origin. But it should be noted that *c* also shows a closer relationship with the (possibly) Canterbury *k*, *i* and *s* than with *x* and *w*, both of which, as we shall see, belong to a different textual tradition. Although the total of shared readings in the *h c* group is somewhat higher than that in the *h i* one, this latter group much more frequently shares a variant that does not appear in any other manuscript.[1] Consequently the relationship between *h* and *i* does not seem to be less intimate than that between *h* and *c*.

Manuscripts *x* and *w* are even more closely related to each other than either *h* and *i* or *h* and *c* are, showing as they do a very high percentage of shared readings including a considerable number of unique ones.[2] This close connection between *x* and *w* is not readily explained by the provenance of the manuscripts, as in the case of the *h i* group. Manuscript *x* comes from Bury St Edmunds but was not written there. The monastery was re-established as late as 1022 and the manuscript must have been there by the middle of the eleventh century. When Bury St Edmunds was refounded monks came from Ely to join the new community,[3] and it seems reasonable to suppose that they brought manuscripts with them. Ely had been refounded by Æthelwold and was in close contact with Winchester;[4] among other donations of the bishop the *Liber Eliensis* records that of the *manerium* of Sudbourne, which Æthelwold had received from King Edgar and his queen for his translation of the Benedictine Rule.[5] It seems possible, therefore, to associate *x* with the Latin text of the Rule as used in Winchester under Æthelwold, and a possible connection between *x* and the Winchester tradition has also been suggested by Mr T. A. M. Bishop on account of the Caroline minuscule script in this manuscript.[6] Manuscript *w*, on the other hand, comes from Worcester and was apparently written there. It has been repeatedly pointed out that there was close collaboration between Winchester and Worcester during the period of the Benedictine reform; for example, the examination of liturgical manuscripts by Professor Gneuss has revealed extensive correspondences between the texts used at Worcester and the Winchester tradition[7] and, more

---

[1] Manuscripts *h* and *c* share only one unique variant, whereas *h* and *i* share nine.
[2] Manuscripts *x* and *w* share twenty unique variants.
[3] See D. Knowles, *The Monastic Order in England. A History of its Development from the Times of St Dunstan to the Fourth Lateran Council 940–1216*, 2nd ed. (Cambridge, 1963), p. 70. See also F. Wormald, *Archaeologia* 91 (1945), 132.   [4] Knowles, *Monastic Order*, pp. 50 and 53.
[5] *Liber Eliensis*, ed. E. O. Blake, Camden 3rd ser. 92 (London, 1962), 111, and see Gneuss, 'Benediktinerregel', p. 270, n. 18.   [6] *English Caroline Minuscule* (Oxford, 1971), pp. xxi–xxii.
[7] *Hymnar und Hymnen im englischen Mittelalter*, Buchreihe der Anglia 12 (Tübingen, 1968), 70–1.

recently, Mr Bishop has shown that a Winchester–Worcester tradition in hand-writing must have developed during the second half of the tenth century, a tradition which differs considerably from that of the scripts in use at Canterbury.[1] These facts may explain why *w* is so closely linked with *x*. As *j* possibly comes from Winchester too, it is interesting to note that it has numerous readings in common both with what I would call the 'Winchester–Worcester group', *x w*, and with the Canterbury *h*. The mid-position which *j* holds between groups *x w* and *h i* might indicate that there were manuscript links between the texts used at Winchester and those used at Canterbury.

A further result of my critical examination is the evidence for a close connection between *O* (*textus interpolatus*) and *g*. They have 64 per cent of common readings, which means that of all *receptus* manuscripts *g* is by far the closest to *O*. In particular *O* and *g* show a comparatively large number of common variants which do not appear in any other manuscript. This seems to confirm Paul Meyvaert's assumption[2] that *g* is probably linked with the earlier English tradition of the *textus interpolatus*, whereas Hanslik[3] thought that the exemplar from which *g* was copied was a *receptus* manuscript imported from France (Fleury). As *s* too has numerous readings in common with *O*, it is obvious that this early English textual tradition must have survived for quite a long time after the *receptus* recension had reached England as a consequence of the Benedictine reform.

The extensive contamination of texts in the Anglo-Saxon manuscripts of *RSB* is bound to complicate the question of the type of *receptus* text that Æthelwold used for his translation. The task becomes even more difficult when we realize that Æthelwold does not normally translate word for word. In order to meet this difficulty I have examined about 120 passages[4] in *RSB* for each of which the Anglo-Saxon *receptus* manuscripts have at least two variant readings that would give a different meaning to the text or context, so that it should be possible to relate the translation of each passage to one of the variants. At first sight the result looks as confusing as that of the investigation of the textual relationships of the Anglo-Saxon manuscripts of *RSB*, as the following examples suggest:

Schröer 25, 21 – 26, 1	to beteran gecyrren
RSB 7.30	converti in melius: *O k x g q w j c s S*
	converti in melius cottidie: *h i*

Schröer 26, 9	lust
RSB 7.33	voluptas: *h g q w i j c S*
	voluntas: *O k x s*

---

[1] *English Caroline Minuscule*, pp. xxi–xxii. [2] 'Textual Transmission', p. 100.
[3] *Benedicti Regula*, p. lxvii. [4] Taken from the list in Gretsch, *Regula*, pp. 129–56.

Schröer 27, 1	geþyld
RSB 7.35	patientiam: $k \, x \, h \, w \, j \, c \, s$
	patientia: $i \, S$
	(omitted) $O \, g \, q$
Schröer 57, 3	gewealde
RSB 33.4	potestate: $h \, g \, S$
	voluntate: $O \, k \, x \, q \, w \, i \, j \, c \, s$
Schröer 91, 7	a
RSB 55.12	semper: $x \, h \, g \, w \, i \, u$
	(omitted): $O \, k \, q \, j \, c \, s \, S$
Schröer 109, 2–3	Be elðeodegum munecum hu hi mon underfon sceal
RSB 61 title	De monachis peregrinis qualiter suscipiantur: $O \, k \, x \, q \, w \, s$
	De monachis peregrinis: $h \, g \, i \, j \, c$
	De sacerdotibus monasterii: u

On closer scrutiny, however, some significant facts emerge:

(1) No Anglo-Saxon manuscript of *RSB* (including *S*, the Cambridge manuscript of Smaragdus's *Expositio*) and consequently no group of manuscripts represents the text from which Æthelwold was translating.[1]

(2) The percentage of Latin readings in each manuscript which agrees with Æthelwold's translation, calculated on the basis of the 120 passages mentioned above, is as follows:[2]

O	57·4	q	63·9	s	69·5
S	59·8	g	64·5	w	70·9
i	60·3	x	68·6	k	71·9
c	63·4	h	69·4	j	72·7

It seems remarkable that x, s, w and j are among the manuscripts closest to the translator's conjectural exemplar, that is the four manuscripts which contain the Latin text side by side with the Old English Rule. This indicates that the two texts were combined from the very beginning, when Æthelwold's translation was first copied to be sent to the reformed monasteries. Moreover we can conclude that the Latin text which accompanied the Old English version in Æthelwold's 'master copy' was largely, if not wholly, identical with the text he had used for his translation. Other readings may have crept in in the course of the transmission, which would account for those variants in $x \, w \, j \, s$ which do not correspond to the Old English rendering.

[1] This result confirms to a large extent Professor Gneuss's tentative findings ('Benediktinerregel', pp. 276–82), which were based on a few specimen variants and on only six of the *receptus* manuscripts.

[2] Fragments i^* and u have again been omitted from the list, as they are too short to provide any reliable evidence of their relationship with the translator's exemplar. According to the comparatively few variant readings which u offers, the text in this manuscript seems to be rather closely connected with that exemplar; see Gretsch, *Regula*, p. 170. But we might find a somewhat different result if u were to contain the complete text of *RSB*.

(3) We have seen that *x* and *w* must have had some kind of connection with Winchester.[1] This assumption is further supported by the fact that they are among the manuscripts with a comparatively high percentage of readings which must have been in Æthelwold's exemplar. Even more important, however, for our argument is the test of the unique readings. There are three such readings in *x* and two more in *x w*, which occur in no other extant English manuscript and on which the corresponding passages in the Old English translation must have been based. No other English manuscript which is closely related to the Old English version (*k h j s*) has any unique reading which is represented in the translation.

(4) As even those Anglo-Saxon manuscripts that are closest to the Old English translation have a considerable number of readings that do not correspond to the Old English, we might look for the exemplar – or something very near it – on the continent, in particular France which seems to have provided numerous books for the Old English Reform movement in the tenth century. Fleury must have been the spiritual centre from which Æthelwold drew a great deal of support. Among the manuscripts collated by Hanslik there is one written at Fleury at the end of the ninth century and exhibiting the *textus receptus*.[2] When we compare the readings of this manuscript with the Old English translation we find that it has 73·8 per cent of those variants that must have been in the translator's exemplar, a percentage slightly higher than that of any English manuscript. This result accords with what we know about the transmission of other texts and the relationship between Fleury and Winchester in general.[3] Professor Gneuss has pointed out that the use of hymns in the Winchester tradition and in the *Regularis Concordia* (whose authorship has been attributed to Æthelwold) follows the regulations of Fleury, whereas the usage of the Canterbury tradition shows closer links with Gorze (Gent). We also have definite evidence that a liturgical sequence which had been especially written for the monastery of Fleury was in use at Winchester.[4] After all this it would seem time to end our doubts about the well-known remarks in *De Abbatibus Abbendoniae*: 'Fecit [Æthelwold] etiam venire [to Abingdon] regulam Sancti Benedicti a Floriaco monasterio.'[5]

5. We cannot exclude the possibility that there was no single exemplar for the Old English Rule. Æthelwold could have based his translation on

[1] See above, pp. 133–4.
[2] Orléans, Bibl. municipale, 273 (322).
[3] See M. B. Parkes, 'The Manuscript of the Leiden Riddle', *ASE* 1 (1972), 217 and n. 3.
[4] See *Hymnar und Hymnen*, pp. 73–4; *Analecta Hymnica Medii Aevi*, ed. G. M. Dreves, C. Blume and H. M. Bannister (Leipzig, 1886–1922) XL, 9 and 150.
[5] *Chronicon Monasterii de Abingdon*, ed. J. Stevenson, Rolls Series (1858), II, 278; cf. Dom Th. Symons, 'Some Notes on English Monastic Origins', *Downside Rev.* 80 (1962), 61–5, and Meyvaert, 'Textual Transmission', p. 103, n. 82.

several Latin manuscripts from which he selected the readings that seemed best to him. If this was so, we need not be surprised at our failure to discover a text that corresponds to Æthelwold's exemplar, and it would be useless to look for such a text in continental manuscripts. But even then, I think, the relationship the Old English Rule has to *x w j s* and the relationship it has to the Fleury manuscript remain significant.

THE MANUSCRIPTS OF THE OLD ENGLISH RULE

The text of the Old English Rule, as we have it now, poses similar problems concerning the history of its transmission and the relationship of the manuscripts. Here we are mainly concerned with two questions: whether the translation was originally intended for a monastery or for a convent and whether Schröer's stemma (see fig. 8) satisfies the standards of modern textual criticism.[1]

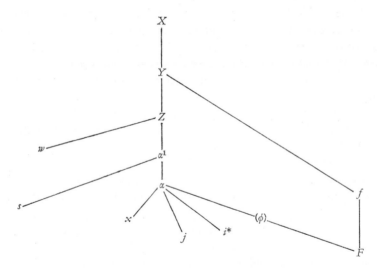

FIG. 8 Schröer's stemma of the manuscripts of the Old English Benedictine Rule

For whom was the translation originally intended?

Schröer was convinced that Æthelwold's translation had originally been intended for monasteries (*X*), that it had then been adapted for use in nunneries (*Y*) and that finally it had been rewritten yet again in a form suitable for monks (*Z*). According to him all the extant manuscripts derive through *Z* from *Y*. But, as he himself admits, on this view there is no

---

[1] The stemma has been taken from Schröer, *Benediktinerregel*, p. xxxiv; it has been supplemented in accordance with Caro's suggestions concerning the position of *i** and *s* in the transmission.

conclusive evidence for the original existence of X. While some scholars, somewhat uncritically, have accepted Schröer's hypothesis,[1] others, from a rather early date, have taken his evidence to mean that the translation was first written not for monasteries but for a nunnery or nunneries.[2] After all, if a 'masculine' original had existed, it seems most unlikely that all the extant manuscripts, each of them representing a 'masculine' version, should go back to a 'feminine' adaptation of this original. Manuscript x, for example, was written within ten or twenty years of the composition of the Old English Rule and it is difficult to see why the original 'masculine' version, if there was such a thing, should not have been available at this time or, come to that, when w, j and s were written in the eleventh century, since far more copies for men's houses (about forty) must have been produced than for nuns' houses (about half a dozen).[3] Thus, if all manuscripts can indeed be shown to derive from a 'feminine' version, it seems reasonable to suppose that this version was the original one.

Unlike the idea of the 'masculine' original which preceded a 'feminine' adaptation, Schröer's second hypothesis – the derivation of all extant manuscripts from a version for nuns – has never been challenged. Schröer supported this theory with a number of readings in x w j u, which, in his view, are traces of such a version.[4] After examining these, however, I consider that they do not afford sufficient proof for his claim.[5] Nor is there any other evidence in addition to that listed by him which indicates such a common source for all our manuscripts. Nevertheless it is clear that there was an Old English version written for nunneries. This cannot be concluded, as one might suppose it could, from WV, the early Middle English version written for the Cistercian nunnery at Wintney in Hampshire, since, although this is adapted for the use of nuns, Schröer[6] himself has shown that it goes back to an Old English exemplar which belongs to the tradition of the 'masculine' version. There is, however, conclusive evidence for the existence of an Old English 'feminine' version in F, which contains, just as the other MSS do, a text of the Old English Rule for monks, but with numerous traces of a 'feminine' exemplar. It can be shown, for instance, that a large number of feminine forms of the personal pronouns have been partly erased

[1] Cf. R. Wülker (1885), G. Caro (1898), G. W. Rohr (1912), K. Malone (1948), C. L. Wrenn (1967); for full references, see Gretsch, *Regula*, p. 181, n. 4.

[2] Cf. S. A. Brook (1898), W. Keller (1900), J. A. Robinson (1923), R. W. Chambers (1932), P. S. Ardern (1951), D. Knowles (1963) and H. Gneuss (1964); for full references, see Gretsch, *Regula*, pp. 182–3, nn. 5–11. Brook and Keller thought that the translation was originally made for the Nunnaminster at Winchester.

[3] See Gneuss, 'Benediktinerregel', pp. 273–4.

[4] This was confirmed by Caro (*EStn* 24, 162) for some of the corresponding passages in s.

[5] Neither does s show traces of a 'feminine' version in the corresponding passages; see Gretsch, *Regula*, pp. 184–94.

[6] *Wintney-Version*, p. xiv.

and changed into masculine forms.[1] Moreover, chs. 1 and 62 in *F* differ from those in all the other manuscripts in having been adapted specifically for the situation in nuns' houses.[2] This manuscript therefore leaves no doubt that there was a version of the Old English Rule for use in nunneries in the tenth century or the eleventh. This is not surprising in view of the significance of this text and of what we know about the knowledge of Latin among nuns in the Middle Ages. It remains, however, to ask which of the two versions was the original one or whether, perhaps, there were two versions from the very beginning.

As has been said before, there is no clue in the manuscripts themselves that would indicate priority of the 'feminine' version. Indeed it seems unlikely that *F*, which is the latest of all the manuscripts, should be the closest to the original. It is true, though, that *F* seems to preserve an older tradition in being the only manuscript to contain Æthelwold's *Historical Postscript*, an account of the English Benedictine reform.[3] But an examination of the text of the Old English Rule in *F* has shown that it has a considerable number of unique variant readings which cannot possibly be original. On the other hand there is no definite proof for the hypothesis that the original translation was identical with the 'masculine' version, although the manuscript transmission would seem to speak for this. The two versions of chs. 1 and 62 might suggest that Æthelwold himself produced a translation for monks as well as one for nuns, particularly since there are no apparent stylistic differences between the versions of these chapters. The *Liber Eliensis* (II. 37) reports that both King Edgar and Queen Ælfthryth commissioned Æthelwold to translate the Rule, which strengthens the case for a double version right from the start, since we know from the *Regularis Concordia* that Edgar was responsible for men's monasteries while Queen Ælfthryth was the patron of the nunneries.[4] But there is no other evidence for the theory that there were two parallel versions written by Æthelwold at or about the same time and the question for whom he translated *RSB* must therefore remain open.

[1] E.g. *he* from *heo*: 13.10, 26.17, 30.4, 31.7 and 31.10; *se* from *seo*: 30.12; and *hys* from *hyre*: 27.2, 46.16 and 49.6.

[2] For the somewhat complicated details see Gretsch, *Regula*, pp. 196–8.

[3] Printed under the title 'Eadgars Establishment of Monasteries', *Leechdoms, Wortcunning and Starcraft of Early England*, ed. T. O. Cockayne, RS (1864–6), III, 432–45. King Edgar's rôle in the reform movement is emphasized. Most scholars are agreed that Æthelwold is the author; see the references Gretsch, *Regula*, pp. 41–2. Recently D. Whitelock ('King Edgar's Establishment of Monasteries', *Philological Essays. Studies in Old and Middle English Language and Literature in Honour of Herbert Dean Meritt*, ed. J. L. Rosier (The Hague, 1970), pp. 125–36) has shown that there is so much agreement in phraseology and vocabulary between the *Postscript* and the Old English Rule that this may almost be taken as proof of Æthelwold's authorship.

[4] Cf. *Regularis Concordia*, p. 2, and see also 'Eadgars Establishment of Monasteries', ed. Cockayne, p. 440.

Schröer's stemma

Schröer based his edition on w for two reasons: he thought that w was written at about the same time as x and that the original text was preserved much more reliably in w than in any other manuscript. It[1] seems certain that he was wrong on the first point. Dr Ker dates w to the first half of the eleventh century and x to the second half of the tenth century:[2] x is therefore by far the oldest of the surviving manuscripts. As to the second claim, a critical examination of the texts has shown that this is not tenable either: Schröer's assumption that w has a striking number of variant readings which must be considered original does not prove true. In most of the passages which he cites as evidence w exhibits either plain errors or unique variants which cannot have been original. As we shall see, w presents neither the best nor the most original text. The following tables are based on an investigation of about 900 words or passages for which there is a significant variant reading in any of the extant manuscripts. Table 2 shows the total number of cases in which a manuscript has a unique variant or a group of manuscripts share a variant. It is noticeable that all combinations that could occur within a total of five manuscripts appear rather frequently. Table 3 shows what percentage of the variants each manuscript shares with each of the other manuscripts. Among the 900 or so variants examined, the individual manuscripts present the following number of scribal errors: x 32 (8); w 55 (39); j 63 (38); s 26 (18); F 63 (57). (The numbers in parentheses show how many of the errors are unique.) Thus w has a considerably larger number of errors and isolated variants (which cannot be original) than x. As compared with all other manuscripts, however, x is obviously the closest to the original. It has the fewest unique readings and (apart from s, which we shall discuss presently) the fewest scribal errors. Moreover each of the other manuscripts consistently shares more variants with x than with any other manuscript.

The value of Schröer's edition is not, however, seriously impaired by the fact that he chose w as his basic manuscript, since he offers a comprehensive and reliable critical apparatus, which even records all the spelling variants.[3] Moreover w is the second oldest manuscript and contains a text which is much closer to the original than that in any of the later j, s and F, as has become clear from the examination of these texts. It seems particularly important in this respect that x and w are closely related to each other, sharing 82·9 per cent of the variant readings, a figure which is not reached by any

---

[1] For Schröer's view of the textual relationships between the manuscripts, see *Benediktinerregel*, pp. xxviii-xli, and cf. the detailed discussion Gretsch, *Regula*, pp. 200–34.

[2] *Catalogue of Manuscripts Containing Anglo-Saxon* (Oxford, 1957), nos. 41 and 353.

[3] Only scribal variation between $þ$ and $ð$ has not been recorded.

TABLE 2

Unique variants		Shared variants					
		2 MSS		3 MSS		4 MSS	
s	450	*j s*	31	*x w j*	63	*x w j F*	338
F	165	*x w*	21	*x w F*	42	*x w j s*	133
j	149	*x j*	19	*x w s*	27	*x w s F*	84
w	82	*w F*	18	*x j F*	25	*x j s F*	70
x	24	*j F*	9	*x j s*	24	*w j s F*	13
		s F	8	*x s F*	19		
		x F	7	*w s F*	11		
		x s	7	*j s F*	11		
		w j	6	*w j s*	5		
		w s	6	*w j F*	4		

TABLE 3

x w	82·9	*w x*	82·9	*j x*	74·7	*F x*	70·7	*s x*	40·4
x j	74·7	*w F*	65·0	*j w*	64·6	*F w*	65·0	*s j*	33·0
x F	70·7	*w j*	64·6	*j F*	56·8	*F j*	56·8	*s w*	32·7
x s	40·4	*w s*	32·7	*j s*	33·0	*F s*	26·1	*s F*	26·1

other combination of two manuscripts. This close relationship is the more remarkable as there are similarly close links between the Latin texts in these manuscripts. We have therefore conclusive proof that *x* and *w* belong to one and the same line of transmission, which presumably points back to Winchester, the place of origin of the translation. This connection with Winchester as well as the early date of these manuscripts may provide a further explanation for the fact that they both offer us the best text of the Old English Rule. Their close links contradict Schröer's opinion that *j* is nearest to *x*, and that *F* is nearest to *w*. Again he is wrong to claim that the text in *F* is nearly as original as that in *w* – drawing a direct line between *F* and one of the hyparchetypes of his 'feminine' version – since *F* has a striking number of isolated variant readings[1] and scribal errors. Obviously contamination increases with the span of time between the original translation and the date of the particular manuscript. This is indicated by the considerably larger number of unique variants in each of the later manuscripts and by the fact that the relationship between two manuscripts becomes less intimate the later they were written.[2]

[1] The numerous cases where *F* shows traces of an exemplar written for nuns have not been included in the number of 165 unique variant readings in *F* recorded in table 2.

[2] Cf., e.g., the percentage of common readings in group *x w* as opposed to groups *j F* and *s F*.

Manuscript *s* holds a peculiar position within the transmission in having by far the largest number of unique readings but the fewest errors. Caro[1] assigns to this manuscript a place in Schröer's stemma which would give it an intermediate position between *w* and *x j F*, since, according to him, it has preserved a considerable number of original readings together with many readings shared with *x j F*. Placing *s* in such a position is unacceptable, not only because Caro's argument is based on Schröer's unreliable stemma but also because his collation of the manuscript and his investigation are so incompetent and sloppy. Caro did not recognize that *s* contains a carefully revised text; it should be pointed out, however, that the revision was of a far more limited kind than that in *u*, which to all intents and purposes could be called a new version. At any rate it is due to a reviser that *s* has such an astonishing number of unique readings while being almost completely free from mistakes. Particularly striking are the many changes in style and sentence structure intended to make the meaning of a passage more lucid.[2] Frequently, however, the changes consist only in a rearrangement of word-order made for no apparent reason.[3] Occasionally the reviser seems to have gone back to the Latin text when making a change.[4] More often, however, his revised passages differ from the corresponding text in the other manuscripts in giving a freer rendering of the Latin original.[5] We can therefore assume that he did not aim at producing a version closer to the Latin Rule than that made by Æthelwold. Owing to the numerous changes *s* has a comparatively low percentage of variants shared with each of the other manuscripts, even with *x*, which seems the closest (only 40·4 per cent of the 900 or so readings). Although the percentage of variants shared between *s* and *j* is only 33 per cent, there seems to be a closer link between these two manuscripts than between *s* and *x*, as *s* and *j* share a striking number of variants which are unique to them as well as a few mistakes which do not occur elsewhere.

When we consider all this evidence, there cannot be the slightest doubt that Schröer's stemma and Caro's supplement to it do not correspond to the facts. Schröer realized that drawing up a stemma was problematic in view

---

[1] *EStn* 24, 163–4.

[2] E.g. (Schröer 6, 1–2) þæt we hine geefenlæcende mid geþylde earfeþa and eahtnesse þolien *x j F [passage omitted from w]*:þæt we hine geefenlæcan mid geþylde and earfoþa and ehtnesse þolien *s*:(RSB Prol. 50) passionibus Christi per patientiam participemur; and (Schröer 55, 19–20) þæt nænig sy gedreued, ne geunrotsige [geunrotsige *x w j F*, geunrotsod *s*] on Godes huse:(RSB 31.19) ut nemo perturbetur neque contristetur in domo dei.

[3] E.g. (Schröer 27, 12) on þysum eallum *x w j F*:on eallum þisum *s*.

[4] E.g. (Schröer 72, 19–20) swa þæt he þa getimbrige and no ne gedrefe þa, ðe hine gehyrað *x w j F*:swa þæt he þa getimbrige, ðe hine geherað *s*:(RSB 47.3) ut aedificentur audientes.

[5] E.g. (Schröer 16, 20) arweorðian *x w i* j G [passage omitted from F]*:lufian *s*:(RSB 4.8) honorare; and (Schröer 20, 4) gefolgiað *x w j [passage omitted from F]*:gefyllað *s*:(RSB 5.8) sequuntur.

of the importance and wide circulation of the text, but the extent of textual contamination is far greater than he was willing to believe. It is probable that each of the forty-six monasteries in existence after the Benedictine reform owned at least one copy of the Old English Rule; yet only two (*x* and *w*) written before the middle of the eleventh century still exist; all the others were written in the later eleventh and twelfth centuries. It seems therefore quite unrealistic to try to base a stemma on this fragmentary transmission and we must content ourselves with ascertaining the relationship of the individual manuscripts to each other.[1]

ÆTHELWOLD'S AIMS AND TECHNIQUES

Literary historians and editors have said very little about the principles that guided Æthelwold in his translation, about the particular techniques and devices he employed and about the overall quality – possibly deficiencies – of his work. These questions are of interest mainly for two reasons: we would like to know something about Æthelwold's knowledge of Latin and his aptitude as a translator, and this in turn would also tell us something about the state of learning in late-tenth-century England or at least at the school of the Old Minster in Winchester. We would also like to know what Æthelwold had in mind when he translated the Rule; his work may be able to tell us something about his audience and about his intentions.

When we attempt a stylistic comparison of the Old English Rule and the Latin original[2] we are struck by the numerous additions Æthelwold introduced. Usually they are fairly brief, ranging from a few words to a few lines. They are particularly frequent in places where the Rule deals with fundamental questions of monastic life, such as the rank and dignity of the members of a monastic community as opposed to conditions in secular life; the precedence that the *opus dei* should take over all other occupations; the monastic vows of obedience, poverty and humility; or the duty of the monastic

---

[1] Schröer does not assign a place in his stemma to *u* because this manuscript offers a completely revised text of the Old English Rule. The manuscript with which *u* has the highest percentage of readings in common is again *x*, but there also seems to be a closer connection between *s* and *u*, as both manuscripts rather frequently share a variant reading which cannot be found in any other manuscript. The *i** and *G* fragments are too short for anything definite to be said about their relationships with the other manuscripts. Each of these fragments has a striking number of unique variants. These might indicate that ch. 4 of the Old English Rule had an even more complicated and widely ramified textual transmission than that of the complete translation. This chapter, with its laconic instructions for the pious conduct of life, was included in manuscripts with miscellaneous contents of a religious nature. In both the manuscripts in question it is found among lives of saints, homilies and prayers of various kinds.

[2] For a more detailed discussion of Æthelwold's translation technique see Gretsch, *Regula*, pp. 235–306.

community to care for the poor.[1] They also take the form of explanatory remarks where Benedict's Latin instructions are not quite clear and easily understandable.[2] There are also frequent explanations of biblical quotations and metaphorical expressions.[3] By far the most numerous additions, however, are of a pleonastic nature, expanding and repeating an idea which had already found sufficiently clear expression in the Latin. While some of these have an antithetical structure, which lends forcefulness and precision to the text, most of them have no particular stylistic effect and leave the impression of a certain diffuseness.[4] Æthelwold seems to have endeavoured to make his translation understandable for every member of a monastic house, including those who had had very little education; and in so doing he may have preferred understandability attained through repetition and explanation to stylistic elegance. This is why all his additions tend to interpret and explain the Latin original. There is not a single case in which the sense of the original has been changed.

The interpretative character of the additions makes one suspect that Æthelwold might have used a commentary on the Rule. Two such commentaries existed at the time. One of these is the *Expositio in Regulam S. Benedicti* by Smaragdus of St Mihiel,[5] which was written before 820 in connection with the reform movement instigated by Benedict of Aniane and was available in England at the time of the tenth-century Benedictine reform, as can be seen from *S*. The other, by Hildemar, a Frankish monk, was composed in about 840 at the monastery of Civate on Lake Como, where Hildemar's

---

[1] Thus we find a rather lengthy addition in the following passage dealing with the rank and dignity of the monks: (*RSB* 2.16) Non ab eo [i.e. ab abbate] persona in monasterio discernatur; (Schröer 12, 7–10) Ne sie fram abbode hada toscead on mynstre gehealden, *þæt is ne sy nan fram him geweorðad for gebyrdum oððe for ylde oþþe for ænigum oþrum þingum, butan for Godes ege anum and for soþes wisdomes gesceade.* The importance of the *opus dei* is stressed: (*RSB* 43.3) Ergo nihil operi dei praeponatur; (Schröer 68, 4–6) Ne sy nan ðing geset toforam þam Godes weorce, *ne nan ðing swa besorh, þæt he his tidsang fore forlæte.*

[2] Thus Benedict demands that the monk who comes late to the divine service should stand in a separate place: (*RSB* 43.6) usque dum completo opere dei publica satisfactione paeniteat. The Old English translation describes this atonement in more detail; cf. (Schröer 68, 13–16) and geendedum tidsancge openlice hreousigende bete, *ðæt is, astrecce hine æt þæs tidsanges ende and mid þære gesewenlican dædbote his gymeleaste eaðmodlice gebete.*

[3] Cf. the following passage, where Æthelwold explains the metaphorical language of a biblical quotation: (*RSB* 2.15) Qui in fratris tui oculo festucam videbas, et in tuo trabem non vidisti (Matthew VII.3); (Schröer 12, 3–6) 'þu gesawe gehwæde mot on þines broðor eage and ne gesawe þone mæstam cyp on þinum agenum eagan.' *þæt is on andgite: þu asceonudest þa læstan gyltas on þine gingran and þa mæstan noldest on þe sylfne.*

[4] Cf. the following passages; in the first the pleonastic addition has an antithetical structure, whereas in the second it is stylistically awkward: (*RSB* 4.49) in omni loco deum se respicere pro certo scire; (Schröer 18, 1–2) he sceal geþencan, *þæt he nahwer Gode dygle ne bið*, ac he hine æghwær gesihþ; and (*RSB* 48.21) Neque frater ad fratrem iungatur horis incompetentibus; (Schröer 74, 22–3) Ne nan broðor wið oþerne ne þeode, *ne mid his geþeodrædenne ne lette* on unþæslicum timan.

[5] Ed. Migne, *Patrologia Latina* 102, cols. 689–932.

pupils wrote down what they had been taught by him about the Rule. This exposition is extant in three recensions one of which has been erroneously ascribed to Paul the Deacon.[1] We do not know if Hildemar's commentary was available to the English reformers; at any rate no extant manuscript of any of the versions of this work was written in Anglo-Saxon England. Comparing Æthelwold's additions with these Latin commentaries is made rather difficult by the relative brevity of the relevant passages in the translation, whereas Smaragdus and Hildemar expound the Rule in a detailed and lengthy manner. There are, nevertheless, a number of cases in which Æthelwold's explanation corresponds to the interpretation that the commentaries provide for the same passage. Such correspondences are of various kinds. Frequently Æthelwold's addition only vaguely resembles the wording of the commentators, but there are also a number of fairly exact agreements which cannot be due to chance. There seem to be particularly close links with the Smaragdus, as can be seen from the following example (my italics):

RSB 7.42: Sed et praeceptum domini in adversis et inuriis per patientiam adimplentes, qui percussi in maxillam praebent et aliam, auferenti tunicam dimittunt et pallium, angariati miliario vadunt et duo

Schröer 27, 20 – 28, 8: Ge eac þurh Godes gebod earfeþa and teonrædena mid geþylde forberað, þæs halgan godspelles cwide gefyllende, þe þus cleopað: 'þonne þu geslegen sie on an gewenge, wænd þæt oðer to; ðam þe þine tunecan þe benæme, læt þinne wæfels to; geneadod to anre mile gange, gang willes twa'; *ðæt is on andgite: Se went oþer hleor to sleandum, se þe god deþ þæm, þe him yfeles uþe, se þe bletsað þæne, þe hine wyrigde, he læt þa hacelan to þæm, þe hine tunecan benæmbe, se gæð sylfwilles twa mila, to anre geneadod, þonne he bið oferswiðed fram þam yfelan, he gewænt þane yfelan to gode.*

Smaragdus, cols. 820–1: Hanc alii justitiae doctores interpretati sunt sententiam. Beatus vero Benedictus tantum ut hoc in loco humilitatis et patientiae nobis daret exemplar, posuit illam, quam qui in adversis et in injuriis veraciter implere conatus fuerit, ad aeternitatis culmen ascendere cito poterit. Nam nullus hanc implere perfecte poterit, nisi qui prius grandis patientiae fundamentum in corde radicaverit, et summae humilitatis prius culmen attigerit. *Qui enim in injuriis irrogatis non reddit malum pro malo,* ille maxillam percutienti unam praebet et aliam. *Ille qui maledictum non reddit pro maledicto,* auferenti tunicam dimittit et pallium. *Ille qui non vincitur a malo, sed vincit in bono malum,* angarianti milliario voluntarie pergit duo.

[1] Cf. W. Hafner, 'Paulus Diaconus und der ihm zugeschriebene Kommentar zur Regula S. Benedicti', *Commentationes in Regulam S. Benedicti,* ed. B. Steidle, Studia Anselmiana 42 (Rome, 1957), 347–58, and Hafner, *Der Basiliuskommentar zur Regula S. Benedicti. Ein Beitrag zur Autorenfrage karolingischer Regelkommentare,* Beiträge zur Geschichte des alten Mönchtums und des Benediktinerordens 23 (Münster, 1959). For comparison with Æthelwold's translation the edition by R. Mittermüller has been used: *Vita et Regula SS. P. Benedicti una cum Expositione Regulae a Hildemaro Tradita* (Regensburg, 1880).

Hildemar covers several pages with his comments on this passage, but, as in other cases, there is not such a noticeable correspondence between his exposition and Æthelwold's addition. It seems justifiable to conclude from this and similar examples that Æthelwold used Smaragdus's *Expositio* for some of his additions and that he may have used it for a number of others.[1] It is not impossible that he also utilized the Hildemar, but this is not very likely.

Next to the frequent additions we notice the numerous double translations of Latin verbs, nouns and adjectives.[2] These doublets in Æthelwold's Rule, however, do not serve the same purpose as the tautological pairs of words in Old English interlinear versions and some prose translations of the period of King Alfred. In these they are usually employed because the translator thinks he cannot adequately reproduce the sense of a Latin word by means of a single Old English one. Æthelwold on the other hand uses doublets for stylistic reasons. This can be deduced from the fact that there are hardly any such pairs in which one or both expressions are loanwords, loan translations or semantic loans, whereas doublets with loans are frequent in other Old English texts.[3] It is also interesting that doublets often occur in the additions, where they cannot have been caused by an attempt to render a difficult word in the Latin. We can assume therefore that Æthelwold was employing doublets in order to express thoughts and facts as clearly and forcefully as possible by means of a suitable rhetorical device.[4] The use of these pairs of words and the employment of explanatory additions are therefore based on the same stylistic principle.

Omissions of words, phrases and sentences found in the Latin original are rare in Æthelwold's translation and in most cases may be mere slips.[5]

[1] Further examples in which Æthelwold may have used Smaragdus's *Expositio* are: Schröer 12, 5–6 = Smaragdus, col. 734 (Hildemar, pp. 99–100); Schröer 12, 15 – 13, 2 = Smaragdus, col. 735 (Hildemar, pp. 101–2); Schröer 28, 16 = Smaragdus, col. 821 (Hildemar, pp. 246–7); Schröer 32, 14–16 = Smaragdus, cols. 829–30 (Hildemar, pp. 278–9); Schröer 66, 19 – 67, 2 = Smaragdus, cols. 878–9 (Hildemar, p. 455); Schröer 105, 20 – 107, 2 = Smaragdus, col. 907 (Hildemar, p. 554).

[2] Cf. (*RSB* 2.7) utilitatis:(Schröer 11, 2) note and nytwyrðnesse; (*RSB* 27.8) erraverat:(Schröer 51, 18–19) losode and dwelede; and (*RSB* 45.1) maiori vindictae:(Schröer 71, 7–8) stiðran and teartran steore.

[3] Cf. H. Gneuss, *Lehnbildungen und Lehnbedeutungen im Altenglischen* (Berlin, 1955), pp. 30–1.

[4] The use of tautological pairs of words for stylistic and rhetorical purposes has also been noticed in several other Old English writers, e.g. Wulfstan (see D. Bethurum, *The Homilies of Wulfstan* (Oxford, 1957), pp. 90–1) and Bishop Werferth and the translator of the Old English Bede (see Fijn van Draat, 'The Authorship of the Old English Bede. A Study in Rhythm', *Anglia* 39 (1916), 319–46). In the case of the Bede translator, however, it has also been claimed that the frequent doublets go back to the practice of interlinear glossing (see S. M. Kuhn, 'Synonyms in the Old English Bede', *JEGP* 46 (1947), 168–70; but see D. Whitelock, 'The Old English Bede', *Proc. of the Brit. Acad.* 48 (1962), 58–9).

[5] Cf., e.g. (*RSB* 16.2) Qui septenarius *sacratus* numerus:(Schröer 40, 5) ðæt seofonfealde getæl; and (*RSB* 23.2) hic secundum domini nostri praeceptum ammoneatur semel et secundo *a senioribus suis*:(Schröer 48, 6–7) þes þyllica æfter Godes gebode sy dyhlice mid wordum tuwa oððe þriwa gemyngod.

It is possible, however, that some are due to textual corruption in the early stages of transmission. Some others may have been caused by gaps in the Latin exemplar of the translator. Only a very few omissions – most of them in ch. 2 – may have been made deliberately, in consideration of the audience for whom the Rule was translated. This audience has been quite clearly defined by Æthelwold himself.[1] According to him the translation of the Rule was meant for English monks (or nuns) with little or no education, those who had no Latin and who therefore would hardly have qualified for the office of abbot (or abbess), since St Benedict himself demands that the abbot should bring a certain amount of education and reading to his task. Therefore some passages in ch. 2 dealing with the duties and qualities expected of an abbot may have been omitted because they were of no special interest to uneducated monks.[2] But even here the number of omissions is too small for us to draw definite conclusions as to Æthelwold's intentions. Considering the fact, however, that Æthelwold expands that part of ch. 2 concerned with the ranks and dignities of the individual monks,[3] we may suppose that the omissions in the same chapter would not have come about by chance.

Completely free translations of Latin words or passages are not very frequent. In some places, where the Old English is not more than a paraphrase of the Latin text, the explanation can be found in an elliptical or difficult hypotactical construction in the Latin.[4] Paraphrasing like this, however, rarely leads to a change of sense. Most of the cases in which the meaning of the original has been changed can be attributed to the translator's negligence. In only two places does the Latin exemplar seem to have been misunderstood.[5] That there are just these two instances is proof of Æthelwold's excellent knowledge of Latin – a knowledge that could not always be expected from a translator, as can be seen from the long list of mistakes collected by Hecht from Bishop Werferth's translation of Gregory's *Dialogues*.[6] Although freely paraphrased expressions and passages in the Old English Rule are not very numerous, Æthelwold does not depend

---

[1] See 'Eadgars Establishment of Monasteries', ed. Cockayne, p. 442.

[2] Cf., e.g., (*RSB* 2.39–40) et ita timens semper futuram discussionem pastoris de creditis ovibus cum de alienis cavet ratiociniis, redditur de suis sollicitus; et cum de monitionibus suis emendationem aliis subministrat, ipse efficitur a vitiis emendatus. This passage is omitted from the Old English Rule; see Schröer 14, 20. The other omissions are found in the following places: *RSB* 2.31–2 = Schröer 14, 4–10; *RSB* 2.33–4 = Schröer 14, 11–12; and *RSB* 46.6 = Schröer 72, 6–7; see Gretsch, *Regula*, p. 272 and n. 64.

[3] Cf. *RSB* 2.16 = Schröer 12, 7–10; *RSB* 2.18 = Schröer 12, 13–14; and *RSB* 2.18 = Schröer 12, 15–13, 2.

[4] Cf, e.g., *RSB* 1.3–5 = Schröer 9, 5–9; and *RSB* 46.1–4 = Schröer 71, 13 – 72, 3.

[5] (*RSB* 43.2) fomitem, cf. Schröer 67, 20 – 68, 4; and (*RSB* 59.5) usu fructuario, cf. Schröer 103, 19 – 105, 1.

[6] *Bischof Wærferths von Worcester Übersetzung der Dialoge Gregors des Grossen*, ed. H. Hecht, Bibliothek der angelsächsischen Prosa 5 (Leipzig–Hamburg, 1900–7), II, 99–121.

narrowly on his exemplar. His aim was to write clear and fluent English prose and he keeps closely to the original as long as he can fulfil this purpose by means of a literal translation. On the other hand he does not hesitate to translate more freely if a too literal rendering would seem unidiomatic. This is why we find freely translated chapters and passages side by side with others which reproduce the original fairly literally. Chs. 8–20, which give an account of the liturgy of the monastic office and form a rather literally translated sequence, are the only exception. It is in these chapters, too, that we find most of the unidiomatic syntactic constructions, such as absolute participles in the dative case, all of them translating Latin ablative absolutes.[1] Elsewhere such syntactic Latinisms are very rare.[2]

Manuscript *u* contains a fragment of a version which, although it is clearly based on Æthelwold's translation, differs from it in so many respects that we can treat it as in effect an independent work.[3] The contribution of this reviser consists in numerous additions and omissions and in changes of syntax and vocabulary. The result is often stylistically inferior to Æthelwold's version. This is particularly true of the syntax; some of the reviser's sentences show that he was unable to master complicated hypotactical constructions.[4] It is also possible to establish some of his principles and intentions. He tends to replace the forms of the optative *sy* and *syn* by *beo* and *beon*;[5] he substitutes sentences with *man* and the verb in the active voice for passive constructions;[6] sometimes he places the predicate in front of the object or a prepositional phrase;[7] several words that seem to be rare or are not found outside the Old English Rule are replaced by what must have been considered more common expressions.[8] None of these changes, however, has been carried out consistently in *u*. The manuscript was written in about the middle of the eleventh century; less than a century – perhaps only a few decades – had elapsed since the original translation had been made. There can be no doubt that Æthelwold was a far better prose writer than this reviser, but it would be interesting to know where and under what conditions the revision was made and if it was of more than local importance.

---

[1] Cf., e.g., (*RSB* 8.4) incipiente luce:(Schröer 33, 1) upasprungenum dægriman.

[2] For a detailed investigation of syntactic Latinisms in Old English, which includes Æthelwold's translation, see M. Scheler, *Altenglische Lehnsyntax. Die syntaktischen Latinismen im Altenglischen* (Ph.D. thesis, Berlin, 1961).

[3] Schröer prints the text of *u* synoptically with that of *w*: *Benediktinerregel*, pp. 78–90 and 94–122, even page numbers.

[4] Cf., e.g., Æthelwold's translation 109, 20 – 111, 2 and *u* 108, 21 – 110, 2.

[5] E.g. (Schröer 83, 5–6) and swa syn on soðre sibbe geferlæhte:and swa beon on soðre sibbe geferlæhte *u*.

[6] E.g. (Schröer 99, 2–3) sy he gelæd eft to nigecumenra monna huse:læde hine man eft to nicumenra manna huse *u*.

[7] E.g. (Schröer 81, 10) mid stilnesse anfealdlice he ingange:he inga mid stilnysse *u*.

[8] E.g. (Schröer 97, 14) gesinlice:georne *u*; and (Schröer 119, 25) syueræte:syfre *u*.

Æthelwold's translation of the 'Regula Sancti Benedicti'

Research in the fields of Old English word geography and word usage has made a great deal of progress during the past few decades[1] and it is now clear that the use of a number of Old English words (or of words with specific meanings) was restricted to certain dialect areas and perhaps also to certain 'schools'. There are expressions that are only or mainly found in Anglian texts, or in West Saxon texts (early and late), or only in early or late West Saxon texts. Again, within the late West Saxon group, there is the so-called 'Winchester group', whose word usage seems to set it apart from other late West Saxon texts. Within this pattern Æthelwold's translation seems to hold a particularly important position. An examination of its vocabulary confirms what we know about the historical background of Æthelwold's work and helps to throw more light on the development of Old English word usage.[2]

As is to be expected, there are no purely Anglian words in the Old English Rule. Most of those words that can be more or less definitely attributed to a particular period or dialect are typically late West Saxon, as (*un*)*acumendlic*, *besargian*, *carful*, *cnapa*, *gedeorf*, *geefenlæcan*, *hæfen*, *hæfenleas* and *heordræden*. Other words seem to be rarely recorded in early West Saxon, while they are frequent in later texts. Examples are *æþelboren*, *gedyrstlæcan*, *leorningcniht*, *gerihtlæcan* and *þæslic* and its derivatives. There are also about twenty loan-words which may have been introduced by Æthelwold, since there is no earlier record of them.[3] Æthelwold's vocabulary is, then, what we might call 'modern' and the Old English Rule is without doubt among the texts that mark the beginning of late West Saxon or 'Standard Old English'. Even more significant, however, is the rôle of Æthelwold's translation in what Professor Gneuss has called the 'Winchester group' of Old English texts. As he pointed out in an earlier volume of this periodical,[4] there are a number of texts that show a striking uniformity and consistency in the use of certain members of groups of synonyms. This group of texts includes the works of Ælfric, the Lambeth Psalter gloss, the Old English glosses to the *Expositio Hymnorum* and the Old English translation of the Rule of Bishop Chrodegang. The standardization of vocabulary usage found in these texts

---

[1] See O. Funke, 'Altenglische Wortgeographie. (Eine bibliographische Überschau)', *Anglistische Studien. Festschrift zum 70. Geburtstag von Professor Friedrich Wild*, Wiener Beiträge zur Englischen Philologie 66 (Vienna, 1958), 39–51, and H. Gneuss, 'The Origin of Standard Old English and Æthelwold's School at Winchester', *ASE* 1 (1972), 75, n. 4.

[2] For a fully documented discussion of the vocabulary of the Old English Rule, see Gretsch, *Regula*, pp. 307–77 and 403–6.

[3] Cf. O. Funke, *Die gelehrten lateinischen Lehn- und Fremdwörter in der altenglischen Literatur* (Halle, 1914), pp. 164–5 and *passim*; see also Gretsch, *Regula*, pp. 364–70.

[4] 'Origin of Standard Old English', pp. 63–83.

was probably introduced and taught at Æthelwold's school at Winchester. If this was so, we should expect to find the beginning of such standardization – if not more than this – in the earliest work of the Old Minster school, the translation of the Rule. We should also expect traces of earlier usage or a less consistent use of synonyms in such a comparatively early text.

All this is exactly what we find. The Old English Rule agrees with the Winchester group in always employing *gylt* and never *scyld*; *modig, modigness* and *modigian* are the normal translation words for *superbia* and its relations; *leahtor* is more frequent than *unþeaw* and is the normal equivalent for Latin *vitium*; *peregrinus* has nearly always been translated by *ælþeodig* and never by *fremed*; and *wuldorbeag* renders *corona* in the sense 'crown of life'. Other words which may also be typically 'Winchester' are *geefenlæcan, gedyrstlæcan, hæfen, hæfenleas, hæfenleast, onhrop* and *gerihtlæcan* (in the sense 'to mend one's ways'). In some cases, however, the Old English Rule differs from the Winchester group. Æthelwold employs *cild* five times for 'boy' but the Winchester word *cnapa* only twice; Latin *gaudere* is rendered by *gefeon* and not by the Winchester word *geblissian* (nor by the older West Saxon word *gefægnian*); and *mægen* is consistently used for *virtus*, 'virtue', whereas the Winchester group prefers *miht* to *mægen*. In translating Latin *filius* by *bearn* (except once by *sunu*) Æthelwold differs not only from the Winchester texts but from almost all Old English texts, which normally employ *sunu*. But even here we find a link with a Winchester text, since the Lambeth Psalter gloss frequently has *bearn* for *filius*. Beside these indications that Æthelwold had retained 'older' words there are a few signs that he was experimenting with Old English synonyms in an attempt to find suitable equivalents for certain Latin terms. Thus he seems to have felt that *cirice* was not the appropriate word for *ecclesia* in the sense of 'community of Christ' and therefore tried a new loan-word, *ecclesia*, as well as a paraphrase *þe gelaðede synd*. The Winchester word in this sense, is *gelaðung* and it is not impossible that this was 'fixed' by Æthelwold or his collaborators at Winchester at some time after *RSB* had been translated. Similarly, the Old English Rule has six different expressions for *discipulus*: *geongra, leornere, underþeod, underþeod leornere, læringman* and *leorningcniht*. The last of these became the preferred word in Winchester texts; *læringman* is not recorded elsewhere and may be a loan-formation devised by Æthelwold. He also introduced the new loan-word *altare* and used it side by side with *weofod*, whereas he seems to have rejected the older loan-word *alter*. Later on a decision must have been made in favour of *weofod*, which became the standard Winchester word.

It seems clear from these examples that Æthelwold's translation represents an early stage in the work of the Winchester school, and it is worth noticing that a slightly earlier Old English psalter gloss, which was probably written at Winchester, shows some striking correspondences with the Old English Rule.[1] An examination of the vocabulary of Æthelwold's translation both confirms what we know about the place of this text in the history of Old English prose and about its date and authorship and helps us better to understand the development of late Old English standardization in language and the rôle of Winchester in this development. It is to be hoped that future research and a new, comprehensive Old English Dictionary will throw more light on this problem.

[1] BM Royal 2.B.v; cf. Gneuss, 'Origin of Standard Old English', p. 79, and Gretsch, *Regula*, p. 374.

Social idealism in Ælfric's *Colloquy*

EARL R. ANDERSON

Ælfric's *Colloquy*[1] is, of course, first and foremost, a dialogue between a master and his pupils to give practice in the use of Latin at a conversational level. The pedagogic intention of the work is evident from the interlocutors' habit of lingering over commonly used words in various grammatical forms: for example, in a few opening lines (2–11) the deponent *loqui* appears as *loqui, loquimur, loquamur* and *loqueris*, together with the noun *locutio*, and within a little more than fifty lines (66–119) we find seven forms of the verb *capere*, two of them occurring four times each and one twice. Yet, equally certainly, this colloquy has more to it than just schoolboy exercises in declensions and conjugations. It has escaped the oblivion that has been the lot of its more humdrum fellows who – to use Garmonsway's personification – were assigned the rôle of literary Cinderellas, labouring 'in obscurity in monastic classrooms to help boys learn their lessons'.[2] It has long been acclaimed for its realism and for its 'sociological picture of the occupational strata'[3] of Anglo-Saxon society; and, in our own day, Stanley B. Greenfield has called attention to its literary merits, 'its fine organization and structure, dramatic in effect, with its pairing and contrasting, for example, of the king's bold hunter and the independent, timid fisherman . . . and with its lively disputation toward the end about which occupation is most essential'.[4] In the present study I hope to demonstrate that it also draws on a background of ideas and that its longevity is partly due to this ingredient. After all, Ælfric's work as a whole is intellectual in character and his various writings are related to one another as parts of a plan systematically pursued,

---

[1] Ed. G. N. Garmonsway, 2nd ed. (London, 1947); all references are to this edition.

[2] Garmonsway, 'The Development of the Colloquy', *The Anglo-Saxons: Studies in some Aspects of their History and Culture presented to Bruce Dickins*, ed. Peter Clemoes (London, 1959), p. 249. On the humble origins of the colloquy as a genre, probably descending from the fourth-century *Ars Grammatica Dosithei Magistri*, see *ibid.* p. 252.

[3] Stanley B. Greenfield, *A Critical History of Old English Literature* (New York, 1965), p. 52. See, e.g., W. Cunningham, *Growth of English Industry and Commerce* (Cambridge, 1890–2) I, 131; A. F. Leach, *Educational Charters and Documents* (Cambridge, 1911), p. xvi; Leach, *Schools of Medieval England* (Cambridge, 1915), p. 91; G. G. Coulton, *Social Life in Britain* (Cambridge, 1919), p. 54; and A. Cruse, *The Shaping of English Literature* (New York, 1927), p. 70. For a discussion of the earlier views of the sociological significance of the *Colloquy*, see ed. Garmonsway, pp. 14–15.

[4] Greenfield, *History*, p. 52.

as has been suggested by Sisam[1] and reiterated by Clemoes in an admirable metaphor:

> Its controlling idea was universal history with Christ's redemption of man at its centre. The conception which moulded Ælfric's writings was in fact that which moulded the Gothic cathedral later. His main structure, as it were, consisted of two series of homilies combining Temporale and Sanctorale, later extended and completed with more Temporale homilies. *De Temporibus Anni*, the *Grammar* and *Colloquy*, and his letters for Wulfsige and Wulfstan and to the monks of Eynsham buttressed this edifice; *Lives* and Old Testament narratives enriched it with stained glass windows; 'occasional' pieces such as the *Letter to Sigeweard* gave it the synthesis of sculpture on the West Front.[2]

All the same, in a work as elementary in purpose as the *Colloquy* ideas in a developed form are not to be expected. They are likely to be at their simplest and, indeed, may remain no more than mere implications. What, then, are some of them?

Eric Colledge has suggested an influence from St Augustine's *Enarratio in Psalmum LXX* for the dialogue between the master and the merchant, in which the merchant defends his profit motive in buying goods abroad and selling them at a higher price in England (149–66). As Colledge points out, Ælfric, in allowing his merchant to justify his profit as the means of providing for himself and his wife and family, adopted Augustine's position that the merchant deserves compensation for his labour, provided that this, and not greed, is his motive.[3] It may be also that, in putting into the merchant's mouth the point that mortal danger, and sometimes shipwreck and loss of goods, is involved in earning his honest profit (155–7), Ælfric was aware of the Roman satirists' position, represented in Horace, Juvenal and Persius,[4] that merchants who undergo maritime perils are motivated by avarice, for his merchant's point of view is, in effect, a denial of this charge.[5]

[1] Kenneth Sisam, *Studies in the History of Old English Literature* (Oxford, 1953), p. 301.

[2] P. A. M. Clemoes, 'The Chronology of Ælfric's Works', *The Anglo-Saxons*, ed. Clemoes, pp. 245–6.

[3] Eric Colledge, 'An Allusion to Augustine in Ælfric's *Colloquy*', *RES* n.s. 12 (1961), 180–1. The importance of Augustine's *Enarratio in Psalmum LXX* in medieval thought has been observed by J. W. Baldwin, in *The Mediaeval Theories of the Just Price*, Trans. of Amer. Philosophical Soc. n.s. 49 (1959), pt 4, esp. 12–16, and in *Masters, Princes and Merchants: the Social Views of Peter the Chanter and his Circle* (Princeton, 1970) I, 262–4 and II, 185–6, nn. 17, 18, 19 and 20.

[4] All these were curriculum authors in Europe in the early Middle Ages; see E. R. Curtius, *European Literature and the Latin Middle Ages*, trans. W. R. Trask (London, 1953), p. 49. There is positive evidence that Horace was read at Winchester in Ælfric's time (see M. Lapidge, 'Three Latin Poems from Æthelwold's School at Winchester', *ASE* 1 (1972), 109); but there is no certain evidence for the study of Juvenal and Persius in late-tenth-century England.

[5] Horace, *carm.* 1.1.13–17 and 3.1.25–6; *serm.* 1.4.25–32; and *epist.* 1.1.42–58 and 1.6.31–8; Juvenal, *sat.* 14.256–302; and Persius, *sat.* 5.132–60; cf. *sat.* 6.75–80. For the Roman satirists' views on merchants, see Ethel Hampson Brewster, *Roman Craftsmen and Tradesmen of the Early Empire* (Menasha, Wisconsin, 1917), pp. 30–9. The position of the Roman satirists was adopted

It is likely that Ælfric's treatment of the baker and the cook was influenced by a tradition of using the merits of these crafts as a topic for school debate. An early example is Vespa's poem, *Iudicium coci et pistoris*, which belongs to the fifth century or earlier[1] and, if Raby is correct in characterizing it as a 'school piece which gives the opportunity for a rhetorical setting forth of the merits of each trade, with proper mythological allusions',[2] more than likely merely followed the conventions of an already existing tradition. As its title suggests, Vespa's *Iudicium*[3] presents a debate between a cook and a baker as to whose occupation is the more useful. The poem proceeds along lines familiar in debate literature: there is a balanced contention on a single subject, each side of the argument is presented with equal force and the outcome is decided by a third party or *iudex*. The *iudex* in this case is Vulcanus, who, as the source of fire, is qualified to understand both sides of the question. Weighing the arguments of each contender, he concludes that flesh and bread are both necessary to sustain life, that the cook and the baker are equals and that their quarrel is neither necessary nor desirable. Direct influence of Vespa on Ælfric is unlikely, since there is no evidence that his poem was known in England,[4] and, in any case, there are more differences than similarities between his treatment of the cook and the baker and Ælfric's. But the school tradition that Vespa represents is another matter. The baker and the cook are juxtaposed in the *Colloquy* and it is in the master's words to the baker that the validity of a craft is called into question for the first time: 'Quid dicis tu, pistor? Cui prodest ars tua, aut si sine te possimus uitam ducere?' (185–6). And the note of contention increases when, instead of addressing the cook directly as he does all the others, the master asks a question about him which demands, and receives, an answer in self-defence:

Quid dicimus de coco, si indigemus in aliquo arte eius?
    Dicit cocus: Si me expellitis a uestro collegio, manducabitis holera uestra uiridia, et carnes uestras crudas, et nec saltem pingue ius potestis sine arte mea habere. (192–6)

by St Ambrose, and much later by Peter the Chanter, who was fond of quoting Horace on this subject; see Baldwin, *Masters, Princes and Merchants* I, 263 and II, 185, n. 12.

In the event of a shipwreck, a merchant could lose everything he had, for it was customary in the early Middle Ages for the prince to seize whatever cargo remained, although earlier Roman law had protected the surviving owners or their heirs; see *ibid.* I, 247–8.

[1] F. J. E. Raby (*A History of Secular Latin Poetry in the Middle Ages*, 2nd ed. (Oxford, 1957) I, 45) associates the poem with the third century. The only evidence for dating the poem, however, is the fact that it appears in the Codex Salmasianus, a collection of Latin poetry of the sixth century and earlier. Vespa's poem must have been written therefore by the sixth century, but no more certain date is possible. For the text see *Anthologia Latina*, ed. A. Riese (Leipzig, 1869–70) I. 1, 140–3.

[2] *Secular Latin Poetry* I, 45.

[3] 'Vespae Iudicium coci et pistoris iudice Vulcano' in ed. Riese.

[4] Vespa's name does not appear in J. D. A. Ogilvy, *Books Known to the English, 597–1066* (Cambridge, Mass., 1967).

But the master is not prepared to accept this as an answer and the cook has to try again:

Non curamus de arte tua, nec nobis necessaria est, quia nos ipsi possumus coquere que coquenda sunt, et assara que assanda sunt.

Dicit cocus: Si ideo me expellitis, ut sic faciatis, tunc eritis omnes coci, et nullus uestrum erit dominus; et tamen sine arte mea non manducabitis. (197–202)

Argument of this sort does not enter into the master's dealings with any other craftsman.

Debate as to the usefulness of baker and cook is but a particular application of a more general tradition of school debate over the relative merits of various crafts and callings, as represented, for instance, in a fragment from Carolingian times, *De navigio et agricultura*.[1] Influence from this wider tradition comes to the fore when the master asks the monk whether there is a wise counsellor among his companions and, on being told that there is, assigns to this counsellor the role of *iudex*: 'Quid dicis tu, sapiens? Que ars tibi uidetur inter istas prior esse?' (211–12). The counsellor's decision in favour of the ploughman as the primary secular craftsman does not go unchallenged: a smith and a carpenter each states his own claim, the smith being answered by the counsellor and the carpenter being challenged by the smith. The result of such difference of opinion is an appeal to all concerned for reconciliation, agreement and diligence in fulfilling one's calling that is similar in kind to the judgement of Vespa's Vulcan:

Consiliarius dicit: O, socii et boni operarii, dissoluamus citius has contentiones, et sit pax et concordia inter uos, et prosit unusquisque alteri arte sua, et conueniamus semper apud aratorem, ubi uictum nobis et pabula equis nostris habemus. Et hoc consilium do omnibus operariis, ut unusquisque artem suam diligenter exerceat, quia qui artem suam dimiserit, ipse dimittatur ab arte. Siue sis sacerdos, siue monachus, seu laicus, seu miles, exerce temet ipsum in hoc, et esto quod es; quia magnum dampnum et uerecundia est homini nolle esse quod est et quod esse debet. (233–43)

We may safely conclude that elements of a school debate tradition concerning crafts have entered into Ælfric's handling of the colloquy form. Perhaps he was merely following precedent; perhaps he made the combination for the first time himself.

In his views on occupational specialization, Ælfric probably was influenced by the topos of the God-given 'gifts of men', a medieval commonplace having its *loci biblici* in such texts as I Corinthians XII.8–10 and Ephesians IV.8 but probably best known through Gregory's *Homilia IX in Evangelia*

---

[1] *Monumenta Germaniae Historica, Poetae Latini Aevi Carolini* 4. 1, 244–6.

on the parable of the talents.[1] Ælfric sometimes used this topos with considerable freedom. For instance he seems to echo it in a discourse on tithes when expanding a statement by Caesarius of Arles, 'De negotio, de artificio, de qualicunque operatione vivis, redde decimas':[2] 'Ælcum men þe ænige tilunge hæfð, oððe on cræfte, oððe on mangunge, oððe on oðrum begeatum, ælcum is beboden þæt hy þa teoðunge Gode glædlice syllan of heora begeatum oððe cræftum þe him God forgeaf.'[3] In the *Colloquy* the topos is not specifically formulated, but it is surely implied in the advice to each man to practise his particular profession, just quoted: 'Et hoc consilium do omnibus operariis . . . nolle esse quod est et quod esse debet' (237–43).

The 'siue sis sacerdos, siue monachus, seu laicus, seu miles' (240–1) depends on a view of society like that expressed in the threefold classification 'oratores, laboratores et bellatores', which Ælfric used in a piece appended to his *Passio Sanctorum Machabeorum*[4] and in his *Letter to Sigeweard* ('On the Old and New Testament').[5] Since both these writings were later in composition it may well be that the *Colloquy* lacks their specific formulation because the unidentified source on which they were based had not yet come into Ælfric's hands.[6] But that his view of society was the same before he acquired this new material as it was afterwards is shown by the counsellor's verdict in the *Colloquy* that the primary secular occupation was the ploughman's (219): just so, in the piece appended to the *Passio Machabeorum* 'laboratores synd þa þe urne bigleofan beswincaᴺ' and their type is *se yrðlincg*[7] and in the *Letter to Sigeweard* 'Laboratores sind þe us bigleofan tiliað, yrðlingas 7 æhte men to þam anum betæhte'.[8] Evidently the ploughman is thought to fulfil most completely the function of the *laborator* in the social ideal of the three mutually supporting estates. Incidentally, Ælfric's three treatments of the topos are nicely complementary in that in the *Passio Machabeorum* it is the *oratores*, as warriors who fight against spiritual foes, that are in the forefront of attention, in the *Letter to Sigeweard* it is the *bellatores*, who defend the kingdom, and in the *Colloquy* it is the *laboratores*, who provide for the material needs of society.

While the ploughman's craft is recognized as the most essential secular occupation, even greater importance is attributed to the *oratores* in the coun-

---

[1] J. E. Cross, 'The Old English Poetic Theme of *The Gifts of Men*', *Neophilologus* 46 (1962), 66–70.

[2] Caesarius of Arles, *Homilia XVI, De Decimis*, Migne, *Patrologia Latina* 67, col. 1079.

[3] *Homilies of Ælfric, a Supplementary Collection*, ed. John C. Pope, Early Eng. Text Soc. 259–60 (London, 1967–8), II, 808, lines 99–102.

[4] *Ælfric's Lives of Saints*, ed. Walter W. Skeat, EETS o.s. 76, 82, 94 and 114 (London, 1881–1900), II, 1120–4, lines 812–62.

[5] *The Old English Version of the Heptateuch, Ælfric's Treatise on the Old and New Testament and his Preface to Genesis*, ed. S. J. Crawford, EETS o.s. 160, repr. (London, 1969), 71–2, 'On the Old and New Testament', lines 1204–20.

[6] I owe this observation to Peter Clemoes.

[7] Ed. Skeat, lines 815 and 819.   [8] Ed. Crawford, lines 1208–9.

sellor's answer to the question, 'Que ars tibi uidetur inter istas prior esse?' (211–12). Probably he reflects a common medieval view when he claims that 'mihi uidetur seruitium Dei inter istas artes primatum tenere, sicut legitur in euangelio: "Primum querite regnum Dei et iustitiam eius, et hec omnia adicientur uobis"' (213–16). But more particularly his answer is in accord with the emphasis on monasticism which was especially marked at the time Ælfric was writing and with the emphasis, within monasticism, on the liturgical life. It is noteworthy that the same scriptural text (Matthew VI.33; cf. Luke XII.31) is used in St Benedict's instructions concerning the characteristics of the abbot: 'Ante omnia, ne dissimulans aut paruipendens salutem animarum sibi commissarum ne plus gerat sollicitudinem de rebus transitoriis et terrenis atque caducis, sed semper cogitet, quia animas suscepit regendas, de quibus et rationem redditurus est. Et ne causetur de minori forte substantia, meminerit scriptum: *Primum quaerite regnum dei et iustitiam eius et haec omnia adicientur uobis*' (II. 33–5).[1] Similarly, the conception of the *seruitium Dei* as one of the *artes*, or crafts, is reminiscent of Benedict's chapter on the instruments of good works, which closes with the statement, 'Ecce haec sunt instrumenta artis spiritalis' (IV. 75). The instruments of good works, such as obedience, humility and chastity, are tools borrowed from God, to be used with care in the 'workshop' and returned on the Day of Judgement (IV. 76–8), just as the tools of manual labour are to be used with care and returned to the monastic storehouse at the end of the day.

The Benedictine Rule is, indeed, the most important and pervasive influence on the *Colloquy*, although it is impossible to tell how far this influence was transmitted directly through Ælfric's familiarity with the Rule itself and how far it resulted from his experience of monastic practices at Winchester and other reformed monasteries in southern England. C. L. White, noting the strength of Ælfric's Benedictine associations, recognizes in the last part of the *Colloquy*, especially in the *horarium* (266–78), an expression of the Benedictine ideal of order in a well-regulated life;[2] but it has not been pointed out that the influence of the Rule extends also to the dialogue on crafts. Earlier scholars, apparently failing to see the importance of rôle-playing in the *Colloquy*, thought that the *pueri* actually belonged to the social orders indicated by their crafts, thus providing evidence for 'an amazing diffusion of education among all classes, boys in all the different occupations,

---

[1] *Benedicti Regula*, ed. Rudolph Hanslik, Corpus Scriptorum Ecclesiasticorum Latinorum 75 (Vienna, 1960); all references are to this edition.

[2] Caroline Louisa White, *Ælfric, a New Study of his Life and Writings* (Boston, 1898), pp. 40–3; cf. *Regula* IX–XIX. For the Benedictine ideal of order see Dom David Knowles, *The Monastic Order in England*, 2nd ed. (Cambridge, 1963), pp. 448–53; Dom Cuthbert Butler, *Benedictine Monachism*, 2nd ed. (London, 1924), pp. 275–90; T. F. Lindsay, *Saint Benedict: his Life and Work* (London, 1949), pp. 114–32; and J. C. Dickinson, *Monastic Life in Medieval England* (London, 1961), pp. 103–9.

ploughboy, gamekeeper . . . merchant, learning Latin of a secular master side by side with a young monk'.[1] Although this view is now discarded, it is still generally assumed that the dialogue on crafts refers to daily life outside the monastery walls. According to C. L. Wrenn, for example, Ælfric treats of 'the ordinary happenings of rustic daily life and occupations' by having each boy 'assume the character of a rural worker – ploughman, smith, fisherman, etc.'. Similarly, G. K. Anderson considers that the *Colloquy* gives the sociologist a 'rare chance to see the common Anglo-Saxon people at work'.[2] Although this more recent sociological view seems plausible enough, quite another possibility is suggested by Garmonsway, who writes that the oblates' dialogue on crafts is 'based on their own observation of the manifold activities of a monastic house'.[3] Garmonsway's position is justified first by the fact that the various crafts described in the *Colloquy* were commonly practised in and around the monastic enclosure, and second by the fact that colloquies typically dealt with subjects 'sensibly related to the many and varied activities of a monastic house', only occasionally ranging beyond its walls.[4]

If we accept Garmonsway's position, it is possible for us to see the unifying theme of the *Colloquy* as an expression of the Benedictine monastic ideal, derived from the Rule, of an orderly and well-regulated life within the confines of an economically self-sufficient community devoted to the service of God – a community separate from the world but at the same time a microcosmic image of it, in which each monastic craftsman contributes in his own way to the general welfare. Earlier English monachism, exemplified by Guthlac and Cuthbert, had been heavily influenced by Celtic – and ultimately Antonine – ideals, stressing the ascetic struggle of the individual for spiritual perfection. By the time of Ælfric, however, the Benedictine ideal of monasticism had become secure in many parts of England, with its stress on the community rather than on the individual, and on the communal *seruitium Dei* rather than on personal asceticism.[5] The ideal of a self-sufficient community is evident in ch. LXVI of the Rule: 'Monasterium autem, si possit fieri, ita debet constitui, ut omnia necessaria, id est aqua, molendinum, hortum uel artes diuersas intra monasterium exerceantur, ut non sit necessitas

---

[1] Leach, *Educational Charters and Documents*, p. xvi.

[2] C. L. Wrenn, *A Study of Old English Literature* (London, 1967), pp. 70–1 and 228; George K. Anderson, *The Literature of the Anglo-Saxons*, 2nd ed. (Princeton, 1966), pp. 316 and 353.

[3] Ed., p. 14.

[4] 'Development of the Colloquy', pp. 255ff. The various activities of the monastic household are well documented: see Dom Justin McCann, *The Rule of Saint Benedict*, 3rd ed. (Latrobe, Penn., 1950), pp. 304–16 and 361–6; R. H. Snape, *English Monastic Finances in the Later Middle Ages* (Cambridge, 1926), p. 13; J. Evans, *Monastic Life at Cluny* (Cambridge, 1927), pp. 67 and 84; Edouard Schneider, *The Benedictines* (London, 1926), pp. 86–101; and Knowles, *Monastic Order*, pp. 466–7.

[5] *Ibid.* pp. 682–5.

monachis uagandi foris, quia omnino non expedit animabus eorem' (LXVI. 6–7). Some manuscripts include a *pistrinum* in the catalogue of necessary utilities.[1] Besides water, the mill, garden and bakery, Benedict elsewhere mentions the kitchen, the cellar and the office (XLVI) and devotes a chapter to the maintenance of tools used in various crafts (XXXII). In the chapter on manual labour (XLVIIII) it is clear that the monks are expected to devote much of their time to work, including field work, for idleness is the enemy of the soul, and the presence of monastic artisans, possessed with special skills, is attested in the chapter *De artificibus monasterii* (LVII), which warns the craftsmen against pride and establishes the policy for hiring their services outside the monastery.

It is obvious, of course, that not all the craftsmen of the *Colloquy* are represented as monks. The merchant has a family to support (163–6), the hunter is a servant of the king (53–5), and the ploughman is a serf on monastic lands (35).[2] The shepherd, faithful to his lord (41–2), and the oxherd, whose duties supplement those of the ploughman (44–7), seem to be servants of the monastery rather than monks; however, there is no reason why the other interlocutors could not be monks skilled in specific crafts: the cobbler, salter, baker, cook, smith and carpenter, particularly, all attest their usefulness to the *collegium* to which they belong. It is difficult to say whether or not the fisherman and fowler could be monks, but it is worth noting that fish was so important to the monastic economy that fishponds were maintained even if there was a river nearby.[3] In any case, whether or not all the craftsmen are monks is of little importance. The main point of the dialogue on crafts is that each member of the fraternity helps the others by his craft: 'et prosit unusquisque alteri arte sua' (235). Each craftsman contributes to Ælfric's little society in order to make that society self-sustaining, in accordance with the Benedictine ideal.

From a modern point of view, we might be tempted to see Ælfric's expression of the Benedictine ethos in the *Colloquy* as an early English Utopia, especially when we reflect that St Benedict, in the Rule, combines a practical Roman talent for government with a profound Christian idealism.[4] The true spirit of the *Colloquy*, however, is not Utopian but pedagogic. In keeping with the spirit of Benedict's request that the Rule be read frequently in the community so that the brethren may not excuse themselves on grounds of ignorance (LXVI. 8), in the *Colloquy* Ælfric offers his pupils a picture of the

[1] Ed. Hanslik, p. 157, note to LXVI. 6.
[2] For serfdom on monastic lands see John Chapman, *St Benedict and the Sixth Century* (London, 1929), pp. 147–75.
[3] D. H. S. Cranage, *The Home of the Monk* (Cambridge, 1934), p. 62.
[4] Gustav Schnürer, *Church and Culture in the Middle Ages*, trans. George J. Undreiner (Paterson, N.J., 1956) I, 159ff.

Rule in its practical application. Thus the demand for correct Latin usage and pronunciation, which was enforced by whipping boys who made mistakes in the oratory (*Regula* XLV), finds expression in the children's request to the master 'ut doceas nos loqui latialiter recte, quia idiote sumus et corrupte loquimur' (*Colloquy* 1–3). The use of corporal punishment for children, to which Benedict devotes a chapter (XXX; cf. XXVIII and XLV), is evident in Ælfric's community, where the boys find it necessary to learn their lessons (7–10) and behave circumspectly (279–83) in order to escape whipping. The master's final advice to his pupils, admonishing them to obedience, reverence and seriousness in all places, especially in the oratory, the cloister and the study (308–15), reflects the spirit of obedience and humility which permeates the Rule (cf. V, VI and VII).

Finally, the children's special dietary allowances and dormitory accommodation, which of course reflect monastic practices in Ælfric's day, are ultimately based on the Rule. *Quadripedum carnes* were forbidden to monks (*Regula* XXXIX); however, the oblate is allowed meat 'quia puer sum sub uirga degens' (*Colloquy* 285–6), in accordance with special provisions for youth, old age and illness (*Regula* XXXVI and XXXVII). After cataloguing the variety of foods available in the monastery (*Colloquy* 285–9), the oblate's assertion that 'Non sum tam uorax ut omnia genera ciborum in una refectione edere possim' (292–3) reflects Benedict's stipulation that only two dishes be served at any one meal (*Regula* XXXVIIII. 1–4); and the boy's claim that he is not a glutton (*Colloquy* 295–7) is in keeping with the general spirit of Benedict's chapter *De mensura ciborum*. The restriction on wine, reserved for the old and wise, and forbidden to those who are young and foolish (*Colloquy* 300–2), accords with Benedict's warning that 'uinum apostatare facit etiam sapientes' (*Regula* XL. 7). The oblate's statement that he sleeps 'in dormitorio cum fratribus' (*Colloquy* 304) accords with the dormitory arrangements described in the chapter *Quomodo dormiant monachi*, where there is even a provision for children predisposed to sleep late in the morning (*Regula* XXII; cf. *Colloquy*, 305–7). These parallels between the *Colloquy* and the Rule, whether they result from direct or indirect transmission, indicate that even the minor details of Ælfric's composition are thematic.

At the beginning of their lesson the oblates ask their master for instruction and practice only in correct Latin usage, not caring about the subject of their discourse, provided only that it would not be idle or shameful (1–6); but the master has more to offer than correct grammar and pronunciation. The disciples' gradual induction into wisdom takes place in three stages, the first two marked off by 'false closures' and the third by the master's concluding advice. In the first and longest phase (1–243) the dialogue on crafts develops into a debate over which craft is most essential.

The dispute is resolved, probably not without influence from the common-places of the 'gifts of men' and the 'three estates' but more especially as an expression of the Benedictine ideal, by an affirmation of the need for a harmoniously unified society which is devoted to the service of God and in which each craftsman works in his own way for the benefit of the whole. In the second phase (244–60) the oblates have revised their educational goals upwards. They are now willing to study diligently to acquire not only a knowledge of correct Latin usage but also wisdom 'quia nolumus esse sicut bruta animalia, que nihil sciunt, nisi herbam et aquam' (250–1). Never-theless an abstract discussion of the quality of wisdom would be beyond their comprehension. As in the dialogue on crafts, in the third phase (261–315) the master must guide his pupils toward an expression of spiritual wisdom in simple and practical terms. The Benedictine ideal of order and the *seruitium Dei* thus find expression in the *horarium* (268–78), and the discussion of the boys' food, drink and sleeping arrangements (284–307) shows in practical terms how an individual benefits from life in a self-sufficient com-munity whose members work together for the common good. By combining an all-pervasive Benedictine idealism with the practical needs of language instruction Ælfric produces a work of art – simple but not pedestrian, thoughtful and yet lively and witty – that is altogether worthy of one of England's most learned and creative teachers.[1]

[1] I am indebted to Stanley B. Greenfield for his encouragement, and to Peter Clemoes for his guidance, in the composition of this paper.

The architectural interest of Æthelwulf's *De Abbatibus*

H. M. TAYLOR

The purpose of this article is to describe the architectural evidence contained in a ninth-century poem which has recently been published in a new critical edition.[1] The poem relates to a Northumbrian abbey dependent on Lindisfarne and its content provides some welcome additions to the present small number of contemporary descriptions of churches and their fittings. The poet, who was a member of the community, describes in some detail two churches of the abbey as well as a greater church which he saw in a vision. The poem is dedicated to Egbert, bishop of Lindisfarne 803–21, who would presumably be familiar with the abbey; and this dedication therefore serves not only to date the poem within the first quarter of the ninth century but also to indicate indirectly that it should be free from the wilder exaggerations that have sometimes brought discredit on contemporary descriptions of buildings.

The poem names six abbots from the time of the foundation of the abbey during the reign of Osred, king of Northumbria 705–16; and it ascribes the first church to the founder and first abbot, Eanmund, while the second church was the gift of the fourth abbot, Sigbald. The earliest of the three extant manuscripts is from the first half of the eleventh century, and the three manuscripts establish a sound text without conjecture in spite of earlier belief that this was not so.[2]

In addition to architectural details of three churches the poem gives some indications about furnishings and fittings and also about the nature of services. While a cautionary word is necessary about borrowing from other writers, particularly from Aldhelm, yet even if the whole of these borrowings were to be deleted (so far as they are known) very little would be lost from the descriptive details of buildings as set out below.[3] Moreover, while there is no reason to believe that the visionary church was based in detail upon any building which the poet had seen, it is hard to imagine that he

---

[1] *Æthelwulf: De Abbatibus*, ed. A. Campbell (Oxford, 1967). I am indebted to Professor Clemoes for having drawn my attention to this publication.   [2] *Ibid.* preface and pp. xiii–xv.

[3] For specific detail about borrowings, see *ibid.* pp. xxxi and xliv–xlviii; for the borrowing from Aldhelm, p. xlvi.

would have provided so much detail unless he had been familiar with some church which possessed at least the general plan that he described.

In what follows I first quote, in translation,[1] all the passages in the poem that bear directly on the churches or their fittings, a separate section being devoted to each of the three churches, while a fourth deals with the fittings and other material possessions of the abbey. There then follow, in a corresponding arrangement, the deductions I draw from these passages.

THE TEXT

The founder's church dedicated in honour of St Peter

The founder's church appears twice, in sections VI and XXI. In both sections it is explicitly stated that it was 'consecrated to God in the name of Peter'; but in the heading of section XXI it is described as 'the chapel of the apostles' (*oratorio apostolorum*) as if its dedication had an alternative form.[2] Apart from this detail, the second reference does not seem to give any architectural or historical information; the following quotations are therefore from section VI. After describing how the founder, Eanmund, sent to a holy bishop in Ireland asking for advice and for an altar-table, the poet continues:

The venerable bishop obeyed and complied: he strengthened the departing (messenger) with words, and enriched him with a sacred gift. A table, consecrated in the name of great Peter to God, sped and strengthened the monastery against the dark enemy. (120–3)

Accordingly, the pious man (i.e. Eanmund) completed the lofty walls of a very beautiful temple, putting sheets of lead outside on the roof,[3] and used all his powers to render this house of the Lord outstandingly adorned. In the centre of the pile, he placed the altar we have just mentioned, which produces for Peter very sweet scents. (143–8)

Abbot Sigbald's church dedicated in honour of the Mother of Christ

The founding of a second church by the fourth abbot, Sigbald, is described in section XIV. More detail is given about this church and its fittings than

---

[1] Apart from a few instances, to each of which attention is drawn, my translation is taken directly from the published text, with kind permission from Professor Campbell and the Oxford University Press, to each of whom my gratitude is here acknowledged. In each case of divergence from the published translation I have given in a footnote the original Latin (OL), Professor Campbell's translation (CT) and my reasons for preferring an alternative. The line numbers of the Latin text are cited after each passage.

[2] The section-headings form part of the original text: *ibid.* p. xxi, n. 3. A dedication to St Peter and St Paul was very common both on the continent and in England and sometimes one or other name came to be abandoned.

[3] OL: *exterius tabulas perfundens tegmine plumbi*; CT: 'putting "tables" outside on the roof of lead'. The use of *tabula* to mean a sheet (of lead) is known in medieval Latin usage in the eleventh century, and it seems the most natural meaning here.

about the founder's church of St Peter. The relevant extracts from the poem are as follows:

He enriched the cell with many gifts, and in his zeal built a church worthy of God. This is the house which the mother of the exalted dignity inhabits and occupies beneath the vast dome of the sky. (432–5)

Built into it there is an altar, which is distinguished by very lovely pictures, in the middle of the sanctuary,[1] and the holy men crown it with foliage when they reserve in the pyx the precious life-giving gift. (436–8)

On the west side are conspicuous those resplendent ministers who make the high heaven lovely with concerted melody. All the saints haunt the midmost floor of the church, and occupy it at all times, mustering in countless troops. (439–43)

For the rest, who should number all the lights throughout that church, which shine in the church and overhead to our true delight? (446–7)

That priest gave many gifts to God. That golden chalice, which he gave in his piety to the church of the great mother, gleams, being covered with gems, and shines, being made with markings of silver. (449–51)

While leaden pieces keep the roof of the church in repair, there also resound to the delight of the brothers metal vessels of copper: these have clappers ringing in hollow rattles. (452–4)

The church in Æthelwulf's vision

The vision recorded in section XXII occupies over one hundred lines of which some sixty have reference to a church and its fittings; and many of these give such vivid and detailed descriptions as to leave a clear impression that the vision was based upon things with which the poet was familiar.

The vision begins with a meeting between the poet and a shining being who acted as his leader; together they crossed a broad plain, to a shining city with high walls. They entered and came to a church.

The enclosures of a sacred church could be seen, and they were fairly laid out in the shape of a cross. And the interior of that building shone with a great light, and its walls were made of very smooth stones. (710–13)

Outside, the building was supported all the way round the wall by large and small *porticus*.[2] Of these, twice two looked towards the four corners of the world, and above touched the top of the wall. (714–17)

---

[1] OL: *porticus in medio*; CT: 'in the midst of a portico'. There is good evidence that the word *porticus* was used by Anglo-Saxon and other early medieval writers with the special meaning of a subsidiary room opening from the main body of a church. This church is specified as having only one altar and the altar is specified as being in the middle of a *porticus*. There therefore seems little doubt that the poet is here using the word to mean the particular subsidiary room that we would describe as the sanctuary. For a discussion of the meaning which Bede attached to this word see G. Baldwin Brown, *The Arts in Early England* II, *Anglo-Saxon Architecture*, 2nd ed. (London, 1925), pp. 88–90, or *Venerabilis Bedae Opera Historica*, ed. C. Plummer (Oxford, 1896) II, 80, 333 and 369.

[2] OL: *porticibus*; CT: 'porticoes'. Here and later I have preferred to use the neutral word *porticus* in order to avoid the danger of words with special meanings such as chapels, aisles, transepts, nave or chancel.

Between them in a row small cells were interspersed. Encircling the temple completely with their bright entrances, these afforded a view into a hall which was very marvellous with marble. (718–20)

The floor of the building beneath the mid-point of the temple roof bore the weight of golden offerings on a wondrous table. A holy cross rose up shining upon a very long stem from the top of the table, and (upon it) emeralds shone full bright. Golden plating blazed there (set) with dark-hued gems. (721–5)

At this point, inside the church, the shining leader disappeared and Æthelwulf was left in dismay to his own resources.

I turned my eyes away, to the right, where there was a chair, which shone, and was becomingly (adorned) with gilt carvings, and a venerable old man had seated himself upon it. Before his face, an altar decked with garlands of golden flowers sent dedicated gifts to God, the highest one, and it had on its top the emblem of a tall cross. This shone with ruddy gold and splendid gems from the east. (732–8)

A sparkling vestment of fine linen covered the top of a tomb, which had the bones of some saint in the heart of its interior. (739–41)

Æthelwulf asked the old man where he could find his former teacher Hyglac. He was told to look to the north, and there he recognized another teacher, Eadfrith.

It was Eadfrith, my teacher in my early years. He was a priest, who was seen as I then saw him with head bent in prayer, venerating in piety the blessed tomb of Cuthbert with body and mind. At his back there sat on a stool, which shone with bright metal, the blessed doctor and reader Hyglac, and he shone brightly, being dressed in white robes. He blessed me with his excellent hands. (750–7)

Eadfrith proceeded from there along the walls of the great church, and he led me into the great and small open *porticus*.[1] (758–9)

In each of these there hung near at hand a censer of shining gold, surrounded on all sides with pillars, and from these incense smoked to the thunderer who sits on high. In all the *porticus*[2] bright waxen lights were burning, honouring the altars with flaming donations. (760–4)

Proceeding at length, we hastened to the west side. The *porticus*[3] there gleamed and shone in high distinction. Here shining with gold flamed a thing marvellously lovely, a consecrated altar, which sent gifts to God, the highest one. Here sapphire set in beryl had made ready a splendid chair, on which the blessed monk had seated himself, whom his venerable parents delighted to call Wulfsig . . . He raised his hand and blessed me with words as I departed. (765–74)

In the company of my venerable guide I slowly made my way up into the roof

---

[1] OL: *porticibus magnis minimis induxit apertis*; CT: 'and he opened the porticoes great and small and let me in'. I have preferred not only to use the neutral word *porticus* (see preceding note), but also to translate *apertis* in the sense 'standing open' rather than to imply of necessity that there were doors which needed to be opened.

[2] See above, p. 165, n. 2.

[3] See *ibid*.

of the church,[1] which gave a view to the north. There many vessels gleamed with wondrous gems, and other ones of gold flashed with changing light, and being made from a precious vein, they could indeed surpass by their comeliness all the metals of the world. (775–80)

Among these a table freshly supplied with various forms of sustenance and foods of all kinds offered the blessing of a meal. He (Eadfrith) took from it a cup (made) from a vein of crystal ore, and drew with his hands the gift of sacred liquid, and gave a drink which he blessed with pious prayers. (781–5)

Eadfrith told the poet that this was a home which God had established for blessed souls who would live there for ever. The poet then awoke, and wrote down what he had seen.

Furnishings and details of life in the monastery

Men hasten from outside to the summons of ringing, and sing songs, which answer one another, to their king. (614–15)

This is the house, lofty and with long walls, which the shining sun illuminates through glass windows, diffusing soft light in the bright church. (620–2)

As the whole sky shines with gleaming stars, so beneath the roof of the church hanging torches dangle their tremulous flames in a number of rows. (625–7)

Many men wished to hang up numerous bowls, which would give soft light in the rectangular church, and others set up ensigns of shining metal which present the revered miracles of the holy Christ. (631–4)

Some gave orders for the writing of sacred books which present the exalted utterances of God the thunderer. (636–7)

And these (books) are covered by plate of bright ductile gold; and similarly men adorned the altars of the blessed church. (639–40)

Shining reliefs of silver (on them wouldst thou see figures stamped with the finger) well display these things. (643–4)

That golden chalice, which I mentioned above in my poem, and the broad paten fairly made from silver show surfaces well engraved with silver. (649–51)

He (Ultan) was a blessed priest of the Irish race, and he could ornament books with fair marking, and by this art he accordingly made the shape of the letters beautiful one by one, so that no modern scribe could equal him. (209–12)

And when the depths of the earth had long been eating his body, it was decided to raise this brother's remains from the grave, and after washing his bones to place them in the inside of a prepared tomb, which stood on the floor of the blessed church. (227–30)

Let me recall with wondrous tales a brother, who could control and shape metals of the iron variety. (278–9)

Then when the psalms of matins had been duly completed, forthwith the hammer

---

[1] OL: *ad culmen cellae*; CT: 'to a high place in the church' (with a footnote that the poet seemed now to be back at the place where he had asked about Hyglac). Elsewhere in the poem *culmen* is used of the roof and we know from records and surviving remains that upper chambers were used for treasuries and other purposes.

rang on the anvil as the metal was struck; and as it flew and smote the empty air, it decked the table of the brothers by beating out vessels.[1] (302–5)

Then the band of brothers placed the limbs of their revered father in a fitting tomb under the roof of the church.[2] (399–400)

While a great crowd gathered, a company placed his limbs for blessed quietude by the figure of the tall cross which he himself had set up.[3] (538–9)

Churches sacred to the parent of heaven and earth now rise everywhere throughout the historic countryside. (149–50)

DEDUCTIONS

The founder's church

The altar-table of this church (or at any rate the part of the altar which was brought from Ireland) was suitable for transport; the altar, and presumably the church itself, was consecrated to God in the name of Peter; the church had lofty walls, and a roof covered with lead; it was adorned to the best of the founder's ability; and the altar was placed in the centre of the pile (*medio sub aggere*).[4]

Abbot Sigbald's church

Like the founder's church, Abbot Sigbald's second church had only one altar. It is explicitly said that the church was dedicated in honour of the Mother of God, i.e. the Virgin Mary. The altar was enriched with pictures and was placed in the middle of the sanctuary.[5] It was crowned with foliage when the sacrament was reserved in the pyx. The church was well provided with lights, throughout and also overhead. Abbot Sigbald had given the church a golden chalice inlaid with silver and enriched with gems. He had roofed the church with lead and had provided bells of copper.

It might be felt that lines 439–43 could be interpreted to mean that the choir had its place at the west while the brethren as a whole were in the middle of the church; but the whole paragraph could suggest that the poet is describing an angel chorus and congregation rather than a body of his fellow monks. This view is strengthened by the lines which follow, not reproduced here. It is, of course, also possible that the poet is describing a painted west wall and decorations in the middle part of the church either on the walls or, less likely, on the floor or ceiling.

---

[1] Lines 278–9 and 302–5 are in a section headed 'Concerning Brother Cwicwine', the worker in iron (*De fratre cuicuino ferrario*). [2] This is the burial of Eanmund, the first abbot.

[3] This is the burial of Sigwine, the fifth abbot.

[4] The interpretation of the word *medio*, even in such apparently clear phrases as *in medio ecclesiae* or *in media ecclesia*, is open to some slight doubt. See, e.g., F. Oswald, 'In Medio Ecclesiae', *Frühmittelalterliche Studien* 3 (1969), 313–26, where the general conclusion is that, while sometimes excavation proves that the geometrical centre is intended, it is sometimes the case that a position anywhere on the central axis was referred to by the words *in medio ecclesiae*.

[5] See preceding note and above, p. 165, n. 1.

The church in Æthelwulf's vision

Even with all the reservations which are necessary in dealing with a vision such as Æthelwulf's, especially when it has links with other visions of churches which in some way represented the world to come or the New Jerusalem, it seems possible to make some deductions about churches which the poet might have seen and which might therefore have provided the inspiration for his vision.

In the first place, the church was laid out in the form of a cross (*crucis in speciem fabricata*) and was faced internally with very smooth stones. The exterior is described in terms which are consistent with a cellular cruciform plan such as is shown in fig. 9. The poet's words do not preclude other plans, but of all those known from surviving Anglo-Saxon churches the one shown in the figure most closely fits the words of the poem. The nave there shown is the temple or building which the poet describes as being supported all round by large and small *porticus*. The sanctuary, the western *porticus* and main cells to north and south are the poet's four large *porticus* which faced the four corners of the world and which above touched the top of the walls. In fig. 9 a single smaller cell is shown in each of the spaces between the main arms, and the lateral cells as a whole are laid out in a row; the words of line 718 (*inter quas modice variantur in ordine celle*) would perhaps be even more closely represented if at least two small cells (instead of only one) were to be placed as shown in fig. 10*a* in each of the spaces between the main arms.

In the plan, the altar of lines 721–5 is shown at the centre of the nave, while the altar and chair of lines 732–8, the tomb and the stool are all shown in the eastern sanctuary where the poet would have seen them on turning to the right if he had entered the church through the main south *porticus*. On either side of the nave and sanctuary, doorways are shown opening to lateral cells, and altars are shown in them (758–64).

Lines 765–80 are the most difficult to convert into a picture without undue stretching or bending of the evidence to fit preconceived ideas. It is clear that the poet saw an altar in a western *porticus* and also an elegant chair on which was seated the monk Wulfsig (who was abbot during part of the poet's time at the abbey). An entrance porch such as is known from the remains at Reculver or at St Augustine's abbey in Canterbury would seem inappropriate for an altar and an abbot's chair; and one is therefore led to think of an arrangement such as is described by Eadmer for Canterbury Cathedral where an altar stood in a western oratory with the archbishop's chair behind it against the western wall of the church.[1]

[1] See H. M. Taylor, 'The Anglo-Saxon Cathedral Church at Canterbury', *ArchJ* 124 (1970), 101–30, esp. fig. 2. See also observations by E. Gilbert and R. Gem in *ArchJ* 125 (1971).

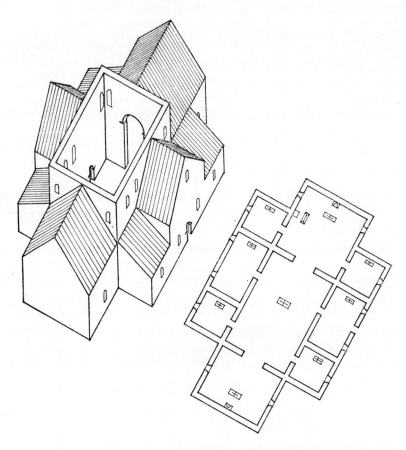

FIG. 9 A possible reconstruction of the church in Æthelwulf's vision. The poet's dream does not serve unambiguously to define a church with this plan or features. But such a plan and features do violence neither to the words of his dream nor to architectural probabilities as they are known from surviving churches of his time. The plan and reconstruction could be regarded as the present author's vision of the flesh and skin of the church described only in skeleton by the poet

Finally there is the room described in lines 780–5 where there were many gleaming vessels decked with jewels, and also food of all kinds. The wording could be taken to describe either a normal meal or the symbolic meal of the Eucharist, even though no altar is mentioned. But in either case it is perhaps closest to the normal meaning of the poet's words if we think of this room as being an upper chamber. There are many surviving upper rooms in western towers and many evidences of galleries over western parts of naves; either of these would also allow for the poet's view to the north.

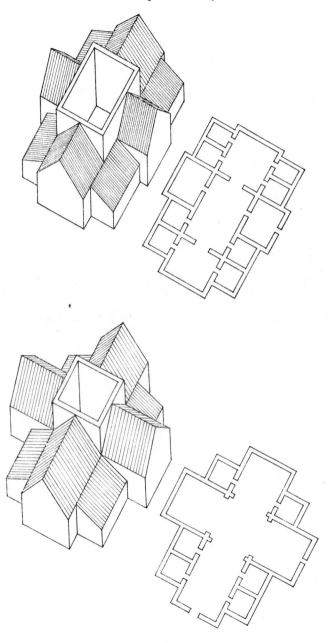

FIG. 10 Other possible reconstructions of the church in Æthelwulf's vision. The upper one differs from fig. 9 only in having the main cells on north and south extended further sideways to emphasize the cruciform plan and in having additional small cells on either side. The lower one shows a transeptal plan with a central tower, of a type which is generally regarded as of later date

H. M. Taylor

Furnishings and details of life in the monastery

The bells in Abbot Sigwald's church, referred to in lines 452–4, appear again in lines 614–15 where their use is specified as summoning the brothers to services. The lofty walls of St Peter's church are again emphasized in lines 620–2, where it is also specified explicitly that the windows are provided with glass. The lighting of the churches is mentioned in four places. In lines 446–7 there is simply an indication of a great number of lights; lines 760–4 specify bright waxen lights; lines 625–7 name torches; and lines 631–4 record the wish of many to hang up bowls that would give soft light to the rectangular church (. . . *plures multi cupiebant pendere caucos, | limpida qui tribuant quadrato lumina templo*). Hanging bowls have long been a subject of considerable controversy in Anglo-Saxon studies, and it is thus of some importance to have a contemporary record of one use to which they were put.[1]

Metal representations of the miracles of Christ are mentioned for the first time in lines 631–4 but ornament on altars and metal vessels is mentioned in several other places. Lines 636–7 and 639–40 mention the writing and ornamentation of books; and lines 209–12 are of special interest in their particular mention of the outstanding excellence of an Irish priest in this craft. Lines 278–9 and 302–5 record the making of iron vessels for the table of the brothers by one of their number, Cwicwine. So far as I know, iron vessels for table use have not yet been discovered, but an iron pan for kitchen use was found on the cathedral car park site at Winchester in 1961 and has been dated to the ninth or tenth century.[2]

It is interesting also to consider in one place the three main references to the burial practices of the abbey. The priest Ultan, the skilled ornamenter of books, had at first been buried deep in the earth, but lines 227–30 describe how a long time later his remains were raised from the grave and his bones were washed and placed in a tomb on the floor of the church. By contrast, the first abbot, Eanmund, was buried under the roof of the church (399–400); while the fifth abbot, Sigwine, was buried beside a tall cross which he had himself set up (538). The apparent difference in practice indicated by the burials of these two abbots may in fact spring from the general principle of associating benefactors in death with the contributions they had made during their lifetime, Eanmund with the church which he had built and Sigwine with the cross which he had set up.

Finally we may note in lines 149–50 the poet's belief that in the early part of the ninth century the land was well covered with churches.

[1] For a recent account of hanging bowls, with a full bibliography and suggestions about other uses and possible development of decoration, see Elizabeth Fowler, 'Hanging Bowls', *Studies in Ancient Europe*, ed. J. M. Coles and D. S. A. Simpson (Leicester, 1968), pp. 287–310.

[2] M. Biddle and R. N. Quirk, 'Excavations near Winchester Cathedral, 1961', *ArchJ* 119(1962), 184–6.

The architectural interest of Æthelwulf's 'De Abbatibus'

Further consideration of the architectural evidence

The visionary church is described explicitly as having walls of stone; by contrast no detail is given about the material of the walls of the two churches of the abbey. It may be that their walls were of wood like those of the church built at Lindisfarne by Finan (bishop 651–61); this was of hewn oak, roofed with thatch; and it was later covered with lead both on its roof and its walls.[1] The poet is explicit that both churches of the abbey had lead roofs and that at least one had windows of glass. Moreover each of these churches had only one altar, whereas the visionary church had many, housed in the many *porticus*. Sigbald's church of St Mary had its altar in a *porticus* and may therefore be visualized as having been of the well-known Northumbrian two-cell plan consisting of a rectangular nave and a rectangular or square sanctuary. Eanmund's earlier church of St Peter could have been of simple rectangular shape since the poet's description does not mention a *porticus* but simply describes the altar as being in the middle of the pile.[2]

The visionary church is explicitly described as having been built in the form of a cross (*crucis in speciem fabricata*). That this does not necessarily involve a transeptal form has already been shown in fig. 9; but churches with a central tower and transepts would of course fit the poet's description so long as they had rows of smaller cells beside the nave and chancel. It has, however, usually been accepted that this more developed transeptal form belongs to a later period, perhaps in the tenth century or the eleventh, and for this reason the simpler form has been shown in fig. 9. For completeness fig. 10 shows two alternatives to the church of fig. 9, either of which would fit the poet's description.

The position of the altar

In all three churches the implication of the poet's words is that the position of the altar (or of certain altars in the visionary church) is in the middle of the room in which it stands. I have given elsewhere an account of both structural and literary evidence for the placing of altars in pre-Viking churches of Anglo-Saxon England at some distance from the east wall rather than against it;[3] and, in spite of the uncertainty to which attention has been directed above,[4] the evidence of this poem is in accord with that conclusion.

[1] Bede, *HE* iii.25.
[2] Evidence for one-cell rectangular wooden churches has been found in England at Stafford (St Bertelin) and at Wharram Percy. Many examples have been recorded on the continent.
[3] H. M. Taylor, 'The Position of the Altar in Early Anglo-Saxon Churches', *AntJ* 53 (1973), 52–8.
[4] P. 168, n. 2.

Towards a revision of the internal chronology of the coinages of Edward the Elder and Plegmund

MICHAEL DOLLEY

A number of years ago it was observed by the present writer[1] that the later issues of King Edward the Elder's two substantive types (Brooke[2] 12 and 13) can be distinguished from the earlier by the fact that they are struck on relatively spread flans. The diameter of typical pieces with the Cuerdale provenance for example is 20–1 mm, while pieces which have very close affinities with the earliest coins of Athelstan have a mean diameter in the region of 22–3 mm. It was further noticed that the coinage of Plegmund, archbishop of Canterbury, exhibits a neat dichotomy between pennies which conform in style and module to late, but not the very latest, coins of Alfred the Great and pennies which patently are contemporary with the later, but not the earlier, coins of Edward the Elder. The hypothesis was further advanced, and seems now generally accepted, that the Canterbury mint was closed as a consequence of the two-pronged Viking attack on Kent in 892 and opened again at least a year or two before the death of Plegmund.[3] It follows that the inception of the last phase of Edward's coinage falls likewise at least a couple of years before the archbishop's demise, an event which is uniformly dated in the numismatic literature to 914.[4] Nor can numismatists altogether be blamed for their consistency in accepting without demur a date proposed without any indication of controversy by so respectable, and indeed magisterial, a work of reference as F. M. Powicke and E. B. Fryde, *Handbook of British Chronology*.[5]

It must be admitted, though, that the 'first and onlie begetter' of this arrangement of Edward the Elder's issues has never been entirely happy about certain aspects of the chronology. Plegmund's second coinage is not so exiguous that it can be confined with plausibility within months rather than

---

[1] *NC* 6th ser. 15 (1955), 'Proceedings', p. xx, but no details there given.
[2] G. C. Brooke, *English Coins*, 3rd ed. (London, 1950).
[3] *Nordisk Numismatisk Årsskrift* 1957–8, 39.
[4] Most recently by P. J. Seaby, *Coins of England and the United Kingdom*, 12th ed. (London, 1973), p. 42, which could plead such recent (1967) and seemingly impeccable academic authority as Sylloge of Coins of the Brit. Isles *Ashmolean* 1, 53–6.
[5] 2nd ed. (London, 1961), p. 209.

years, and 912, if not indeed 910, has always seemed a perilously early *terminus post quem non* for those of Edward's coins which are not patently late. There are numerous regal coins which are demonstrably 'post-Cuerdale' but which by no means conform to the module of the Plegmund pieces on spread flans, and it has been particularly worrying that none of the archiepiscopal coins appears to exhibit any of the transitional features observable in quite a number of pennies of Edward which are neither characteristically early nor typically late. In other words, before 912 far too many coins have had to be fitted in which present either early or intermediate features, while for the rest of the reign the number of coins which have had to be spread out over more than a decade is much too small. The rare coins of Brooke type 2 are a case in point. The module and style suggest a date towards 920, but beside them coins of the same type and of identical work exhibit the name of Plegmund and so presumably fall before 914, taking with them not only the Edward the Elder pieces of Brooke type 2 but also at least a proportion of the larger flan coins of types 12 and 13.

The dilemma is a real one, and none the less real for being for too long avoided. Fortunately it can now be resolved in the light of a paper in the first (1972) volume of this publication.[1] Miss O'Donovan gives the *obit* of Archbishop Plegmund as 2 August 923 and supports this unqualified rejection of the traditional 914 dating by an appeal to J. Armitage Robinson, *The Saxon Bishops of Wells* (London, 1918), pp. 56–8.[2] It is only too clear that the case for 914 depended on totally unreliable evidence. For the numismatist the implications of this new chronology are as momentous as welcome. In the first place it is now possible to arrange Edward's coins in three distinct groupings – 'early', 'intermediate' and 'late' – which are far more appropriate to the material than the old dichotomy. Datings at this stage cannot hope to be more than approximate, but little violence would appear to be done to the evidence by the provisional assumption that the first phase of the regal coinage ends *c*. 910 and the second *c*. 920. That the Canterbury mint on this telling re-opens a decade later than was previously postulated seems to present no difficulties for the historian, while the fact that at least three of the archiepiscopal moneyers went on to strike for Athelstan is, if anything, more compatible with the hypothesis that they had been striking for the archbishop as recently as the early 920s. Easily the most important consequence of the revised dating, however, is its implication that it was Athelstan and not Edward the Elder who broke with tradition and banished from English coins the names of the southern primates. 2 August 923 as

[1] M. A. O'Donovan, 'An Interim Revision of Episcopal Dates for the Province of Canterbury, 850–950: Part I', *ASE* 1 (1972), 23–44.
[2] *Ibid*. pp. 26 and 31.

the date of Plegmund's death does not require us to suppose – as the earlier date did – that his successor Athelm was effectively in possession of the metropolitan see at Edward's death on 17 July 924. Athelm's sojourn at Canterbury was relatively brief – he in turn died on 8 January 926 – and it could well be significant that he introduced his nephew Dunstan to Athelstan's court, not to Edward's.[1] A new reign, conceivably *sede vacante* into the bargain, might well have been the occasion for a rigorous application of the apparently novel principle 'that there is to be one coinage over all the king's dominion':[2] it should have been recognized that an element of uncharacteristic indecision was involved in the belief that the collected, if conservative, Edward restored to the coins the name of Plegmund *c.* 912 after an interval of perhaps twenty years only to abolish the privilege a couple of years later. It would have been quite in character, though, for the reforming Athelstan, with his almost monomaniac preoccupation with uniformity, to insist that the king's name and none other appear on all coin of the realm.

Further discussion of these and other numismatic implications of Miss O'Donovan's revision of the date of Plegmund's death can safely be left to Mr C. E. Blunt, whose forthcoming monograph on the coinage of Athelstan promises to be a turning-point in our understanding of the English coinages of the tenth century. It is sufficient here to have emphasized how well the numismatic evidence accords with Miss O'Donovan's interpretation of the documentary sources.

[1] F. M. Stenton, *Anglo-Saxon England*, 3rd ed. (Oxford, 1971), p. 446.
[2] II Athelstan 14; *English Historical Documents c. 500–1042*, ed. D. Whitelock (London, 1955), p. 384.

The Icelandic saga of Edward the Confessor: its version of the Anglo-Saxon emigration to Byzantium

CHRISTINE FELL

The fourteenth-century compiler of the saga of Edward the Confessor, *Saga Játvarðar konungs hins helga*, supplemented his material on the king[1] with history, anecdote and legend on various topics. His final chapter contains an account of the Anglo-Saxon emigration to Byzantium after the Norman Conquest. No historian doubts that this event took place. There is fairly full documentation from Byzantium itself and the accounts of the Anglo-Norman chronicler Orderic and the hagiographer Goscelin are not unknown. But in general the medieval chroniclers in England make no reference to it and the scholars who have worked on *Játvarðar saga*, perhaps insufficiently aware of supporting Byzantine evidence, have tended to dismiss the account as a fabrication. Gudbrand Vigfusson calls it 'an extraordinary story'.[2] Professor Jón Helgason writes, with a characteristic touch of fine disdain, that 'the saga concludes with the episode of Earl Sigurðr of Gloucester, who after the Conquest left England, together with other English malcontents, and with the Greek emperor's consent settled in a country six days' journey north-east of Constantinople. Here they gave the towns such English names as London and York. The source of this far-fetched story is unknown.'[3] H. L. Rogers says no more than 'evidently a similar tradition was known to the Anglo-Norman Ordericus Vitalis'.[4]

One of the places where the *Játvarðar saga*'s contribution to the evidence might have been analysed in full is in the *Væringjasaga* of Sigfús Blöndal, subtitled *Saga Norræna, Rússneskra og Enskra Hersveita í Þjónustu Miklagarðskeisara á Miðöldum*. Yet in spite of the inclusion here of the word *enskra* the book deals only slightly with the English presence in Constantinople and *Játvarðar saga* is described as 'bersýnilega full af ýkjum'.[5]

---

[1] On this see my 'The Icelandic Saga of Edward the Confessor: the Hagiographic Sources', *ASE* 1 (1972), 247–58.
[2] *Icelandic Sagas*, ed. Gudbrand Vigfusson, Rolls Series (1887), 1, xvii.
[3] *Byskupa Sǫgur*, ed. Jón Helgason, Corp. Cod. Islandicorum Medii Aevi 19 (Copenhagen, 1950), 22.
[4] H. L. Rogers, 'An Icelandic Life of St Edward the Confessor', *SBVS* 14 (1953–7), 259.
[5] 'Clearly full of ambiguities', Sigfús Blöndal, *Væringjasaga* (Reykjavík, 1954), p. 218.

In any case Blöndal, wishing to prove that Scandinavians not English were most prominent in the Varangian guard in the eleventh and twelfth centuries, naturally minimizes the English element. In his article on Nabites the Varangian he puts his viewpoint clearly: 'We must conclude that there was a strong Scandinavian element in this particular regiment [the Varangian guard] during the period of the Comneni, and I think it can be proved, that the majority were Norsemen, not English, at any rate until the reign of Manuel Comnenus, probably all the way down to 1204.'[1] Following this theory Blöndal attempts to demonstrate that Anna Comnena's 'Thule' refers to the Scandinavian countries rather than England and that the man she names Nabites must have been a Norwegian or an Icelander. The result of Blöndal's not unnatural lack of interest in the English contingent among the Varangians is that he has done no more than give passing mention to *Játvarðar saga* in his text and quote it in his footnotes.

R. M. Dawkins in an article on the later history of the Varangian guard attempts to put the *Játvarðar saga* version into perspective by suggesting that its sources were twofold: on the one hand the fact that 'many Englishmen did go to serve in Constantinople after the conquest of their own country' and on the other hand 'some distorted tradition of the Goths in the Crimea'.[2] He allows a paragraph for analysis of the details, but it is clear that he too does not take the saga very seriously, since he dismisses it as 'a curious story'. He refers to a different version of the saga in the *Flateyjarbók* manuscript, but in fact *Flateyjarbók* has no differences at this point.

The least cavalier treatment of the *Játvarðar saga* account is in the 1852 edition of the saga.[3] Here parallels from Ordericus Vitalis are cited in the footnotes and the places on the emigrants' route from England to Greece are identified. Mistrust of the sagas had not at that date become a fashion.

The story deserves a fuller summary than Jón Helgason's, which records its least probable details. It tells how William's rule was hated by English chieftains, who tried to persuade Svein of Denmark to come to their aid against him. But William bought off Svein with tribute. Therefore a number of Englishmen under the leadership of Sigurðr, earl of Gloucester, rather than endure William's rule longer, sold their land and left England. The route which they took is recorded in some detail. Eventually they arrived in Sicily, where they heard that the Emperor Kirjalax (Alexius) had just come to power and that Byzantium was under attack. Knowing that Scandinavians who went into service in Byzantium had received great honour, they thought

---

[1] Sigfús Blöndal, 'Nabites the Varangian', *Classica et Mediaevalia* 2 (1939), 147.

[2] R. M. Dawkins, 'The Later History of the Varangian Guard: Some Notes', *Jnl of Roman Stud.* 37 (1947), 42.

[3] C. C. Rafn and Jón Sigurdsson, 'Saga Játvarðar Konúngs hins Helga', *Annaler for Nordisk Oldkyndighed og Historie* (1852), 3–43.

it would be to their advantage to go there. Accordingly they did so, and won Alexius's gratitude by fighting a victorious battle on his behalf. They stayed for some time in Byzantium, where Alexius offered to make them members of his bodyguard, an offer which some of them accepted. Others wanted land of their own. Alexius refused to give them land already owned by his people, but told them of territory north-east across the Black Sea, formerly under Byzantine rule, now occupied by the heathens. Some of the English sailed north, took this land for themselves and named their settlements there after English towns. They would not accept *Pálsbók*, the form of religion current in Byzantium, but looked for bishops and clergy from Hungary.[1]

A very great service has been done to the scholarship of this subject by Miss Krijnie Ciggaar, who has drawn our attention to a previously un-noticed Latin account of the Anglo-Saxon emigration.[2] This occurs in an unpublished section of the *Chronicon universale anonymi Laudunensis*, a world chronicle which ends at the year 1219, was written by an English monk of the Premonstratensian order at Laon and survives in two thirteenth-century manuscripts, Phillipps 1880 now in the Deutsche Staatsbibliothek, Berlin, and Paris, BN Lat. 5011. There can be no doubt that the account of the Anglo-Saxon emigration in *Játvarðar saga* is based on the one in this chronicle. In a later article I hope to discuss how far the *Chronicon Laudunensis* was a major source for most of *Játvarðar saga*'s non-hagiographic material. Here I limit myself to a discussion of the section on the Anglo-Saxons in Byzantium.

A comparison of the *Játvarðar saga* account with the *Chronicon* manuscripts reveals that the two have in common many details shared by no other text. Both of them specify the ranks of the leaders involved, the numbers of earls and barons who emigrated and the number of ships which they took. The journey through the Mediterranean with stopping-places at Septem on the north African coast and at Majorca and Minorca is described in both but not elsewhere. The arrival in Byzantium and the honour accorded to the emigrants by Alexius is confirmed by Ordericus and by the Byzantine evidence, but the final passage, concerning the English emigrants' voyage six days' sailing distance across the Black Sea to a land which they called New England and in which they gave their settlements the names of English towns, is found only in this chronicle and saga. A rejection of Greek Ortho-doxy in favour of the Latin rites of the Hungarian church is also found in both texts.[3] In addition the general order and grouping of material follows the same pattern in both.

[1] Vigfusson, *Icelandic Sagas*, pp. 398–400.
[2] Miss Ciggaar's article, which includes a transcript of the relevant sections of the *Chronicon Laudunensis* and lists previous publication of the manuscripts, is to appear shortly in *Revue des Études Byzantines*.
[3] See my 'A Note on *Pálsbók*', *Med. Scandinavia* (forthcoming).

But though there is this close correspondence in the general outline of material that is found in no other source, especially in the New England section, there is not a close textual resemblance. Sometimes it is possible to see parallel of sentence to sentence and there are a number of places where links between the Latin and Norse vocabulary are obvious and interesting, but in general the Icelandic author has drastically shortened his material and conveys in a phrase the Latin of a sentence or a paragraph. For example, the Latin names three leaders of the emigration and then says: '(H)ii tres fuerunt heroes quos anglici corrupto idiomate herles uocant . . . (F)uerunt et alie dignitatis uiri qui a suis drenc nominabantur que dignitas prima fuit post heroes hos possumus non indigne barones uocitare.'[1] The Icelandic for this and more is: 'Þar vóru fyrir þrír jarlar ok átta barúnar.' Yet in spite of this extreme contraction the Icelandic retains not only the information of the original but the direct verbal links of *jarlar* and *barúnar*.[2] Or again, there is another example in the description of the land which the emigrants called *Nova Anglia*. We learn from both Icelandic and Latin that this land is six days' sailing distance north-east of Byzantium, that it was once under Byzantine rule but subsequently had been conquered and settled by pagans and that some of the English stayed in Byzantium itself while others set sail for this land, killed the pagans and named the country England and the settlements after English towns. When we are told in both texts of the land's fertility we can once again see the hand of the Icelandic translator at work in cutting down the verbosity of his original. The Latin reads: 'Est autem regio pascuis uberrima. fontes salubres flumina piscosa. Saltus ameni. Agri fertiles. fructus gustu iocundi', but the Icelandic simply: 'er þat hinn bezti landkostr'.

Yet there are also a number of places where the Icelandic offers us slightly more information than the Latin. In the earlier part of the story the Latin starts the account of the voyage from England with the voyagers' arrival at Septem. The Icelandic gives additional detail for the first part of the route, mentioning *Matheus nes*, *Galizu land* and *Nörva sund*. In the New England section it is only the Icelandic version which tells us that the English obtained the promise from Alexius that if they won back this land from the heathen it should belong to them free of dues or tribute, and further it is only the Icelandic which tells us that the settlements called after English towns were named London and York.

---

[1] My transcripts are from Phillipps 1880. My thanks are due to the Deutsche Staatsbibliothek, Berlin, for permission to use this manuscript.

[2] The saga writer cannot have failed to recognize the term *drenc* borrowed into Old English from ON *drengr*. But in the *Chronicon* it is equated with a specific rank, a meaning which it acquired in late Old English and which survives into Middle English. ON *drengir* would not have suggested to the audience a rank equivalent to *barúnar*, but rather either the personal followers of the *jarl* (in which case there would have been more than eight) or the general body of emigrants whose presence is covered by the term *mikit lið ok fritt*.

In addition to the differences imposed on the texts by contraction in some areas and expansion in others there are places where the actual information given is different. The Icelandic names the foremost of the three earls as 'Sigurðr jarl af Glocestr' while the Latin calls him 'Stanardus', though still 'comes cladicestrie'; in the Icelandic eight barons are said to emigrate, in the Latin a list of twelve names is given; in the Icelandic the ships number 'hálft fjórða hundrað', in the Latin 'ducentis et triginta quinque'; in the Icelandic the English hear the news about the Greek emperor's troubles with heathen invaders while they are on the island of 'Sikiley', in the Latin when they arrive 'ad sardiniam'.

Perhaps the most complicated range of variants is found right at the beginning of the tale, before the emigration takes place, when negotiations with Svein of Denmark are in process. The Latin text says that two embassies went to the Danish king, one from the English rebels and one from William. 'Godwinus iunior', brother of that Harold who was killed by the Normans, and Haveloch 'de regia stirpe dacorum ortus' went on the first, and Helsinus, abbot of Ramsey, on the second. The Icelandic translator distinguishes the two embassies, one from the rebels and one from William, but he does not name anyone on the first mission and he puts both Godwine and a bishop (not abbot) on the second. He does not name the bishop, he omits Haveloch and he calls Godwine not brother of Harold but 'Guðini ungi Guðinason', giving the same identity but using a different method of identification.[1] On the other hand the 'rex dacorum' is not named in the Latin, but the saga writer is quite clear that he is Svein Ulfsson. And, again, the Icelandic is more precise than the Latin about the purpose of the first embassy to Svein. The Latin merely says that the two were sent to the Danish king 'ut eis subuectaret auxilium opportunum', the Icelandic has the invitation that if Svein will come to England with a Danish army the English will fight against William and accept Svein's rule.

All these differences in the two accounts need more explanation than mere carelessness or laziness on the part of the Icelandic translator, even though this is the last chapter of the saga and his abrupt conclusion might indicate that he was getting tired of the subject. When he adds information it is often possible to explain it away as general knowledge. The route between England and the Straits of Gibraltar was a common one for Vikings; the names London and York were well known, and the fact that Svein Ulfsson ruled the Danes at the time of the Norman Conquest could readily be learned from the kings' sagas. Similarly it could be argued that the well-read author of *Játvarðar saga* certainly knew enough English history to identify a brother of Harold as a son of Godwine, and that the name *Sigurðr*, especially coupled

---

[1] The *Flateyjarbók* reading is 'Guðina junga Ballduinasun jarls'.

with *jarl*, would naturally fall more easily from an Incelander's pen than *Stanardus*. Yet such explanations do not seem to me adequate, even if we accept that certain points are either misreadings or additions of no significance. It is surprising that in the Latin text after we have been told of the great fleet amassed by the emigrants the next sentence should begin 'Et uenientes apud septam'. It is more likely that the scribe omitted a sentence about leaving England and following the west coast of France and Spain for the first part of the journey than that there should be so abrupt a transition. I do not discount the possibility that an Icelandic translator, faced with this awkward connection, bridged it himself with the sentence: 'Þeir fóru fyrst suðr um sjó, ok síðan vestr fyrir Matheus-nes, ok svá út fyrir Galizu-land; en þaðan fóru þeir til Nörva-sundz, ok út yfir sundin til höfuð-borgar þeirrar er Septem heitir.' But my reading of Old Norse does not include other references to 'Matheus nes', which is a perfectly acceptable translation for 'pointe de saint Mathieu'. The Breton headland is still called by this name, and it would certainly be the first notable landmark to anyone going 'south across the sea' from the west coast of England. One would also expect textual justification for the description of Septem as 'höfuð-borg' rather than just 'borg' and for the accurate placing of it 'út yfir sundin'.

If we add up the differences in names the total is impressive. It is to be expected that an Icelander would translate 'Willelmus rex anglie benignissimus' as 'Viljálmr bastharðr' and that Contantinople would become 'Miklagarðr' and Alexius 'Kirjalax inn mikli', though even here the Icelandic adds a rider without authority from the Latin, 'ok hafði ný-tekit við riki'. The saga writer adds the name of one person (Svein Ulfsson) and of five places, three on the route to Byzantium and two in New England. He changes one place-name (Sicily) and one personal name (Sigurðr). The last of these is the most challenging. If we accept that 'Sigurðr jarl af Glocestr' was copied from a Latin reading 'Stanardus . . . comes cladicestrie', we are faced with the unlikely situation that the translator, baffled by the personal name, could yet unhesitatingly and accurately render *cladicestria* as *Glocestr*. Besides, the saga's *Sigurðr* is a good deal more probable than the chronicle's *Stanardus*. *Stanardus* occurs quite frequently in Domesday Book but is not attached to any person of note in English history of the mid-eleventh century. *Sigurðr*, or in its more usual English form *Siward*, is on the other hand the name of two distinguished opponents of William. There were two Siwards who joined Hereward's resistance at Ely, Siward of Maldon and Siward Barn. 'Siwardus de Maldune, socius Ærewardi', appears with that appellation in the *Liber Eliensis*[1] and as 'de Meldona tegnus' and 'tegnus et cognatus

---

[1] *Liber Eliensis*, ed. E. O. Blake, Camden 3rd ser. 92 (London, 1962), 291.

regis', landowner of great estates in Essex and Suffolk, according to a number of entries for those counties in Domesday Book.[1] After Ely he disappears from English records. Siward Barn appears more frequently in historical sources. The *Anglo-Saxon Chronicle* tells us that in 1071 'com se bisceop Egelwine ond Siward Bearn ond fela hund manna mid heom in to Elig'.[2] Both the *Anglo-Saxon Chronicle* and later sources tell us that all the outlaws surrendered to William except Hereward and those who remained with him. Siward is not named among them.[3] Simeon of Durham adds to the story the detail that in 1070 Siward Barn, in the company of Prince Edgar and his family, left York, stayed with the Danes (presumably the Danish fleet in the Humber) and then found hospitality at the court of Malcolm of Scotland.[4] Orderic knows of a Siward 'tribunus Merciorum' connected with the Scottish house. Gaimar claims that Siward and Bishop Æthelwine left Scotland by sea in new ships in order to join the Ely rebellion, thus linking the information in the *Anglo-Saxon Chronicle* with Simeon's.[5] Domesday Book tells us that Siward Barn owned impressive estates not only in Gloucestershire, but widely throughout Mercia, enjoying *sac* and *soc* in Lincolnshire and Nottinghamshire.[6]

Even if Siward Barn were not Orderic's 'tribunus Merciorum' it is clear that he was a man of some standing, and if he brought hundreds of men to Ely he had a considerable following. If we wish to associate him with the saga writer's earl of Gloucester, leader of the Anglo-Saxon emigration, the pattern of hostility to William and reliance on Danish help is right, the name is right and the locality is right. Also it is very clear from Byzantine as well as European sources that the leader of the emigration must have been a man of some distinction, since there is on record a complaint to the Greek emperor concerning the honour accorded to 'the foreigner who has come to

---

[1] Olof von Feilitzen, *The Pre-Conquest Personal Names of Domesday Book* (Uppsala, 1937), pp. 361–3.

[2] This is the E text. (*Two of the Saxon Chronicles Parallel*, ed. J. Earle and C. Plummer (1892–9) I, 208). The D text has the name form *Sigwarð*.

[3] The only piece of evidence against Siward's leadership of the emigration is Florence of Worcester's statement that Siward Barn was one of the prisoners released by William on his deathbed in 1087. But Florence may have been relying on nothing more than the *Anglo-Saxon Chronicle*'s list of rebels against William and the issue could have been confused by the presence of two Siwards at Ely. The Durham charters including Siward Barn in the witness-lists are forgeries. On the other hand recent scholarship mentioning the leader of the emigrants as 'Siward, dont les chroniques ont conservé le nom' has as its sole source *Játvarðar saga*, translated into Latin by Thormodus Torfæus in 1711, quoted from there by the nineteenth-century historian Augustin Thierry and adopted uncritically as late as 1953 by R. Janin, *La Géographie Ecclésiastique de l'Empire Byzantin* (Paris, 1953), p. 591.

[4] *Symeonis Monachis Opera Omnia*, ed. Thomas Arnold, RS (1882–5) II, 190.

[5] Gaimar, *Lestorie des Engles*, ed. Sir Thomas Duffus Hardy and Charles Trice Martin, RS (1888–9) I, 231.

[6] In *VCH Warwickshire* I, 282–3 J. H. Round draws together the estates held by Siward Barn. See also von Feilitzen, *Pre-Conquest Personal Names, s.n. Sigeweard*.

us from England'.[1] But there is no direct proof that Siward Barn is the saga's *Sigurðr*, and since the saga is the only source to offer this name it would be absurd to press this suggestion further. The point I wish to emphasize is that whereas some evidence can be adduced in favour of a *Sigurðr* none at all can be offered for *Stanardus* beyond the existence of the name. Von Feilitzen records a number of entries under *Stanheard*, mostly with the qualification 'liber homo'. He adds 'Among later bearers we may note . . . two Colch[ester] burgesses in 1086 . . . and a great number of peasants under Bury St Edmunds . . . 1087–98.'[2] It is clear enough that there was a fair amount of class-consciousness in the Anglo-Saxon choice of names, and *Stanheard* is not found in the family trees of Anglo-Saxon kings or nobles. *Siward/Sigeweard* is inherently a more likely name for a man of distinguished birth, a *jarl* or a *comes*.

Whether saga or chronicle or neither is accurate on this point, there are a number of other places where the chronicle's accuracy can certainly be faulted, and not all its errors are taken into the Icelandic text. In listing the emigrants the Latin text names one as earl of Lichfield, a title not created at the time of the emigration. The Icelandic omits this reference. The messengers sent by the English to ask for Danish help against William – Godwine, brother of Harold, and Haveloch – are both suspect. Harold had a son called Godwine, but we do not know of a brother of that name, and Haveloch is a character of Middle English romance.

Perhaps most curious of all is the evident confusion in the chronicler's reports between the Scandinavians and the English in Byzantium. It is to be expected that Byzantine sources should not always be clear about the distinctions between tribes of northern barbarians, but it seems odd in a European chronicler. After the account of the colony in New England the writer of the *Chronicon* adopts without explanation the term 'angli orientales'. I am not sure what he means by this, but from the placing it looks like a distinction in his mind between those who had settled New England, the 'noui angli', and those who had stayed in Byzantium. At any rate he puts the description of the events concerning the 'angli orientales' after his account of the English emigration. He says that the messenger sent by Alexius to obtain tribute from the 'angli orientales' was killed by them and Alexius in revenge intended to kill 'omnes anglos', for fear of which many of them crossed to New England and many of them took to piracy. It is one of the 'angli orientales' called *Hardigt/Hardigch* (both spellings are in Phillipps

---

[1] A. A. Vasiliev, 'The Opening Stages of the Anglo-Saxon Immigration to Byzantium in the Eleventh Century', *Annales de l'Institut Kondakov* 9 (1937), 65. Anyone working in this field must be deeply indebted to Vasiliev's research. I have relied heavily on this article for the Byzantine material.

[2] Von Feilitzen, *Pre-Conquest Personal Names*, p. 372.

1880) who kills a lion, who is 'fortissimus omnium anglorum' and who is raised to a position of eminence by the emperor.

Most of these references to 'angli orientales' fit much better with what we know of the Scandinavian Varangians than anything we know of the English. Hardigt, who was not mentioned in the first list of emigrants, must in fact be the Norwegian Harald Hardrada, who adopted for his stay in Byzantium the pseudonym Nordbrigt. *Hardigt* looks like a mixture of his real name and his alias. Scandinavia knows a tradition whereby Harald while in Byzantium killed a great serpent,[1] whereas in William of Malmesbury as in the *Chronicon* the adversary is a lion.[2] William of Malmesbury is nearly as confused as the *Chronicon*. In his version the name is *Haroldus Harvagra*, a confusion which is common in English sources. It is the name not the identity that is mistaken, since William correctly calls him brother of Olaf and refers to his service under the Greek emperor. William also tells us that Harald was thrown to the lion 'pro stupro illustris foeminae'. Sigfús Blöndal is scathing about this: 'We can treat lightly the piece of information given by William of Malmesbury that the cause of Harald's imprisonment was an illicit love affair with a high born lady.'[3] Blöndal is more concerned with establishing facts than linking traditions and he points out that a Greek source hints at Harald's problems without stating them and that Saxo's version of the imprisonment is that Harald was 'homicidii crimine damnatus'. William's story may not be factually accurate, but the sagas are eloquent on the subject of Maria, 'ein mær, ung ok fríð'. According to Snorri she was the niece of the empress Zoe.[4] *Morkinskinna* and *Flateyjarbók* have long accounts of Harald and Maria, *Morkinskinna* including a charming story of how Maria's quick-wittedness actually prevented Harald from being charged with her seduction. Snorri more austerely tells us only that Harald asked for Maria's hand in marriage, but all three sources are agreed that Zoe was angry, that the Varangians believed this was because she had wanted Harald herself and that the embezzlement charges which led to Harald's imprisonment resulted from Zoe's anger on this account. Blöndal has failed to find any Maria in Byzantium who will fit and he is inclined to think, if I read him rightly, that the charge of seduction is a romantic story to cover up the real matter of misappropriation of public money, rather than that, as the sagas have it, the monetary charge was invented by Zoe for the reasons outlined. Whatever the facts behind the story, it is clear that William of

---

[1] *Morkinskinna*, ed. C. R. Unger (Christiania, 1867), pp. 12–13; *Flateyjarbók*, ed. G. Vigfusson and C. R. Unger (Christiania, 1860–8) III, 304–5.
[2] William of Malmesbury, *De Gestis Regum Anglorum*, ed. William Stubbs, RS (1887–9) II, 318.
[3] Sigfús Blöndal, 'The Last Exploits of Harald Sigurdsson in Greek Service', *Classica et Mediaevalia* 2 (1939), 13.
[4] *Heimskringla*, ed. Bjarni Aðalbjarnarson, Íslenzk Fornrit 26–8 (Reykjavík, 1941–51), III, 85.

Malmesbury knew something not unlike the tradition that reached Iceland and that both William and the author of the *Chronicon* had heard tales of King Harald similar to those in the sagas, even though neither had the name right and most of the detail is different. The difference of detail demonstrates clearly that their sources for this material are independent. Their accounts link with each other in mentioning the lion, not serpent, but have links with the sagas that are separate and unrelated. It is the other half of the charge than William's that is known to the author of the *Chronicon*. He reports a quarrel over tribute money between the emperor and the 'angli orientales'. Snorri's story is that Zoe claimed Harald had 'misfarit með Grikkjakonungs fé' and he was imprisoned, but was subsequently released from prison to lead a Varangian rebellion against the emperor responsible. In the *Chronicon* the emperor, after threatening to kill 'omnes anglos', penitently recalled them. Again the details are unlike, but a quarrel over money, a Varangian rebellion and an eventual peaceful settlement seem to be the facts behind the two variant accounts. The most startling connection of all is that we know Harald Hardrada to have been given the rank of *manglabites* and subsequently of *spatharokandidates* (colonel) by the emperor.[1] This is recorded in Byzantine sources. The *Chronicon Laudunensis* tells us that: 'Imperator uero eum principem omnium custodum suorum constituit et non multo post ducem naualis exercitus ordinauit.' If we sum up the points that Hardigt and Harald Hardrada have in common they are the name, the killing of a lion/serpent, the trouble over taxes and the appointment to a specific rank by the emperor. This is, I think, enough to establish their identity, especially as William of Malmesbury's story shows that distorted tales of Harald Hardrada's exploits had filtered through to English chroniclers.

I conclude that the term 'angli orientales' was the result of someone's distinction between English and Norwegian Varangians. The common Icelandic term for Norwegian was *austrænn*, 'easterner', and it may be that whoever carried the report to north-west Europe (perhaps some Anglo-Dane in the train of Wulfric of Lincoln[2]) might have picked up the term and the story of Harald from one of the Icelanders so frequently found in the Varangian bodyguard. The chronicler himself obviously failed to understand the nature of the distinction and believed that he was writing about two groups of English emigrants. This belief has confused his chronology. Anything concerning Harald Hardrada in Byzantium probably happened in the

[1] Blöndal, 'Last Exploits', p. 2, and Gustav Storm, 'Harald Haardraade og Væringerne i de græske Keiseres Tjeneste', *Historisk Tidsskrift* 2nd ser. 4 (Christiania, 1884), 369–70.

[2] As E. A. Freeman pointed out (*The History of the Norman Conquest*, 2nd ed. (Oxford, 1870–9), p. 847), it is an interesting comment on the haphazard nature of our sources that we hear of Wulfric's embassy only because he donated relics of St John Chrysostom to Abingdon. The record is in *Chronicon Monasterii de Abingdon*, ed. Joseph Stevenson, RS (1858), II, 46–7.

decade 1035 to 1045. He died at Stamford Bridge in 1066, the very year in which William's seizure of the English crown turned English minds in the direction of Byzantium. Even so the English probably did not arrive there for another decade, when they had given up all hope of help against William from Svein of Denmark. Even if we accept the story of the colonization of New England it had not taken place at the time when the 'angli orientales' refused to pay tribute and in the face of the emperor's anger 'plurimi eor*um* ad nouos anglos tr*an*sier*unt*'.

Clearly we must not believe all we read in the *Chronicon Laudunensis*. But it is evident that the chronicler has had access to some genuine material from Byzantium. His muddled account is based on fact, however much decorated with fiction. One of our problems is to decide how far we can hope to disentangle the two. Another is to decide the precise nature of the textual relationship between the *Chronicon* and *Játvarðar saga*.

It is evident that the saga writer was not interested in Hardigt and probably never even associated him with Harald Hardrada. He ignores the *Chronicon*'s distinction between 'noui' and 'orientales angli'. I doubt whether he noticed it, for the only fact he takes from the account of the 'angli orientales' is to the effect that disliking the authority of the Greek patriarch they turned to the Roman church of Hungary, but he inserts this into his account of the English inhabiting New England. Still the saga writer knows about Scandinavian Varangians and he introduces them in his own way. When the English exiles reach Sicily and hear of the hostilities against Byzantium their hopes are roused because 'langan tíma áðr höfðu Norðmenn þar stór-miklar sæmðir, þeir er mála-menn gjörðuz'. Later, when in both Latin and Icelandic texts the emperor issues an invitation to the English to become the imperial bodyguard, it is only the Icelandic that adds 'svá sem siðvenja Væringja var til, þeirra sem á mála gengu'. Again it can be argued that of course the saga writer would be sufficiently well educated to make these additions, but it cannot be denied that he has produced a more coherent, and in some respects more informed, account than the *Chronicon*'s. All his additions make good sense, the additional information they provide, where we can check it, is accurate, and the saga is free of a number of the chronicle's more glaring errors. I do not think that all this can be attributed to a combination of good luck and general knowledge. It is more likely that the saga writer had in front of him an earlier, less muddled, possibly shorter, text than the present recension of the *Chronicon*. I think that this source provided him with at least some of the names absent in the extant manuscripts of the *Chronicon* (certainly *Matheus nes* and *Glocestr*), that *Siwardus* not *Stanardus* was an original reading and that such delightful details as the introduction of Haveloch are the whimsical interpolations of a later scribe. The possibility that both *Chronicon* and saga versions of the emigration derive independently from another source altogether is ruled out by the close correspondence between other stories shared by the two, though it is true that these all occur in the same section of the *Chronicon*. We must assume, in fact, that the saga's source was, if not a recension of the whole work, at any rate a fairly large piece of historical writing subsequently incorporated into the *Chronicon* wholesale.

I think, however, that we are also entitled to conclude that the recension from which *Játvarðar saga* derives was not particularly close to the one in the extant manuscripts of the *Chronicon*. These manuscripts, Phillipps 1880 and BN Lat. 5011, present the same version except for orthographical variants, mainly in names. Lat. 5011 has generally been assumed to be a direct and almost contemporary copy of Phillipps 1880.[1] Certainly Phillipps 1880 looks marginally closer to Old English originals in the spelling of names than Lat. 5011 does. Phillipps 1880, for example, has *Vlfchetel*, *Godwinus* and *Alsino*, where Lat. 5011 has *Vlchetel*, *Godwinus* and *Helsino*. It is probable that we have only the one recension in these two manuscripts, but we have very little hope of establishing the relation of this part of Phillipps 1880 to a hypothetical original. Miss Ciggaar argues the closeness of the account to the event from the use of a present tense describing one of the emigrants in Byzantium, 'Coleman hic uir sanc*tus* consta*n*tinopoli habet te*m*pl*um*', but, as she is herself aware, this is a small point on which to build. All we are entitled to posit is an account of the Anglo-Saxon emigration, perhaps not longer after the event than Wulfric of Lincoln's return visit as ambassador from Alexius to Henry I early in the twelfth century, this account being later incorporated into an early version or source of the *Chronicon Laudunensis*. From such a source, or earlier version, are derived (perhaps at some removes) the accounts in Phillipps 1880 and *Játvarðar saga*.

Before Miss Ciggaar's entry into this field of research the *Chronicon* account had been overlooked and the *Játvarðar saga* was, as we have seen, considered negligible and even absurd. At first sight the provision of a respectable Latin chronicle as a source for the saga would seem to go some way towards vindicating the saga writer of the charges levelled against him. Unfortunately this source turns out to be even more full of difficulties than the saga. In the saga account we have a certain amount of information supported elsewhere, together with some found only in the saga itself, but, unlike the *Chronicon*, the saga is not full of demonstrable errors mixed in with this material. But there is also material in both saga and chronicle that is clearly accurate, and it is time for us to turn to those parts of the story which have full supporting evidence from Byzantium and from other European sources. In this way we may hope finally to arrive at a reasonable

[1] Details will appear in Miss Ciggaar's forthcoming article in *Revue des Études Byzantines*.

assessment of their value and validity. As far as possible I shall treat the version shared by the *Chronicon Laudunensis* and *Játvarðar saga* as one, referring to it as the *CL/JS* version, and concentrate on the material they have in common, not their differences.

CL/JS are certainly not derived from any of our previously known sources on the post-Conquest Anglo-Saxon emigration to Byzantium. The two other northern references are much slighter, lacking accumulation of detail and any hint whatsoever of the New England colony. The Byzantine evidence is of course centred on the presence of the English in Constantinople, not on the circumstances of the emigration.

The earlier of the two other northern references is in Goscelin's *Miracula de Sancto Augustino Episcopo Cantuariensi in Anglia*.[1] This work cannot have been written very long after the event since Goscelin died at the beginning of the twelfth century. The other account is in the *Historic Ecclesiastica* of Ordericus Vitalis, finished in 1141. Orderic refers three times to the emigration, his first and fullest reference being in bk IV, ch. 3 (the second and third are in bk VII, ch. 5 and bk IX, ch. 5).[2] Goscelin's reference is brief and casual since he is not interested in the emigration itself, but in the devotion of one of the protagonists to St Augustine. The two reasons for trusting his account are his closeness to the event and the absence of any political or ecclesiastical propaganda value in his anecdote. For him, if not for us, it is immaterial that the people involved in his story are English emigrants to Byzantium: what matters is that, once there, one of them built a church in honour of St Augustine. If we look at the statements of both Goscelin and *CL/JS* we can see that there are several details where their accounts reinforce each other. Goscelin begins: 'Prima ex Normannis regnatore Angliae Willelmo Angliam captante, vir honorificus de curia et nutritura B. Augustini, cum multis Optimatibus patriae profugis, Constantinopolim transmigravit.' The general statement that after the Norman Conquest numbers of Englishmen emigrated to Byzantium is the same as in *CL/JS* and as in Ordericus Vitalis. The phrase 'multis optimatibus' suggests that the earls, barons, host of followers and hundreds of ships in *CL/JS* are not quite the fabrication they appear at first sight. Though the number of ships is considerable, the *Anglo-Saxon Chronicle* has no lack of references to ships by the hundred in its reports of Danish invasions. For example, it tells us that in 1076 200 ships came from Denmark with their leaders Cnut Sveinsson and Earl Hakon on board. There is no reason to distrust the *CL/JS* version on this point. Goscelin confirms the general statement that there were large numbers of

---

[1] *Acta Sanctorum Maii* VI (Antwerp, 1688), 410.

[2] Ordericus Vitalis, *Historia Ecclesiastica*, ed. Augustus le Prévost (Paris, 1838–55) II, 171–2, and III, 169 and 490. For the first of Orderic's references see also *The Ecclesiastical History of Orderic Vitalis* II, bks III and IV, ed. Marjorie Chibnall (Oxford, 1969), 202–4.

high-ranking men involved in the exile and the *Anglo-Saxon Chronicle* indicates that though the numbers of ships may be exaggerated they are not fantastic, even if there are 115 more ships in *JS* than in *CL*. If we turn to the other north-European account, that of Ordericus Vitalis, we find that he as well as Goscelin confirms the *CL/JS* statement that chieftains of high rank were involved in the emigration. He introduces them as 'pulchrae juventutis flore uernantes' and makes a later reference to Englishmen who 'cum proceribus regni Albionem reliquerant'. Orderic agrees with *CL/JS* that the exiles went by sea. His phrase is 'per Pontum in Thraciam navigaverant' and A. A. Vasiliev has demonstrated that since Orderic uses the word *pontus* as a common noun for 'sea' this should not be understood as referring to a route by way of the Black Sea, *Pontus Euxinus*.[1] Orderic and *CL/JS* all claim that the English met with a particularly favourable reception from Alexius because they arrived when he was fighting off invaders and their help was necessary to him, though in *CL/JS* these invaders are heathens (Turks) and in Orderic's account they are Normans. All sources are agreed that after this some of the English were willing to stay in the service of Alexius and that Alexius honoured them highly. *CL* may look over-stated: 'Custodia*m* sui corporis. et vxoris sue et filior*um* suor*um* et vniuerse regie stirpis eis credidit et eor*um* heredibus i*m*perium defendendu*m* scripto sigillato co*n*firmauit.' But Orderic has a similar emphasis: 'et eisdem principale palacium cum regalibus thesauris tradidit . . . et ipsi ac haeredes eorum sacro imperio fideliter famulati sunt; et cum magno honore inter Traces Cesari et senatui populoque kari usque nunc persisterunt'. Thus *CL/JS* are confirmed by the other two northern accounts and where these two do not offer support it is because of their greater brevity rather than because they contradict anything.

CL/JS are further supported by the Byzantine sources. Anna Comnena writes in her *Alexiad* of 'the Varangians from Thule (by these I mean the axe-bearing barbarians)' and of 'the barbarians from the island of Thule'.[2] She has this to say of the Varangians: 'they regard loyalty to the emperors and the protection of their persons as a family tradition, a kind of sacred trust and inheritance handed down from generation to generation'. The old question of whether Varangian here means the Scandinavian or English contingent and Thule means Scandinavia or Britain or just northern barbarian countries in general has been re-opened by Jonathan Shepard.[3] He argues convincingly that Anna uses the term Thule for Britain, and it follows from this that her comments on the barbarians from Thule relate to the English

---

[1] Vasiliev, 'Opening Stages', p. 53.
[2] Anna Comnena, *Alexiad*, trans. E. R. A. Sewter (Harmondsworth, 1969), pp. 95–6 and 100.
[3] Jonathan Shepard, 'The English and Byzantium', *Traditio* 29 (1973), 53–92.

Varangians. Documentary evidence from Byzantium also demonstrates that shortly after the accession of Alexius the Varangian bodyguard began to be identified as English. Byzantine sources listing the nationalities serving in Byzantium do not mention Anglo-Saxons between 1070 and 1080 but include them in a list of 1088. The Sicilian chronicler Geoffrey of Malaterra, whose history of Sicily ends with the year 1099, records an important semantic development in his famous phrase 'Angli vero, quos Waringos appellant'.[1] Northern and Byzantine emphasis on the high regard the emperor had for his English-Varangian bodyguard is remarkably confirmed by the letter of complaint written by one Nikoulitza, *c.* 1080:

Foreigners, unless they are of the royal house in their own country, you should not promote to high rank nor trust with great offices of State, for you will by so doing stultify both yourself and your own Greek men of rank. For if you honour the foreigner who has come to us from England by making him head of a department of state or general, what office of command will you have to give to the Roman?[2]

The evidence from Byzantine sources put forward by Vasiliev and fully and effectively deployed by Shepard leaves us in no doubt that there were large numbers of emigrant Englishmen in Byzantium by the end of the eleventh century.

Since all northern sources agree that the reason for the emigration was hostility to William who took the throne in 1066 and since all sources, northern and Byzantine, imply that the English reached Constantinople after the accession of Alexius who came to his throne in 1081, it becomes necessary to probe the time-gap more fully. There is of course no discrepancy in the Byzantine material which simply records the existence of the English mercenaries after their arrival. Orderic tells us that the English were welcomed by Alexius because he was fighting the Norman, Robert Guiscard, and certainly they must have been there by then, for Anna Comnena's reference to the barbarians from Thule who supported her father on his campaigns corroborates Orderic. It is likely, though, that they had arrived before Alexius's accession, and *CL* in spite of its confusion can probably give us the facts. *CL* is the only source to put an explicit date on the arrival: 'Acta sunt hec anno domini MLXXV.' On the other hand *CL/JS* also say that the English reached Byzantium in the reign of Alexius, when Byzantium was under siege from the Turks, or at any rate heathens. Since Alexius was not on the throne in 1075 one of these statements must be wrong. Probably the name of Alexius, so much more widely known than his predecessors, has

---

[1] Geoffrey of Malaterra, *De Rebus Gestis Rogerii Calabriae et Siciliae Comitis*, ed. E. Pontieri, Rerum Italicarum Scriptores 5.1, 2nd ed. (Bologna, n.d.), 74.

[2] Vasiliev, 'Opening Stages', p. 65.

clung to the tale and confused the chronology. Byzantium was besieged by the Turks in the reign of Michael Parapinaces (1071–8) and that this was known to the western world is shown by the Pope's appeal in 1074 for western Christian to help Byzantine Christian. *CL/JS* and Orderic appear to contradict each other, since Orderic tells us that Alexius warmly welcomed the English because of the Norman threat and *CL/JS* say that their favourable reception was because of their help against the Turkish threat. It is reasonable to conclude that the English took part in both campaigns and that the only error in *CL/JS* here is the use of the name Alexius instead of Michael as that of the reigning emperor when they arrived.

We still have the space 1066 to 1075 to account for and neither Orderic nor Goscelin is any help. But it is particularly clear in *JS* and implied in *CL* that it was not until all hope of help from Denmark was at an end that the English decided on emigration. If we look at the *Anglo-Saxon Chronicle* we find that Svein of Denmark made an abortive attempt against William in 1070, Hereward's Ely resistance was in 1071 and the Breton plot of 1075 attempted to enlist Danish help but without success. In 1076 according to English and Icelandic sources, but in 1074 according to Danish ones, Svein died. The failure of the so-called Breton plot in which it is clear that English as well as Bretons were involved had severe consequences. Earl Waltheof was executed and the plotters were mutilated or banished. Perhaps we should link the banishment in the *Anglo-Saxon Chronicle* with the voluntary emigration in Goscelin, Orderic and *CL/JS*. But even without this link it is clear that all hope of help from Denmark must have been at an end by the mid-1070s and the saga's statement that the emigration took place after the English were convinced that the Danes would not help them against William makes good sense in terms of the actual historical situation. The saga writer seems to be the only one aware of the time-gap involved and the need for explanation. When the English reach Byzantium he reminds us 'Þetta var nokkurum vetrum eptir fall Haraldz konungs Guðinasonar'. Orderic, for example, tells us of the English embassy to Svein and of the emigration but fails to make any connection between the two. The saga provides an acceptable time-scheme and it seems very likely that the emigration took place sometime during the mid-1070s, whether or not 1075 is precisely accurate for the date of their arrival.

Geographically too the *CL/JS* account has some validity. The places on the voyage through the Mediterranean (and in the case of the saga down the west coasts of France and Spain) are accurately given. In the description of New England we are told that the land lies north-east from Byzantium across the Black Sea, which is the direction of the Crimean peninsula. *CL/JS* claim that this land is six days' sailing distance from Byzantium. This is also the timing that the geographer pseudo-Scylax gives for such a voyage. He estimates the distance from the mouth of the Black Sea to the Danube as three days' and nights' sail and the distance from the Danube to the southern tip of the Crimea as a sail of a further three days and nights. *CL* similarly divides the distance into 'bis tridua nauigatione'. *CL/JS* also tell us that this land had formerly been under Byzantine rule but that at the time when Alexius offered it to the English it had been conquered and settled by pagans. R. M. Dawkins thinks that this statement fits very well with the loss of Kherson to the Russian Vladimir in 988. In fact Vladimir handed it back to Byzantium on the occasion of his baptism and it was certainly Byzantine-administered territory for much of the eleventh century. But it was also under constant threat from heathen invasion (the contemporary wave was the Pechenegs) and politically it was far too important to Byzantium to be readily surrendered. If the Varangians were no longer needed as a defence in Byzantium itself or its immediate environs, the Crimea would be an excellent outpost for them to hold. This accords with the Byzantine habit of establishing Varangians on the empire's borders. Geoffrey of Malaterra tells us of Castoria in Macedonia, 'Trecenti enim Waringi in eadem urbe habitabant, custodes ab imperatore deputati, quorum praesidio et opere non minimum defensabatur.'[1]

Orderic writes that Alexius had a town built at a place called Chevetot for the English, and this is usually identified with the unnamed 'stronghold by the sea' which Anna Comnena says that Alexius built to threaten Turkish Nicomedia and is thought to be Kibotos, a place less than one day's sail from Byzantium. It is possible that the *CL/JS* account of New England is some distorted version of this episode. But it is at least equally possible that, when they were no longer needed at Kibotos to keep an eye on the Turks in that region, the English were offered the defence and occupation of the Crimea on some such terms as *CL/JS* put forward.[2] If the English did make an attempt to settle a land six days' sail north-east of Byzantium it is not surprising that they should have named their settlements after remembered towns in England in the traditional manner of pioneers and exiles. Mr Shepard has found in the Crimea the traces of names indicating Varangian settlement (including a possible 'London') surviving into the late Middle Ages.[3] But it is not to be expected that linguistic and racial identity could have been preserved for any length of time and it should cause no surprise

---

[1] Pontieri, *De Rebus Gestis*, p. 75.

[2] I am indebted to Professor Donald Bullough of the University of St Andrews for arguing this case. He writes (in a personal communication): 'To offer Kherson to the "Foreign Legion" which was no longer needed at Kibotos fits so neatly that I am inclined once again to give the saga even more credit than you have done.'

[3] For this material see a forthcoming article by Jonathan Shepard, 'Another New England?'.

that our records are so few and so dubious. Some of the difficulties concerning the evidence for Varangians in Byzantium itself have been neatly outlined by Robert Byron:

Up till 1865, tombstones of the Varangians still existed on a tower in the vicinity [of Bogdan Serai]. In that year, the request of the British ambassador that they might be removed to the British cemetery at Scutari prompted the Turks to use them for building purposes. The copies of the inscriptions which were taken, were accidentally burnt in 1870.[1]

CL/JS are clearly not sources correct in every detail. But our accounts of the Anglo-Saxon emigration are few and we do not have anything more reliable to set against this version and to use in preference. Orderic and Goscelin are short; Goscelin is not even intended to be more than a miraculous anecdote and Orderic is notoriously unreliable. We have here one more major version to add to the ones we know and some of what it says is consistent with what we know from elsewhere. Where it provides new information this should not be dismissed out of hand. There is nothing unreasonable in supposing that the author or compiler of *CL* had access to genuine material on the English Varangians, even if it reaches us distorted by his own incomprehension. *Játvarðar saga* in comparison emerges with the credit of being a short, sensible and coherent version, lacking many of the complications and confusions which disfigure the *Chronicon*. Whether the credit goes to the compiler of *Játvarðar saga* himself or whether, as I have tried to demonstrate, he was working from a more competent original, there can be no doubt that the version he gives deserves more attention and less derision than it has previously been accorded.

[1] Robert Byron, *The Byzantine Achievement* (London, 1929), p. 147, n. 1.

Kinship in Anglo-Saxon England

H. R. LOYN

There is a great text in the Welsh laws that tells us that a man who killed another, and who wished to make proper amends, paid one-ninth of his victim's blood-price to the offended kindred. His mother and father paid another ninth, and his brothers and sisters a further ninth again. The remaining two-thirds was to be found by the kindred to the seventh degree – some recensions say the ninth – and two-thirds of that in turn was to come from the paternal kin, one-third from the maternal.[1] The blood-feud group in other words was ego-centred, differed from individual to individual, and was elaborate in structure. Descendants of the great-grandparents of great-grandparents on both sides would be involved.

The lawyers of western Norway, the men of the fjords, the Gulathing, were even more specific. They tell how the blood-price, the wergild was to be paid. We follow patiently, even placidly, to the third knee. There are minor complications, but when the principle is grasped that for purposes of payment and of receipt of compensation descent through the paternal kin is reckoned as one degree more potent than descent through the maternal, things are straightforward. The son of a maternal aunt was grouped with the son of a paternal uncle's son, and both were to receive half a mark from the slayer, if the slain man were of *hauld* rank. As such they were equivalent to another group: the son of a father's paternal uncle, a mother's maternal uncle, and the son of a sister's daughter. The complexity increases as the degree of kinship decreases. The lawman does his best for us. He did his sums well with only a rare slip. At the fourth knee, we are told, kinsmen received in the maternal kin $18\frac{2}{3}$ pence a head, the same as the fifth knee on the paternal side. At the tenth knee the compensation had dwindled to $2\frac{2}{15}$ pence on the maternal side. At the thirteenth the paternal kinsman received one penny only, with a pitiful $\frac{2}{3}$ of a penny for the corresponding rank on the maternal side. Dare we say 'de minimis non curat lex'?[2]

---

[1] *Llyfr Iorwerth*, ed. Aled Rhys Wiliam (Cardiff, 1960), par. 106. *Cyfreithiau Hywel Dda: Llyfr Blegywryd*, ed. S. J. Williams and J. Enoch Powell (Cardiff, 1942), p. 32; *The Laws of Hywel Dda (The Book of Blegywryd)*, trans. Melville Richards (Liverpool, 1954), pp. 45–6. I am grateful to my colleague, Morfydd Owen, for help with these references and for much valuable discussion of problems connected with the Welsh laws.

[2] L. M. Larson, *The Earliest Norwegian Laws* (New York, 1935), esp. pp. 153–8, 'Laws 225–35 of the Gulathing'. Also B. Phillpotts, *Kindred and Clan* (Cambridge, 1913), pp. 58–9.

H. R. Loyn

It is the complete contrast with anything that can be found in Anglo-Saxon law that has in part prompted this article. For nowadays when so much emphasis is properly put on the comparative method and on the inner workings of society such a contrast demands investigation. Why is it that we have from Anglo-Saxon England so little information about the workings of the outer rings of the kindred, with what Mr T. Charles-Edwards has recently termed, in a delightful domestic image, the outer peelings of the onion's skin?[1]

To begin with our terminology is weak. Miss Lorraine Lancaster long ago discussed the evidence, analysing the Anglo-Saxon terms for the nuclear family, for the collateral and affinal groups.[2] She remarks cogently on the dearth of special Old English terms for cousin. The Anglo-Saxon language can take you back in a straight line to your *sixta fæder*, your 'sixth father', your grandfather's grandfather's grandfather, but sideways movement was feeble and cumbersome, poor stuff by the side of the Welsh compounds for second, third, and more remote cousins.[3] In Anglo-Saxon there was little more than a general *nefa* which could mean nephew, grandson, or step-son, or *fæderan sunu*, a father's brother's son, or *suhterga*, a nephew or cousin. Even the occasional and excessively rare poetic compounds dealt with the immediate family. *Suhtergefæderan* and *suhtorfædran* expressed the relationship between nephew and uncle, *aþumswerian*, perhaps most significant of all, between father-in-law and son-in-law.[4] We have nothing in other words outside the nuclear family but the generalized degrees of kindred.

It is, of course, well known that there are dangers in arguing too strongly from negative evidence. Society is not articulate on its routine common-places. What is known by all is explained by none. There is danger too in arguing to a false comparative method. Twelfth- and thirteenth-century Scandinavia, Wales and Ireland are different in structure and in methods of recording from tenth- and eleventh-century England. A touch of sophisti-cated antiquarianism can so easily make the whole world kin. But it is at least possible that we have in these differences evidence of contrast in social growth and in institutional development between England and the Scandi-navian and Celtic world.

---

[1] In a paper delivered to the Welsh Laws Seminar of the Board of Celtic Studies at Cardiff in the summer of 1971. T. Charles-Edwards has since written an acute paper on 'Kinship, Status and the Origins of the Hide', *Past and Present* 56 (1972), in which he stresses the essential social dis-tinction between the paternal and maternal kindreds of the laws and the more compact descent-groups, agnatic and patrilocal, which he calls 'lineages'.

[2] Lorraine Lancaster, 'Kinship in Anglo-Saxon Society' pts I and II, *Brit. Jnl of Sociology* 9 (1958), 234–48 and 359–77. Also D. A. Bullough, 'Early Medieval Social Groupings: the Terminology of Kinship', *Past and Present* 45 (1969), 3–18, esp. 14–15.

[3] T. Charles-Edwards, 'Some Celtic Kinship Terms', *Bull. of the Board of Celtic Stud.* 24 (1970–2), 105–22.   [4] *Beowulf* 84 (*aþumswerian*); also 1164 and *Widsith* 46.

Examination of some known and recognized difficulties and agreed conclusions about kinship in Anglo-Saxon England may help to further discussion of this possible contrast. It is, for example, generally accepted that the dominant trend in late Old English society is one by which the authority of the secular lord increases at the expense of the kindred. Lordship and kingship are the twin forces operating to bring about a more highly organized community. The royal concern with the establishment of a general peace well illustrates this process. Athelstan in his London decrees was gravely concerned about kindreds that were so strong, whether noble or common, that they refused the king his rights and stood up for a thief – a reflection of his specific anxieties in Kent about the man who was so rich or of so great a kindred (*tantae parentelae*) that he could not be punished nor would he desist from wrong-doing.[1] Athelstan was also naturally concerned with secular lords who protected their dependants illegally, and three-quarters of a century later when Æthelred, Wulfstan and Cnut busied themselves over matters of general order the emphasis was placed almost exclusively on the danger to peace of the over-weening lord, the *stræc* men who protected their own men as well as they were able, either of free or of unfree status.[2] These fears were balanced by more positive action. Lordship itself received consistent support as a peace-inclining institution. The lawyers tried to ensure that each man had a true legal guarantor. A secular lord took his own household under his *borh*, his legal protection. If a man were convicted of perjury, his *healsfang*, his first payment of wergild, a tenth of his blood-price, was to be forfeit to the king or to his *landrica*. A cowardly deserter in battle, on land or on the sea, forfeited his life and all his possessions; the lord was to take his possessions and the land he had previously given him, and his bookland was to pass to the king.[3] Steady pressure was diminishing the legal sanctions attributable to kinship.

Yet kinship remained immensely strong in ordinary social life. The literature of the period provides much powerful evidence of the validity and potency of kinship ties. A man's whole status could depend on his position in a free kindred. A stranger passing to new lands was expected to declare his kindred. The great epic *Beowulf*, still copied and read in the late tenth century and early eleventh (though composed at least two centuries earlier), provides a splendid example. Beowulf lands on the Danish coast

---

[1] VI Ath. 8. 2 and III Ath. 6; F. Liebermann, *Die Gesetze der Angelsachsen*, 3 vols. (Halle, 1903–16) I, 178 and 170 (this collection referred to hereafter as Liebermann). References to individual law-codes are given in the form of standard abbreviations. Cf. also VI Ath. 12. 2; Liebermann I, 183, where the possibility that a kin will not redeem a man or stand surety for him is explored.

[2] II Cnut 20. 1; Liebermann I, 322–4. Athelstan's concern appears notably in his Grately decrees, II Ath. 3; Liebermann I, 152.

[3] II Cnut 31, 37, 77 and 77. 1; Liebermann I, 334, 338 and 364.

and is asked by the coastguard to make known his lineage (his *frum-cyn*), and he replies:

> We are of the kin (*gumcynnes*) of the people of the Geats
> And hearth-companions to Hygelac.
> My father was well-known among the people,
> A noble warrior, Ecgtheow by name.[1]

The presence of Beowulf's party is then announced to Hrothgar, the Danish king, who says that he knew Beowulf, *cnihtwesende*, when he was a boy, and that he knew both his father and his mother. The Danish messenger from court is able to report back to Beowulf that all is well, that his *æþelu*, his kindred, is known.[2] Even so Beowulf's first words to Hrothgar show how intertwined are still the concepts of noble lineage and service: 'All hail, Hrothgar. I am the kinsman (*mæg*) and the kinsman-thegn (*magoðegn*) of Hygelac.'[3] To some measure, of course, this is a commonplace of the western world. When St Alban, in Bede's account of the martyrdom, was accused of harbouring a priest, the judge asked him 'cuius familiae uel generis es', a phrase which the ninth-century Anglo-Saxon translator renders 'hwylces hiredes 7 hwylces cynnes' ('which household and which kin').[4] The warriors at Maldon made their kin known and also their service before they went into battle.[5] And some of it is just a little like George Eliot's comment in the opening paragraph of *Silas Marner* 'How was a man to be explained unless you at least knew someone who knew his father and his mother?' The social need for good family or at worst known family is almost universal in relatively settled communities.

Yet there was more than simple knowledge of family to be traced in Anglo-Saxon sources. A deep interest in genealogy also existed. In the West Saxon royal house descent from the sixth-century Cerdic was essential in a king. Chroniclers and scholars could not resist the further step of tracing the dynasty through a succession of Germanic epic figures to the Old Testament genealogies and ultimately to Noah and so to Adam himself. Dr Sisam has shown us brilliantly how even in their historic ranges these genealogies must be treated with caution. To go beyond great-grandfathers is seldom necessary. An accepted mythological background was used by dynasty after dynasty as it established temporary military superiority over other folk.[6] The stated line of descent from Egbert to Ingeld is to be trusted; from Ingeld back to Cerdic it is defensible; beyond Cerdic all is fiction.

[1] *Beowulf* 260ff.   [2] *Ibid.* 372.   [3] *Ibid.* 407–8.
[4] Bede, *Historia Ecclesiastica*, ed. C. Plummer (Oxford, 1896) I. 7. *The Old English Version of Bede's Ecclesiastical History*, ed. T. Miller, Early Eng. Text Soc. o.s. 95 (London, 1890), p. 36.
[5] *The Battle of Maldon*, especially Ælfwine (210ff.), Leofsunu (244ff.) and Byrhtwald (311ff.).
[6] K. Sisam, 'Anglo-Saxon Royal Genealogies', *Proc. of the Brit. Acad.* 39 (1953), 287–346, esp. 320–2.

This is far from meaning that we should be scornful of exact family knowledge in depth. The Chronicle gives us Offa's genealogy through Pybba *s.a.* 755. It is the twelfth-century William of Malmesbury who has preserved the link from Pybba to Penda, *adnepos* in the fifth generation.[1] Knowledge of kin was treasured when status depended on it, and not only at the royal level. The landholding class absolutely had an intense interest in kindred-right, a right which affected so many matters concerning the transmission of land. Alfred ruled bluntly that if a man had bookland, and his kindred had left it to him, the bookland was not to be sold outside the kindred, provided that there was written evidence that the first donor had forbidden this to happen.[2] The will of Æthelgifu, rediscovered and edited in this last generation, makes a significant distinction between land that came to the widow as a result of her marriage (and of her husband's acquisition) and her own inherited land. The former, after her death, was allotted to St Albans; the inherited land passed back to her kinsfolk.[3] Examples can be multiplied at every turn through to the Conquest; and yet even here some reservations are essential. Eadnoð, King Alfred's contemporary, contended with the powerful bishop of Worcester and succeeded in keeping the owner-ship of an estate in the *mægþ* or kindred. He did so, however, only after agreeing to pay to the bishop the substantial sum of forty mancuses together with a promise of an annual payment of fifteen shillings of pure money, and only after failing to find a kinsman willing to take on the duties of a priest in the diocese. Eadnoð's success, formerly used to illustrate the tenacity of principles of kin ownership, serves rather to illustrate the much more generalized principle of kindred interest in the transmission of land.[4]

Much more illuminating are in fact the discursive charters of Æthelred's reign. There is, for example, the Brabourne charter from Kent.[5] In 996 Æthelred assigned estates in Kent to his mother in return for another estate at Cholsey. He explained how the Kentish land had come to him. Early in his reign it had been held by Wulfbold who, on the death of his father, had seized an estate belonging to his stepmother. The king summoned him. He failed to appear. His wergild was assigned to the king. Again the king summoned him, and again he failed to appear. Wulfbold then made matters worse, seizing another estate at Bourne, owned by his kinsman, Brihtmær. A third and fourth summons were ignored, and on each occasion his

[1] William of Malmesbury, *De Gestis Regum Anglorum*, Rolls Series (1887–9) I, 84, ch. 86: 'quinto genu Pendae adnepos'.

[2] Alf 41; Liebermann I, 74.

[3] *The Will of Æthelgifu*, trans. and examined by D. Whitelock, with N. Ker and Lord Rennell for the Roxburghe Club (Oxford, 1968), esp. ch. III (by D. Whitelock) and ch. VII (by Lord Rennell).

[4] *Select Historical Documents of the Ninth and Tenth Centuries*, ed. F. E. Harmer (Cambridge, 1914), no. 15, pp. 25–7. P. H. Sawyer, *Anglo-Saxon Charters* (London, 1968), no. 1446.

[5] *Anglo-Saxon Charters*, ed. A. J. Robertson, 2nd ed. (Cambridge, 1956), LXIII, pp. 128–30.

wergild was assigned to the king. Finally an impressive assembly was held at London at which Æthelwine, earl of East Anglia, and all the witan were present. Wulfbold's property was declared forfeit and Wulfbold himself placed in the king's mercy. Nevertheless – a telling aside on Æthelred's authority – Wulfbold retained all his lands *ungebet* until he died, presumably in his bed.

This was not the end of the affair. Wulfbold left a widow with a son – both more turbulent than he. Eadmer, a cousin of Wulfbold (his uncle's son) and a king's thegn, took possession of Bourne with fifteen companions. The widow descended and killed them all. This proved too much: the whole apparatus of king and church moved into cumbersome action, Æthelgar, the archbishop of Canterbury, intervened, the wrongdoers were evicted, and at long last the estates passed to the king.

The Brabourne charter provides an elusive record as well as a violent one. So many themes of a type more familiar from poetry than from diplomatic evidence are to be found: provision for widows, the anger of a stepson, a cousin of the true kin (*riht cyn*) ready to assert his rights, a dispute between kinsmen resolved in violence, a bootless crime. The epic ingredients are there in earthy mould, Hrothulf and Hrethric in the home counties. But the land-owning kin is not shown, and the same is true of other Anglo-Saxon land-books, no matter how promising. These are family squabbles. They treat of kinship only obliquely. The much more limited question of family inheritance is at the centre of their concern. These is no evidence for the existence of a territorial clan in Anglo-Saxon charters.

Personal status, genealogy, land: there are glimpses of kinship in action but little that can be called conclusive. There remains one important source of evidence, the evidence of the law-books, that offers greater hope of understanding. In the later laws especially, some of it under Scandinavian influence, direct and indirect, there is much of direct value. Definitions had to be made, regulations established. Not that the compilations were always as helpful as they might be. Much was taken for granted. It is difficult, for example, to keep the blood-feud group distinct from the kindred, and so to separate function from substance. The laws are practical documents. They do not pause to reflect on the substance of kinship. They describe rather kinship in action. Function predominates, and four practical matters receive, as might be expected, special attention: the feud, wergild payments, marriage arrangements and succession to land.

With the feud we touch on one of the mainsprings of early society. A kindred was responsible for a member's status. It was also responsible for his safety, or for arranging for vengeance, or for the payment of compensation. At this level the kindred was in closest contact with the rising power of the state, and out of contact, often developing into conflict, came elucidation.

The laws give a clear picture of attempts to control the feud. The struggle was not completely successful, nor could it ever be in areas like parts of Northumbria remote from royal authority or at times when new Scandinavian irruptions forced communities to barter head for head. King Edmund in the 940s was the most precise in his attempts to fix a legal curb on the feuding spirit. He ordered that a slayer was to bear the feud unless he was able to pay compensation within a twelvemonth, that his kindred was to have the right to abandon him and to refuse to pay compensation with him, that his kinsfolk were then to be exempt from the feud unless they protected the slayer or gave him food, and that if any of the offended kin took vengeance on any man except the slayer he would incur the hostility of the king and threat of forfeiture.[1] This declared right to opt out of kindred obligations is sure proof that a higher authority was present, able to give the general protection formerly exercised by the kin. Kingship in action trimmed the power of the kindred, and indicates the predominance of legal concepts quite different from those operating between kinsman and kinsman.

Even more information is given about wergild, in its purest form the blood-price, the sum paid in just compensation for a slaying. In origin the wergild was intimately connected with the feud or the threat of the feud, with the buying-off of the spear, the death-price. By the end of the Anglo-Saxon period it was generalized to the point where free society was grouped into two principal classes according to the weight of their wergilds, the two-hundred shilling men, the ceorls, and the noblemen with their compensation price of twelve-hundred shillings. The wergild was still something of a developing institution. According to the *Leges Henrici Primi* of the early twelfth century even a slave had a small wergild, and a freeman could make up his own mind about the desirability of helping an unfree kinsman.[2] Wergild was also used increasingly as a convenient unit of account, an assessment to forfeiture, a penalty, for example, imposed for non-appearance at the royal summons. Law-worthiness had to be bought back again. High rank, as always, could be expensive.

Our best insight into wergild in its original meaning comes from an anonymous document of the early eleventh century, preserved in the *Textus Roffensis*, a compact document, business-like, showing some skill in drafting

---

[1] II Em; Liebermann I, 186–90. The kin is permitted to desert (*forlete*) an offender and refuse to pay for him, p. 186. The tone of Edmund's statements is so much firmer and more systematic than, for example, earlier Frankish royal laws that at times struck 'glancing blows' against the feud: cf. J. M. Wallace-Hadrill, 'The Blood-Feud of the Franks', *The Long-Haired Kings* (London, 1962), pp. 121–47, esp. 130 ff.

[2] Hn. 70. 2 (in Wessex) and 70. 5b; Liebermann I, 587–8. *Leges Henrici Primi*, ed. L. J. Downer (Oxford, 1972), pp. 218 and 220.

and some practical sense.[1] It may be significant of the generalized nature of wergild that the author felt obliged to start with simple definitions, and he tells us solemnly that a twelve-hundred man's wergild is 1200 shillings and a two-hundred man's 200 shillings. With equal solemnity he tells us that if a man is slain he is to be paid for with his blood-price. But there then follows rare and precious detail on the procedures of payment, in line of descent from Edmund's decrees. We learn that a slayer, if he pledges himself to pay the wergild, is to find a surety (*wærborh*) thereto, and that for a twelve-hundred man, twelve men are to act as sureties, eight from the paternal kin and four from the maternal. When that is done the king's *mund* (translated *pax* in *Quadripartitus*) is to be raised, and all from both kindreds shall vow to the mediator with hands clasped on one weapon that the king's *mund* shall stand. From that day within twenty-one days 120 shillings was to be paid for a twelve-hundred man. This was the *healsfang*, the neck-price, the ten per cent deposit which belonged to the children, the brothers and the father's brother, and which (the document tells us with special emphasis) belonged to no kinsman save those within that knee. Twenty-one days later *manbot*, compensation to the lord, was to be paid, and twenty-one days later again *fihtwite*, the penalty for fighting.[2] After that the further instalments of wergild proper were to be paid, starting with the *frumgyld*, twenty-one days after the fighting penalty, and then so forth so that full payment was made in the time that wise men appointed until with amity full friendly accord was reached. A ceorl's wergild was to be paid in similar order.

The value of this document is self-evident. Although new alien institutions were present – the hand of the king and written custom – the formality and public solemnity of ancient ritual is clearly apparent. Known custom lay behind the documents. Rational definition was its object, even a certain flexibility in the presence of a mediator and of the wise men who were to appoint the timing of the wergild payment. Most important of all it gives precious information about the inner kindred, the *healsfang* group. It is uncertain how much institutional importance we should give to this precise group, somewhat barely clipped to the brothers and children, with the *fædera*, the father's brother, as the active agent. At worst it is nice to know that all patrilinear uncles are not wicked. The group is analogous to a similar grouping in the *Leis Willelme* where, on death by violence, ten shillings from the *healsfang* was to be paid to the widow and orphans and the rest to be divided among *les orfenins* and *les parenz*.[3] The existence of a hardship group was recognized. We are clearly dealing with a society where great emphasis is placed on the individual and his household and the inner kin. The document also provides us with proof that both paternal and

---

[1] *Wer.*; Liebermann i, 392–4.   [2] *Ibid.* p. 392.   [3] *Leis Willelme* 9; Liebermann i, 498.

maternal kin participated in the composition group, and that the kindred could, if it so willed, refuse to support an offender. Formal feuding and compensation arrangements were indeed not as primitive as used to be believed. It is perfectly understandable why Liebermann at one point suggested that a kindred constituted a virtual court of equity.[1] Men must reach a decision before they pay or decide to act as compurgators.

There remained a problem which vexed contemporaries as it vexes us now. If the possession of a sound kin was so desirable what of the man with no kin? He may have been rare but was assuredly not unknown. The same problem was faced in other societies. In Scotland in the early modern period pretence of blood or the place of his dwelling could bind a man to his chief.[2] It is exceedingly likely that a man with no effective inner kin was reckoned as kinless, that is to say not the bare *healsfang* group but an effective inner kin back to a common great-grandfather, with the quality of effectiveness dependent on residence and accessibility, not necessarily at all on affection. The Anglo-Saxons found their answer to the kinless man in the *gegildan* or *geferan* who weave in and out of the laws, 'associates' as we may innocuously render them. In Alfred's laws if a man without paternal kin slew a man his maternal kin was to pay a third of the wergild, his associates a third, and he himself the other third. If he had no maternal kin, the payment was to be shared, a half from his associates and a half from himself. If he were slain himself, half of the compensation was to go to his associates and a half to the king, the protector of the kinless.[3] As late as the reign of Æthelred a priest charged with the blood-feud had to swear with his kindred, and if he possessed no kindred with his associates – though the escape-hatch of ordeal by consecrated bread was open to him.[4] A monk was a different case. One graphic phrase explained all: rule-law destroyed kin-law.[5]

Under normal circumstances a kindred gave support and standing, fed a man if he were in prison, took on responsibility for the baptism of infants, looked after orphans, guarded the insane and the deaf-and-dumb, and curbed evil-doers. When under Athelstan the kin was empowered to bring a lordless member from whom no redress could be exacted into the protection of a lord[6] we have the clearest evidence of the path along which society was

---

[1] Liebermann II (Glossär), p. 654, *s.v. Sippe*, 19.

[2] G. Donaldson, *Scotland, James V to James VII* (Edinburgh and London, 1965), pp. 12–15, and T. C. Smout, *A History of the Scottish People, 1560–1830* (London, 1969), pp. 38–42: both stress the importance of the surname (sometimes carrying with it 'pretence of blood') and of tenurial ties.

[3] Af. 27, 27.1 and 28; Liebermann I, 66.

[4] VIII Eth. 23ff. and I Cnut 5. 2b and c; Liebermann I, 266 and 286. Also VIII Eth. 33; Liebermann I, 267 – the king acts as 'mæg' and 'mundbora, buton he elles oðerne hæbbe'.

[5] VIII Eth. 25 and I Cnut 5. 2d; Liebermann I, 266 and 286 'gæð of his mægðlage þonne he gebyhð to regollage'.

[6] II Ath. 2; Liebermann I, 150.

developing. Law dealt more readily with lords than with kindreds. Yet the kindred naturally continued to exercise control over one vastly important aspect of social life: marriage. Problems of marriage are sorely complicated by canonical rulings, some of which were based on personal and faulty readings of authorities on the forbidden relationships to the sixth or seventh degree of kinship, what Maitland called a maze of flighty fancies and mis-applied logic.[1] Marriage in fact remained essentially a secular business. Even in the short late text, preserved for us again in the *Textus Roffensis*, no more is said on the religious side than that there should by rights be a priest.[2] And on consanguinity there is the astonishing and almost casual statement that: 'It is well to take care that one knows that they are not too closely related – lest one afterwards puts asunder what was previously wrongly joined together.'[3]

The legal onus lay on the prospective groom to show by pledge and surety that he could maintain his bride properly, pay the remuneration proper for her upbringing, grant an adequate gift in return for her suit, and grant adequate provision for her if she should live longer than he. If he could promise all these things to the satisfaction of the bride-to-be's kindred, they then set about betrothing their kinswoman to him. She herself had some considerable say in the matter. Arrangements had to be pleasing to her as well as to her kin.[4]

One social and legal fact is certain. Marriage did not interfere with her birth-price. A woman remained with the status she had acquired by birth. She kept her own wergild and did not take that of her husband. If guilty of homicide, penalties were imposed according to her birth-price. Her children followed their father's kin. The Anglo-Saxons were in this sense strongly patrilinear; but so did the mother follow her own father's kindred. Her married state was certainly honourable. She could expect a substantial morning-gift, a competence in life, and provision for widowhood. She did not necessarily suffer if her husband did wrong. *Domesday Book* tells us that in Nottinghamshire and Derbyshire a thegn having sake and soke who had forfeited his land would nevertheless leave half to his legal wife and legiti-mate children, the other half only to be divided between the king and the earl.[5] Marriage was still a secular business, and as such a matter of prime concern to the kindred, again one may well believe the active inner kin.

Linked with the whole question of marriage and marriage settlements is the problem of the kindred and the holding of land. It has already been

---

[1] F. Pollock and F. W. Maitland, *History of English Law before the Time of Edward I*, 2nd ed. (Cambridge, 1968) II, 389.

[2] *Wif* 8; Liebermann I, 442. Also *English Historical Documents* I, ed. D. Whitelock (London, 1955), p. 431.   [3] *Wif* 9; Liebermann I, 444.

[4] *Wif* 1; Liebermann I, 442 'hit swa hire 7 freondan gelicige'.   [5] *Domesday Book* I, 280 b.

suggested that the evidence for ownership of land by a kindred is strictly limited, and that the evidence for the existence of a territorial clan is non-existent. The important second code of Cnut lays down that in case of intestacy the property is to be divided justly among the wife, children, and close kinsmen, each in proportion to what belongs to them. But the lord is to take his heriot first, and the lord is to be responsible for the just division.[1] It has long and rightly been an axiom of Anglo-Saxon studies that one of the chief objects of booking land was to give testamentary freedom, to permit it to be bequeathed outside the kin. But there is a vital distinction to be made between land subject to customary testamentary obligation within the kin and land owned by a kindred. Of the former there is ample evidence. This was folkland, land preferably passing in the male line of descent on the spear side and not the spindle, and presumably the type of land in question in the code of Cnut. Of the latter there are only traces and these in records from the earlier period. The laws of Ine tell us that if an heir of tender age succeeds, the kin shall take possession of the chief holding, providing for the widow and children, but not permitting the land to pass to the widow and so out of the kin. Until the majority of the eldest son the paternal kin exercised protection over him. If a widow remarried within her 'true year' her morning-gift was to revert to the first husband's kin.[2] But in the legal record generally, and increasingly after the reign of Alfred, the king, the individual landlord and the compact inner kin dominate the scene. It seems likely indeed that in early historic times the territorial clan, if it ever reached that status, was swallowed up in the rising kingdoms and sub-kingdoms of the so-called Heptarchy.

For it is too easy in dealing with these fringe anthropological matters to forget the all-important time factor. In Anglo-Saxon England kindreds were not given enough time to develop into full-fledged land-owning institutions. Tribal institutions in their more mature form in Celtic and Scandinavian lands needed a long period of weak state authority to nurture them. England was a wealthy country, strong in arable land, which Wales and Norway were not. The surplus was enough to permit kingship to flourish before tribal institutions were fully mature. The results may be seen in the laws with their traces of such tribal institutions, half-grown. Kinship and kindred principles are strong socially but hesitant in their own legal right. The legal being of the kindred depended greatly on the active tutelage of the king, personal lordship, and territorial organization. Even the blood-feud

---

[1] II Cnut 70 and 70. 1; Liebermann I, 356.
[2] II Cnut 73a; Liebermann I, 360. Cf. V Atr 21. 1 and VI 26. 1 (Liebermann, I, 242 and 254), Ine 38 (Liebermann I, 104–6); also *Hlothære and Eadric* 6 (Liebermann I, 10), where the child and his property were to be protected by the father's kindred, though the child himself was to go with his mother.

itself failed to reach that stage in formal institutional growth, untrammelled by superior folk-principles, that it achieved elsewhere in other communities with their details of payments to the seventh or ninth knee. Maitland with typical prescience and precision read much into the petition of the men of Kerry in Montgomeryshire that they may live under English law because that law has suppressed the blood-feud and does not punish the innocent together with the guilty.[1] The heart of the matter lies there. The territorial unity of England in the tenth century, made possible by the superior economic resources of the easterners, was no idle *imperium*. It was the unity of a kingdom in which, when all allowance is made for regional peculiarities, for the customs of Northumbria and the Land of the Five Boroughs, for the distinction of Mercia from Wessex and of the Danelaw from English England, the fundamental principles of folk-law in matters of preserving peace, supervising the church, enjoying the rule of justice, could be asserted. Alfred when he drew up his great law-code prefaced it by snatches of Old Testament law, and highlighted the negative golden rule. Do not unto others what you would not wish them to do unto you. The law is Christian. The Germanic dooms are commentaries upon it in individual practical instances. The theocracy of Edgar and the unhappy Æthelred is reminiscent of Ottonian Germany. In neither community, German nor English, was there opportunity for a growth of tribalism in the late tenth century. In both the *jus legale* triumphed over the *jus naturale cognatorum*.[2] The *Leges Henrici Primi* tells us further that the division of the law of England was triune: the one of Wessex, the other of Mercia, and the third of the Danelaw, and that beyond all this should be recognized the 'tremendum regie maiestatis . . . imperium quod praeesse iugiter legibus'.[3] The tremendous dominion of the royal majesty of Henry I was surely in the writer's mind, and yet his examples take us back well into the Saxon past, above all to the special pleas of the king already outlined in the laws of Cnut. The peace-keeping apparatus, in theory at least, was firmly in royal hands before 1066.[4]

---

[1] *History of English Law* I, 221 n. (1st ed. p. 200).

[2] Hn. 4. 4; Liebermann I, 548: 'omne autem ius aut naturale cognatorum est aut morale extraneorum aut legale ciuium'. *Leges Henrici Primi*, ed. Downer, p. 82. K. J. Leyser, 'The German Aristocracy from the Ninth Century to the Early Twelfth Century', *Past and Present* 41 (1968), 25–53, provides an invaluable guide to the German situation. The key development appears to have been from large family groups, conscious of nobility by descent from a great ancestor, into more closely-knit families by the end of the eleventh century and the beginning of the twelfth (*ibid.* pp. 32–3). Attention should also be drawn to the seminal article on this theme by L. Génicot, 'La Noblesse au Moyen Age dans l'Ancienne "Francie"', *Annales* 17 (1962). The lesser landowners of the eastern counties in late-tenth-century England already appear to have the attributes of closely-knit family groups.

[3] Hn. 6. 2 and 2a; Liebermann I, 552. *Leges Henrici Primi*, p. 96.

[4] Hn. 10–13; Liebermann I, 555–9. *Leges Henrici Primi*, pp. 108–18, a section based on the laws of Cnut with some additions from earlier codes. D. A. Bullough, 'Anglo-Saxon Institutions and

And there we have an important clue to the social situation. In a relatively wealthy complicated community, royal law and secular lordship could whittle away the *raison d'être* of an organized kindred as a legal institution. Bookland gave better title to land. Charters, then writs, ensured the continuity of good title. Writs offered possible instruments for the articulation of government. The apparatus of tithing, hundred, and shire provide a framework for greater security and hope of redress. Guild organization flourished in towns and townships. Social ties of kinship, at least to the four-degree kin, remained strong under normal circumstances as they were to for centuries to come. But the formal institutional life of the kin was atrophied, if not stifled at birth, by the strength of territorial lordship and Christian kingship.

Early English Society', *Annali della Fondazione Italiana per la Storia Amministrativa* 2 (Milan, 1968), 647–59, in a paper directly prompted by his reappraisal of Chadwick's work, makes many acute observations relevant to this theme (esp. p. 658) that the absence of the notion that all non-royal land was held of a superior was a social fact to the advantage of the monarchy. The monarchy, with church support, was indeed well poised to move into all manner of indeterminate areas in late Anglo-Saxon England.

Anglo-Saxon charters: the work of the last twenty years

NICHOLAS BROOKS

1973 is an auspicious year for the study of the charters of the pre-Conquest period. At the time of writing,[1] the publication of Professor A. Campbell's *Anglo-Saxon Charters I, The Charters of Rochester* is imminent. This is the first volume in a series in which the entire corpus of pre-Conquest charters is to be edited with full critical apparatus, with detailed analysis of their diplomatic, palaeographical, topographical and linguistic features and with extensive glossaries and indices. Professor Campbell's volume is part of a collaborative enterprise organized by a committee of The British Academy and The Royal Historical Society. When the series is complete, historians will no longer need to reiterate W. H. Stevenson's famous dictum, 'It cannot be said that the Old English charters have yet been edited.'[2] One significant feature of the scheme deserves to be noted here; each volume will cover the charters of an archive that was in existence towards the end of the Old English period. Thus there will be one volume for Rochester, another for Christ Church, Canterbury, another for Exeter, another for Burton Abbey, and so on. Small archives will be grouped together with others from the same region or diocese to form suitable volumes. In this way the organization of the edition will itself reveal the local character of Anglo-Saxon charters which is so marked throughout their history. It will also bring to light the work of forgers for individual churches developing their claims to particular lands and rights by means of charters of apparently widely differing dates.

Any collaborative enterprise of this type takes many years to complete. It cannot be overemphasized that the full value of the edition will be realized only when the series is all in print. Here, then, is the task for this generation of pre-Conquest historians. Here is the ideal training for the best of our research students. When one considers the contribution made to early medieval studies on the continent by historians trained by editing volumes of diplomata for the Monumenta Germaniae Historica, or for the Chartes et Diplomes series of the Académie des Inscriptions et Belles Lettres, the

---

[1] This review covers the period up to the end of August 1973.
[2] *The Crawford Collection of Early Charters and Documents*, ed. A. S. Napier and W. H. Stevenson (Oxford, 1895), p. viii.

opportunities and prospects which the new series presents are clear. Few research subjects are so well defined, or so educative in the different disciplines that they involve, or so exciting in the discoveries that await the painstaking scholar, than the title-deeds of a single major beneficiary. The completion of the new edition will depend upon the willingness of today's scholars to take their part in the work, and to train and direct their research students to it.

In one sense, therefore, the last two decades may be seen as an interregnum in charter studies – a lull between the publication in 1952 of the late Miss F. E. Harmer's *Anglo-Saxon Writs*[1] and the start of the new edition of the entire corpus of pre-Conquest charters. But they have also been years in which much fundamental work has been done, and in which major differences in approach and interpretation have become apparent. It is not surprising that the pre-Conquest charters should have become the subject of controversies. The Anglo-Saxon royal diplomas are unique in Europe in bearing no outward signs of validation, neither any seal, nor autograph subscriptions, nor autograph crosses, nor even the name of the scribe. Their form is not that of a public act issued from a 'public' or royal chancery, but of a private deed of a particularly primitive and peculiarly religious form. Their authenticity was purely religious and ecclesiastical – hence the pictorial and verbal invocations to God, and the pious preambles and anathemas, even in grants to laymen; hence too the use in the earliest charters of uncial and majuscule scripts that were normally reserved for sacred books, and the association of charters with gospel books and with ceremonies at the altar of an important church. Such charters were the products of a large number of ecclesiastical scriptoria whose diplomatic needs to be studied separately. In the absence of a comprehensive and critical edition, the difficulty of establishing the authenticity of these texts, especially when the majority only survive in late and often corrupt copies, will be evident.

The novice may best be introduced to charter problems by means of Professor Whitelock's introduction to the 'Charters and Laws' and her translations and comments upon selected documents.[2] Sir Frank Stenton's more discursive survey of the Latin diplomas[3] demonstrates with *élan* how a combination of rigorous but wide-ranging criticism and a sympathetic and informed judgement can wring important historical evidence from the most unpromising materials. In addition to these general introductions there are now available a number of basic manuals, which help to clear the path of the scholar or of the layman, who is interested in a particular charter or in those

---

[1] *Anglo-Saxon Writs*, ed. F. E. Harmer (Manchester, 1952).
[2] *English Historical Documents* I, ed. Dorothy Whitelock (London, 1955), pp. 337–55 and 440–556.
[3] F. M. Stenton, *The Latin Charters of the Anglo-Saxon Period* (Oxford, 1955).

of a particular period or region. Professor Sawyer's *Anglo-Saxon Charters: an Annotated List and Bibliography*[1] is an invaluable work of reference. Every extant charter is listed (in addition to many 'lost charters'), and for each charter Professor Sawyer has provided a brief description of its content, a list of the surviving manuscripts (up to 1800), an estimate of the date of their scripts, references to all printed editions, translations and facsimiles, and a bibliography of all significant discussions of the charter, together with a brief indication of the gist of the views of most of the cited authors. The value of this handbook has been immeasurably increased by the inclusion of the judgements of N. R. Ker and T. A. M. Bishop on the date of the script of all 'apparent originals' and of Professor Whitelock on the authenticity of many of the most difficult documents. Properly used as a guide to the original sources and to the secondary literature, and not as an alternative to them, the *Bibliography* saves many hours of misguided searching in libraries and is a constant stimulus to effective research. It is to be hoped that scholars will respond to the editor's plea to send him corrections and additions, and that it will be possible to keep this manual up to date at regular intervals.

The second major enterprise of the last two decades and one that is still in progress has been the work of Professor Finberg and of his pupil, Dr Hart, in providing local historians with handlists, county by county, of all the pre-Conquest charters concerned with lands or rights therein, both charters that are extant and those that are known to have once existed. Beginning in 1953 with Devon and Cornwall, Professor Finberg has covered in turn the counties of the West Midlands and of Wessex; Dr Hart has been responsible for Essex and the counties of eastern England;[2] a volume for northern England and the north Midlands is promised, and it is to be hoped that a scholar will be found to take on the large task of calendaring the charters of the south-eastern counties. The great value of these lists lies in the amount of accurate and new topographical work they incorporate, and in the way they enable historians of the local society and economy to see at a glance how many of the estates in the pre-Conquest charters of their area have been located, and how much work in this field remains to be done. The opportunity has also been taken in each county list to publish usable texts of any charters that have hitherto been unprinted – something for which all pre-Conquest historians are in their debt. A controversial feature of the later volumes in the scheme has been the grading of the charters by a system of stars to indicate degrees of authenticity. Professor Finberg's belief that earlier

[1] Ed. P. H. Sawyer, R. Hist. Soc. Guides and Handbooks 8 (London, 1968).
[2] H. P. R. Finberg, *The Early Charters of Devon and Cornwall* (Leicester, 1953, 2nd ed. 1963); Finberg, *The Early Charters of the West Midlands* (Leicester, 1961); Finberg, *The Early Charters of Wessex* (Leicester, 1964); C. R. Hart, *The Early Charters of Essex* (Leicester, 1957, 2nd ed. 1971); and Hart, *The Early Charters of Eastern England* (Leicester, 1966).

scholars have been unduly critical and cautious in discussing the authenticity of the bulk of the pre-Conquest charters has led him to adopt a 'deliberately conservative and lenient standard of criticism'.[1] A glance at Professor Sawyer's *Bibliography* soon shows how frequently the handlists mark documents as authentic, or as in large part authentic, which have hitherto been considered spurious. It is a moot point, of course, whether the paralysis of research that may result from the over-critical condemnation of difficult charters is worse than the wasted effort and misguided conclusions that result from the acceptance as genuine of spurious and interpolated texts. Local historians would perhaps be better served if the remaining volumes in the series included references to Professor Sawyer's *Bibliography* and a brief indication of any considerations which have led the compiler to a more 'lenient' view of an individual charter.

One indispensable guide remains to be written, namely a manual of Anglo-Saxon diplomatic. Diplomatic has for so long been a neglected branch of English historical scholarship that it is not surprising that we lack an English Tessier, Dölger or Bresslau.[2] Until the charters have been re-edited, the scholar who attempted any such survey would indeed be sticking his neck out. But the need for this to be done is all the more acute since scholars of repute have questioned the methods of diplomatic and their applicability to pre-Conquest documents.[3] This is the more surprising since two model studies of all the 'apparent originals' of a limited period and category have shown what can be achieved even in well worked fields. T. A. M. Bishop and P. Chaplais, in their facsimile edition of all the royal writs of the eleventh century that survive on single sheets of parchment, built upon the foundations laid by Miss Harmer.[4] They emphasized that however much the pre-Conquest writs may take the form of administrative messages, they are in practice notifications of royal grants, which conferred title to rights and properties. Not only were writs therefore preserved in the beneficiary's archives along with his other title-deeds but on occasion they were also written by a scribe of the beneficiary.[5] The assumption that Anglo-Saxon royal writs were *in toto* the products of a royal 'chancery' was thus shown to be false. Mr Bishop and Dr Chaplais also established that Edward the Confessor had but one royal seal (that hitherto known as his second seal),

[1] Finberg, *Wessex*, p. 20. Cf. Finberg, *West Midlands*, p. 14.
[2] G. Tessier, *Diplomatique Royale Française* (Paris, 1962); F. Dölger, *Byzantinische Urkundenlehre* (Munich, 1968); and H. Bresslau, *Handbuch der Urkundenlehre für Deutschland und Italien*, 3 vols., 2nd ed. (Leipzig, 1912–31).
[3] F. Barlow, *The English Church 1000–1066* (London, 1963), p. 127, n. 2, and Finberg, *Wessex*, p. 199, and 'Fact and Fiction from Crediton', *West Country Historical Studies* (Newton Abbot, 1969), pp. 65–9.
[4] *Facsimiles of English Royal Writs to AD 1100*, ed. T. A. M. Bishop and P. Chaplais (Oxford, 1957).
[5] *Ibid.* pp. xii–xiii and pls. xviii and xxiiib.

and that the other seals purporting to be his, and the documents to which they are attached, are forgeries. The abbey of Westminster was revealed as a prolific centre of forged seals and forged writs in the middle years of the twelfth century.[1]

The second work to show the value of meticulous attention to the extant originals consists of two volumes in the series Chartae Latinae Antiquiores in which Dr A. Bruckner has re-edited with facsimiles all the extant Anglo-Saxon charters whose script may be assigned to a date before 800.[2] In addition to providing an exact text of these charters with full critical apparatus, Dr Bruckner has surveyed the diplomatic of the extant originals in the introduction to vol. IV. Following the practice of this series, this introduction carries no annotation, and scholars should therefore study the somewhat fuller version that Dr Bruckner has published with copious footnotes in the *Archivalische Zeitschrift*.[3] Particularly valuable is his attention to the evidence for the procedures by which the diplomas were produced and delivered, and his demonstration of how frequently the authenticity of 'apparent originals' can be placed beyond reasonable doubt by detecting and explaining changes of script or of ink, confirmatory endorsements, and traces of preliminary drafts. Though we may doubt Dr Bruckner's belief that some of the attestations in certain diplomas have autograph crosses, and may also regret the omission from the facsimiles of the endorsements that are later than 800, his work breaks new ground and serves as a reproach to the neglect of most British scholars. Only the sumptuous edition of the recently discovered will of Æthelgifu by Professor Whitelock, Dr Ker and Lord Rennell shows in a comparable way how much can be learnt when original documents are edited with full studies of their internal and external characteristics.[4]

The other major contribution to Anglo-Saxon diplomatic has been the revolutionary series of articles by Dr P. Chaplais, who may be said to have inherited the mantle of W. H. Stevenson.[5] Fundamental to all his work is the plea which he made in 1965 for an exact and rigorous terminology. A charter in which any attempt at deception can be detected is called a 'forgery'. 'Original' is used only to refer to a charter in contemporary script on a single

---

[1] *Ibid.* pp. xx–xxiii.
[2] *Chartae Latinae Antiquiores*, ed. A. Bruckner and R. Marichal III and IV (Olten, 1963 and 1967).
[3] A. Bruckner, 'Zur Diplomatik der älteren angelsächsischen Urkunden', *Archivalische Zeitschrift* 61 (1965), 11–45.
[4] *The Will of Æthelgifu*, trans. and examined by Dorothy Whitelock, with Neil Ker and Lord Rennell, for the Roxburghe Club (Oxford, 1968).
[5] P. Chaplais, 'The Origin and Authenticity of the Royal Anglo-Saxon Diploma', *Jnl of the Soc. of Archivists* 3 (1965–9), 48–61; 'The Authenticity of the Royal Anglo-Saxon Diplomas of Exeter', *Bull. of the Inst. of Hist. Research* 39 (1966), 1–34; 'The Anglo-Saxon Chancery: from the Diploma to the Writ', *Jnl of the Soc. of Archivists* 3 (1965–9), 160–76; 'Some Early Anglo-Saxon Diplomas on Single Sheets: Originals or Copies?', *ibid.* 315–36; and 'Who Introduced Charters into England? The Case for Augustine', *ibid.* 526–42.

sheet of parchment and displaying no suspicious features. 'Copy' refers to a charter which also has no suspicious features, but which is not in a contemporary hand. Charters on single sheets, but which through insufficient palaeographical and diplomatic analysis cannot yet be placed in one of these categories, are termed 'apparent originals'.[1] The great merit of this classification is that it concentrates attention on the period and context in which the extant charters were produced rather than on their purported date. It also helps to discourage what in the absence of a critical edition must be regarded as the besetting sin of Anglo-Saxon historians, namely their use of those parts of spurious charters that fit their theories on the grounds that the anachronistic features of the document are 'later interpolations' in a charter that is basically genuine.

Dr Chaplais's conclusions on how the authenticity of the earliest surviving diplomas can be established are notably similar to those reached at the same time by Dr Bruckner.[2] Nonetheless it is startling to discover that there are still major discoveries to be made about such famous and well studied charters as King Hlothar's grant of 679 to the abbey of Reculver[3] (where Dr Chaplais shows that the witnesses were added by a different but contemporary scribe) or the grant of Œthelræd to Æthelburh, abbess of Barking, in March 687(?).[4] In this charter not only the list of witnesses but also the boundary clause was written by a later scribe, who alone used the late spellings *Œdel-* and *Hædde* whose presence in this charter once caused philologists such trouble. Both charters can now be accepted as originals – Hlothar's grant in its entirety, Œthelræd's as far as the unfinished corroboration clause 'Et ut firma et inconcussum sit donum'. The bounds and witnesses of Œthelræd's charter were added about a century later; they were probably copied from a scribal memorandum on a separate piece of parchment stitched to the original. Dr Chaplais has drawn attention to the traces of stitching that can still be detected along the bottom edge of the charter.

Dr Chaplais's examination of the diplomatic of the earliest originals has led him to re-open the question of the date when 'landbooks' or charters were first introduced to England. He argues the case for Augustine as the originator, even though (like earlier scholars) he can find neither originals nor copies of authentic charters before the 670s.[5] The obvious objection to Dr Chaplais's theory – namely that it is inconceivable that churches would all be so negligent of their earliest deeds as to fail to copy them before they

[1] Chaplais, 'Diplomas of Exeter', p. 3.   [2] Chaplais, 'Some Early Diplomas', *passim*.
[3] BM Cotton Augustus ii. 29; *Facsimiles of Ancient Charters in the British Museum*, ed. E. A. Bond (London, 1873–8; henceforward cited as *BMFacs*) i, 1, and *Cartularium Saxonicum*, ed. W. de Gray Birch (London, 1885–93; henceforward cited as *BCS*), no. 45.
[4] Augustus ii. 29; *BMFacs* i, 2 and *BCS* 81.
[5] Chaplais, 'Origin and Authenticity', pp. 49–52, and 'Augustine', *passim*.

disintegrated through age and damp – is less powerful when one considers how few English churches have an uninterrupted history from before the age of Archbishop Theodore.[1] Consequently his case relies on the accumulation of indirect evidence. It might, however, have been strengthened had he discussed the purported grant of King Æthelberht to the church of Rochester in the year 604. W. Levison drew attention to the formulae drawn from Italian private deeds in this charter, though he found the unique address to the king's son, Eadbald, anomalous.[2] But the address to Eadbald may be a point in its favour rather than the reverse; we know too little of Kentish politics to reject the possibility that Eadbald had some authority in west Kent during his father's lifetime.[3] If the boundaries in English indicate that the charter as it stands is a forgery, their brevity suggests that it was an early one. And if forged, it is strange indeed that the forger resisted the temptation to record the presence of Augustine himself and to date the charter by the era of the incarnation. Whatever may be made of this Rochester charter, Dr Chaplais has an important point when he stresses that the form of Old English diplomas implies a very primitive secretarial organization, such as we might expect amongst the earliest missionaries. The absence of any means of validation and also the variety of formulae amongst the earliest originals would be surprising if the diploma had been recently introduced by Archbishop Theodore, who is known to have had at least one notary, the aptly named Titillus, in his *familia*.[4]

Religious in form, the pre-Conquest charter was also, Dr Chaplais argues, ecclesiastical in production. He stresses that Anglo-Saxon diplomas were always written in monastic or episcopal scriptoria, and frequently drafted by high-ranking ecclesiastics. There were, of course, royal writers and king's priests, who could write letters for the king when required. But he challenges the view that any pre-Conquest English king ever had a royal 'chancery' – that is, a permanent central royal secretariat staffed by scribes who specialized in royal business. The demonstration that ninth-century royal diplomas were

---

1 The only churches to be considered are Canterbury, Rochester, London and Winchester and the monasteries of St Augustine's and Lyminge. The new edition, when it covers these churches, should show whether there are local archival reasons why authentic charters of the early seventh century have not been preserved in these houses.

2 *BCS* 3; W. Levison, *England and the Continent in the Eighth Century* (Oxford, 1946), pp. 223–5. As Levison points out, the address to Eadbald is misleadingly printed by Birch. It consists simply of 'Ego Æthelberhtus rex filio meo Eadbaldo'. The following words belong to the proem.

3 Compare the otherwise unknown King Æthelwald (*adulwaldi*) who was converted by Bishop Justus, and was probably a subordinate king in (west) Kent during the reign of Eadbald. See P. Hunter Blair, 'The Letters of Pope Boniface V and the Mission of Paulinus to Northumbria', *England before the Conquest: Studies in Primary Sources presented to Dorothy Whitelock*, ed. Peter Clemoes and Kathleen Hughes (Cambridge, 1971), pp. 7–8.

4 Titillus wrote the acts of the Synod of Hertford, preserved by Bede (*HE* iv.5); *Bede's Ecclesiastical History of the English People*, ed. B. Colgrave and R. A. B. Mynors (Oxford, 1969), p. 352.

for the most part produced in episcopal scriptoria is welcome, and is likely to be reinforced when the new edition of the charters gets under way.[1] But it is for the tenth and eleventh centuries that Dr Chaplais's views are most revolutionary. He accepts the evidence accumulated by R. Drögereit that for about a generation from 931 many royal diplomas, even though they concern estates in widely separated parts of the kingdom, were produced in a single scriptorium. But he is unwilling to interpret this as a royal chancery, an organ of government reflecting the growing power of the West Saxon dynasty. Instead he has drawn attention to Dr Ker's demonstration that one of the so-called 'royal' scribes who wrote such 'chancery' diplomas was the Winchester writer responsible for the 951 annal in the Parker Chronicle (Cambridge, Corpus Christi College 173), and that the script of five of the other seven 'royal' scribes (Chaplais nos. 2, 3, 5, 7 and 8) may together with the hand of the annals from 925 to 955 in the Parker Chronicle be regarded as the typical script of the Winchester scriptorium.[2] The concentration of charter-writing in the episcopal *familia* at Winchester was doubtless an administrative convenience, not least because there were so few other centres of literacy in the kingdom and because the bishop of Winchester would normally be in attendance at important meetings of the witan with some of his *familia*. But Winchester was never the only scriptorium which produced charters for the English kings. Indeed the first 'chancery' scribe who wrote originals of the years 931 and 934 used a very different script from the Winchester type, and his spelling of personal names and of the Old English bounds of the estates shows that he was not a West Saxon.[3] A group of charters concerning Mercian and East Anglian estates and ranging in date from 940 to 956, which are drafted in rhythmical and alliterative prose and in formulae quite distinct from those of the Winchester scriptorium, must be regarded as the products of a Midland writing-office.[4] Moreover Dr Chaplais has shown how, when the tenth-century reformation of monastic life got under way in England, royal diplomas began once more to be written in monasteries – at Glastonbury in the 950s and at Abingdon in the 960s.[5]

---

[1] Chaplais, 'Origin and Authenticity', pp. 58–9. Evidence that the writing of ninth-century royal diplomas concerning lands in Kent was organized on a strictly diocesan basis was presented in my unpublished Oxford D.Phil. thesis, 'The Pre-Conquest Charters of Christ Church, Canterbury' (1969). The point should be established by the volumes in the new edition for Rochester and Christ Church.

[2] Chaplais, 'Origin and Authenticity', pp. 59–61, and N. R. Ker, *Catalogue of Manuscripts Containing Anglo-Saxon* (Oxford, 1957), p. lix.

[3] *BCS* 677 and 702; *BMFacs* III, 3 and 5. The dialect forms are more common in *BCS* 702 than in *BCS* 677, so it is possible that they are not a guide to the scribe's origin, but have been copied into *BCS* 702 from a scribal memorandum listing the bounds and the witnesses, which had been written in the region of the estate, i.e. in Sussex or Kent.

[4] *BCS* 746, 751, 771, 772, 773, 815, 876, 882, 883, 884, 890, 893, 909, 911, 937 and 1346.

[5] Chaplais, 'Anglo-Saxon Chancery', pp. 163–5.

No scholar has succeeded in proving the existence of a centralized chancery in the later decades of the tenth century, and it is to be expected that the volumes of the new edition will establish the activities of many local monastic and episcopal scriptoria in the last century of Anglo-Saxon England.

Dr Chaplais has also provided a new and far more satisfying interpretation of the development of the royal writ. Like Professor Barraclough, he is not willing to conclude that the royal writ was already in use under King Alfred from Alfred's reference to a man who receives his lord's 'ærendgewrit and hys insegel', and from his use in the preface to the *Pastoral Care* of an opening protocol that is close to the address and greeting of the writs of the eleventh century.[1] The 'lord's letter and his seal' may refer to a letter sealed 'close', but Dr Chaplais argues that it more probably means a letter and a loose seal carried by the bearer as a sign of credence. He does not deny that the formulae of the royal writs may be much older than the eleventh century, but explains their appearance in set form already in the earliest writs of certain authenticity – those of King Cnut for Christ Church, Canterbury – as the result of their long use for purely oral messages. He argues that the motive for recording the king's message to the courts in writing was not the king's desire for efficient government, but the beneficiaries' wish for a permanent record of their acquisitions. Thus the earliest authentic writs were written on spare leaves of gospel books at Christ Church by contemporary Canterbury scribes.[2] There is no reason to suppose that these gospel entries are copies of sealed originals. They are rather the only record of notifications of the king's grants made orally in the shire court. Their authenticity was guaranteed by their presence in a gospel book on the altar at Christ Church. Thus it is that none of the 'writs' that were entered into gospels have been preserved as sealed 'originals', and conversely the one Christ Church writ which has been preserved on a single sheet of parchment with the king's seal,[3] was not copied into any extant gospel book. It did not need any authentication beyond the royal seal.

With this picture of the writ deriving its formulaic phraseology from generations of oral messages to the folk-courts, but being recorded in writing only when beneficiaries insisted upon a more permanent testimony than the memory of those present in the court, the last evidence for a royal 'chancery'

---

[1] *Ibid.* pp. 166–76; Harmer (*Writs*, pp. 10–13) argued for writs in Alfred's time. G. Barraclough ('The Anglo-Saxon Writ', *History* n.s. 39 (1954), 193–215) understood *insegel* to mean a signet-ring carried as a sign of credence, and stressed that the use of comparable epistolary protocols does not prove that the royal writ as we know it later was already being used for the same purposes in Alfred's reign. The reference to 'your lord's *ærendgewrit* and his *insegel*' is from *King Alfred's Old English Version of St Augustine's Soliloquies*, ed. H. L. Hargrove, Yale Stud. in Eng. 12 (New Haven, 1902), 23.

[2] Harmer, *Writs*, nos. 26, 27, 28, 29, 30 and 35.

[3] BM Campbell Charter xxi.5; Harmer, *Writs*, no. 33.

in the Anglo-Saxon period disappears. Doubtless one of the members of the king's household had custody of the royal seal, which from Edward the Confessor's reign, and perhaps already from Cnut's,[1] was being used to authenticate writs. Equally some of the king's priests may on occasion have been asked to write royal writs, though it is not until the very end of William I's reign that the extant originals provide clear evidence for a royal scribe. Until that time *Empfängerausstellung* seems to have been the general rule.[2] As Professor Barraclough observed, the development of the royal chancery from the royal chapel was a very slow one, scarcely complete before the thirteenth century.[3] Though some of the seeds of this development may be discerned in the reign of Edward the Confessor, we must beware of exaggerating the Anglo-Saxon administrative and bureaucratic capacity.

No other scholar has ranged so widely over the entire field of pre-Conquest charters as Dr Chaplais, and it is to be hoped that he will be persuaded to give us the manual of Anglo-Saxon diplomatic that he alone of present-day scholars is qualified to write. His judgements may on occasion be too severe. For example it is difficult to accept that the two papal privileges to King Cenwulf of Mercia, whose corruptions Levison corrected, are the work of a Winchcombe forger who somehow had access both to a genuine privilege of Pope Paschal I and to a copy of the papal formula-book, the *Liber Diurnus*; for a forgery which did not even name the estates which the monastery of Winchcombe wished to claim would not only be incompetent but also motiveless.[4] But to err on the side of rigour is a good fault if pre-Conquest diplomatic is to achieve a sure foundation.

The work of other scholars has been limited to particular aspects of the charters, to individual texts, or to groups of charters. Often important work has been incidental to research on much wider subjects. Thus the interests of German scholars in the concepts of kingship and of imperial rule has led to a series of studies of the regnal styles in English charters.

---

[1] Harmer (*Writs*, pp. 94–101) follows Bresslau in suggesting that the double-sided English royal seal originated with Cnut, who had two kingdoms, and that its design was modelled on the (one-sided) seal of Emperor Conrad II, whose coronation in 1027 Cnut attended. Dr Chaplais ('Anglo-Saxon Chancery', p. 175) draws attention to the numismatic evidence that Edward's seal may have been the work of the German engraver, Theodoric, who, it is suggested, made the dies for the coins of the later part of Edward the Confessor's reign. See R. H. M. Dolley and F. Elmore Jones, 'A New Suggestion Concerning the So-Called Martlets in the Arms of St Edward', *Anglo-Saxon Coins: Studies presented to F. M. Stenton*, ed. R. H. M. Dolley (London, 1961), pp. 215 and 220. The two positions are not incompatible.

[2] Bishop and Chaplais, *Facsimiles*, pp. xii–xiii, xvi–xix and pls. ix and xxv a. Their tentative suggestion that the similar hands of BM Cotton Augustus ii.80 and Campbell Charter xxi.5 (pls. i and v) might represent 'the style of the royal chancery script' under Edward the Confessor is doubted by Dr Chaplais in his more recent article, 'Anglo-Saxon Chancery', p. 175.

[3] Barraclough, 'Anglo-Saxon Writ', pp. 213–15.

[4] BCS 337 and 363; Chaplais, 'Some Early Diplomas', pp. 335–6. Compare Levison's judgement in *England and the Continent*, pp. 255–8.

R. Drögereit's attempt to show that the use of imperial styles by Anglo-Saxon kings was a chimera, on the grounds that styles using *imperator* and *imperialis* occurred only in spurious charters, was received with enthusiastic masochism in England.[1] But his analysis of the charters – wilful in its neglect and distortion of palaeographical evidence, in casting doubt by false associations, and in its failure to suggest any motive or occasion for the forgery of so many charters (most of them grants to laymen) from almost a dozen different archives – has been justly criticized by Mr E. John and by Dr E. Stengel.[2] Of particular interest in view of Alcuin's rôle in the creation of Charlemagne's empire is Dr Stengel's demonstration of the links between the title 'divina largiente rector et imperator Merciorum regni' in a charter of King Cenwulf of 798 and the letters of Alcuin of the later 790s.[3] There will still remain doubt, however, about the significance of imperial titles in English charters. Are we really to understand them as proof of a non-Roman concept of empire among the Anglo-Saxon (let alone the Celtic) peoples of Britain? Do they imply rule over other kingdoms, or even a claim to universal rule within the *orbis Britanniae*? Or are they simply attempts to ring the changes among the various Latin words for royal lordship available to the drafters of charters? Hanna Vollrath-Reichelt has recently taught us to use the evidence for overlordship with care and precision.[4] Of particular note is her emphasis on the fact that after 785 King Offa ruled in Kent, not as overlord, but as king (of the Mercians); but her denial that Offa had ever claimed to control (or to confirm) the booking of land in Kent in the 760s and 770s, when there were still native kings on the Kentish throne, involves the rejection on quite inadequate grounds of the charters of 764 and 765 from the Rochester cartulary and is based upon an incomplete analysis of the evidence for Offa's quashing of the charters of King Egbert II of Kent.[5]

[1] R. Drögereit, 'Kaiseridee und Kaisertitel bei den Angelsachsen', *Zeitschrift der Savigny-Stiftung für Rechtsgeschichte*, Germ. Abt. 69 (1952), 24–73. Drögereit's arguments on the 'imperial' charters of the tenth century were summarized by H. R. Loyn, 'The Imperial Style of the Tenth-Century Anglo-Saxon Kings', *History* n.s. 40 (1955), 111–15.

[2] E. John, *Land Tenure in England* (Leicester, 1958), pp. 95–8; 'An Alleged Worcester Charter of the Reign of Edgar', *Bull. of the John Rylands Lib.* 41 (1958), 60–3; and *Orbis Britanniae* (Leicester, 1966), pp. 52–6; and E. E. Stengel, 'Imperator und Imperium bei den Angelsachsen', *Deutsches Archiv für Erforschung des Mittelalters* 16 (1960), 15–72, repr. E. E. Stengel, *Zum Kaisergedanken im Mittelalter* (Cologne, 1965), pp. 289–342.

[3] *BCS* 289; Stengel, 'Imperator', pp. 38–54 and 69–72. A better edition of this charter using ultra-violet photography is in Bruckner and Marichal, *Chartae* III (no. 191).

[4] H. Vollrath-Reichelt, *Königsgedanke und Königtum bei den Angelsachsen bis zur Mitte des 9 Jahrhunderts*, Kölner Historische Abhandlungen 19 (Cologne, 1971).

[5] Ibid. pp. 151–76. Miss Reichelt's rejection of *BCS* 195 and 196 is not based on any analysis of their diplomatic; neither the somewhat inflated style of *BCS* 195 nor the attestation of the otherwise unknown bishop, Badenoth, in *BCS* 196 constitutes grounds for suspicion. Her analysis of the 'Aldhun affair' involves a very forced interpretation of *BCS* 332 and she ignores the fact that Offa quashed not only Egbert's grants to Aldhun and to Christ Church (*BCS* 293) but also his grants to Rochester. Compare *BCS* 227 and 228 with *BCS* 257.

The land-law that lies behind the pre-Conquest charters, the nature and origin of 'bookland' and 'folkland', have again become subjects of controversy in recent years. Mr E. John has argued the relevance of Professor E. Levy's studies of Vulgar Roman law to a proper understanding of English bookright, and stressed that the creation of hereditary right and the power of alienation were the essence of the legal changes brought about in the 'booking' of an estate. But the deliberately 'disputatious' aim of his work, and the slipshod or too brief discussion of many of the key charters, antagonized his readers and did no service to his case.[1] His recent restatement of his view that folkland was land which was held precariously and which reverted to the king at the death of the tenant is constructive, if regrettably brief, and a welcome challenge to pre-Conquest historians to re-examine their assumptions about early English society and land-law.[2] Another long-overdue contribution to this subject has been the attempt of Miss Vollrath-Reichelt to relate the evidence of the English charters to current German assumptions about the nature of early medieval lordship over land, and about the meaning of such terms as *folc* and freeman.[3] In accord with one school of thought she interprets folkland as *fiskalland*, that is land directly dependent upon the king in his capacity as leader of the *folc* and settled by *Königsfreien*, who owed services and dues to the king. And it is entirely typical of this school, with its delight in the paradoxes of unfree, and even semi-free, freedom, that she should argue, in the face of the evidence of numerous immunity clauses,[4] that the 'secular services' of the charters were not owed by all the people, the whole *gens*, but only by the king's (free) men on *fiskalland* (folkland). These works have demonstrated the need for a far more extended treatment of pre-Conquest land-law; it will need of course a deep knowledge of the English charters, but it will also have to take account of current continental scholarship on Germanic and Vulgar Roman law, and of the works of the adherents of the *Königsfreien* school and of their many Italian, French and German critics; it will need, too, to study the development of the Anglo-Saxon immunity, which so far has been systematically examined only in relation to the reservation of the three military burdens.[5]

[1] John, *Land Tenure*. See the important reviews by D. Whitelock (*Amer. Hist. Rev.* 66 (1960–1), 1009–10, and further correspondence, *ibid.* 67 (1961–2), 582–4) and H. R. Loyn (*History* n.s. 46 (1961), 233–5).

[2] E. John, 'Folkland Reconsidered', *Orbis Britanniae*, pp. 64–127.

[3] Vollrath-Reichelt, *Königsgedanke*, pp. 65–8 and 192–225.

[4] The references from Anglo-Saxon diplomas were collected by W. H. Stevenson, 'Trinoda Necessitas', *EHR* 29 (1914), 689, n. 3. See also Nicholas Brooks, 'The Development of Military Obligations in Eighth- and Ninth-Century England', *England before the Conquest*, ed. Clemoes and Hughes, pp. 69–70 and 76–8.

[5] E. John, 'The Imposition of Common Burdens on the Lands of the English Church', *Bull. of the Inst. of Hist. Research* 31 (1958), 117–29, repr. *Land Tenure*, pp. 64–79, and Brooks, 'Development', pp. 69–84.

Few aspects of charter studies have been advanced so much in the last twenty years as the study of the actual estates that are the subject of the grants.[1] Most Anglo-Saxon royal diplomas include a description of the boundaries of the land granted, and careful topographical research can therefore reveal the extent and shape of a pre-Conquest estate, and hence can help to fill in our picture of the exploitation of the land and the development of settlement. Since the pioneering studies of Dr T. R. Thomson and of Professor Finberg, the principles of such topographical study and of its publication have gradually been clarified. Firstly, as Professor Finberg has justly emphasized, no Anglo-Saxon diploma has been correctly understood until the estate has been precisely located, its extent and character understood. His own works have repeatedly shown that the identifying of the boundaries of a charter may lead to a radically new understanding of the document's purpose.[2] Equally, however, the bounds of a charter cannot be studied in isolation from the diplomatic, the palaeography and the language of the charter. One of the more common forms of forgery of pre-Conquest charters was the addition of a lengthy set of boundaries to early charters, which originally had only the briefest indication of the neighbouring properties on north, south, east and west or had no boundary clause at all. It is hazardous to assume that a boundary clause, whose form and language are later than the purported date of the charter to which it belongs, nonetheless represents accurately an estate that was granted at the date borne by the charter. For on the rare occasions when both an original and a later version with modernized bounds survive the additions of the forger can be detected.[3] Two things are needed above all others by the student of Anglo-Saxon bound-

---

[1] Studies of the bounds of individual charters in the last twenty years are too numerous to be fully listed here. Amongst the more important are: T. R. Thomson, 'The Early Bounds of Purton and a Pagan Sanctuary', *Wiltshire Archaeol. Mag.* 55 (1954–5), 353–63; 'The Bounds of Ellandune *c.* 956', *ibid.* 56 (1955–6), 265–70; 'The Early Bounds of Wanborough and Little Hinton', *ibid.* 57 (1958–70), 203–11; and (with R. E. Sandell) 'Saxon Land Charters of Wiltshire', *ibid.* 58 (1961–3), 442–6; H. P. R. Finberg, 'The Treable Charter', *Devon and Cornwall*, pp. 20–31; 'The Hallow-Hawling Charter', *West Midlands*, pp. 184–96; 'Some Crediton Documents Re-examined', *AntJ* 48 (1968), 59–86, repr. with emendations as 'Fact and Fiction from Crediton', *West Country Studies*, pp. 29–69; and 'Two Acts of State', *ibid.* pp. 11–28; M. Gelling, 'The Boundaries of the Westminster Charters', *Trans. of the London and Middlesex Archaeol. Soc.* n.s. 11 (1954), 101–4; C. Hart, 'Some Dorset Charter Boundaries', *Proc. of the Dorset Nat. Hist. and Archaeol. Soc.* 86 (1964), 158–63; and D. J. Bonney, 'Two Tenth-Century Charters Concerning Lands at Avon and Collingbourne', *Wiltshire Archaeol. Mag.* 64 (1969), 56–64.

[2] Finberg, 'Treable Charter', 'Hallow-Hawling Charter' and 'Some Crediton Documents'.

[3] As for example *BCS* 335 of the year 811, which survives in two versions: BM Cotton Augustus ii. 10 of *saec. ix* (*1*) and BM Stowe Charter 10 of *saec. x* (*2*), which includes boundaries of two additional estates. An object lesson in the need to study the boundaries of charters in conjunction with the diplomatic, palaeographical and linguistic evidence (or with the collaboration of experts in these fields) is provided by the way in which Professor Finberg has had to retract the exciting conclusions that he first drew from the bounds of *BCS* 1331 and of the Treable charter of 976. Compare Finberg, *Devon and Cornwall*, pp. 20–31, with *West Country Studies*, pp. 44–61.

aries: the linguistic skill and knowledge to interpret them correctly, and a current knowledge of and access to the area, so that the difficulties of the bounds can be solved by repeated walking in various seasons and weathers. Work from maps, old and new, is an essential preliminary, but identifications based on map-work alone without field-work will always be incomplete and often mistaken. At the end of the day it is likely that there will still remain some points along a boundary that defy identification, where place-names have passed out of use or where the bounds themselves are trees that have long since died, or small ponds, swampy places, copses and the like, which have long since been drained or cut down and cleared away. It is therefore essential for the benefit of future workers in the field that accurate Ordnance Survey grid references are given for each bound that has been located, and that those that are positively identified should be distinguished from inter-mediate points whose location is dependent upon them. A willingness to admit the uncertain areas of an identification is vital. For the historian may reasonably doubt an identification which, for example, claims that the estate covers an area that was still assessed at the time of the Domesday Survey at a far larger number of hides than the assessment in the charter itself, more than two centuries earlier.[1] When an estate is eventually located there-fore, it must make historical and geographical sense.

Pre-Conquest charters often contain essential information for solving the chronological problems of Anglo-Saxon history. Indeed they are often the only evidence for dating the pontificates of bishops and the reigns of kings. In recent years work on these problems has been resumed. Mary Anne O'Donovan has put all historians of the English church in the age before the monastic revival in her debt by setting out with exemplary clarity the evi-dence for the order of succession and the dating of the bishops of all the English sees of the southern province during the period from 850 to 950.[2]

[1] Professor Finberg's identification of the bounds of the famous South Hams charter of 846 (*BCS* 451), by which King Æthelwulf booked twenty hides of land to himself, makes the estate cover an area which in 1086 was assessed at more than three times this number of hides. Yet there is evidence to suggest that the hidage assessment of Devon and of Cornwall was remark-ably stable in the tenth and eleventh centuries, for the four Devon boroughs in the Burghal Hidage are given a garrison drawn from 1,534 hides, which equals the combined assessment of Devon and Cornwall in Domesday Book. For the Burghal Hidage, see A. J. Robertson, *Anglo-Saxon Charters* (Cambridge, 1939), p. 246. We can scarcely avoid the conclusion that men from Cornwall had to go to help defend and repair the boroughs in west Devon, and that the assessment of these shires remained unchanged over nearly two centuries. To maintain Professor Finberg's identification of the bounds of the South Hams charter, one would need to suppose that the assessment of this part of Devon was drastically increased between 846 and the early tenth century, when the Burghal Hidage was compiled. Evidence for such increases in assessment is entirely lacking.

[2] M. A. O'Donovan, 'An Interim Revision of Episcopal Dates for the Province of Canterbury, 850–950', *ASE* 1 (1972), 23–44 and 2 (1973), 91–113. See also Dorothy Whitelock, 'The Pre-Viking Age Church in East Anglia', *ASE* 1 (1972), 1–22, esp. 19–22.

Kenneth Harrison has re-investigated the numerous problems connected with the use of indictions and of the era of the incarnation. Of particular importance is his demonstration that use of the Year of Grace is not necessarily a cause for suspicion in charters earlier than Bede's *Ecclesiastical History*. Incarnational dating occurs in a small number of Mercian, Kentish and West Saxon charters associated with Bishop Wilfrid, all of which have features suggesting that despite some corruptions they may be copies of authentic texts.[1] Wilfrid, of course, had championed the Roman cause at the Synod of Whitby, when the Easter tables of Dionysius, based on the era of the incarnation, were adopted. Equally important is Mr Harrison's analysis of the dating clauses of charters of the second half of the eighth century and of the ninth; he shows that the drafters of these charters began their incarnation year at Christmas, and that they seldom, if ever, made any allowance, when calculating the indiction, for the fact that the indiction properly began in September. It would seem that their normal practice was simply to read the indiction number from the Dionysiac Tables.[2] The effect of Mr Harrison's work is to reduce the significance of the indiction in England. But, in the view of the subsequent all-conquering rôle of the 'Bedan' indiction on the continent through the work of Anglo-Saxon missionaries and scholars, there remains much to be done to determine how and when the equinoctial indiction beginning on 23 or 24 September was transmitted from the east Mediterranean, where it is found until the mid-fifth century, to England in the seventh century or the eighth.[3] Indeed in the light of the work

---

[1] K. Harrison, 'The *Annus Domini* in some Early Charters', *Jnl of the Soc. of Archivists* 4 (1970–3), 551–7. He discusses *BCS* 42, 43, 51 and 72. Only *BCS* 42 has no evident connection with Wilfrid. Yet it shows Wilfrid's friend and protector, King Æthelred of Mercia, intervening in Kent by force in January 691 ('dum ille infirmaverat terram nostram') at a time when the see of Canterbury was vacant. Wilfrid was by this time again running into difficulties with the Northumbrian king, and his biographer claims that he had been offered the succession to the see of Canterbury by Archbishop Theodore himself. See *Life of Bishop Wilfrid by Eddius Stephanus*, ed. B. Colgrave (Cambridge, 1927), pp. 86–92. The problem of the succession to the see of Canterbury after Theodore's death will be fully discussed in my *Early History of the Church of Canterbury*, in preparation.

[2] K. Harrison, 'The Beginning of the Year in England *c.* 500–900', *ASE* 2 (1973), 51–70. I am grateful to Mr Harrison for showing me a typescript of his article in advance of publication.

[3] V. Grumel ('La Chronologie Byzantine', *Traité d'Études Byzantines*, ed. P. Lemerle 1 (Paris, 1958), 193–205) has the best discussion of the use of the autumn equinox as the beginning of the civil year, and hence of the indiction, in the eastern Roman Empire; he also shows its association with the feast of the conception of St John the Baptist (24 September in the west, 23 in the east), and with the birth of Emperor Augustus (23 September), and fixes as precisely as possible the change from the equinoctial indiction to that beginning on 1 September. Long after this change eastern liturgical calendars continued to record the beginning of the indiction and the conception of St John on 23 September. The most likely source of the transmission of the equinoctial indiction to England is, as Grumel suggests, a Roman calendar with some eastern entries. An English calendar of *saec. xi* (2) (Cambridge, University Library, Kk. v. 32) has under 24 September an addition of *saec. xi–xii*, 'Hic incipiuntur indictiones et finiuntur'. See *English Kalendars before AD 1100*, ed. F. Wormald, Henry Bradshaw Soc. 72 (London, 1933), 78. The source may, however, have been Bede rather than calendar tradition.

of Levison, and more recently of Mr D. P. Kirby, Dr Chaplais and Mr Harrison, it is fair to question whether anyone seeking to comprehend *de novo* the dating of Archbishop Theodore's synods of Hertford and Hatfield would ever reach R. L. Poole's conclusion that they used the misnamed 'Greek' indiction, beginning on 1 September, and that they must therefore be dated 672 and 679 in preference to Bede's dates of 673 and 680.[1] If we could accept that the two synods used the equinoctial indiction and that Bede dated them correctly, then we no longer need to explain how the 'Bedan' indiction replaced the 'Greek' indiction in England and went on to triumph over it on the continent at a time when Mr Harrison has shown the indiction to have had little importance in England.

Charters, wills, writs and the like, written in the vernacular, and Latin charters with substantial Old English boundaries, are a vital, but as yet inadequately used, source for the development of English as a vehicle for written prose, for the analysis of the different English dialects, and for the dissemination of 'classical' West Saxon in the tenth century. A start has recently been made in the study of the syntax of the Old English charters,[2] but progress on the various dialects of the extant charters of the ninth and tenth centuries has been hampered by uncertainty about the provenance of charters. Sweet's analysis and classification of the charters extant in manuscripts earlier than *c.* 900 has remained in use, even though Sweet himself knew that it was inadequate.[3] He knew that the scribes of some charters that he had listed as 'Mercian-Kentish' and 'Saxon-Kentish' had also written some that he had listed as purely 'Kentish'.[4] It is therefore scarcely surprising that difficulties and doubts should have arisen over identifying and distinguishing the Mercian and Kentish dialects in the ninth century.[5]

---

[1] R. L. Poole, *Studies in Chronology and History* (Oxford, 1934), pp. 38–55. Levison (*England and the Continent*, pp. 265–79) and Harrison ('Beginning of the Year', pp. 55–9) have destroyed Poole's theory that Bede's Year of Grace began on 24 September. D. P. Kirby ('Bede and Northumbrian Chronology', *EHR* 78 (1963), 517–18) has drawn attention to the difficulties of fixing the date of the Synod of Hatfield from the regnal years of the kings listed in the protocol; in particular he notes that Kentish charters (*BCS* 36 and 44) suggest that King Hlothere succeeded in 674 rather than 673. Cf. Bede, *HE* IV.17. This, together with Bede's date for Æthelred of Mercia's succession (675; *HE* v.24), points to the synod having taken place in 680 not 679. Chaplais ('Some Early Diplomas', pp. 324–5) emphasized that Bede's indiction both began *and ended* on 24 September, i.e. the change occurred on the 24th, probably at sunset; Bede could therefore regard an event which happened on 24 September as occurring on the last day of the old indiction, and he therefore dated the Synod of Hertford 673 rather than 672. Taken together these facts explain why Bede dated these councils 673 and 680, and suggest that he was right to do so. The only evidence for the 'Greek' indiction in England may therefore be a chimera.

[2] C. Carlton, *Descriptive Syntax of the Old English Charters*, JL ser. practica 3 (The Hague, 1970).

[3] *Oldest English Texts*, ed. H. Sweet, Early Eng. Text Soc. o.s. 83 (London, 1885), 420–60.

[4] *Ibid.* p. 424.

[5] Thus the charters described by Sweet as 'Kentish' (*ibid.* pp. 443–53; nos. 34 and 37–44) were regarded as pure West Mercian by R. Vleeskruyer (*The Life of St Chad* (Amsterdam, 1953), p. 47), but as Kentish with some influence of Mercian spelling by A. Campbell (*Old English*

The new edition of the pre-Conquest charters will use diplomatic and palaeographical tests to identify the scriptoria where the charters were written. A new and firmly based classification of the Old English material in the charters will then be possible. Charters, of course, like books, could be written in one region in the dialect of another,[1] but when it has been established where they were written, one of the uncertainties in the study of dialects will have been removed.

If the study of the language of the vernacular charters has been hampered by inadequate analysis and classification, that of the Latin of the charters has been largely neglected. Yet there is a rich field of study here for any who will analyse the grammar and the orthography of the 'apparent originals'. No one who has examined those of the ninth century will doubt Alfred's statement that at his accession there were very few south of the Humber who could translate a letter from Latin to English, and that he could not recall a single one south of the Thames. Later, under King Athelstan, when Latinity had improved and had become inflated with 'hisperic' style, there is much to be learned, as Professor Bullough has recently demonstrated, from the study of its sources and vocabulary.[2] Here too the new edition should act as a spur to research by showing how varied was the Latin written in different centres throughout the Anglo-Saxon period. Indeed it will be possible to analyse not only the Latin styles of a number of English scriptoria but also the development of their script. At present the writings of E. A. Lowe, N. R. Ker and T. A. M. Bishop contain invaluable scattered clues to the provenance and date of charter hands, and to the scripts of individual houses at key periods;[3] may we look forward to the prospect of a series of studies of Anglo-Saxon scriptoria using charter evidence as their foundation?

One of the most profitable lines of approach to the charters in recent years, and one which itself anticipates the concept of the new edition, has come from the study of monastic cartularies and narratives. Since the bulk of purportedly pre-Conquest charters has been preserved only in such collections,

---

Grammar (Oxford, 1964), §§ 307 and 314, and *The Vespasian Psalter*, ed. D. H. Wright and A. Campbell, EEMF 14 (Copenhagen, 1967), 85–6), and as Kentish by R. M. Wilson ('The Provenance of the Vespasian Psalter Gloss: the Linguistic Evidence', *The Anglo-Saxons: Studies in some Aspects of their History and Culture presented to Bruce Dickins*, ed. P. Clemoes (London, 1959), pp. 302–4.

[1] K. Sisam, 'Canterbury, Lichfield, and the Vespasian Psalter', *RES* n.s. 8 (1956), 1–10 and 113–31.

[2] D. A. Bullough, 'The Educational Tradition in England from Alfred to Ælfric: Teaching Utriusque Linguae', *Settimane di Studio del Centro Italiano di Studi sull'Alto Medioevo* 19 (1972), 466–78.

[3] E. A. Lowe, *English Uncial* (Oxford, 1960), and *Codices Latini Antiquiores* 11: *Great Britain and Ireland*, 2nd ed. (Oxford, 1972); Ker, *Catalogue*; and T. A. M. Bishop, 'Notes on Cambridge Manuscripts', *Trans. of the Cambridge Bibliographical Soc.* 2 (1954–8), 185–99 and 323–36, and 3 (1959–63), 93–5 and 412–23; 'A Charter of King Edwy', *Bodleian Lib. Record* 6 (1957), 369–73; and *English Caroline Minuscule* (Oxford, 1972).

it is essential to understand the occasion, the motives and the methods of their compilation. The pioneering work of Dr Ker and of the late Professor Wormald on Hemming's cartulary and on the Sherborne cartulary set the standard in this field.[1] More recently Dr E. O. Blake has re-edited the *Liber Eliensis* with a foreword and critical notes by Professor Whitelock.[2] Book II of this work of the mid-twelfth century is based upon a wide range of pre-Conquest charters and vernacular records of various types, most of which there is every reason to accept as authentic. They provide an invaluable picture not only of the fluctuating fortunes of the Ely endowment but also of East Anglian administrative, legal and monetary practice. The preliminary studies of the cartulary of the cathedral priory of Winchester (BM Add. 15350) by Professor Finberg and Dr Hart have also stressed the importance of examining cartularies in their own right.[3] But the number of grants to laymen in this cartulary, which concern lands that have not yet been shown to have ever belonged to, or even to have been claimed by, Winchester, does not prove, as Dr Hart argues, that 'the royal archives' were kept at Winchester and that copies of all charters issued from a royal (Winchester) scriptorium were preserved in them. There is no evidence at all that royal diplomas were normally issued in duplicate in the Anglo-Saxon period, one for the donor and one for the donee. And charters that have no known connection with the house where they were preserved are not a problem unique to Winchester. On the contrary most major pre-Conquest churches have such charters, if they have preserved a substantial number of original charters or have a cartulary whose compiler did not restrict himself to grants to his own house. It is simpler to accept the traditional and well documented conclusion that laymen who received charters often placed them for safe-keeping in an important church[4] than to credit the Anglo-Saxon monarchy with bureaucratic procedures that would put them more than two centuries in advance of all other secular governments in western Europe.

The charters of the monasteries of the tenth-century reformation in England have been the especial interest of Mr E. John,[5] and they present par-

---

[1] N. R. Ker, 'Hemming's Cartulary: a Description of the Two Worcester Cartularies in Cotton Tiberius A.xiii', *Studies in Mediaeval History presented to F. M. Powicke*, ed. R. W. Hunt, W. A. Pantin and R. W. Southern (Oxford, 1948), pp. 49–75, and F. Wormald, 'The Sherborne Cartulary', *Fritz Saxl Memorial Essays*, ed. D. J. Gordon (London, 1962).

[2] *Liber Eliensis*, ed. E. O. Blake, R. Hist. Soc., Camden 3rd ser. 92 (London, 1962).

[3] Finberg, *Wessex*, pp. 16–18 and 214–48, and Hart, 'The *Codex Wintoniensis* and the King's *Haligdom*', *Land, Church, and People: Essays presented to H. P. R. Finberg, Agricultural Hist. Rev.* 18 Supplement (1970), 7–38.

[4] Stenton, *Latin Charters*, pp. 19–20. Compare Robertson, *Anglo-Saxon Charters*, no. 78, where a layman even gets the settlement of a land dispute entered into the gospel book of the local cathedral church (Hereford).

[5] E. John, 'An Alleged Worcester Charter of the Reign of Edgar', *Bull. of the John Rylands Lib.* 41 (1958), 54–80; 'St Oswald and the Tenth-Century Reformation', *JEH* 9 (1958), 147–68, repr.

ticularly acute problems of criticism. On the one hand these monasteries themselves acted as scriptoria where charters were drafted and written,[1] so that arguments for and against their authenticity cannot necessarily be decided by appeal to the charters of other houses. On the other hand monastic reform, as Mr John has rightly stressed,[2] frequently involved a tenurial revolution which meant that the subsequent history of the house was one of endless litigation. In these circumstances there was always a motive for forgery, and we must regard with particular suspicion any 'apparent original' to a reformed monastery, whose script is later than its purported date. We should not therefore be surprised that Mr John's interpretation of many of these charters has proved controversial. In particular his attempt to prove that the cathedral community of Worcester was reformed in 964 along Æthelwoldian lines (i.e. by sudden and forcible ejection of recalcitrant clerks in favour of monks) rests upon his belief that a considerable genuine stratum can be distinguished in the forged *BCS* 1135, the so-called *Altitonantis* charter.[3] But Professor Darlington and Professor Sawyer have since shown in detail and beyond all reasonable doubt that this charter is a compilation of the twelfth century and that no part of it can be reliably used as evidence for the tenth. Professor Sawyer has further demonstrated that the witness-lists of Bishop Oswald's leases do not support any theory of sudden reform at Worcester.[4] On the contrary they show that the composition of the community was only gradually changed, that there were two main periods of recruitment – 964–5 and 969–77 – and that its members, even by the end of Oswald's life, were more frequently called clerks than monks.

With *Altitonantis* must also fall Mr John's interpretation of the military and judicial privileges of the liberty of Oswaldslow, which is dependent upon it.[5] Of greater value is his discussion of a group of charters granting wide privileges to a number of reformed houses, particularly those of Æthelwold's connection; they have formulae in common and have been usefully styled the *Orthodoxorum* charters from the first word in most of their

Orbis Britanniae, pp. 234–48; 'The King and the Monks in the Tenth-Century Reformation', *Bull. of the John Rylands Lib.* 42 (1959), 61–87, repr. *Orbis Britanniae*, pp. 154–80; 'Some Latin Charters of the Tenth-Century Reformation', *RB* 70 (1960), 333–59; 'Some Alleged Charters of King Edgar for Ely', *Orbis Britanniae*, pp. 210–33; and 'The Church of Winchester and the Tenth-Century Reformation', *Bull. of the John Rylands Lib.* 47 (1964–5), 404–29.

1 John, *Orbis Britanniae*, pp. 207–9 and 228, and 'Church of Winchester', pp. 405–7, and Chaplais, 'Origin and Authenticity', p. 60, and 'Anglo-Saxon Chancery', p. 165.

2 John, 'King and Monks', *passim.*

3 John, 'St Oswald', and 'The Altitonantis Charter', *Land Tenure*, pp. 162–7.

4 R. R. Darlington, *The Cartulary of Worcester Cathedral Priory*, Pipe Roll Soc. 76 (1962–3), xii–xix, and P. H. Sawyer, 'Charters of the Reform Movement: the Worcester Archive', forthcoming in the publication of the *Regularis Concordia* Conference of 1970. I am indebted to Professor Sawyer for showing me a copy of his article before publication.

5 John, *Land Tenure*, pp. 80–139.

preambles.[1] Such general grants of privileges, particularly when they are also *pancartae* – that is when they include general confirmations of listed estates – were always liable to alteration and improvement by forgers. Mr John admits that some of the *Orthodoxorum* group are, in Dr Chaplais's terminology, forgeries. But he makes a good case on diplomatic and historical grounds for the authenticity of Æthelred's privilege of 993 to Abingdon and of Edgar's privilege of 972 to Pershore.[2] If his conclusions can be supported by the necessary close examination of the script and of the external characteristics of these charters in the light of other charters and books from these houses, the diplomatic of the monastic reform movement will have received a welcome foundation in a sea of uncertainty. Mr John has also argued, against the view of Dr Blake and Professor Whitelock, that a case can be made out for the authenticity of the Ely 'foundation privilege', *BCS* 1266; his arguments have been strengthened by Professor Pope's demonstration that the style of the vernacular version of this charter leaves little room for doubt that it was composed by Ælfric.[3] This, of course, does not rule out the possibility that *BCS* 1266 is an early forgery, and we still need an adequate explanation of why, if Ely possessed an authentic original of 970, it was necessary for this to be redrafted in bilingual form as though that had been its original appearance.

Such doubts are unlikely to be resolved until the relevant volumes of the new edition of the pre-Conquest charters have appeared in print, with the necessary combination of diplomatic, linguistic, palaeographical and topographical analysis. In the meantime it is evident that sure progress in charter studies can come only from comparable collaboration between experts in these different disciplines. Thus few will be convinced by Professor Finberg's valiant attempt to salvage the credit of the charters of 844 and 854 purporting to belong to Æthelwulf's *decimatio* of his estates;[4] for Professor Finberg justifies setting aside the diplomatic evidence that these charters are full of formulae of the late tenth and early eleventh centuries by quoting Sir Frank Stenton in such a way as to make it seem that Sir Frank had believed that such analysis was valueless;[5] he fails to explain why the only charter of this

---

[1] John, 'Some Latin Charters'. The charters are *BCS* 1046, 1047, 1187, 1282 and 1284 and *Codex Diplomaticus Aevi Saxonici*, ed. J. M. Kemble, 6 vols. (London, 1839–48; henceforward cited as *KCD*), no. 684.

[2] *KCD* 684 and *BCS* 1282. Cf. Chaplais, 'Anglo-Saxon Chancery', p. 165.

[3] John, 'Some Alleged Charters'; *Liber Eliensis*, ed. Blake, pp. 414–15; and J. Pope, 'Ælfric and the Old English Version of the Ely Privilege', *England before the Conquest*, ed. Clemoes and Hughes, pp. 85–113.

[4] Finberg, *Wessex*, pp. 187–213.

[5] *Ibid*. p. 199. The quotation comes from Stenton, *Latin Charters*, p. 15, where Sir Frank was criticizing Stevenson's hasty and unbalanced comments upon some of the Muchelney charters; but Stenton's overall appreciation of Stevenson's methods of detailed diplomatic analysis is shown on pp. 7–10 of the same work.

series which survives as an 'apparent original' is in a hand of *saec. xi*, or why these charters contradict the evidence of the Anglo-Saxon Chronicle and of the Rochester *decimatio* charter, *BCS* 486, that the tithing occurred in 855. Solution of the problems of Æthelwulf's *decimatio* will be achieved only by combining detailed analysis of the diplomatic and palaeography of the charters with study of the history of the archives where they have been preserved, and with wider historical considerations, in particular with an examination of the comparable measures of Carolingian rulers, whose interpretation is, of course, equally controverted.

It is fitting, in view of the aims of this periodical, that a review of recent work on charters should end with a plea for collaboration between scholars in different disciplines, between diplomatists and topographers, palaeographers and linguists. Few if any scholars have such mastery of all these skills that they can do without such expert help. It is only through collaboration that the new edition will be achieved, and that the more bitter controversies of the last generation will lead to constructive and sure conclusions in this most stimulating, but most difficult of fields.

Bibliography for 1973

MARTIN BIDDLE, ALAN BROWN, T. J. BROWN, PETER A. CLAYTON and PETER HUNTER BLAIR

This bibliography is meant to include all books, articles and significant reviews published in any branch of Anglo-Saxon studies during 1973. It excludes reprints unless they contain new material. It will be continued annually. Addenda to the bibliographies for 1971 and 1972 are included at the appropriate places; one that concerns a book or article is preceded by an asterisk and specifies the year of publication. A.B. has been mainly responsible for sections 2, 3 and 4, T.J.B. for section 5, P.H.B. for section 6, P.A.C. for section 7 and M.B. for section 8. Peter Clemoes has been coordinating editor.

The following abbreviations are used where relevant (not only in the bibliography but also throughout the volume):

AB	*Analecta Bollandiana*
ABR	*American Benedictine Review*
AHR	*American Historical Review*
AntJ	*Antiquaries Journal*
ArchJ	*Archaeological Journal*
ASE	*Anglo-Saxon England*
ASNSL	*Archiv für das Studium der neueren Sprachen und Literaturen*
BGDSL	*Beiträge zur Geschichte der deutschen Sprache und Literatur*
BNJ	*British Numismatic Journal*
BROB	*Berichten van de Rijksdienst voor het Oudheidkundig Bodemonderzoek*
CA	*Current Archaeology*
CCM	*Cahiers de Civilisation Médiévale*
CHR	*Catholic History Review*
DUJ	*Durham University Journal*
E&S	*Essays and Studies by Members of the English Association*
EC	*Essays in Criticism*
EconHR	*Economic History Review*
EEMF	Early English Manuscripts in Facsimile
EHR	*English Historical Review*
ELN	*English Language Notes*
EStn	*Englische Studien*
ESts	*English Studies*
IAF	*Issledovanija po Anglijskoj Filologii*
IF	*Indogermanische Forschungen*

JBAA   *Journal of the British Archaeological Association*
JEGP   *Journal of English and Germanic Philology*
JEH   *Journal of Ecclesiastical History*
JL   Janua Linguarum
JTS   *Journal of Theological Studies*
MA   *Medieval Archaeology*
MÆ   *Medium Ævum*
MLN   *Modern Language Notes*
MLQ   *Modern Language Quarterly*
MLR   *Modern Language Review*
MP   *Modern Philology*
MS   *Mediaeval Studies*
N&Q   *Notes and Queries*
NC   *Numismatic Chronicle*
NM   *Neuphilologische Mitteilungen*
PMLA   *Publications of the Modern Language Association of America*
PQ   *Philological Quarterly*
RB   *Revue Bénédictine*
RES   *Review of English Studies*
SAP   *Studia Anglica Posnaniensia*
SBVS   *Saga-Book of the Viking Society for Northern Research*
SN   *Studia Neophilologica*
SP   *Studies in Philology*
TLS   *Times Literary Supplement*
TPS   *Transactions of the Philological Society*
TRHS   *Transactions of the Royal Historical Society*
YES   *Yearbook of English Studies*
ZAA   *Zeitschrift für Anglistik und Amerikanistik*
ZDA   *Zeitschrift für deutsches Altertum und deutsche Literatur*
ZVS   *Zeitschrift für vergleichende Sprachforschung*

1. GENERAL AND MISCELLANEOUS

[Anon.] 'Thomas Charles Lethbridge, Esq., M.A.', *AntJ* 52, 448–9
   'Professor Francis Wormald, C.B.E. . . .', *AntJ* 52, 456–9
Braddy, Haldeen, 'England and English before Alfred', *Costerus* 7, 27–46
Brown, Alan K., 'Old English Research in Progress 1972–1973', *NM* 74, 520–9
   'Old English Bibliography 1972', *OE Newsletter* 6. 2, 27–45
Clemoes, Peter, *et al.*, ed., *ASE* 2, 'Preface' (ix–x) and 'Bibliography for 1972'
   (303–33)
Collins, Rowland L., Robert S. Cox, Robert T. Farrell, Milton McCormick Gatch,
   Oliver J. H. Grosz, Matthew Marino and Joseph B. Trahern, 'The Year's
   Work in Old English Studies 1972', *OE Newsletter* 7. 1, 9–45
Eliason, Norman E., 'Kemp Malone, 14 March 1889–13 October 1971', *Amer.*
   Speech 44, 163–5

Jackson, Kenneth, 'Nora Kershaw Chadwick 1891–1972', *Proc. of the Brit. Acad.* 58, 537–49

*Jankuhn, Herbert, 'Die Glaubwürdigkeit des Tacitus in seiner *Germania* im Spiegel archäologischer Beobachtungen', *Der altsprachliche Unterricht* (1972) 142–51

Kahrl, Stanley J., ed., *OE Newsletter* 6. 2 and 7. 1 [including 'Elegy, Composed upon the B.U. Bridge' in Old English, by Penn Szittya, and two Old English crossword puzzles by Ann Harleman Stewart]

Ker, Neil, 'Kenneth Sisam 1887–1971', *Proc. of the Brit. Acad.* 58, 409–28 [with a bibliography]

Klingenberg, Heinz, *Runenschrift – Schriftdenken – Runeninschriften*, Germanische Bibliothek 3. Reihe (Heidelberg)

Lipp, Frances, 'The Teaching of Introductory Old English in the U.S. and Canada: some Comments on the 1972 Survey', *OE Newsletter* 6. 2, 7–26

Major, Kathleen, 'Doris Mary Stenton 1894–1971', *Proc. of the Brit. Acad.* 58, 525–35

*Oizumi, Akio, and Taé Okada, trans., *A Handbook of Old English* by Fernand Mossé [in three parts], *Doshisha Stud. in Engl* 3 (1972), 191–262, and 4 (1972), 87–133, and Monograph 1 (1972), Department of English, Doshisha University, Kyoto

Pyles, Thomas, 'Kemp Malone, Onomatologist', *Names* 21, 131–2

Riché, Pierre, *Éducation et Culture dans l'Occident Barbare VIe–VIIIe Siècle*, 3rd ed. rev. (Paris)

Sandgren, Folke, 'The Published Writings of Olof von Feilitzen, 1931–1972: a Bibliography', *Otium et Negotium: Studies in Onomatology and Library Science presented to Olof von Feilitzen*, ed. Folke Sandgren (Stockholm), pp. 254–8

Welsford, Enid, E. H., *In Memoriam Nora K. Chadwick 1891–1972* (Cambridge)

West, Philip, J., 'Medieval Style and the Concerns of Modern Criticism', *College Eng.* 34, 784–90

2. OLD ENGLISH LANGUAGE

Adžiašvili, Š. D., 'Remeclennaja terminologija v drevneanglijskom jazkye (terminologija prjadenija i tkačestva) [Handicraft Terms in Old English: the Terminology of Spinning and Weaving]', *Vestnik Moskovskogo Universiteta*, ser. X, *Filologija* 5, 63–75

*Antonsen, Elmer H., 'The Proto-Germanic Syllabics (Vowels)', *Toward a Grammar of Proto-Germanic*, ed. Frans van Coetsem and Herbert L. Kufner (Tübingen, 1972), pp. 117–40

*Arngart, O., see sect. 6

Ball, C. J. E., and A. F. Cameron, 'Some Specimen Entries for the Dictionary of Old English', *Zeitschrift für Dialektologie und Linguistik* Beiheft 9, 46–64

*Bammesberger, Alfred, 'Altenglisch *gedægeþ* in Napier XLIV', *ZVS* 86 (1972), 190–2

'Altenglisch *hlæfþe*', *ZVS* 86 (1972), 307–11

Bammesberger, Alfred, 'Zu altenglisch *berofan* in *Genesis* 2078b', *Die Sprache* 19, 205–7

'Das anglische Verb *lioran/leoran*', *ZVS* 87, 272–82

Barnes, Mervin, and Helmut Esau, 'Germanic Strong Verbs: a case of Morphological Rule Extension?', *Lingua* 31, 1–34

*Beck, Heinrich, and Klaus Strunk, 'Germanisch *armaʒ* und vedisch *árma-* (I und II)', *Festschrift für Hans Eggers*, ed. Herbert Backes (Tübingen, 1972), 18–41

*Beckers, Hartmut, *Die Wortsippe '*hail*' und ihr sprachliches Feld im Altenglischen*, Münster diss (1971)

*Bennett, William H., 'Prosodic Features in Proto-Germanic', *Toward a Grammar of Proto-Germanic*, ed. Frans van Coetsem and Herbert L. Kufner (Tübingen, 1972), pp. 99–116

Bergmann, Rolf, *Verzeichnis der althochdeutschen und altsächsischen Glossenhandschriften: mit Bibliographie der Glosseneditionen der Handschriftenbeschreibungen und der Dialektbestimmungen*, Arbeiten zur Frühmittelalterforschung 6, Univ. Münster (Berlin and New York)

Brown, Alan K., 'Some Further Etymologies of *Heifer*', *Neophilologus* 57, 94

'*Neorxnawang*', *NM* 74, 610–23

Burchfield, R. W., 'Four-Letter Words and the O.E.D.', *Zeitschrift für Dialektologie und Linguistik* Beiheft 9, 84–9 [repr. from *TLS* 13 October 1972, p. 1233]

Burgschmidt, Ernst, and Dieter Götz, *Historische Linguistik: Englisch* (Tübingen)

Cameron, Kenneth, 'Early Field-names in an English-Named Lincolnshire Village', *Otium et Negotium: Studies in Onomatology and Library Science presented to Olof von Feilitzen*, ed. Folke Sandgren (Stockholm), pp. 38–43

*Coetsem, Frans van, 'The Germanic Consonant Shift: Compensating Processes in Language', *Lingua* 30 (1972), 203–15

'Proto-Germanic Morphophonemics', *Toward a Grammar of Proto-Germanic*, ed. F. van Coetsem and Herbert L. Kufner (Tübingen, 1972), pp. 174–209

Cox, B. H., 'Leicestershire Moot-Sites: the Place-Name Evidence', *Trans. of the Leicestershire Archaeol. and Hist. Soc.* 47, 14–21

Cruz, Juan Manuel de la, 'A Late 13th Century Change in English Structure', *Orbis* 22, 161–76

Dickins, Bruce, see sect. 6

Dodgson, John McN., 'Two Coals to Newcastle', *Otium et Negotium: Studies in Onomatology and Library Science presented to Olof von Feilitzen*, ed. Folke Sandgren (Stockholm), pp. 46–8

see sect. 6

Dolley, Michael, 'The Forms of the Proper Names Appearing on the Earliest Coins Struck in Ireland', *Otium et Negotium: Studies in Onomatology and Library Science presented to Olof von Feilitzen*, ed. Folke Sandgren (Stockholm), pp. 49–65

*Düwel, Klaus, 'Die Runeninschrift auf der silbernen Scheibe von Liebenau', *Die Kunde* (Niedersächsischer Landesverein für Urgeschichte) 23 (1972), 134–41

Eichman, Th. L., 'Althochdeutsch *sinnan* "streben nach", sanskritisch *san-, sā-* "gewinnen", und hethitisch *sanh-* "erstreben"', *ZVS* 87, 269–71

*Ek, Karl-Gustav, *The Development of OE ȳ and ēo in South-Eastern Middle English*, Lund Stud. in Eng. 42 (1972)

Erickson, Jon, '*An* and *na þaet an* in Late Old English Prose: some Theoretical Questions of Derivation', *Archivum Linguisticum* 4, 75–88

*Fellows Jensen, Gillian, *Scandinavian Settlement Names in Yorkshire*, Navnestudier udgivet af Institut for Navneforskning 11 (Copenhagen, 1972)

Fellows Jensen, Gillian, 'Place-Name Research and Northern History: a Survey with a Select Bibliography of Works Published since 1945', *Northern Hist.* 8, 1–23

*Field, John, *English Field Names: a Dictionary* (Newton Abbot, 1972)

Foley, James, 'Assimilation of Phonological Strength in Germanic', *A Festschrift for Morris Halle*, ed. Stephen R. Anderson and Paul Kiparsky (New York)

Forsberg, Rune, '*Ætstealles beorh*: a Place-Name Crux Reconsidered', *SN* 45, 3–19

Frank, Roberta, and Angus Cameron, ed., *A Plan for the Dictionary of Old English* (Toronto) [Roberta Frank, 'The Dictionary of Old English Conference', pp. 1–7; Helmut Gneuss, 'Guide to the Editing and Preparation of Texts for the Dictionary of Old English', pp. 9–24; Angus Cameron, 'A List of Old English Texts', pp. 25–306; Richard L. Venezky, 'Computational Aids to Dictionary Compilation', pp. 307–27; C. J. E. Ball and Angus Cameron, 'Some Specimen Entries for the Dictionary of Old English', pp. 329–47

Gelling, Margaret, 'Further Thoughts on Pagan Place-Names', *Otium et Negotium: Studies in Onomatology and Library Science presented to Olof von Feilitzen*, ed. Folke Sandgren (Stockholm), pp. 109–28

Gneuss, Helmut, 'Vorarbeiten und Vorüberlegungen zu einem neuen Wörterbuch des Altenglischen', *Festschrift Prof. Dr Herbert Koziol zum siebzigsten Geburtstag*, ed. Gero Bauer, Franz K. Stanzel and Franz Zaic, Wiener Beiträge zur englischen Philologie 75 (Vienna and Stuttgart), 105–15

Hallander, Lars-G., 'Old English *dryht* and its Cognates', *SN* 45, 20–31

Hamp, Eric P., 'A Semantic Archaism', *Ling. Inquiry* 4, 246–51 [*dōgor*]

*Heeroma, Klaas, 'Zur Raumgeschichte des Ingwäonischen', *Zeitschrift für Dialektologie und Linguistik* 39 (1972), 267–83

Heeroma, Klaas, 'Fries *fean* in ingweoons perspectief', *Us Wurk* 21–2, 37–44

Heller, L. G., 'Late Indo-European Water Deity as Spearman: Greek *Triton* and Old English *gārsecg*', *Names* 21, 74–7

Hoard, James E., and Clarence Sloat, 'English Irregular Verbs', *Language* 49, 107–20

Jasanoff, Jay H., 'The Germanic Third Weak Class', *Language* 49, 850–70

Kabell, Aage, 'Uber einige Verba für *tun* in den germanischen Sprachen', *ZVS* 87, 26–35
see sect. 8*i*

Kim, Suksan, 'Long Consonants in Old English', *Linguistics* 102, 83–90

King, Robert D., 'Rule Insertion', *Language* 49, 551–78

Knapp, Frizt Peter, 'Althochdeutsch *biscof* – altfranzösisch *(e)vesque* – altgallo-italienisch **vescof*', *Die Sprache* 19, 180–97

Kolb, Eduard, '*Elmet*: a dialect Region in Northern England', *Anglia* 91, 285–313 [*efes*]

*Kristensson, Gillis, 'A Note on Old English *slagu* "slag, dross"', *SN* 44 (1972), 274–7

*Kufner, Herbert L., 'The Grouping and Separation of the Germanic Languages', *Toward a Grammar of Proto-Germanic*, ed. Frans van Coetsem and Herbert L. Kufner (Tübingen, 1972), pp. 71–97

*Kuhn, Hans, *Kleine Schriften 3: Namenforschung; Sonstiges* (Berlin and New York, 1972)

*Kuryłowicz, Jerzy, 'Notes de Conjugaison II (6. Verbes Germaniques en -*e*-)', *Biuletyn Polskiego Towarzystwa Językoznawczego* 29 (1971), 13–17

*Lehmann, Winfred P., 'Proto-Germanic Syntax', *Toward a Grammar of Proto-Germanic*, ed. Frans van Coetsem and Herbert L. Kufner (Tübingen, 1972), pp. 239–68

see sect. 3*bi*

*Lowe, Pardee, Jr, 'Germanic Word Formation', *Toward a Grammar of Proto-Germanic*, ed. Frans van Coetsem and Herbert L. Kufner (Tübingen, 1972), pp. 211–37

*McLintock, D. R., '"To Forget" in Germanic', *TPS* (1972), 79–93

Marcq, Phillippe, 'Structure du Système des Prépositions Spatiales dans le *Béowulf*', *Études Germaniques* 28, 1–19

Marino, Matthew, see under Collins, Rowland L., sect. 1

*Markey, Thomas L., 'Germanic Terms for Temple and Cult', *Studies for Einar Haugen*, ed. Evelyn Scherabon Firchow *et al.*, JL Ser. Maior 59 (The Hague and Paris, 1972), 365–78

'The Place-Name Element -*hurst* (-*horst*)', *Naamkunde* 4 (1972), 26–35

*Matthews, C. M., *Place Names of the English-Speaking World* (New York, 1972)

Mezger, Fritz, 'Germ. **ga-laga-* n.: An. *lǫg* n. Pl. "geltendes Recht, Gesetz(e), Satzung, Bestimmung(en)"', *ZVS* 87, 22–5

*Miedema, H. T. J., 'Thor en de Wikingen in Friesland: Oudfries **thôresdey*, "donderdag"', *Naamkunde* 4 (1972), 1–20

'Nederlands *keen*, engels *chine*, fries *sein*', *Naamkunde* 4 (1972), 40–5

Miedema, H. T. J., 'Ist die altfriesische Präposition *til* ein altnordisches Lehnwort der Wikingerzeit?', *Us Wurk* 21–2, 173–80

Migaćev, V. A., 'O Nekotoryx postulatax sravitel'noj grammatiki germanskix jazykov (kritika kompozicionnoj teorii dental'nogo preterita) [Some Postulates of Comparative Germanic Grammar: a Critique of the Theory of the Compounded Dental Preterite]', *Filologičeskie Nauki* 74, 63–71

*Mitchell, Lawrence, 'Old English as an SVO Language: Evidence from the Auxiliary', *Papers in Ling.* 5 (1972), 183–201

*Moulton, William G., 'The Proto-Germanic Non-Syllabics (Consonants)', *Toward a Grammar of Proto-Germanic*, ed. Frans van Coetsem and Herbert L. Kufner (Tübingen, 1972), pp. 141–73

Munske, Horst Haider, *Der germanische Rechtswortschatz im Bereich der Missetaten: Philologische und sprachgeographische Untersuchungen, I: Die Terminologie der älteren westgermanischen Rechtsquellen*, Studia Linguistica Germanica 8. 1 (Berlin and New York)

Nummenmaa, Liisa, *The Uses of 'So' 'Al So' and 'As' in Early Middle English*, Mémoires de la Société Néophilologique de Helsinki 39

O'Neil, Wayne, 'Some Remarks on Old and Middle English Stress', *A Festschrift for Morris Halle*, ed. Stephen R. Anderson and Paul Kiparsky (New York), pp. 158–65

Page, R. I., 'Anglo-Saxon Scratched Glosses in a Corpus Christi College, Cambridge, Manuscript', *Otium et Negotium: Studies in Onomatology and Library Science presented to Olof von Feiltzen*, ed. Folke Sandgren (Stockholm), pp. 209–15 see sect. 8*i*

Pak, Tae-Yong, 'Position and Affrication in Northumbrian Old English', *Neophilologus* 57, 74–82

Peeters, Christiaan, 'On English *lie*, Old English *lēogan*, "mentiri"', *ESts* 54, 58–9 'A Note on the West Germanic Gemination', *Linguistics* 98, 65–7 'On the Sequence *-ow-* before *j* and before Vowel in Germanic', *Word* 26, 278–81

*Penzl, Herbert, *Methoden der germanischen Linguistik*, Sprachstrukturen A.1 (Tübingen, 1972) 'Methods of Comparative Germanic Linguistics', *Toward a Grammar of Proto-Germanic*, ed. Grans van Coetsem and Herbert L. Kufner (Tübingen, 1972), pp. 1–42

*Polomé, Edgar C., 'Germanic and the Other Indo-European Languages', *Toward a Grammar of Proto-Germanic*, ed. Frans van Coetsem and Herbert L. Kufner (Tübingen, 1972), pp. 43–69

Ponomarenko, L. O., 'Šljaxy zapozyčennja z latyns'koi movy v anglijs'ku [Methods of Borrowing from Latin into English]', *Inozemna Filolohija* 30, 16–21

*Purdy, D. W., 'Did Old English Have a Definite Article?', *York Papers in Ling.* 2 (1972), 121–4

*Ramat, Paolo, 'Die Analyse eines morphosemantischen Feldes: die germanischen Modalverben', *IF* 76 (1971), 174–202

Rhee, F. van der, 'De *i*-umlaut in het Oudfries', *Taal en Tongval* 25, 127–30

Richards, Melville, 'Welsh Influences on some English Place-Names in North East Wales', *Otium et Negotium: Studies in Onomatology and Library Science presented to Olof von Feilitzen*, ed. Folke Sandgren (Stockholm), pp. 216–20

Rigold, S. E., see sect. 8*e*

Robinson, Fred C., 'Old English *Awindan, Of*, and *Sinhere*', *Festschrift Prof. Dr Herbert Koziol zum siebzigsten Geburtstag*, ed. Gero Bauer, Franz K. Stanzel and Franz Zaic, Wiener Beiträge zur englischen Philologie 75 (Vienna and Stuttgart), 266–71 'Syntactical Glosses in Latin Manuscripts of Anglo-Saxon Provenance', *Speculum* 48, 443–75 see sect. 3*biii*

*Ross, Alan S. C., '*I*- and *U*-Adjectives in Germanic', *TPS* (1972), 94–100

Ross, Alan S. C., 'Supplementary Note to "A Connection between Bede and the Anglo-Saxon Gloss to the Lindisfarne Gospels?" [*JTS* 20, 482–94]', *JTS* 24, 519–21 [a summary of *Eng. Philol. Stud.* 13, 49–72, A. S. C. Ross and Constance O. Elliott, 'Aldrediana XXIV: the Linguistic Peculiarities of the Gloss to St John's Gospel']

Runge, Richard M., 'The Phonetic Realization of Proto-Germanic /r/', *ZVS* 87, 228–47

*Sandred, Karl Inge, 'New Light on an Old English Landmark' [in Birch *Cart. Sax.* 260 (*Textus Roffensis*)], *Namn och Bygd* 59 (1971), 37–9

Schabram, Hans, 'Das altenglische *superbia*-Wortgut', *Festschrift Prof. Dr Herbert Koziol zum siebzigsten Geburtstag*, ed. Gero Bauer, Franz K. Stanzel and Franz Zaic, Wiener Beiträge zur englischen Philologie 75 (Vienna and Stuttgart), 272–9

Scheler, Manfred, 'Zum Bedeutungswandel des englischen *to show* ("schauen > zeigen")', *ASNSL* 209, 357–61

Scragg, D. G., see sect. 5

Seebold, Elmar, 'Die Stammbildungen der idg. Wurzel *ueid- und deren Bedeutungen (2. Teil)', *Die Sprache* 19, 158–79 [*edwitan*]

*Seltén, Bo, *The Anglo-Saxon Heritage in Middle English Personal Names: East Anglia 1100–1399* I, Lund Stud. in Eng. 43 (1972)

Sokolova, M. N., 'Signification des Termes *ham* et *tun* dans les Documents Anglo-Saxons', *CCM* 16, 123–32

Sprockel, Cornelis, *The Language of the Parker Chronicle II: Word-Formation and Syntax* (The Hague)

Starck, Taylor, and J. C. Wells, *Althochdeutsches Glossenwörterbuch: mit Stellennachweis zu sämtlichen gedruckten ahd. und verwandten Glossen*, fasc. 1 and 2 (Heidelberg, 1972–3)

Stewart, Ann Harleman, 'The Old English "Passive" Infinitive', *Jnl of Eng. Ling.* 7, 57–68

Tops, Guy A. J., 'Indo-European *a*, *o* > Germanic *a*; Indo-European *ā*, *ō* > Germanic *ō*', *Orbis* 22, 138–50

*Trutmann, Albertine, *Studien zum Adjektiv im Gotischen*, Quellen und Forschungen zur Sprach- und Kulturgeschichte der germanischen Völker 47 (Berlin and New York, 1972)

*Vachek, Josef, 'On One Point of Old English Phonology', *Prague Stud. In Eng.* 14 (1971), 133–42

Waterhouse, R., see sect. 3*c*

*Wentersdorf, Karl P., 'The Semantic Development of O.E. *dreorig* and *dreorigian*', *SN* 44 (1972), 278–88

Wentersdorf, Karl P., see sect. 3*biii*

West, Fred, 'Some Notes on Word Order in Old and Middle English', *MP* 71, 48–53

Zimmermann, Rüdiger, 'Structural Change in the English Auxiliary System: on the Replacement of *Be* by *Have*', *Folia Linguistica* 6, 103–17

3. OLD ENGLISH LITERATURE

a. General

Cameron, Angus, see under Frank, Roberta, and Angus Cameron, sect. 2

Gneuss, Helmut, see sect. 2

    see under Frank, Roberta, and Angus Cameron, sect. 2

Grose, M. W., and Deirdre McKenna, *Old English Literature*, Literature in Perspective (London and Totowa, New Jersey)

Grosz, Oliver, J. H., see under Collins, Rowland L., sect. 1

*Markland, Murray, 'The Task Set by Valor', *Costerus* 5 (1972), 103–15

The Oxford Anthology of English Literature I: The Middle Ages through the Eighteenth Century (New York, London and Toronto)

Page, R. I., 'Anglo-Saxon Texts in Early Modern Transcripts', *Trans. of the Cambridge Bibliographical Soc.* 6, 69–85

*Partridge, A. C., *English Biblical Translations* (London, 1972)

Quennell, Peter, and Hamish Johnson, *A History of English Literature* (London)

Scragg, D. G., see sect. 5

b. Poetry

i. General

Adams, Percy G., 'The Historical Importance of Assonance to Poets', *PMLA* 88, 8–18

*Conner, Patrick W., 'Schematization of Oral-Formulaic Processes in Old English Poetry', *Lang. and Style* 5 (1972), 204–20

Doane, A. N., '"The Green Street of Paradise": a Note on Lexis and Meaning in Old English Poetry', *NM* 74, 456–65

Finnie, W. Bruce [letter to editor about Percy G. Adams, 'The Historical Importance of Assonance to Poets', *q.v.*], *PMLA* 88, 1183–4

Gardner, Thomas, 'How Free was the *Beowulf* Poet?', *MP* 71, 111–27

Hacikyan, A., 'The Runes of Old English Poetry', *Revue de l'Université d'Ottawa* 43, 53–76

Keenan, Hugh T., '*Exodus* 312a: Further Notes on the Eschatological "Green Ground"', *NM* 74, 217–19

*Kennedy, Charles W., *The Earliest English Poetry: a Critical Survey* (1943; repr. with a new foreword by James P. Pettegrove, London, 1972)

*Kühlwien, Wolfgang, 'Entropie und Redundanz in der angelsächsischen Poesie', *Linguistics* 68 (1971), 13–28

*Kurath, Hans, 'A Note on Alliterative Practices in Germanic Verse', *Studies for Einar Haugen*, ed. Evelyn Scherabon Firchow *et al.*, JL Series Maior 59 (The Hague and Paris, 1972), 321–2

*Kuryłowicz, Jerzy, 'Podstawy językowe metryki starogermańskiej, [Linguistic Bases of Old Germanic Metre]', *Biuletyn Polskiego Towarzystaw Językoznawczego* 30 (1972), 3–15

Kyte, E. Clemons, 'On the Composition of Hypermetric Verses in Old English', *MP* 71, 160–5

*Lehmann, W. P., 'Comparative Constructions in Germanic of the OV Type', *Studies for Einar Haugen*, ed. Evelyn Scherabon Firchow *et al.*, JL Ser. Maior 59 (The Hague and Paris, 1972), 323–30

Lewis, Richard A., 'Old English Poetry: Alliteration and Structural Interlace', *Lang. and Style* 6, 196–205

'Alliteration and Old English Metre', *MÆ* 42, 119–30

Rollinson, Philip B., 'The Influence of Christian Doctrine and Exegesis on Old English Poetry: an Estimate of the Current State of Scholarship', *ASE* 2, 271–84

Trahern, Joseph B., see under Collins, Rowland L., sect. 1

Utley, Francis Lee, 'The Oral Formula: its Critics and its Extensions', *Stud. in Med. Culture* 4, 9–18

Whitman, F. H., 'A Major Compositional Technique in Old English Verse', *ELN* 11, 81–6

*Wienold, Götz, see sect. 3*biii*

ii. 'Beowulf'

Alexander, Michael, *'Beowulf': a Verse Translation* (Harmondsworth)

Bandy, Stephen C., 'Cain, Grendel, and the Giants of *Beowulf*', *Papers on Lang. and Lit.* 9, 235–49

Berkhout, Carl T., *'Beowulf* 3123b: under the Malice-Roof', *Papers on Lang. and Lit.* 9, 428–31

Braswell, Laurel, 'The Horn at Grendel's Mere: *Beowulf* 1417–41', *NM* 74, 466–72

Caldwell, Robert A., *'Beowulf* vv. 413b–414', *MÆ* 42, 131–2

*Cassidy, Frederic C., 'Beowulf: *Icge* and *Incge* Once More', *Studies for Einar Haugen*, ed. Evelyn Scherabon Firchow *et al.*, JL Ser. Maior 59 (The Hague and Paris, 1972), 115–18

*Collinder, Björn, 'On the Translation of Epics', *Sprachkunst* 3 (1972), 327–32

Condren, Edward I., *'Unnyt* Gold in *Beowulf* 3168', *PQ* 52, 296–9

Cox, Robert S., see under Collins, Rowland L., sect. 1

Evans, W. O., 'The Case for Sir Gawain Re-Opened', *MLR* 68, 721–33 [remark on *Beowulf*, pp. 732–3]

Gardner, Thomas, see sect. 3*bi*

Hanning, Robert W., 'Sharing, Dividing, Depriving: the Verbal Ironies of Grendel's Last Visit to Heorot', *Texas Stud. in Lang. and Lit.* 15, 203–13

*Hart, T. E., *Tectonic Design, Formulaic Craft and Literary Execution: the Episodes of Finn and Ingeld in 'Beowulf'*, Amsterdamer Beiträge zur älteren Germanistik 2 (1972)

Lendinara, Patrizia, see sect. 3*biii*

Lewis, Richard A., see sect. 3*bi*

Liggins, Elizabeth M., 'Revenge and Reward as Recurrent Motives in *Beowulf*', *NM* 74, 193–213

Marcq, Philippe, see sect. 2

*Moorman, Charles, *Kings and Captains: Variations on a Heroic Theme* (Lexington, Kentucky, 1971)

Nelson, Marie, '*It is More Honorific to Give* . . .', *NM* 74, 624–9 [*Beowulf* 1008–49]

Ohba, Keizo, 'Hroðgar's "Sermon" and Beowulf's Death', *Annual Reports of Studies, Doshisha Women's College of Liberal Arts, Kyoto* 24, 1–19

Opland, Jeff, 'A *Beowulf* Analogue in *Njálssaga*', *Scandinavian Stud.* 45, 54–8

*Porsia, Franco, see sect. 4

*Puhvel, Martin, 'The Deicidal Otherworld Weapon in Celtic and Germanic Mythic Tradition', *Folklore* 83 (1972), 210–19

Puhvel, Martin, 'The Blithe-Hearted Morning Raven in *Beowulf*', *ELN* 10, 243–7

Richards, Mary P., 'A Reexamination of *Beowulf* ll. 3180–3182', *ELN* 10, 163–7

Robinson, Fred C., see sect. 2

Rosier, James L., 'The Two Closings of *Beowulf*', *ESts* 54, 1–6

Stevens, Peter, 'The *Beowulf* Poet is Alive and Well', *Canadian Lit.* 55, 99–102

Wentersdorf, Karl P., see sect. 3*biii*

Whallon, William, Margaret Goldsmith, Charles Donahue *et al.*, 'Allegorical, Typological or Neither? Three Short Papers on the Allegorical Approach to *Beowulf* and a Discussion', *ASE* 2, 285–302

Wrenn, C. L., ed., *Beowulf with the Finnesburg Fragment*, rev. by W. F. Bolton (London and New York)

iii. Other poems

Anderson, Earl R., 'Voices in *The Husband's Message*', *NM* 74, 238–46

'The Sun in *The Battle of Brunanburh*, 12b–17a', *N&Q* 20, 362–3

Bammesberger, Alfred, see sect. 2

Berkhout, Carl T., and James F. Doubleday, 'The Net in *Judith* 46b–54a', *NM* 74, 630–4

Bollard, J. K., 'The Cotton Maxims', *Neophilologus* 57, 179–87

Bosse, Roberta Bux, 'Aural Aesthetic and the Unity of *The Seafarer*', *Papers on Lang. and Lit.* 9, 3–14

Calder, Daniel G., 'The Art of Cynewulf's *Juliana*', *MLQ* 34, 355–71

'Two Notes on the Typology of the OE *Exodus*', *NM* 74, 85–9

Campbell, A. P., '*The Seafarer:* Wanderlust and our Heavenly Home', *Revue de l'Université d'Ottawa* 43, 235–47

Cherniss, Michael D., 'The Cross as Christ's Weapon: the Influence of Heroic Literary Tradition on *The Dream of the Rood*', *ASE* 2, 241–52

Cochran, Robert, '*Deor*', *Ball State Univ. Forum* 14, 79–80

Frankis, P. J., 'The Thematic Significance of *enta geweorc* and Related Imagery in *The Wanderer*', *ASE* 2, 253–69

Godden, M. R., see sect. 3*c*

Goedhals, J. B., 'Byrhtnoth and *The Battle of Maldon*', *Unisa Eng. Stud.* 11, 1–7

Hill, Thomas D., 'Vision and Judgement in the Old English *Christ III*', *SP* 70, 233–42 [with a suggestion on *The Dream of the Rood*]

Jones, Frederick G., 'The Hypermetric Lines of the *Rune Poem*', *NM* 74, 224–31

*Langosch, Karl, 'Die Vorlage des *Waltharius*', *Festschrift Bernhard Bischoff zu seinem 65. Geburtstag*, ed. Johanne Autenrieth and Franz Brunhölzl (Stuttgart, 1971), pp. 226–59

Lee, Anne Thompson, '*The Ruin*: Bath or Babylon? A Non-Archaeological Investigation', *NM* 74, 443–55

Lendinara, Patrizia, '*Maxims I*, 146–151: a Hint of Funeral Lamentation', *NM* 74, 214–16

Macrae-Gibson, O. D., 'The Literary Structure of *The Riming Poem*', *NM* 74, 62–84

Malmberg, Lars, 'Poetic Originality in *The Wanderer* and *The Seafarer*', *NM* 74, 220–3

Murdoch, Brian, 'An Early Irish Adam and Eve: *Saltair na Rann* and the Traditions of the Fall', *MS* 35, 146–77

Mushabac, Jane, '*Judith* and the Theme of *Sapientia et Fortitudo*', *Massachusetts Stud. in Eng.* 4, 3–12

Page, R. I., see sect. 3*a*

Pinsker, Hans, 'Neue Deutungen für zwei altenglische Rätsel', *Anglia* 91, 11–17

Regan, Catharine A., 'Evangelicalism as the Informing Principle of Cynewulf's *Elene*', *Traditio* 29, 27–52

Roberts, Jane, '*Guðlac A, B,* and *C*?', *MÆ* 42, 43–6

Robinson, Fred C., 'Anglo-Saxon Onomastics in the Old English *Andreas*', *Names* 21, 133–6

Scragg, D. G., see sect. 5

Solo, Harry J., 'The Twice-Told Tale: a Reconsideration of the Syntax and Style of the Old English *Daniel*, 245–429', *Papers on Lang. and Lit.* 9, 347–64

Szittya, Penn R., 'The Living Stone and the Patriarchs: Typological Imagery in *Andreas*, lines 706–810', *JEGP* 72, 167–74

Talentino, Arnold V., '"Causing City Walls to Resound": *Elene* 151b', *Papers on Lang. and Lit.* 9, 189–93

Trask, Richard M., 'Doomsday Imagery in the Old English *Exodus*', *Neophilologus* 57, 295–7

Vickrey, John, '*Exodus* and the Tenth Plague', *ASNSL* 210, 41–52

Wentersdorf, Karl P., 'On the Meaning of O.E. *dreorig* in *Brunanburh* 54', *NM* 74, 232–7

'On the Meaning of O.E. *heorodreorig* in *The Phoenix* and Other Poems', *SN* 45, 32–46

Whatley, Gordon, 'Cynewulf and Troy: a Note on *Elene* 642–61', *N&Q* 20, 203–5

*Wienold, Götz, '*Deor*: Über Offenheit und Auffüllung von Texten', *Sprachkunst* 3 (1972), 285–97

c. Prose

*Bammesberger, Alfred, see sect. 2

Besserman, L. L., 'A note on the Source of Aelfric's Homily on the Book of Job', *ELN* 10, 248–52

Cross, J. E., 'Portents and Events at Christ's Birth: Comments on Vercelli V and VI and the Old English Martyrology', *ASE* 2, 209–20

Dalbey, Marcia A., 'Patterns of Preaching in the Blickling Easter Homily', *ABR* 24, 478–92

Farrar, Raymon S., 'Structure and Function in Representative Old English Saints' Lives', *Neophilologus* 57, 82–93

Gatch, Milton McCormick, see under Collins, Rowland L., sect. 1

Godden, M. R., 'An Old English Penitential Motif', *ASE* 2, 221–39
'The Development of Aelfric's Second Series of Catholic Homilies', *ESts* 54, 209–16

Gretsch, Mechthild, *Die Regula Sancti Benedicti in England und ihre altenglische Übersetzung*, Texte und Untersuchungen zur englischen Philologie 2 (Munich)

Horgan, Dorothy M., 'The Relationship Between the O.E. MMS. of King Alfred's Translation of Gregory's *Pastoral Care*', *Anglia* 91, 153–69

Kim, Suksan, 'A Collation of the Old English MS Hatton 20 of King Alfred's *Pastoral Care*', *NM* 74, 425–42

Page, R. I., see sect. 3*a*

Proppe, Katherine, 'King Alfred's *Consolation of Philosophy*', *NM* 74, 635–48

Richards, Mary P., see sect. 5

Schabram, Hans, see sect. 2

Schnall, Uwe, see sect. 8*i*

Scragg, D. G., see sect. 5

Sprockel, Cornelis, see sect. 2

Squires, Ann, 'Some Curious Abbreviations in the Durham Ritual', *N&Q* 20, 403–9

Szarmach, Paul E., ed., 'Vercelli Homily XX', *MS* 35, 1–26

Waterhouse, R., 'Semantic Development of Two Terms within the *Anglo-Saxon Chronicle*', *Studia Germanic Gandensia* 14, 95–106 [*fyrd* and *here*]

4. ANGLO-LATIN, LITURGY AND OTHER LATIN ECCLESIASTICAL TEXTS

*Alfonsi, L., *La letteratura latina medievale* (Milan, 1972)

Arngart, O., see sect. 5

Bede, *The Lives of the Abbots of Wearmouth*, trans. P. Wilcock (1818, repr. Newcastle 1973)

*Bieler, Ludwig, 'Towards a Hiberno-Latin Dictionary', *Archivum Latinitatis Medii Aevi* 38 (1972), 248–55

Bonner, Gerald, see sect. 6

Brückmann, J., 'Latin Manuscript Pontificals and Benedictionals in England and Wales', *Traditio* 29, 391–458

Campbell, James, see sect. 6

Derolez, René, see sect. 6

Dumville, D. N., 'Biblical Apocrypha and the Early Irish: a Preliminary Investigation', *Proc. of the R. Irish Acad.* 73C, 299–338

Finch, Chauncey E., 'The Riddles in Cod. Barb. Lat. 1717 and Newberry Case MS f 11', *Manuscripta* 17, 3–11

*Gardner, Frank Cook, *The Pilgrimage of Desire: a Study of Theme and Genre in Medieval Literature* (Leiden, 1971)

Gatch, Milton McCormick, see under Collins, Rowland L., sect. 1

Gretsch, Mechthild, see sect. 3*c*

Korhammer, P. M., see sect. 5

McNamara, Martin, 'Psalter Text and Psalter Study in the Early Irish Church (A.D. 600–1200)', *Proc. of the R. Irish Acad.* 73C, 201–98

*Porsia, Franco, 'Note per una riedizione ed una rilettura del *Liber Monstrorum*', *Annali* della Facoltà di Lettere e Filosofia, Università di Bari, 15 (1972), 317–38

Richter, Michael, *Canterbury Professions* (with a palaeographical note by T. J. Brown), Canterbury and York Soc. 67

Robinson, Fred C., see sect. 2

Steadman, J. M., 'April–Aphrodite in Bede's *De Temporum Ratione*: a Note on the *Reverdie*', *N&Q* 20, 409

*Turner, D. H., ed., *The Claudius Pontificals, from Cotton MS. Claudius A. iii in the British Museum*, Henry Bradshaw Soc. 97 (1971)

*Winterbottom, Michael, 'Three Lives of Saint Ethelwold', *MÆ* 41 (1972), 191–201

5. PALAEOGRAPHY, DIPLOMATIC AND ILLUMINATION

Arngart, O., 'On the Dating of Early Bede Manuscripts', *SN* 45, 47–52

Baines, Arnold H. J., see sect. 6

*Bill, E. G. W., *A Catalogue of Manuscripts in the Lambeth Palace Library MSS. 1222–1860*, with a Supplement to M. R. James's *Descriptive Catalogue of the Manuscripts in the Library of Lambeth Palace*, by N. R. Ker (Oxford, 1972)

Brückmann, J., see sect. 4

Campbell, A., ed., *Anglo-Saxon Charters I: Charters of Rochester* (London)

Edden, Valerie, 'Early Manuscripts of Virgiliana', *The Library* 5th ser. 28, 14–25 [contains list of manuscripts of Servius's commentary, some of them associated with Anglo-Saxon continental centres]

*Erbes, Roslyn Rensch, 'The Development of the Medieval Harp: a Re-examination of the Evidence of the Utrecht Psalter and its Progeny', *Gesta* 11. 2 (1972), 27–36

Harrison, Kenneth, 'The *Annus Domini* in Some Early Charters', *Jnl of the Soc. of Archivists* 4, 551–7

Hunter, Michael, 'The Facsimiles in Thomas Elmham's History of St Augustine's, Canterbury,' *The Library* 5th ser. 28, 215–20

Korhammer, P. M., 'The Origin of the Bosworth Psalter', *ASE* 2, 173–87

Lester, G. A., 'A Possible Early Occurrence of Moses with Horns in the Benedictional of St Æthelwold', *Scriptorum* 27, 30–3

Lutz, Cora E., 'A Manuscript Fragment from Bede's Monastery', *Yale Univ. Lib. Gazette* 48, 135–8

Mellinkoff, Ruth, 'The Round, Cap-Shaped Hats Depicted on Jews in BM Cotton Claudius B.iv', *ASE* 2, 155–65

Nordenfalk, Carl, 'The Diatessaron Miniatures Once More', *Art Bull.* 55, 532–46
'The Draped Lectern: a Motif in Anglo-Saxon Evangelist Portraits', *Intuition und Kunstwissenschaft: Festschrift für Hanns Swarzenski* (Berlin), pp. 81–100

Pächt, Otto, and J. J. G. Alexander, *Illuminated Manuscripts in the Bodleian Library Oxford*, 3: *British, Irish, and Icelandic Schools with Addenda to Volumes 1 and 2* (Oxford)

Page, R. I., see sects. 2, 3*a* and 8*i*

Park, Marlene, 'The Crucifix of Fernando and Sancha and its Relationship to North French Manuscripts', *Jnl of the Warburg and Courtauld Insts.* 36, 77–91

Richards, Mary P., 'On the Date and Provenance of MS Cotton Vespasian D. xiv, ff. 4–169', *Manuscripta* 17, 31–5

Richards, Melville, 'The "Lichfield" Gospels (Book of "Saint Chad")', *National Lib. of Wales Jnl* 18, 135–46

Robinson, Fred. C., see sect. 2

*Sandred, Karl Inge, see sect. 2

Schapiro, Meyer, 'The Miniatures of the Florence Diatessaron (Laurentian MS Or. 81): Their Place in Late Medieval Art and Supposed Connection with Early Christian and Insular Art', *Art. Bull.* 55, 495–531

Scragg, D. G., 'The Compilation of the Vercelli Book', *ASE* 2, 189–207

Soell, Werner, J., 'Lindisfarne e os seus evangelhos', *Estudos*, Rio Grande do Sul, 33, 65–9

Turner, D. H., see sect. 4

6. HISTORY

Albrechtsen, E., see sect. 8*a*

*Arngart, O., 'On the *Ingtūn* Type of English Place Name', *SN* 44 (1972), 263–73

Baines, Arnold H. J., 'The Boundaries of Over Winchendon', *Records of Buckinghamshire* 19, 169–73 [based on bounds in the 'foundation charter' of St Frideswide's, Oxford, P. H. Sawyer, *Anglo-Saxon Charters* (London, 1968), no. 909]

Beresford, M. W., and H. P. R. Finberg, *English Medieval Boroughs, a Hand-List* (Newton Abbot)

*Bethell, Denis, 'Richard of Belmeis and the Foundation of St Osyth's', *Trans. of the Sussex Archaeol. Soc.* 3rd ser. 2. 3 (1971), 299–328

Bonner, Gerald, 'Bede and Medieval Civilization', *ASE* 2, 71–90

*Brooke, Christopher, 'Gregorian Reform in Action: Clerical Marriage in England, 1050–1200', *Medieval Church and Society: Collected Essays* (New York, 1972), pp. 69–99

Cameron, Kenneth, see sect. 2

Campbell, A., see sect. 5

Campbell, James, 'Observations on the Conversion of England: a Bede Commemorative Review', *Ampleforth Jnl* (Summer), pp. 12–26

Campbell, Miles W., 'Emma, Reine d'Angleterre, Mère Dénaturée ou Femme Vindicative?', *Annales de Normandie* 23, 99–114

Clarke, H. B., 'Domesday Slavery (Adjusted for Slaves)', *Midland Hist.* 1. 4, 37–46 [review article on H. C. Darby and I. B. Terrett, *The Domesday Geography of Midland England*, 2nd ed. (Cambridge, 1971); R. Welldon Finn, *Domesday Studies: the Norman Conquest and its Effects on the Economy* (London, 1971);

and Roy Millward and Adrian Robinson, *Landscapes of Britain: the West Midlands* (London, 1971) and *Landscapes of Britain: the Welsh Marches* (London, 1971)]

Claude, Dietrich, 'Beiträge zur Geschichte der frühmittelalterlichen Königsschätze', *Early Med. Stud.* 7, 5–24 (*Antikvariskt arkiv* 54)

Cox, B. H., see sect. 2

Cutler, Kenneth E., 'Edith, Queen of England, 1045–1066', *MS* 35, 222–31

*Darby, H. C., *The Domesday Geography of Eastern England*, 3rd ed. (Cambridge, 1971)

*Darby, H. C., and I. B. Terrett, *The Domesday Geography of Midland England*, 2nd ed. (Cambridge, 1971)

Davies, Wendy, '*Unciae:* Land Measurement in the *Liber Landavensis*', *Agricultural Hist. Rev.* 21, 111–21

'*Liber Landavensis*: its Construction and Credibility', *EHR* 88, 335–51

'Middle Anglia and the Middle Angles', *Midland Hist.* 2. 1, 18–20

Davison, B. K., see sect. 8*b*

Derolez, René, 'British and English History in the *Liber Floridus*', *Liber Floridus Colloquium* (Ghent), pp. 59–70

Dickins, Bruce, '*Fagaduna* in Orderic (A.D. 1075)', *Otium et Negotium: Studies in Onomatology and Library Science presented to Olof von Feilitzen*, ed. Folke Sandgren (Stockholm), pp. 44–5

Dodgson, John McN., 'Place-Names from *hām*, Distinguished from *hamm* Names, in Relation to the Settlement of Kent, Surrey and Sussex', *ASE* 2, 1–50

see sect. 2

Dumville, David N., 'A Paraphrase of the *Historia Brittonum*: Two Fragments', *Bull. of the Board of Celtic Stud.* 25, 101–5

'A New Chronicle-Fragment of Early British History', *EHR* 88, 312–14

Fellows Jensen, Gillian, see sect. 2

*Field, John, see sect. 2

Fisher, D. J. V., *The Anglo-Saxon Age c. 400–1042* (London)

Gelling, Margaret, see sect. 2

Gibbs, Marion, 'The Decrees of Agatho and the Gregorian Plan for York', *Speculum* 48, 213–46

Godfrey, John, 'The Evolution of the Early English Parish', *Hist. Mag. of the Protestant Episcopal Church* 42, 437–50

Gould, Jim, 'Letocetum, Christianity and Lichfield (Staffs.)', *Trans. of the South Staffordshire Archaeol. and Hist. Soc.* 14, 30–1

*Grierson, Philip, *English Linear Measures: an Essay in Origins* (Stenton Lecture 1971, Reading, 1972)

Harrison, Kenneth, 'The Beginning of the Year in England, c. 500–900', *ASE* 2, 51–70

'The Primitive Anglo-Saxon Calendar', *Antiquity* 47, 284–7

'The Synod of Whitby and the Beginning of the Christian Era in England', *Yorkshire Archaeol. Jnl.* 45, 108–14

see sect. 5

Bibliography for 1973

Hart, Cyril, 'Athelstan "Half King" and his Family', *ASE* 2, 115–44

Hawkes, Christopher and Sonia, ed., *Greeks, Celts, and Romans: Studies in Venture and Resistance* (Archaeology into History 1, London) [for parallels with late and sub-Roman Britain, see Johanna Haberl, 'The Last of Roman Noricum: St Severin on the Danube']

Higgitt, J. C., 'The Roman Background to Medieval England', *JBAA* 3rd ser. 36, 1–15

Historical Association, *Annual Bulletin of Historical Literature* 56: *Publications of the Year 1970* (London) [Sect. 4, The Earlier Middle Ages, 500–1200, is relevant]

King, Edmund, 'Domesday Studies', *History* 58, 403–9 [review article on H. C. Darby, *The Domesday Geography of Eastern England*, 3rd ed. (Cambridge, 1971); H. C. Darby and I. B. Terrett, *The Domesday Geography of Midland England*, 2nd ed. (Cambridge, 1971); R. Welldon Finn, *The Norman Conquest and its Effects on the Economy* (London, 1971) and *The Making and Limitations of the Yorkshire Domesday*, Borthwick Papers 41 (York, 1972); and Sally Harvey, 'Domesday Book and its Predecessors', *EHR* 86 (1971), 753–73]

Kirby, D. P., 'Bede and the Pictish Church', *Innes Rev.* (Spring), pp. 6–25

Kolb, Eduard, see sect. 2

Krüger, Karl Heinrich, 'Königskonversionen im 8. Jahrhundert', *Frühmittelalterliche Studien* 7, 169–222

Musca, Giosue, *Il Venerabile Beda storico dell'Alto Medioevo* (Bari)

O'Donovan, Mary Anne, 'An Interim Revision of Episcopal Dates for the Province of Canterbury, 850–950: Part II', *ASE* 2, 91–113

Page, R. I., see sect. 8*i*

Pearce, Susan M., 'The Dating of some Celtic Dedications and Hagiographical Traditions in South Western Britain', *Trans. of the Devonshire Assoc.* 105, 95–120

Richards, Melville, see sect. 2

Richter, Michael, see sect. 4

Rigold, S. E., see sect. 8*e*

Rowland, T. H., *Anglo-Saxon Northumbria* (Newcastle upon Tyne)

Sadovskaja, M. S., 'Voprosy istorii rimskoj Britanii v anglijskoj istoričeskoj literature [Problems of the History of Roman Britain in English Historical Literature]', *Vestnik drevnej Istorii*, Akad. Nauk SSSR, 125, 217–30

*Sandred, Karl Inge, see sect. 2

Shepard, Jonathan, 'The English and Byzantium: a Study of their Role in the Byzantine Army in the Later Eleventh Century', *Traditio* 29, 53–92

Sokolova, M. N., see sect. 2

Storey, R. L., *Chronology of the Medieval World, 800–1491: the Events of Six Centuries Year by Year* (New York)

Thomas, Charles, see sect. 8*a*

Wainwright, F. T., *Scandinavian England*, ed. H. P. R. Finberg (London and Chichester)

Ward, John Hester, 'The British Sections of the *Notitia Dignitatum*: an Alternative Interpretation', *Britannia* 4, 253–63

Bibliography for 1973

*Welldon Finn, R., *The Making and Limitations of the Yorkshire Domesday*, Borthwick Papers 41 (York, 1972)

Whitelock, Dorothy, 'The Appointment of Dunstan as Archbishop of Canterbury', *Otium et Negotium: Studies in Onomatology and Library Science presented to Olof von Feilitzen*, ed. Folke Sandgren (Stockholm), pp. 232–47

7. NUMISMATICS

[Anon.] 'Eadred Halfpenny Found in Oxford', *Seaby's Coin and Medal Bull.* 1973, 57

'Coin is One of Only Four', *Seaby's Coin and Medal Bull.* 1973, 330–1 [Eadred halfpenny found in Oxford]

'An Offa Penny from Luton', *Seaby's Coin and Medal Bull.* 1973, 373 [moneyer Alhmund]

'Saxon Sceatta from Houghton Regis, Beds.', *Seaby's Coin and Medal Bull.* 1973, 441

Blunt, C. E., 'The Sevington Hoard, of 1834', *BNJ* 41, 7–13 [forty-nine pence of Cenwulf (796–821) and Æthelwulf (839–58)]

'The Origins of the Mints of Hertford and Maldon', *BNJ* 41, 21–6 [includes corpus of coins attributable to the mints from Athelstan to Edward the Martyr]

'A Small Parcel from the Dorking (1817) Hoard', *BNJ* 41, 179 [three pieces of Æthelwulf and seven of Æthelberht]

'The Origins of the Stafford Mint', *Otium et Negotium: Studies in Onomatology and Library Science presented to Olof von Feilitzen*, ed. Folke Sandgren (Stockholm), pp. 13–22

Briggs, C. S., and Michael Dolley, 'An Unpublished Hoard from North County Dublin with Pennies of Eadgar', *Seaby's Coin and Medal Bull.* 1973, 47–50 (see also note by A. C. Ganter, 89–90)

British Numismatic Society, 'Publications Noticed, and Accessions to the Library, 1972', *BNJ* 41, 195–8 [with lists of articles of Anglo-Saxon numismatic interest, and important notes and comments]

Canham, R. A., see sect. 8c

*Dolley, Michael, 'The Mythical Element in the 1882 Bishophill (York) Find of Anglo-Saxon Coins', *Annual Report of the Yorkshire Philosophical Soc.* 1971, 88–101 [see also below, *Pirie, E.]

Dolley, Michael, 'Some Irish Evidence for the Date of the *Crux* Coins of Æthelred II', *ASE* 2, 145–54

'A Hiberno-Norse Penny Misattributed to the 1834 Hoard from Kirk Michael', *Numismatic Circular* 81, 2

'An Unexpected "Mint" in the Hiberno-Norse Imitative Series', *Numismatic Circular* 81, 44 [imitation of the Helmet issue of Æthelred II struck at Dublin; based on evidence of three specimens in Copenhagen, Oslo and Uppsala respectively]

'A "New" Moneyer for "Winchester" in the Hiberno-Norse Imitative Series', *Numismatic Circular* 81, 186 [a specimen in the Statens Historiska Museum, Stockholm, which copies a Winchester penny of the moneyer Byrhsige]

Bibliography for 1973

'The Eadgar Millenary – a note on the Bath Mint', *Seaby's Coin and Medal Bull.* 1973, 156–9

'The Anglo-Saxon Coin' [a cut halfpenny of Edward the Martyr], see Sheridan, Ken, 'Seventh Report . . .', sect. 8*b*

see sect. 2

Dolley, Michael, and Elsa Lindberger, 'A Parcel of Later Anglo-Saxon Pennies with a Putative Finnish Hoard-Provenance', *NC* 7th ser. 13, 126–33 [thirteen specimens, nine whole pennies and four fragments, probably from two different hoards: 1834 Raisio (Reso) find and 1880 Espinge find. Æthelred II (three), Reso find; Harold I (nine), Espinge find. All in the Royal Coin Cabinet, Stockholm]

Dolley, Michael, and Tuukka Talvio, 'A Further Die-Link in the Anglo-Scandinavian Imitative Series', *Numismatic Circular* 81, 138 [two coins of the reign of Cnut in the Helsinki Cabinet]

'A Note on the Earliest Finnish Coin Hoard with Anglo-Saxon Pennies', *Suomen Museo* 80, 25–8

Grinsell, L. V., *The Bath Mint: an Historical Outline* (with a section on the moneyer's names by Mrs V. J. Smart) (London)

Grinsell, L. V., C. E. Blunt and Michael Dolley, *Bristol and Gloucester Museums: Ancient British Coins and Coins of the Bristol and Gloucestershire Mints*, Sylloge of Coins of the British Isles 19 (London)

Little, M. J., 'Cricklade Mint', *Cricklade Hist. Soc. Bull.* 8, 4–6

*Metcalf, D. M., 'The "Bird and Branch" Sceattas in the Light of a Find from Abingdon', *Oxoniensia* 37 (1972), 51–65

Pagan, H. E., 'An Unpublished Fragment of a Coin of Ceolwulf II', *BNJ* 41, 14–20

*Pirie, E., 'A Further Note on Coins from the Bishophill (York) Find of 1882', *Annual Report of the Yorkshire Philosophical Soc.* 1971, 101–2 [see also above, *Dolley, Michael]

Smart, Veronica J., 'A New Edward the Confessor Transitional Arm-Sceptre Penny', *Numismatic Circular* 81, 138–9

'Cnut's York Moneyers', *Otium et Negotium: Studies in Onomatology and Library Science presented to Olof von Feilitzen*, ed. Folke Sandgren (Stockholm), pp. 221–31

8. ARCHAEOLOGY

a. General

Albrectsen, E., 'Angler, saxere jyder og fynboer i det 5. århundrede', *Fynske Minder* 1972, 31–42

British Museum, Department of Medieval and Later Antiquities, 'Acquisitions, January 1970 to December 1971: *c.* 400–*c.* 1100', *Brit. Museum Quarterly* 37, 83–4

Council for British Archaeology, *Archaeological Bibliography for Great Britain and Ireland 1971* [contains a full bibliography covering national and local periodicals and dealing with all periods]

British Archaeological Abstracts 6 [covers material published 1 July 1972– 30 June 1973]

Council for British Archaeology, Groups 12 and 13, *Archaeol. Rev.* 7 [surveys work done in 1972, including (sect. 7) early medieval *c.* 450–1000]

de Boone, W. J., 'An Early Mediaeval Grave Field on the Beumelerberg near Garderen', *BROB* 20–1, 249–92 [discusses possible contacts with Anglo-Saxon England in pagan period]

Dickson, Alison C., and David A. Hinton, 'A Gazetteer of the Late Saxon and Medieval Objects in the Department of Antiquities, Ashmolean Museum, Oxford', *Oxoniensia* 37, 192–6

Farrell, Robert T., see under Collins, Rowland L., sect. 1

Haseloff, Günther, 'Zum Ursprung der germanischen Tierornamentik: die spätrömische Wurzel', *Frühmittelalterliche Studien* 7, 406–42 ['Daniel in the lions' den']

Hoskins, W. G., *English Landscapes: How to Read the Man-Made Scenery of England* (BBC, London)

*Jankuhn, Herbert, see sect. 1

McWhirr, Alan, ed., 'Archaeology in Leicestershire and Rutland, 1970–1972', *Trans. of the Leicestershire Archaeol. and Hist. Soc.* 47, 62–76 [includes Anglo-Saxon finds]

Moorhouse, Stephen, compiler, 'The Yorkshire Archaeological Register: 1972', *Yorkshire Archaeol. Jnl* 45, 198–208 [includes Anglo-Saxon discoveries]

Philp, Brian, *Excavations in West Kent 1960–1970* (Dover) [includes accounts of excavations of Anglo-Saxon settlements at Darenth and Lower Warbank, Keston, and of the Anglo-Saxon cemetery at Polhill, Dunton Green]

Rowley, Trevor, and Max Davies, *Archaeology and the M.40 Motorway* (Dept for External Studies, Oxford) [includes brief accounts of Anglo-Saxon discoveries]

Thomas, Charles, 'Irish Colonists in South-West Britain', *World Archaeology* 5, 5–13

*[Various] 'Archaeological Notes', *Trans. of the Essex Archaeol. Soc.* 3rd ser. 2. 3 (1971), 328–41 [recent discoveries, including Anglo-Saxon material]

Webster, Leslie, E., 'Medieval Britain in 1971: I. Pre-Conquest', *MA* 16, 147–70 [survey of archaeological work]

Wilson, Catherine M., 'Archaeological Notes, 1971', *Lincolnshire Hist. and Archaeology* 7, 3–13 [includes Anglo-Saxon and Saxo-Norman discoveries]

Wilson, D. R., 'Roman Britain in 1972: I Sites Explored', *Britannia* 4, 271–323 [includes references to Anglo-Saxon discoveries on Roman sites]

Wiltshire Archaeological Society, 'Wiltshire Archaeological Register for 1971', *Wiltshire Archaeol. Mag.* 67, 167–87 [includes early medieval *c.* 450–1000]

b. Towns and other major settlements

*Addyman, P. V., 'Excavations at Baile Hill, York', *Chateau Gaillard* 5 (1972), 7–12

Addyman, Peter, 'Saxon Southampton: a Town and International Port of the 8th to the 10th Century', *Vor- und Frühformen der europäischen Stadt im Mittelalter*, ed. Herbert Jankuhn, Walter Schlesinger and Heiko Steuer (Göttingen), pp. 218–28

*Aldsworth, Fred, and David Hill, 'The Burghal Hidage – Eashing', *Surrey Archaeol. Collections* 68 (1971), 198–201

[Anon.] 'Why is Oxford at Oxford?', *CA* 3, 316–21 [includes recent work at Dorchester on Thames]

'York', *CA* 4, 45–52 [excavations in 1972]

'Dover: the Battle of the By-Pass; the Painted House; Summary', *CA* 4, 81–8 [includes some Anglo-Saxon material]

'Exeter', *CA* 4, 102–10 [excavations in 1971–3]

[Barker, P. A.] 'Wroxeter', *CA* 4, 111–16 [sub- and post-Roman buildings]

Biddle, Martin, 'Winchester: the Development of an Early Capital', *Vor- und Frühformen der europäischen Stadt im Mittelalter*, ed. Herbert Jankuhn, Walter Schlesinger and Heiko Steuer (Göttingen), pp. 229–61

Biddle, Martin, and Daphne M. Hudson with Carolyn Heighway, *The Future of London's Past: a Survey of the Archaeological Implications of Planning and Development in the Nation's Capital* (Worcester) [surveys the current state of knowledge of Anglo-Saxon London, with maps and bibliography]

Chichester Civic Society, Excavations Committee, *Report for 1973* (Chichester) [contains accounts of Anglo-Saxon discoveries in Chichester]

City of London, Guildhall Museum, *Archaeology in the City of London: an Opportunity* (London)

Davison, B. K., 'The Burghal Hidage Fort of *Eorpeburnan*: a Suggested Identification', *MA* 16, 123–7

'Castle Neroche: an abandoned Norman Fortress in South Somerset', *Proc. of the Somersetshire Archaeol. and Nat. Hist. Soc.* 116, 16–58 [first earthwork might be late Saxon]

Durham, Brian, Tom Hassall, Trevor Rowley and Caroline Simpson, 'A Cutting across the Saxon Defences at Wallingford, Berkshire 1971', *Oxoniensia* 37, 82–5

Fleming, S. J., and D. Stoneham, 'The Subtraction Technique of Thermoluminescent Dating', *Archaeometry* 15, 229–38 [discusses TL date of A.D. 755 ± 155 for hearth below York Minster]

Fletcher, John, and Roy Switzur, 'North Elmham: the Dating', *CA* 4, 25–8

Fowler, P. J., K. S. Gardner and P. A. Rahtz, 'Cadbury Congresbury, Somerset. A Summary Interim Report on Excavations, 1968 and 1970–3', *Bristol Archaeol. Research Group Bull.* 4, 244–9

Green, C. J. S., 'Excavations for the Dorchester Excavation Committee, Interim Report, 1972: Site 3, Poundbury Camp', *Proc. of the Dorset Nat. Hist. and Archaeol. Soc.* 94, 80–1

Harrison, A. C., 'Rochester East Gate, 1969', *Archaeologia Cantiana* 87, 121–57 [with implications for pre-Conquest Rochester]

Haslam, Jeremy, 'The Excavation of a Section across Aldersgate Street, City of London, 1972', *Trans. of the London and Middlesex Archaeol. Soc.* 24, 78–84

Hassall, T. G., 'Excavations at Oxford 1971: Fourth Interim Report', *Oxoniensia* 37, 137–49

Bibliography for 1973

Hassall, T. G., *et al.*, 'Roman Finds from the Radcliffe Science Library Extension, Oxford, 1970–71', *Oxoniensia* 37, 38–50 [discusses Saxon charter evidence relating to Roman Oxford]

Hirst, Susan, and Philip Rahtz, 'Hatton Rock 1970', *Trans. of the Birmingham and Warwickshire Archaeol. Soc.* 85, 160–77

Laing, Lloyd, 'The Mote of Mark', *CA* 4, 121–5

Platt, Colin, *Medieval Southampton. The Port and Trading Community*, A.D. *1000–1600* (London)

Radford, C. A. Ralegh, 'Excavations at Cricklade: 1948–1963', *Wiltshire Archaeol. and Nat. Hist. Mag.* 67, 61–111

*Royal Commission on Historical Monuments, *An Inventory of the Historical Monuments in the City of York* 2, *The Defences* (London, 1972) [includes an important account and discussion of the Anglo-Saxon and Viking defences]

Schove, D. Justin, 'Dates for *Hamwih* and Old Windsor', *CA* 4, 44

Sheridan, Ken, 'Sixth Report of Excavations at Tamworth, Staffs. (1971). A Section of the Saxon and Medieval Defences, Albert Road', *Trans. of the South Staffordshire Archaeol. and Hist. Soc.* 14, 32–7

'Seventh Report of Excavations at Tamworth, Staffs.: a Section through the Northern Defences Excavated by Dr F. T. Wainwright in 1960', *Trans. of the South Staffordshire Archaeol. and Hist. Soc.* 14, 38–44

Simpson, Caroline, *Wallingford. The Archaeological Implications of Development: a Survey* (Oxfordshire Archaeological Unit, Oxford) [includes survey of Anglo-Saxon town and its surroundings]

Sittingbourne and Swale Archaeological Group, 'The Castle Rough Training Project – 1972, Part 1', *Kent Archaeol. Rev.* 31, 15–19 [site shown *not* to be fort erected by Hæsten (*ASC, s.a.* 893)]

Toms, G. S. S., '2a St Alkmund's Place – A Late Saxon and Medieval Site in Shrewsbury', *Trans. of the Shropshire Archaeol. Soc.* 59. 1, 32–42

Wade-Martins, Peter, 'North Elmham', *CA* 4, 22–5

[West, Stanley E., gen. ed.] *Ipswich. The Archaeological Implications of Development* (The Scole Committee, Bury St Edmunds) [includes survey of Anglo-Saxon Ipswich and its surroundings]

York Archaeological Trust, *Interim: Bull. of the York Archaeol. Trust* 1. 1–3 [contains accounts of Anglo-Saxon and Viking discoveries at York in 1972–3, and wider discussion]

c. Rural settlements, agriculture and the countryside

Addyman, P. V., 'Late Saxon Settlements in the St Neots Area', *Proc. of the Cambridge Ant. Soc.* 64, 45–99

[Addyman, P. V.] 'Chalton. The Excavation of an Anglo-Saxon Village', *CA* 4, 55–61

Addyman, P. V., D. Leigh and M. J. Hughes, 'Anglo-Saxon Houses at Chalton, Hampshire', *MA* 16, 13–31

[Anon.] 'Abingdon', *CA* 3, 332

'West Stow' and 'West Stow: the Reconstruction', *CA* 4, 151–8

Avery, Michael, and David Brown, 'Saxon Features at Abingdon', *Oxoniensia* 37, 66–81

Canham, R. A., 'Shepperton: Excavations at Saxon County Junior School', *Surrey Archaeol. Soc. Bull.* 98, 4 [coin of Offa, pottery etc.]

Champion, Sara, *Andover. The Archaeological Implications of Development* (Andover) [includes survey of Anglo-Saxon settlement in Andover area]

Cunliffe, Barry, 'Saxon and Medieval Settlement-Pattern in the Region of Chalton Hampshire', *MA* 16, 1–12

Drury, P. J., 'Preliminary Report: the Romano-British Settlement at Chelmsford, Essex: *Caesaromagos*', *Essex Archaeology and Hist.* 3rd ser. 4, 3–29 [includes sub-Roman and possible Anglo-Saxon material]

Hewlett, Geoffrey, 'Reconstructing a Historical Landscape from Field and Documentary Evidence: Otford in Kent', *Agricultural Hist. Rev.* 21, 94–110

Hewlett, G. P., and Jane Hassell, 'Bishop's Waltham Dikes', *Proc. of the Hampshire Field Club and Archaeol. Soc.* 28, 29–40

*Hurst, J. G., 'The Changing Medieval Village in England', *Man Settlement and Urbanism*, ed. Peter J. Ucko, Ruth Tringham and G. W. Simbleby (London, 1972), pp. 531–40

Miles, Henrietta and Trevor, 'Trethurgy', *CA* 4, 142–7

Morrison, I. A., '*Jarlshof*. The Marine Environment of a Viking Settlement', *Nautical Archaeology* 2, 382–4

Mynard, D. C., 'Caldecotte, Shrunken Medieval Village', *Milton Keynes Jnl of Archaeology and Hist.* 2, 7–8

Le Patourel, H. E. Jean, and P. Wood, 'Excavation at the Archbishop of York's Manor House at Otley', *Yorkshire Archaeol. Jnl* 45, 115–41

Philp, Brian, see sect. 8*a*

Rodwell, Warwick and Kirsty, 'The Roman Villa at Rivenhall, Essex: an Interim Report', *Britannia* 4, 115–27 [includes fifth-century Anglo-Saxon structures, pottery and glass]

Smith, M., 'A Section across the Fleam Dyke', *Proc. of the Cambridge Ant. Soc.* 64, 30–3

d. Pagan cemeteries and Sutton Hoo

Denston, C. B., 'Saxon Human Remains from Horseheath', *Proc. of the Cambridge Ant. Soc.* 64, 28–30

Detsicas, A. P., 'Excavations at Eccles, 1971: Tenth Interim Report', *Archaeologia Cantiana* 87, 101–10 (see also 227–8) [includes brief account of pagan and later Anglo-Saxon cemetery]

Durham, Brian, and Trevor Rowley, 'A Cemetery Site at Queensford Mill, Dorchester', *Oxoniensia* 37, 32–7 [sub- or post-Roman cemetery]

*Evans, Angela, see under *Greenhill, Basil, sect. 8*f*

Hawkes, Sonia Chadwick, 'The Dating and Social Significance of the Burials in the Polhill [Kent] Cemetery', Brian Philp, *Excavations in West Kent 1960–1970* (Dover), pp. 186–201

Müller-Wille, M., 'Pferdegrab und Pferdeopfer im frühen Mittelalter. Mit einem

Bibliography for 1973

Beitrag von H. Vierck: Pferdegräber im angelsächsischen England', *BROB* 20–1, 119–248

Myres, J. N. L., and Barbara Green, *The Anglo-Saxon Cemeteries of Caistor-by-Norwich and Markshall, Norfolk,* (Reports of the Research Committee of the Society of Antiquaries of London 30, London)

Philp, Brian, see sect. 8*a*

Slow, Dorothy, and Margaret Warhurst, 'The Faussett Collection at Liverpool', *Antiquity* 47, 231

e. Churches, monastic sites and Christian cemeteries

Cunningham, C. J. K., and J. W. Banks, 'Excavations at Dorchester Abbey, Oxon.', *Oxoniensia* 37, 158–64 [possible pre-Conquest burials]

Fernie, E. C., 'Enclosed Apses and Edward's Church at Westminster', *Archaeologia* 104, 235–60

Hickmore, M. A. S., *St Peter's Church, Monkwearmouth* (Newcastle upon Tyne)

*Huggins, P. J., K. N. Bascombe and Rhona M. Huggins, 'Waltham Abbey. Monastic Site and Prehistoric Evidence 1953–1967', *Trans. of the Essex Archaeol. Soc.* 3rd ser. 2. 3 (1971), 216–66

Jesson, Margaret, compiler, *The Archaeology of Churches* (Council for British Archaeology, London)

Rigold, S. E., 'Roman Folkestone Reconsidered', *Archaeologia Cantiana* 87, 31–41 [with discussion of the Anglo-Saxon minster and the place-name element *stān* in Kent]

Rodwell, Warwick and Kirsty, 'Rivenhall', *CA* 4, 14–18 [discovery of Anglo-Saxon church]

Smith, T. P., *The Anglo-Saxon Churches of Hertfordshire* (London and Chichester)

Taylor, H. M., 'The Society's [i.e. The Society of Antiquaries] Research Projects: II. Archaeological Investigation of Churches in Great Britain', *AntJ* 53, 13–15
'The Position of the Altar in Early Anglo-Saxon Churches', *AntJ* 53, 52–8
'J. T. Irvine's Work at Bradford-on-Avon', *ArchJ* 129, 89–118

f. Ships and seafaring

*Bass, George F., ed., *A History of Seafaring Based on Underwater Archaeology* (London and New York, 1972)

*Greenhill, Basil, ed., *Three Major Ancient Boat Finds in Britain,* National Maritime Museum (London, 1972) [Valerie Fenwick *et al.* on Graveney, pp. 9–17; Angela Evans on Sutton Hoo, pp. 26–44]

g. Sculpture on bone, stone and wood

Andersson, Aron, 'Gravetenen från Botkyrka och korset från Granhammar', *Fornvännen* 68, 1–12 [mentions English hog-back stones and suggests English iconographical sources]

*Becker, Alfred, *Franks Casket: zu den Bildern und Inschriften des Runenkästchens von Auzon,* Regensburger Arbeiten zur Anglistik und Amerikanistik 5 (Nürnberg, 1972) [also as Regensburg diss. (1973)]

Bibliography for 1973

*Beckwith, John, *Ivory Carvings in Early Medieval England* (London, 1972)

Coatsworth, Elizabeth, 'Two Representations of the Crucifixion on Late Pre-Conquest Carved Stones from Bothal, Northumberland', *Archaeologia Aeliana* 5th ser. 1, 234–6

Lang, James T., 'Some Late Pre-Conquest Crosses in Ryedale, Yorkshire: a Reappraisal', *JBAA* 3rd ser. 36, 16–25

Morris, C. D., 'An Anglo-Saxon Grave-Slab from Hurworth, Co. Durham', *Archaeologia Aeliana* 5th ser. 1, 236–40

Pattison, Ian R., 'The Nunburnholme Cross and Anglo-Danish Sculpture in York', *Archaeologia* 104, 209–34

*Vandersall, Amy L., 'The Date and Provenance of the Franks Casket', *Gesta* 11.2 (1972), 9–26

h. Metal-work and other minor objects

Brown, P. D. C., and F. Schweizer, 'X-ray, Fluorescence Analysis of Anglo-Saxon Jewellery', *Archaeometry* 15, 175–92

Farrant, Nicholas, 'Two Weapons from the Thames', *Trans. of the London and Middlesex Archaeol. Soc.* 24, 157–8 [a seventh-to-ninth century *seax*]

Hawkes, Sonia Chadwick, 'A Late Roman Buckle from Tripontium', *Trans. of the Birmingham and Warwickshire Archaeol. Soc.* 85, 145–59

Mottram, Sophia, 'The West Dereham Ring', *AntJ* 52, 340–4

Okasha, Elisabeth, 'A Rediscovered Medieval Inscribed Ring', *ASE* 2, 167–71

Philp, Brian, 'Saxon Gold Ring Found at Dover', *Kent Archaeol. Rev.* 31, 10

Tylecote, R. F., 'The Pit-Type Iron-Smelting Shaft Furnace; its Diffusion and Parallels', *Early Med. Stud.* 6, 42–7 (*Antikvariskt arkiv* 53)

i. Inscriptions

*Becker, Alfred, see sect. 8*g*

*Düwel, Klaus, see sect. 2

Kabell, Aage, '*Harja*', *ZDA* 102, 1–15

Klingenberg, Heinz, see sect. 1

Okasha, Elisabeth, see sect. 8*h*

Page, R. I., *An Introduction to English Runes* (London)

Schnall, Uwe, *Die Runeninschriften des europäischen Kontinents*, Bibliographie der Runeninschriften nach Fundorten, ed. Wolfgang Krause, 2. Teil, Abhand-lungen der Akademie der Wissenschaften in Göttingen, phil.-hist. Klasse, 3. Folge, 80 (Göttingen)

*Vandersall, Amy L., see sect. 8*g*

j. Pottery and glass

Addyman, P. V., B. G. Hopkins and G. T. Norton, 'A Saxo-Norman Pottery-Kiln Producing Stamped Wares at Michelmersh, Hants.', *MA* 16, 127–30

Everson, Paul, 'Some Anglo-Saxon Potters in North Lincolnshire', *Lincolnshire Hist. and Archaeology* 7, 16–19

Moorhouse, Stephen, 'Early Medieval Pottery from Westbury, East Meon, Hamp-shire', *Proc. of the Hampshire Field Club and Archaeol. Soc.* 28, 41–8

Myres, J. N. L., 'A Fifth-Century Anglo-Saxon Pot from Canterbury', *AntJ* 53, 77–8

Parsons, David, 'Two Nineteenth-Century Anglo-Saxon Finds from Lincolnshire', *AntJ* 53, 78–81

Pile, J. S., and K. J. Barton, 'An Early Medieval Rubbish-Pit at Catherington, Hampshire', *Proc. of the Hampshire Field Club and Archaeol. Soc.* 29, 49–56

Sanders, H. P., 'Pore-Size Distribution Determinations in Neolithic, Iron Age, Roman and Other Pottery', *Archaeometry* 15, 159–61 [includes pagan Saxon material]

k. Musical instruments

*Erbes, Roslyn Rensch, see sect. 5

9. REVIEWS

Aitken, A. J., Angus McIntosh and Hermann Pálsson, ed., *Edinburgh Studies in English and Scots* (London, 1971): Dieter Mindt, *Anglia* 91, 246–9

Alcock, Leslie, *Arthur's Britain: History and Archaeology, A.D. 367–634* (London, 1971): *CA* 4, 77; D.L.T.B. and J.A.G.-C., *Jnl of the R. Soc. of Antiquaries of Ireland* 102, 108–9; *Elizabeth Fowler, MA* 16, 219–21; Kenneth Jackson, *Antiquity* 47, 80–1; Thomas Jones, *Studia Celtica* 7, 184–6; D. P. Kirby, *Archaeologia Cambrensis* 121, 117–22; N. L., *Proc. of the Somersetshire Archaeol. and Nat. Hist. Soc.* 116, 117–18; J. D. A. Ogilvy, *ELN* 11, 57; Charles Thomas, *ArchJ* 129, 245–6

'*By South Cadbury is that Camelot . . .'. Excavations at Cadbury Castle, 1966–70* (London, 1972): *CA* 3, 330; N. L., *Proc. of the Somersetshire Archaeol. and Nat. Hist. Soc.* 116, 117–18; Philip Rahtz, *History* 58, 423

Alexander, Michael, *The Earliest English Poems* (Berkeley and Los Angeles, 1970): J. Verdonck, *ESts* 54, 97

Alexandrovicz, S., in *Acta Baltico-Slavica* 7 (Bialystok, 1970) [Wulfstan's voyage]: Raymond Schmittlein, *Revue Internationale d'Onomastique* 25, 239–40

Alfonsi, L., *La letteratura latina medievale* (Milan, 1972): Giuseppe Cremascoli, *Aevum* 47, 370–2

Ashe, Geoffrey, ed., *The Quest for Arthur's Britain* (London, 1968): A. D. Saunders, *MA* 16, 218–19

Autenrieth, Johanne, and Franz Brunhölzl, ed., *Festschrift Bernhard Bischoff* (Stuttgart, 1971): G. S., *Deutsches Archiv für Erforschung des Mittelalters* 28, 558–60; Hubert Silvestre, *Revue d'Histoire Ecclésiastique* 68, 511–17

Bailey, Terence, *The Processions of Sarum and the Western Church* (Toronto, 1971): Andrew Hughes, *Jnl of the Amer. Musicological Soc.* 26, 334–5; Richard W. Pfaff, *Speculum* 48, 337–9

Barber, Richard, *The Figure of Arthur* (London, 1970): R. H. C. Davis, *EHR* 88, 871

Barker, Philip, and James Lawson, 'A Pre-Norman Field System at Hen Domen, Montgomery', *MA* 15 (1971), 58–72: I. Dąbrowska, *Kwartalnik Historii Kultury Materialnej* 21, 344–6

Bibliography for 1973

Barlow, Frank, *Edward the Confessor* (London and Berkeley and Los Angeles, 1970):
D. L. Farmer, *Canadian Jnl of Hist.* 7, 273–4; Bernhard W. Scholz, *CHR* 59,
536–7

Barlow, Frank, et al., *Leofric of Exeter* (Exeter, 1972): G. R. Dunstan, *JEH* 24,
65–6; David Knowles, *AntJ* 53, 128

Beckwith, John, *Ivory Carvings in Early Medieval England* (London, 1972): *TLS*
16 November, p. 1394

Benning, Helmut A., *Die Vorgeschichte von neuenglisch 'duty'* (Frankfurt, 1971):
Gillis Kristensson, *Linguistics* 99, 118–20

Benveniste, E., *Le Vocabulaire des Institutions Indo-Européennes* (Paris, 1969): Oswald
Szemerényi, *Jnl of Hellenic Stud.* 92, 215–17

Beresford, Maurice, and John G. Hurst, ed., *Deserted Medieval Villages: Studies*
(London, 1972): David Crossley, *Yorkshire Archaeol. Jnl* 45, 217; R. H. C.
Davis, *EHR* 88, 886–7; Christopher Dyer, *Midland Hist.* 1. 4, 55–6; P. D. A.
Harvey, *History* 58, 437–8; Colin Platt, *AHR* 78, 416–17

Berger, R., ed., *Scientific Methods in Medieval Archaeology* (Berkeley and Los Angeles,
1970): Michel de Bouard, *Revue Archéologique* 1973, 170–1; Lawrence Butler,
EHR 88, 688–9

Bessinger, Jess B., Jr, and Philip H. Smith, Jr, *A Concordance to 'Beowulf'* (Ithaca,
1969): G. Bourquin, *Études Anglaises* 26, 221–2

Biddle, Martin, and Daphne M. Hudson with Carolyn Heighway, *The Future of
London's Past* (Worcester, 1973): Nicholas Farrant and Harvey Sheldon,
London Archaeology 2, 87–9

Bill, E. G. W., *A Catalogue of Manuscripts in the Lambeth Palace Library* (Oxford,
1972): *TLS* 2 March, p. 248

Bishop, T. A. M., *English Caroline Minuscule* (Oxford, 1971): Ludwig Bieler, *MÆ*
42, 154–6; K. W. Humphreys, *The Library* 28, 252–3

Blindheim, Charlotte, and Roar L. Tollness, *Kaupang, Vikingenes handelsplass*
(Oslo, 1972): Sigard Greig, *Fornvännen* 68, 216–19

Bloomfield, Morton W., *Essays and Explorations: Studies in Ideas, Language, and
Literature* (Cambridge, Mass., 1970): Heinz Bergner, *Anglia* 91, 111–13

Blunt, C. E., F. Elmore Jones and R. P. Mack, *Collection of Ancient British,
Romano-British and English Coins Formed by Mrs Emery May Norweb, Part I,*
Sylloge of Coins of the British Isles 16 (London, 1971): H. E. P[agan], *BNJ*
41, 190

Bolgar, R. R., ed., *Classical Influences on European Culture AD 500–1500* (Cambridge,
1971): P. McGurk, *Jnl of Hellenic Stud.* 92, 259–60

Bouman, A. C., *Patterns in Old English and Old Icelandic Literature* (Leiden, 1962):
K. Roelandts, *Leuvense Bijdragen* 62, 120

Bowen, E. G., *Britain and the Western Seaways* (London, 1972); Leslie Alcock,
History 58, 251

Branigan, K., *Latimer: Belgic, Roman, Dark Age and Early Modern Farm* (Chesham,
1971): R. Goodburn, *AntJ* 53, 119–21

Brown, William H., Jr, *A Syntax of King Alfred's Pastoral Care* (The Hague, 1970):
David L. Shores, *ESts* 54, 163–6

Bruce, F. F., *The English Bible: a History of Translations from the Earliest English Versions to the New English Bible* (New York, 1970): Bruce M. Metzger, *Jnl of the Amer. Acad. of Religion* 41, 672

Bruce-Mitford, R. L. S., *The Sutton Hoo Ship-Burial: a Handbook* (2nd ed., London, 1972): Hermann Ament, *Germania* 51, 289–90; Birgit Arrhenius, *Fornvännen* 68, 59–60; P. J. Tester, *Archaeologia Cantiana* 87, 247–8; David M. Wilson, *JBAA* 36, 121

Butler, R. M., ed., *Soldier and Civilian in Roman Yorkshire* (Leicester, 1971): Jochen Garbsch, *Germania* 51, 263–4 [esp. 264]; Mark Hassall, *AntJ* 53, 118–19; R. G. Livens, *History* 58, 72; H. U. Nuber, *Bonner Jahrbücher* 172, 658–62 [esp. 662]; A. L. F. Rivet, *EHR* 88, 408–9; C. B. Rüger, *Britannia* 4, 338–41; J. B. Whitwell, *ArchJ* 129, 243–4

Cameron, Angus, Roberta Frank and John Leyerle, ed., *Computers and Old English Concordances* (Toronto, 1971): R. T. Farrell, *MÆ* 41, 293–4; Michael J. Preston, *YES* 3, 264–5

Campbell, Alistair, *Skaldic Verse and Anglo-Saxon History* (London, 1971): Forrest S. Scott, *MÆ* 42, 203–4

Cardona, George, Henry M. Hoenigswald and Alfred Senn, ed., *Indoeuropean and Indoeuropeans* (Philadelphia, 1970): Carroll E. Reed, *Mod. Lang. Jnl* 57, 52–3

Carlton, Charles, *A Descriptive Syntax of the Old English Charters* (The Hague, 1970): E. A. Ebbinghaus, *General Ling.* 13, 53; Teresa Retelewska, *Studia Anglica Posnaniensia* 4, 220–2; David L. Shores, *ESts* 54, 166–7; Aleksander Szwedek, *Linguistics* 99, 115–18

Chaney, William A., *The Cult of Kingship in Anglo-Saxon England* (Manchester and Berkeley, 1970): Clinton E. Albertson, *CHR* 59, 534–5; C. Warren Hollister, *AHR* 78, 80–1; H. M. S., *Deutsches Archiv für Erforschung des Mittelalters* 28, 611–12

Chibnall, Marjorie, ed. and trans., *The Ecclesiastical History of Orderic Vitalis* III (Oxford, 1972): *EHR* 88, 879–80; Frank Barlow, *MÆ* 42, 156–8; Walter Ullmann, *JTS* 24, 287–8

The Ecclesiastical History of Orderic Vitalis IV (Oxford, 1973): *TLS* 10 August, p. 937

Christensen, Aksel E., *Vikingetidens Danmark: paa oldhistorisk Baggrund* (Copenhagen, 1969): Sidney L. Cohen, *Speculum* 48, 123–5

Clark, Cecily, ed., *The Peterborough Chronicle 1070–1154*, 2nd ed. (Oxford, 1970): Rossell Hope Robbins, *ASNSL* 209, 149–50

Clemoes, Peter, and Kathleen Hughes, ed., *England before the Conquest: Studies in Primary Sources presented to Dorothy Whitelock* (Cambridge, 1971): *Speculum* 48, 600; Eric John, *History* 58, 254–5; J. N. L. Myres, *AntJ* 53, 126–8; V. J. S[mart], *BNJ* 41, 189–90; Leslie Webster, *MA* 16, 223–5; David M. Wilson, *JBAA* 36, 109–10

Clemoes, Peter, *et al.*, ed., *Anglo-Saxon England* I (Cambridge, 1972): Cecily Clark, *ESts* 54, 378–81; H.D., *Revue d'Histoire Ecclésiastique* 68, 681–3; H. R. Loyn, *JEH* 24, 407–8; J. D. A. Ogilvy, *AHR* 78, 1434–5; J. M. Wallace-Hadrill, *EHR* 88, 874; David M. Wilson, *JBAA* 36, 103; C. E. Wright, *Antiquity* 47, 245–6

Bibliography for 1973

Comitatus 1 and 2 (1970 and 1971): Patrizia Lendinara, *Annali, Sezione Germanica* (Naples) 16, 242–3

Cox, Betty S., *Cruces of 'Beowulf'* (The Hague, 1971): G. Bourquin, *Études Anglaises* 26, 223; Cecily Clark, *ESts* 54, 403–4; Patrizia Lendinara, *Annali, Sezione Germanica* (Naples) 15, 209–11; James L. Rosier, *Speculum* 48, 740–1

Crépin, André, *Histoire de la Langue Anglaise* (Paris, 1967): Herbert Koziol, *ASNSL* 209, 394–6

Crittall, Elizabeth, ed., *A History of Wiltshire* 1 pt 2 (London, 1973): *TLS* 15 June, p. 668

Cross, J. E., *The Literate Anglo-Saxon: on Sources and Disseminations* (London, 1972): E. G. S., *N&Q* 20, 282

Cunliffe, Barry, *The Regni* (London, 1973): *TLS* 10 August, p. 932

Darby, H. C., *The Domesday Geography of Eastern England*, 3rd ed. (Cambridge, 1971): Edmund King, see sect. 6

Darby, H. C., and I. B. Terrett, *The Domesday Geography of Midland England*, 2nd ed. (Cambridge, 1971): H. B. Clarke, see sect. 6; Edmund King, see sect. 6

Dodgson, J. McN., *The Place-Names of Cheshire* I–III (Cambridge, 1970–1): O. Arngart, *SN* 44, 435–8 [III only]; Guy Fourquin, *Revue Historique* 506, 497 [II only]; Gillis Kristensson, *ESts* 54, 92–6

The Place-Names of Cheshire IV (Cambridge, 1972): Basil Cottle, *RES* 24, 193–4; Kelsie B. Harder, *Names* 20, 295–6

Dolan, J. R., *English Ancestral Names* (New York, 1972): Margaret M. Bryant, *Names* 21, 53–6

Dumas-Dubourg, F., *Le Trésor de Fécamp et le Monnayage en Francie Occidentale pendant la Seconde Moitié du Xe Siècle* (Paris, 1971): C. E. B[lunt], *BNJ* 41, 185–6 [with discussion of English coins and coins of English type in the hoard]

Els, T. J. M. van, *The Kassel Manuscript of Bede's 'Historia Ecclesiastica Gentis Anglorum' and its Old English Material* (Assen, 1972): O. Arngart, *SN* 45, 173–4; A. F. Beringause, *Names* 21, 51–2; A. Campbell, *MÆ* 42, 153–4; J. D. A. Ogilvy, *ELN* 11, 121

Faiss, Klaus, *'Gnade' bei Cynewulf und seiner Schule* (Tübingen, 1967): Hartmut Beckers, *ASNSL* 209, 398–9

Fellows Jensen, Gillian, *Scandinavian Settlement Names in Yorkshire* (Copenhagen, 1972): Margaret Gelling, *N&Q* 20, 144–6

Field, John, *English Field Names: a Dictionary* (Newton Abbot, 1972): Basil Cottle, *RES* 24, 317–19; Conrad M. Rothrauff, *Names* 21, 199–200

Finberg, H. P. R., ed., *The Agrarian History of England and Wales* 1 pt 2 (Cambridge, 1972): *TLS* 25 May, p. 592; G. W. S. Barrow, *Scottish Hist. Rev.* 52, 195–6; D. J. Bonney, *JBAA* 36, 104; A. R. Bridbury, *EconHR* 26, 518–24; H. B. Clarke, *The Local Historian* 10, 312–13; G. E. Fussell, *Technology and Culture* 14, 491–3; Nigel Harvey, *Geographical Jnl* 139, 547–8; Eric John, *Agricultural Hist. Rev.* 21, 135–9; P. J. Reynolds, *Britannia* 4, 342–4

Finkenstaedt, Thomas, Ernst Leisi and Dieter Wolff, *A Chronological English Dictionary* (Heidelberg, 1970): Wilhelm Kesselring, *Die Neueren Sprachen* 1973, 673–5

Fisher, John H., ed., *The Medieval Literature of Western Europe: a Review of Research, Mainly 1930-60* (New York, 1966): J. A. W. B., *MÆ* 41, 240-1

Förstemann, Ernst, *Altdeutsche Personennamen, Ergänzungsband* von Henning Kaufmann (Hildesheim, 1968): Joachim Göschel, *Leuvense Bijdragen* 61, 251-4

Fowler, P. J., ed., *Archaeology and the Landscape: Essays for L. V. Grinsell* (London, 1972): Leslie Alcock, *History* 58, 412-13; Brian K. Davison, *JBAA* 36, 104-5; Ann Dornier, *ArchJ* 129, 221-3

Fowler, Roger, ed., *Wulfstan's Canons of Edgar*, EETS 266 (1972): Alistair Campbell, *N&Q* 20, 103-4

Frere, Sheppard, *Britannia: a History of Roman Britain* (London, 1967): Barbara Trojak, *Eos* 59, 183-6

Verulamium Excavations 1: Ronald Jessup, *Amer. Jnl of Archaeology* 77, 105

Galster, Georg, *The Royal Collection of Coins and Medals, National Museum, Copenhagen. Part IV*, Sylloge of Coins of the British Isles 18 (London, 1972): J. D. B[rand], *BNJ* 41, 190-2

Gardner, Frank Cook, *The Pilgrimage of Desire: a Study of Theme and Genre in Medieval Literature* (Leiden, 1971): Stephen A. Barney, *Speculum* 48, 359-62

Gasser, Raphaela, *Propter lamentabilem vocem hominis: Zur Theorie der Volkssprache in althochdeutscher Zeit*, Zürich diss., 1969: Klaus Matzel, *ZDA* 102, 11-15

Gatch, Milton McC., *Loyalties and Traditions: Man and his World in Old English Literature* (New York, 1971): Edward B. Irving, Jr, *Speculum* 48, 147-50; T. A. Shippey, *YES* 3, 263-4

Gelling, Margaret, *The Place-Names of Berkshire* 1 (Cambridge, 1972): Gillian Fellows Jensen, *N&Q* 20, 117-18; Kelsie B. Harder, *Names* 21, 269-71

Gimson, A. C., *An Introduction to the Pronunciation of English*, 2nd ed. (London, 1970): Klauss Faiss, *Linguistics* 95, 112-17

Girvan, Ritchie, *'Beowulf' and the Seventh Century*, 2nd ed. (London, 1971): G. Bourquin, *Études Anglaises* 26, 222; R. T. Farrell, *MÆ* 41, 292-3; Patrizia Lendinara, *Annali, Sezione Germanica* (Naples) 15, 211-12

Goetz, Hans-Georg, *Geschichte des Wortes 'rūn (rune)' und seiner Ableitungen im Englischen*, Göttingen diss., 1964: Hartmut Beckers, *ASNSL* 209, 397

Goldsmith, Margaret E., *The Mode and Meaning of 'Beowulf'* (London, 1970): G. Bourquin, *Études Anglaises* 26, 223-4; Martin Green, *Style* 7, 69-73; Nicolas Jacobs, *NM* 74, 551-7

Göller, Karl Heinz, *Geschichte der altenglischen Literatur* (Berlin, 1971): Gero Bauer, *Germanisch-Romanische Monatsschrift* 23, 119-21; Martin Lehnert, *ZAA* 21, 309-10

Gradon, Pamela, *Form and Style in Early English Literature* (London, 1971): A. J. Bliss, *RES* 24, 197-9; D. S. Brewer, *Anglia* 91, 388-92; Dieter Mehl, *Erasmus* 25, 222-7; E. G. Stanley, *YES* 3, 265-7; John Stephens, *Southern Rev.* 6, 180-6; P. B. Taylor, *ESts* 54, 383-5

Greenfield, Stanley B., *The Interpretation of Old English Poems* (London and Boston, 1972): André Crépin, *Études Anglaises* 26, 350; Margaret E. Goldsmith, *Essays in Criticism* 23, 298-302; Pamela Gradon, *N&Q* 20, 342-4; Bruce Mitchell, *RES* 24, 319-21; R. M. Wilson, *English* 21, 27

Grinsell, L. V., *The Bath Mint: an Historical Outline* (London, 1973): Anthony Gunstone, *Bristol Archaeol. Research Group Bull.* 4, 234

Grohskopf, Bernice, *The Treasure of Sutton Hoo: Ship-Burial for an Anglo-Saxon King* (New York, 1970): Sandra A. Glass, *Archaeology* 26, 74–5

Grose, M. W., and Deirdre McKenna, *Old English Literature* (London, 1973): André Crépin, *Études Anglaises* 26, 349

Grünberg, M., *The West-Saxon Gospels: a Study of the Gospel of St Matthew with Text of the Four Gospels* (Amsterdam, 1967): Paule Mertens-Fonck, *ESts* 54, 59–60

Gunstone, A. J. H., *Ancient British, Anglo-Saxon and Norman Coins in Midlands Museums*, Sylloge of Coins of the British Isles 17 (London, 1971): Margaret Gelling, *Trans. of the Birmingham and Warwickshire Archaeol. Soc.* 85, 218–19

Hachmann, Rolf, *Die Goten und Skandinavien* (Berlin, 1970): Norbert Wagner, *ZDA Anzeiger* 102, 283–307

Hallander, Lars-G., *Old English Verbs in '-sian'* (Uppsala, 1966): G. Bourquin, *Études Anglaises* 26, 346

Hanowell, Manford, *Maxims I und Maxims II: Untersuchungen zur gedanklichen und formalen Struktur*, Münster diss., 1971: Patrizia Lendinara, *Annali, Sezione Germanica* (Naples) 15, 218–19

Hardinge, Leslie, *The Celtic Church in Britain* (London, 1972); W. H. C. Frend, *AntJ* 53, 121–2; P. McGurk, *History* 58, 251–2

Hart, Cyril, *The Hidation of Northamptonshire* (Leicester, 1970): J. C. Holt, *EHR* 88, 617–18

The Early Charters of Essex, rev. ed. (Leicester, 1971): Eric John, *Agricultural Hist. Rev.* 21, 80

Hartung, Albert E., ed., *A Manual of Writings in Middle English 1050–1500* III (New Haven, 1972): M. W. B., *Speculum* 48, 186

Harvey, Sally, 'Domesday Book and its Predecessors', *EHR* 86 (1971), 753–73: Edmund King, see sect. 6

Hauck, Karl, *Goldbrakteaten aus Sievern* (Munich, 1970): Torsten Capelle, *Deutsches Archiv für Erforschung des Mittelalters* 29, 279

Heighway, C. M., ed., *The Erosion of History* (London, 1972): Ann Hamlin, *ArchJ* 129, 223–4

Hill, David, and Margaret Jesson, ed., *The Iron Age and its Hill-Forts* (Southampton, 1971): S. S. Frere, *Britannia* 4, 341–2

[Hoops, Johannes] *Reallexikon der germanischen Altertumskunde*, 2nd ed. 1. 1–3 (Berlin, 1968–71): Jere Fleck, *Scandinavian Stud.* 45, 376–9

Huber, Wolfgang, *Heliand und Matthausexegese: Quellenstudien insbesondere zu Sedulius Scottus* (Munich, 1969): D. H. Green, *MLR* 68, 441–2

Hunter Blair, Peter, *The World of Bede* (London and New York, 1970): Grover A. Zinn, Jr, *Jnl of the Amer. Acad. of Religion* 41, 603–5

Huppé, Bernard F., *The Web of Words* (Albany, 1970): Martin Green, *Style* 7, 64–8; Patrizia Lendinara, *Annali, Sezione Germanica* (Naples) 15, 219–20

Ilkow, Peter, *Die Nominalkomposita der altsächsischen Bibeldichtung* (Göttingen, 1968): Gerhard Cordes, *ZVS* 86, 324–5; P. Valentin, *Études Germaniques* 28, 217–18

Jackson, Kenneth Hurlstone, ed., *The Gododdin* (Edinburgh, 1969): J. E. Caerwyn Williams, *Studia Celtica* 7, 194–200

Joly, André, *Negation and the Comparative Particle in English* (Quebec, 1967): John P. Hughes, *Word* 26, 297–300

Jones, C. W., ed., *Bedae Venerabilis Opera Pars II: Opera Exegetica I: Libri Quattuor in Principium Genesis usque ad Nativitatem Isaac et eiectionem Ismahelis Adnotationum*, Corpus Christianorum Series Latina 118A (Turnhout, 1967): P. Meyvaert, *JEH* 24, 198–200

Jones, Gwyn, *Kings, Beasts and Heroes* (London, 1972): Rachel Bromwich, *RES* 24, 465–7; André Crépin, *Études Anglaises* 26, 350–1; D. Wyn Evans, *MLR* 68, 884–5; Valerie M. Lagorio, *Manuscripta* 17, 37–8; Ruth P. M. Lehmann, *JEGP* 72, 438–40; J. D. A. Ogilvy, *ELN* 10, 290–1; Hermann Pálsson, *Scandinavica* 12, 62; Barbara Raw, *N&Q* 20, 429–30; R. M. Wilson, *English* 21, 27

King, Robert D., *Historische Linguistik und generative Grammatik* (Frankfurt, 1971): Jochem Schindler, *Die Sprache* 19, 84–6

Klindt-Jensen, Ole, *The World of the Vikings* (London, 1971): Gwyn Jones, *History* 58, 77

Knowles, David, C. N. L. Brooke and Vera C. M. London, ed., *The Heads of Religious Houses: England and Wales 940–1216* (Cambridge, 1972): G. Constable, *JEH* 24, 63–4; R. H. C. Davis, *EHR* 88, 878–9; Beryl Smalley, *MÆ* 42, 192–3; William Urry, *JTS* 24, 285

Knowles, David, and R. Neville Hadcock, *Medieval Religious Houses: England and Wales*, 2nd ed. (London, 1971): B. Benabarre, *Studia Monastica* 14, 270; William D. Carpe, *Church Hist.* 42, 125; Ian B. Cowan, *Scottish Hist. Rev.* 52, 196–7

Krämer, Peter, *Die Präsensklassen des germanischen schwachen Verbums* (Innsbruck, 1971): Elmar Seebold, *BGDSL* (Tübingen) 94, 434–5

Kristensson, Gillis, *Studies on Middle English Topographical Terms* (Lund, 1970): Herbert Voitl, *ASNSL* 210, 177–9

Krüger, Karl Heinrich, *Königsgrabkirchen der Franken, Angelsachsen und Langobarden bis zur Mitte des 8. Jahrhunderts* (Munich, 1971): H. M. S., *Deutsches Archiv für Erforschung des Mittelalters* 29, 333–4; J. M. Wallace-Hadrill, *EHR* 88, 410

Kuhn, Hans, *Kleine Schriften* I (Berlin, 1969): Joachim Göschel, *IF* 76 (1969), 319–23

Kleine Schriften I and II (Berlin, 1969 and 1971): K. Roelandts, *Leuvense Bijdragen* 62, 81–4

Kleine Schriften I–III (Berlin, 1969–72): Heiko Uecker, *Zeitschrift für Deutsche Philologie* 92, 444–7

Kuryłowicz, Jerzy, *Die sprachlichen Grundlagen der altgermanischen Metrik* (Innsbruck, 1970): Fredrik Otto Lindeman, *Kratylos* 16, 97–8; Raffaella del Pezzo, *Annali, Sezione Germanica* (Naples) 15, 223–4

Lacroix, Benoît, *L'Historien au Moyen Âge* (Montreal and Paris, 1971): Bernhard Walter Scholz, *Speculum* 48, 765–7

Bibliography for 1973

László, Gyula, *Steppenvölker und Germanen: Kunst der Völkerwanderungszeit* (Vienna, 1970): Wilhelm Holmqvist, *Fornvännen* 68, 57–9
Leake, Jane Acomb, *The Geats of 'Beowulf': a Study in the Geographical Mythology of the Middle Ages* (Madison, 1967): G. Bourquin, *Études Anglaises* 26, 222–3
Lee, Alvin A., *The Guest-Hall of Eden: Four Essays on the Design of Old English Poetry* (New Haven, 1972): Norman E. Eliason, *MP* 71, 187–8; P. O. E. Gradon, *N&Q* 20, 26–8; Stanley B. Greenfield, *JEGP* 72, 122–6; Micheline Larès, *Études Anglaises* 26, 86–7; Bruce Mitchell, *RES* 24, 195–6; Elizabeth S. Sklar, *Criticism* 15, 371–3; L. Whitbread, *ESts* 54, 381–2
Lindeman, Fredrik Otto, *Les Origines Indo-Européennes de la 'Verschärfung' Germanique* (Oslo, 1964): J. Fourquet, *Bull. de la Société de Linguistique de Paris* 67, 231–3; Gernot Schmidt, *ZVS* 87, 289–94
Lindemann, J. W. Richard, *Old English Preverbal 'Ge-': its Meaning* (Charlottesville, 1970): M. L. Samuels, *MÆ* 41, 289–92; E. G. Stanley, *Anglia* 91, 493–4
Ljublinskaja, A. D., *Latinskaja paleografija* (Moscow, 1969): V. Vodoff, *Le Moyen Âge* 79, 181–4
Lot, Ferdinand, *Recueil des Travaux Historiques* 11 (Geneva and Paris, 1970): André Joris, *Le Moyen Âge* 78, 591–2
Lowe, E. A., *Codices Latini Antiquiores*, Supplement (Oxford, 1971) and *Palaeographical Papers 1907–1965*, ed. Ludwig Bieler (Oxford, 1972): Dom Hubert Dauphin, *Revue d'Histoire Ecclésiastique* 68, 112–15
  Palaeographical Papers 1907–1965 (Oxford, 1972), ed. Ludwig Bieler: Chauncey E. Finch, *Manuscripta* 17, 115; Emmanuel Poulle, *Bibliothèque de l'École des Chartes* 131, 251–3; G. S., *Deutsches Archiv für Erforschung des Mittelalters* 28, 273–4
Loyn, Henry R., ed., *A Wulfstan Manuscript, containing Institutes, Laws and Homilies, BM Cotton Nero A. i*, EEMF 17 (Copenhagen, 1971): G. Storms, *ESts* 54, 497
Makaev, È. A., *Struktura slova v indoevropejskix i germanskix jazykax* (Moscow, 1970): Raimo Anttila, *Language* 49, 701–4
Marsh, Henry, *Dark Age Britain: some Sources of History* (Newton Abbot, 1970): R. Ian Jack, *Jnl of Religious Hist.* 7, 165–6
Matthews, C. M., *Place Names of the English-Speaking World* (New York, 1972): Kelsie B. Harder, *Names* 21, 112–14
Mayr-Harting, Henry, *The Coming of Christianity to Anglo-Saxon England* (London, 1972): Joseph F. Kelly, *Theological Stud.* 34, 321–3; D. P. Kirby, *History* 58, 252–3; J. N. L. Myres, *JTS* 24, 271–3; Richard W. Pfaff, *Church Hist.* 42, 123–4; Dunstan Pontifex, *Downside Rev.* 90, 76–7
McKisack, May, *Medieval History in the Tudor Age* (Oxford, 1971): C. E. Wright, *MÆ* 42, 196–202
Meid, Wolfgang, *Das germanische Präteritum* (Innsbruck, 1971): Alfred Bammesberger, *Anglia* 91, 245–6; Albert L. Lloyd, *Language* 49, 479–82
Michaelis-Jena, Ruth, *The Brothers Grimm* (London, 1970): W. F. H. Nicolaisen, *Jnl of Amer. Folklore* 86, 297–8
Millward, Roy, and Adrian Robinson, *Landscapes of Britain: the West Midlands* (London, 1971) and *Landscapes of Britain: the Welsh Marches* (London, 1971): H. B. Clarke, see sect. 6

Milojčić, V., ed., *2. Kolloquium über spätantike und frühmittelalterliche Skulptur* (Mainz, 1971): David M. Wilson, *AntJ* 53, 124–5

Mindt, Dieter, *Der Wortschatz des Lambeth Homilies: das Adjektiv* (Brunswick, 1971): Martin Lehnert, *ZAA* 21, 202

Mitchell, P. D., *Catalogue of the R. P. V. Brettell Collection of Coins of Exeter and Civil War Issues of Devon. Glendining and Co. 28 October 1970* (London, 1970) [includes introductory essay 'The Exeter Mint and its Moneyers', by I. H. Stewart]: J. D. B[rand], *BNJ* 41, 190–2

  Catalogue of the Important Collection of Anglo-Saxon Silver Pennies, formed by F. Elmore Jones. Glendining and Co. 12 and 13 May 1971 (London, 1971): J. D. B[rand], *BNJ* 41, 190–2

Moorman, Charles, *Kings and Captains: Variations on a Heroic Theme* (Lexington, 1971): T. R. Henn, *MLR* 68, 141–2; Joan Turville-Petre, *MÆ* 42, 204

Morris, John, *The Age of Arthur* (London, 1973): *CA* 4, 77; Leslie Alcock, *Antiquity* 47, 329–30; A. G. R[ook], *Hertfordshire Archaeol. Rev.* 7, 137–8

Morton, Catherine, and Hope Muntz, ed., *The 'Carmen de Hastingae Proelio' of Guy, Bishop of Amiens* (Oxford, 1972): L. Van Acker, *Latomus* 31, 1118; Frank Barlow, *EHR* 88, 616–17; J. Boussard, *Bibliothèque de l'École des Chartes* 131, 269–71; C. Warren Hollister, *AHR* 78, 671; Bruce Webster, *Archaeologia Cantiana* 87, 245

Mossop, H. R., *The Lincoln Mint c. 890–1279* (ed. Veronica Smart, Newcastle upon Tyne, 1970): Gillian Fellows Jensen, *BNJ* 41, 186–9

Müller, Günter, *Studien zu den theriophoren Personennamen der Germanen* (Cologne, 1970): G. N., *ZVS* 87, 283–4

National Maritime Museum, *The Development of the Boat: a Select Bibliography* (London, 1971): Paul Johnstone, *Antiquity* 47, 83–4

Nicolaisen, W. F. H., ed., *The Names of Towns and Cities in Britain* (London, 1970): Hartmut Beckers, *Beiträge zur Ortsnamenforschung* 8, 53–4; Thomas Pyles, *Linguistics* 102, 122–4

Nummenmaa, Liisa, *The Uses of 'So', 'Al So' and 'As' in Early Middle English* (Helsinki, 1973): Matti Rissanen, *NM* 74, 764–7

Okasha, Elisabeth, *Hand-List of Anglo-Saxon Non-Runic Inscriptions* (Cambridge, 1971): Janet M. Bately, *Antiquity* 47, 155–6; Lawrence Butler, *Yorkshire Archaeol. Jnl* 45, 222

Orrick, Allan H., ed., *Nordica et Anglica: Studies in Honor of Stefán Einarsson* (The Hague, 1968): Allen H. Chappel, *Linguistics* 71, 103–8

Owen, Dorothy M., *Church and Society in Medieval Lincolnshire* (Lincoln, 1971): Elisabeth G. Kimball, *Speculum* 48, 396–7

Pächt, Otto, and J. J. G. Alexander, *Illuminated Manuscripts in the Bodleian Library, Oxford* III (Oxford, 1973): *TLS* 15 June, p. 699

Page, R. I., *An Introduction to English Runes* (London, 1973): *TLS* 14 December, p. 1545

Partridge, A. C., *English Biblical Translation* (London, 1972): *TLS* 2 March, p. 243

Pearson, Lucien Dean, trans., *Beowulf* (Bloomington, 1965): G. Bourquin, *Études Anglaises* 26, 222

Peters, Edward, *The Shadow King: 'Rex Inutilis' in Medieval Law and Literature, 751–1327* (New Haven, 1970): D. H. Green, *MLR* 68, 929–31

Petersson, H. Bertil A., *Anglo-Saxon Currency: King Edgar's Reform to the Norman Conquest* (Lund, 1969): Norbert Kamp, *Deutsches Archiv für Erforschung des Mittelalters* 29, 279–80

Piebenga, G. A., *Een studie over het werk van Rasmus Rask, in het bijzonder over zijn 'Frisisk Sproglære'* (Leeuwarden, 1971): H. T. J. Miedema, *Leuvense Bijdragen* 61, 258–61

Pilch, Herbert, *Altenglische Grammatik* and *Altenglischer Lehrgang* (Munich, 1970): Herbert Koziol, *ASNSL* 209, 139–42; M. Perrelet-Bridges and P. B. Taylor, *Linguistics* 102, 118–22

Pohl, Frederick J., *The Viking Settlements of North America* (New York, 1972): *Terrae Incognitae* 4, 133–5

Powell, J. Enoch, and Keith Wallis, *The House of Lords in the Middle Ages* (London, 1968): R. C. van Caenegem, *Le Moyen Âge* 78, 579–80

Pye, N., ed., *Leicester and its Region* (Leicester, 1972): W. Kirk, *Midland Hist.* 2.2, 119–21

Raffel, Burton, *The Forked Tongue* (The Hague, 1971): Derek Bowman, *MLR* 68, 628–9

Reaney, P. H., *The Origin of English Surnames* (London, 1967): Roger Lass, *Foundations of Lang.* 9, 392–402

Rebsamen, Frederick R., *'Beowulf is my Name' and Selected Translations of other Old English Poems* (San Francisco, 1971): Patrizia Lendinara, *Annali, Sezione Germanica* (Naples) 15, 231

Ringbom, Håkon, *Studies in the Narrative Technique of 'Beowulf' and Lawman's 'Brut'* (Åbo, 1968): Karl Reichl, *ASNSL* 210, 180–2

Rissanen, Matti, *The Uses of 'One' in Old and Early Middle English* (Helsinki, 1967): Hans Heinrich Meier, *ASNSL* 209, 147–9

Rohde, Eleanour Sinclair, *The Old English Herbals* (1922; repr. London, 1972): *TLS* 26 January, p. 102

Rosier, James L., ed., *Philological Essays in Honour of Herbert Dean Meritt* (The Hague, 1970): Peter H. Salus, *Linguistics* 109, 116–20

Royal Commission on Historical Monuments (England), *An Inventory of Historical Monuments in the County of Dorset* II.1 and 2 (London, 1970): R. Allen Brown, *Ant J* 53, 131–3

Ryding, William W., *Structure in Medieval Narrative* (The Hague, 1971): Morton W. Bloomfield, *Speculum* 48, 584–7

Sancti Bonifacii Epistolae: Codex Vindobonensis 751 der österreichischen Nationalbibliothek, Faksimileausgabe (Graz, 1971): Paul Meyvaert, *Speculum* 48, 552–3

Sawyer, P. H., *The Age of the Vikings*, 2nd ed. (London, 1972): Barbara E. Crawford, *Scottish Hist. Rev.* 52, 81–2

Schabram, Hans, *Superbia: Studien zum altenglischen Wortschatz* I (Munich, 1965): Lars-G. Hallander, *SN* 45, 171–2

Schmitt, Ludwig Erich, ed., *Kurzer Grundriss der germanischen Philologie bis 1500* (Berlin, 1970 and 1971): G. Beltrán, *Studia Monastica* 14, 345–6; Martin

Lehnert, *ZAA* 21, 307–9; Herbert Penzl, *Zeitschrift für Dialektologie und Linguistik* 40, 208–10; Ilpo Tapani Piirainen, *NM* 74, 546–51

Schwab, Ute, *Die Sternrune im Wessobrunner Gebet, Beobachtungen zur Lokalisierung des clm 22053, zur Hs. BM Arundel 293 und zu Rune Poem V. 86–89* (Amsterdam, 1972): E. G. S., *N&Q* 20, 402|

See, Klaus von, *Germanische Heldensage: Stoffe Probleme, Methoden* (Frankfurt, 1971): David Blamires, *MLR* 68, 931–2; Ernst Alfred Philippson, *JEGP* 72, 62–4

Seebold, Elmar, *Vergleichendes und etymologisches Wörterbuch der germanischen starken Verben* (The Hague, 1970): Fredrik Otto Lindeman, *BGDSL* (Tübingen) 94, 429–34; Herbert Penzl, *Language* 49, 181–4

Seltén, Bo, *The Anglo-Saxon Heritage in Middle English Personal Names, East Anglia 1100–1399* I (Lund, 1972): Gillian Fellows Jensen, *N&Q* 20, 199–200

Seymour, Richard K., *A Bibliography of Word Formation in the Germanic Languages* (Durham, N. C., 1968): Horst H. Munske, *Zeitschrift für Dialektologie und Linguistik* 39, 341–3

Sheehan, Michael M., *The Will in Mediaeval England* (Toronto, 1963): Jacques Boussard, *Revue Historique de Droit Français et Étranger* 50, 622–5

Shippey, T. A., *Old English Verse* (London, 1972): F. Diekstra, *Neophilologus* 57, 314–15; Stanley B. Greenfield, *N&Q* 20, 24–6; R. M. Wilson, *English* 21, 27

Shores, David L., *A Descriptive Syntax of the Peterborough Chronicle from 1122 to 1154* (The Hague, 1971): Robert D. Stevick, *Speculum* 48, 789–93

Simpson, Jacqueline, trans. and ed., *Icelandic Folktales and Legends* (Berkeley and Los Angeles, 1972): Joseph Harris, *Stud. in Short Fiction* 10, 295–7

Sjölin, Bo, *Einführung in das Friesische* (Stuttgart, 1969): J. de Rooij, *Taal en Tongval* 24, 73; Arne Spenter, *IF* 76, 356–61

Smit, Johannes Wilhelmus, *Studies on the Language and Style of Columba the Younger (Columbanus)* (Amsterdam, 1971): Günter Bernt, *Gnomon* 45, 90–3 [Bede and Alcuin]

Southern, R. W., *Western Society and the Church in the Middle Ages* (Middlesex, 1972): Rhys W. Hays, *Church Hist.* 42, 556–7

Stenton, F. M., *Anglo-Saxon England* 3rd ed. (Oxford, 1971): Guy Fourquin, *Revue Historique* 506, 497–8; Niels Lund, *Historisk Tidsskrift* (Copenhagen) 6, 320–1

Strang, Barbara M. H., *A History of English* (London, 1970): Broder Carstensen, *Die Neueren Sprachen* 1973, 568–9

Sutherland, C. H. V., *English Coinage 600–1900* (London, 1973): D. F. Allen, *Antiquity* 47, 328–9

Szövérffy, Josef, *Weltliche Dichtungen des lateinischen Mittelalters* I (Berlin, 1970): K. L., *Mittellateinisches Jahrbuch* 8, 270–2

Thomas, Charles, *Britain and Ireland in Early Christian Times, AD 400–800* (London, 1971): Leslie Alcock, *MA* 16, 217–18; E. G. Bowen, *Studia Celtica* 7, 186–8; J. A. G.-C., *Jnl of the R. Soc. of Antiquaries of Ireland* 102, 110; P. A. Rahtz, *History* 58, 75–6

Bibliography for 1973

The *Early Christian Archaeology of North Britain* (London, 1971): E. G. Bowen, *Studia Celtica* 7, 186–8; D.L.T.B. and J.A.G.-C., *Jnl of the R. Soc. of Antiquaries of Ireland* 102, 108–10; L. A. S. Butler, *Northern Hist.* 8, 161; Peter Hunter Blair, *EHR* 88, 614; Ann Hamlin, *ArchJ* 129, 244–5; Jean Lassus, *Revue Archéologique* 1973, 375–6; P. A. Rahtz, *History* 58, 75–6

Tinkler, John Douglas, *Vocabulary and Syntax of the Old English Version in the Paris Psalter: a Critical Commentary*, JL, series practica 67 (The Hague, 1971): Klaus R. Grinda, *Anglia* 91, 494–9

Todd, Malcolm, *The Coritani* (London, 1973): *TLS* 10 August, p. 932

Trutmann, Albertine, *Studien zum Adjektiv im Gotischen* (Berlin and New York, 1972): Elmar Seebold, *Kratylos* 16, 189–94

Turner, Hilary L., *Town Defences in England and Wales* (London, 1971): G. H. Martin, *History* 58, 429–30; W. Gwyn Thomas, *Archaeologia Cambrensis* 121, 122–4

Vachek, J., 'On One Point of Old English Phonology', *Prague Stud. in Eng.* 14 (1971): C. J. E. Ball, *N&Q* 20, 101–2

Visser, F. Th., *An Historical Syntax of the English Language* iii.1 (Leiden, 1969): Broder Carstensen, *Die Neueren Sprachen* 1973, 44–5; Heinz W. Viethen, *Anglia* 91, 371–8

Vogüé, Adalbert de, *La Règle de Saint Benoît: Commentaire Historique et Critique* (Paris, 1971): J. M. Wallace-Hadrill, *JTS* 24, 267–71 and 599–600

Vollrath-Reichelt, Hanna, *Königsgedanke und Königtum bei den Angelsachsen bis zur Mitte des 9. Jahrhunderts* (Cologne and Vienna, 1971): Kurt-Ulrich Jäschke, *Archiv für Kulturgeschichte* 54, 397–8; H. R. Loyn, *Revue d'Histoire Ecclésiastique* 68, 143–5; H. M. S., *Deutsches Archiv für Erforschung des Mittelalters* 28, 611

Vriend, Hubert Jan de, *The Old English 'Medicina de Quadrupedibus'* (Tilburg, 1972): André Crépin, *Études Anglaises* 26, 348–9; Anne Hudson, *RES* 24, 250

Wallace-Hadrill, J. M., *Early Germanic Kingship in England and on the Continent* (Oxford, 1971): Kurt-Ulrich Jäschke, *Archiv für Kulturgeschichte* 54, 395–7; H. M. S., *Deutsches Archiv für Erforschung des Mittelalters* 28, 610–11

Weinstock, Horst, *Mittelenglisches Elementarbuch* (Berlin, 1968): Gero Bauer, *ASNSL* 209, 142–6

Welldon Finn, R., *The Norman Conquest and its Effects on the Economy, 1066–1086* (London, 1971): H. B. Clarke, see sect. 6; Sally Harvey, *Archives* 10, 124–5; Edmund King, see sect. 6

The Making and Limitations of the Yorkshire Domesday, Borthwick Papers 41 (York, 1972): Edmund King, see sect. 6

Wienold, Götz, *Formulierungstheorie – Poetik – strukturelle Literaturgeschichte am Beispiel der altenglischen Dichtung* (Frankfurt, 1971): Patrizia Lendinara, *Annali, Sezione Germanica* (Naples) 16, 271–7; James W. Marchand, *JEGP* 72, 236–8

Wiley, Raymond A., ed., *John Mitchell Kemble and Jakob Grimm: a Correspondence, 1832–1852* (Leiden, 1971): Murray Peppard, *JEGP* 72, 96–7

Wilson, R. M., *The Lost Literature of Medieval England* 2nd ed. (London, 1970): Peter Genzel, *ZAA* 21, 85–6

Winterbottom, Michael, ed., *Three Lives of English Saints* (Toronto, 1972): Helmut
  Gneuss, *N&Q* 20, 479–80; G. S., *Deutsches Archiv für Erforschung des Mittel-*
  alters 29, 261
Wolff, Philippe, *Western Languages, AD 100–1500* (New York and London, 1971):
  Jack Fellman, *Speculum* 48, 795–6
  Sprachen die wir sprechen: ihre Entwicklung aus dem Lateinischen und Germanischen
  von 100–1500 n. Chr. (Munich, 1971): Kurt Baldinger, *Zeitschrift für romanische*
  Philologie 89, 300–2
Yamaguchi, Hideo, *Essays toward English Semantics*, 2nd ed. with app. [pp. 556–74,
  'A Study of Wulfstan's *Sermo Lupi ad Anglos*'] (Tokyo, 1969): Stephen Ull-
  mann, *Lingua* 31, 71–3